ON THE KARAKORAM HIGHWAY

STEPHEN LORD graduated from Trinity College, Oxford, then worked in banking for 12 years, living in Japan and the USA for most of that time. He loved the travel and living overseas but ultimately opted for camping and travelling under his own steam rather than a life of luxury hotels and sitting in taxis and offices.

He has toured in Asia, North America and Europe on mountain- and touring-bikes. He also enjoys kayak-touring and long-distance walking but always comes back to cycle-touring, believing that the combination of a bike and a tent gives unsurpassed freedom. Between trips he's based in London.

Adventure Cycle-Touring Handbook
First edition: 2006; second edition: 2010

Publisher
Trailblazer Publications
The Old Manse, Tower Rd, Hindhead, Surrey, GU26 6SU, UK
Fax (+44) 01428-607571
info@trailblazer-guides.com
www.trailblazer-guides.com

British Library Cataloguing in Publication Data
A catalogue record for this book is available from the British Library

ISBN 978-1-905864-25-6

Editors: Chris Scott & Nicky Slade
Series Editor: Patricia Major
Typesetting: Nicky Slade
Layout: Nicky Slade
Proofreading: Jim Manthorpe
Cartography: Nick Hill
Index: Jane Thomas

Global travel by bicycle is unpredictable and can be dangerous.
Every effort has been made by the author, contributors and the publisher to ensure that
the information contained herein is as accurate as possible. However, they are unable
to accept responsibility for any inconvenience, loss or injury sustained by anyone
as a result of the advice and information given in this guide.

Printed on chlorine-free paper by D2Print (☎ +65-6295 5598), Singapore

★ TRAILBLAZER

Adventure Cycle-Touring
HANDBOOK

STEPHEN LORD

with contributions by
TOM ALLEN, TIM BARNES, JEAN BELL, ALASTAIR BLAND
ANTONY BOWESMAN, TIM BREWER, ADAM CHALUPSKI
ADRIAN COOKE, JANNE CORAX, PHILIP DAVIS
BASTIEN DEMANGE, MARK ELLIOTT, EDWARD GENOCHIO
PETER GOSTELOW, SIMON HILL, ROY HOOGENRAAD
BJÖRN JOSK & EVEN VERRELST, DOMINIQUE KERHUEL
TOM KEVILL-DAVIES, IGOR KOVŠE, SCOTT MORRIS
TIM MULLINER, ÁLVARO NEIL, STEVE PELLS
SALVA RODRIGUEZ, LUKA ROMIH & MANCA RAVNIKAR
FRIEDEL ROTHER & ANDREW GRANT, CHRIS SCOTT
LUKE SKINNER, CAMERON SMITH, PETER SNOW CAO
SONYA SPRY & AALDRIK MULDER, LAURA STONE
TIM & CINDIE TRAVIS, PETER VAN GLABBEEK
RAF VERBEELEN, JONATHAN WAITE, BILL WEIR
AMAYA WILLIAMS & ERIC SCHAMBION
DAVE WODCHIS, PAUL WOLOSHANSKY

TRAILBLAZER PUBLICATIONS

Acknowledgements

One of the unexpected pleasures of writing a book such as mine is getting to know and become friends with the many contributors who have shared experience and expertise to make it a better book. First and foremost, my thanks go to everyone who has contributed to this book in ways both large and small. By having many voices and many nationalities I hope to have captured the the spirit of independent travel. I welcome more people getting in touch to offer opinions or possibly extend or improve the coverage of this book, which will necessarily always be a short guide to a very large subject.

It never feels entirely right offering lavish praise to one's editor: the editor is the person who won't let you go till the book is done, and done properly but Chris Scott has had a huge influence on the book and made it much stronger all round. Chris has a 'take no prisoners' approach to editing but has made a bigger contribution in thinking and arguing through every aspect of bikes and touring, and the book is all the more robust for it. If Chris is the bad cop, Nicky Slade gets my thanks for being the good cop; greater patience has no woman. Thanks also to the 'wise men' of the first edition who were available to offer comments and assistance with the second edition. Peter Quaife gave me great photos from his gruelling west Tibet ride. Philip Davis is always spot-on with his advice and Steve Pells continues to reign as the master of everything to do with bicycle wheels. Robb Maciag, who is now a published author in Poland, was most generous in making photos available to me and talking over many aspects of the book and has spruced up my website. Good luck to Robb and Ania on their big bike ride through Asia beginning this spring.

Thanks to Dewi Jones at 🖳 www.cyclewales.net, a bike mechanics' school in Snowdonia, for his advice and the training he gave myself and Philip Davis last year. As the book goes to press we are both back at CycleWales on a wheel-building course, then building bikes for ourselves. My best wishes to all at 🖳 www.bigfootbikes.com, my local bike shop, whom I regularly entertain and amuse with stupid questions, and good luck to former owner Roger Sims who sold up and sets out this April with his wife on their round the world ride.

Lastly and most important, thanks to everyone at Trailblazer for their friendship and support: Bryn Thomas for his unflagging support and the attention he has given the book over the past few years, Caroline for her work in promoting the book, Patricia Major for help with the stories, Nick for his work on the maps and Jim Manthorpe for proofreading the manuscript. In an age when guidebooks are written by nameless slaves and rushed to press, any aspiring travel writer would be fortunate indeed to have a publisher like Trailblazer.

A request

Every effort has been made by the author and the publisher to ensure that the information contained in this book is as up to date and accurate as possible. Nevertheless things will change; even before the ink is dry. If you notice any changes or omissions that you think should be included in the next edition of this book, please write to the author at stephen@adventurecycle-touringhandbook.com or c/o Trailblazer (address on p2).

Updated information and a whole lot more at:
www.adventurecycle-touringhandbook.com

Front cover photo: Approaching Karakul Lake, Karakoram Highway, Xinjiang, China
(Photo © Pawel Opaska)

Back cover photos: (top) KKH © Cameron Smith; (bottom) roadsign, Pakistan © Stephen Lord

CONTENTS

INTRODUCTION

PART 1: PRACTICALITIES

Planning and preparation What kind of trip? 9
Research: Online and in print 11

Documentation, money and information Passports and visas 13
Money 14

Health on the road Inoculations 17 – Other health hazards 18 – Sunburn
and sunstroke 19 – Altitude sickness 20 – Other hygiene issues 21
A healthy diet 21 – Learning to pace yourself 22

What bike? Narrowing down your choices 23 – Touring bikes 25
Mountain bikes 25 – Expedition touring bikes 27 – Recumbents 28
Tandems 28 – Frame material 29 – Component groups 30

Choosing a new bike Surly Long Haul Trucker 31 – Bruce Gordon
Bicycles 32 – Thorn Raven Tour & Nomad S&S 32 – Koga-Miyata 33
Roberts Roughstuff 34 – Thorn Sherpa 34 – Mid-range MTBS 35
HP Velotechnik Street Machine GTE 35 – Marin Muirwoods 36 – Other
dream bikes worth considering 36 – BYOB: Build your own bike 36

Adapting a used mountain bike 37

Gears, brakes and wheels Gears 39 – Choosing brakes 42 – Wheels 44
Bottom brackets and headsets 48

Comfort stations! Suspension forks 49 – Finding the sweet spot 51
Love in the saddle 53 – Handlebars 54

Racks and panniers Racks 56 – Panniers 59

Other bike accessories and tools 60 – How much stuff? 62

Transporting your bike by air 65

Clothing Layering 69 – Footwear 72

Camping Tents 73 – Bike touring tents 75 – Sleeping bags 79 – Stoves 80
Carrying Water 82 – Treating drinking water 82 – Kitchen essentials 83
Toilet bag: some suggestions 84 – Other useful camping gadgets 84

GPS 85

PART 2: ROUTE OUTLINES

Europe
Western Europe 89 – Eastern Europe and the Balkans 95

Asia **Russia** 97 – Roads & routes in Russia 103 – **Turkey** 105 – **Lebanon, Syria & Jordan** 107 – Some routes 109 – **Georgia, Armenia & Azerbaijan** 111 – **Iran** 115 – **Central Asia** 116 (Turkmenistan 120 Uzbekistan 120 – Kazakhstan 121 – Kyrgyzstan 122 – Tajikistan 123 The Pamir Highway 124) – **Afghanistan** 124 – **Northern Pakistan** and the Karakoram Highway 126 – **India** 131 (The Himalayan foothills 133 Sikkim & Darjeeling 133 – Rajasthan and the West 134 – The South 135 The Interior 135 – The East Coast 135 – The North-east 136) Ladakh, Spiti & Kinnaur 138 – **China** 141 – Cycling across China 141 **Tibet** 144 (The Friendship Highway: Lhasa to Kathmandu 146 The Tibetan epic: Kashgar to Lhasa 150 – Eastern Tibet: Lhasa to Markham 153 – Leaving Tibet: south to Zhongdian & Dali on the Yunnan Highway) – Cycling in China's south-west 157 – **Mongolia** 159 – From Mongolia to China 160 – Crossing the Gobi 160 – **South-East Asia** 163 **Vietnam** 165 – **Cambodia** 166 – **Thailand** 167 – **Laos** 169 – **Malaysia** 170 **Singapore** 171 – **Indonesia** 171 (Sumatra 172) – **Myanmar** 173 – **Japan** 175

Australasia **Australia** 178 – The Nullabor Plain 179 – South-Western Australia 180 – South Australia & Victoria 181 – An Outback Tour 181 **New Zealand** 184

North, Central & South America
Canada 187 – **USA** 188 (Pacific Coast Highway 190 – Alternative routes 192 The Great Divide 195) – **Cuba** 198 – **Baja California** 199 – **Central America** 203 – **South America** 204 – **Patagonia** 208 (Carretera Austral 210) **Bolivia** 212 – **Peru** 215 – **Ecuador** 215 – **Colombia** 215

Africa **North Africa** 217 (Trans-Sahara 222 – Morocco & Western Sahara 223 Tunisia 223 – Mauritania 224) – **Cairo to Cape Town** 224 (Egypt 225 Sudan 225 – Ethiopia 226 – Kenya 226 – Tanzania 226 – Malawi 226 Zambia 227 – Namibia 227 – South Africa 229 – Botswana 229) **West & Central Africa** 229 (Guinea 230 – Mali 230 – Ghana 231 – Togo 231 Nigeria 231 – Cameroon 231 – Gabon 232 – Congo-Brazzaville 232)

PART 3: TALES FROM THE SADDLE

The Hungry Cyclist	Tom Kevill-Davis	233
England to Australia	Tim Brewer	241
High in Ladakh and the Spiti Valley	Stephen Lord with Chris Scott	249
Desert Blitz – across Libya on a transit visa	Peter Gostelow	255
On the run in Tibet	'Corsair'	259
A long day to Sihanoukville	Jonathan Waite	267
No pay, no pass: on the edge in Central Africa	Amaya Williams	273
Now check your brakes	Edward Genochio	276
Tour fatale? Extracts from the diary	Igor Kovše	280
The Great Fig Hunt	Alastair Bland	288

APPENDICES A: Bicycle maintenance 292 – B: Staying in touch on the road 303

CONTRIBUTORS 304 – **GLOSSARY** 306 – **INDEX** 307

INTRODUCTION

Adventure cycle-touring

Why are so many people going bike touring these days? A minority pastime during the heyday of the car, cycling has once again become a popular choice for travelling – especially for long overseas trips.

Britain's CTC, the Cyclists' Touring Club, began life over 130 years ago during the first cycle-touring craze in the 1870s. Then, as now, the bicycle offered a revolutionary way of touring: you go exactly where you want, when you want, and all under your own steam. This was before the age of the car and walking or riding a horse were the only other options until the bicycle. In 1885 the Rover Safety Bicycle came along, and for all the innovation since then, most modern touring bicycles would be recognisable to a Victorian, as would their derailleur gears.

Bike touring is undergoing a boom at the moment but it is really one of many periodic rediscoveries. Bicycle design, components and gear are evolving to suit the changing needs and tastes of people. It's a combination of experimentation and using tried and tested designs, such as the 'diamond' frame of the Rover Safety Bicycle. The *Adventure Cycle-Touring Handbook* is all about looking at what people are choosing and using: what kind of bikes, what gear and what destinations are being chosen by today's bike tourers.

There are many reasons for taking a bike on your next long trip. My own guess as to why bike touring is back in fashion is that many travellers get burned out by backpacking, which really amounts to travelling by bus and train for most of the time. Buses are certainly fast but they go from one

Joff Summerfield left London in 2006 to ride round the world on a penny farthing he designed and built himself. He carried with him a small stone from the grave of Thomas Stevens, the first person to ride round the world (1884-7), revisiting Stevens' grave to put back the stone upon his return to London in 2008.

noisy town to another, leaving little possibility of exploring the spaces in between, the places where the bus doesn't stop.

Others use bikes to go even further off the beaten track: they want to go where buses don't go at all and perhaps where other vehicles cannot get to either. Paul Woloshansky built his own racks to carry extra gear after being told all too often: 'There's a prettier way to go but there's nothing out there at all'. Other adventurers, such as Sweden's Janne Corax (see p145), have said the same thing: there were times when there was no other way of getting to where they wanted to go. You couldn't get there on foot and you couldn't get there in a truck. It was possible only on a bicycle.

Half the adventure, though, is in the riding itself. Being out in the fresh air and seeing much more than is possible from a bus or train window is always a good feeling, whether you are wandering around France or riding across India. Many of today's cycle tourists are interested in the riding but not that interested in bikes. It's a means of transport and a way to carry bags comfortably, while sitting down and enjoying the view. Not everyone is drawn to the high passes of the Andes or the Himalaya but they are all enjoying that same sense of freedom and all that comes with it – unexpected discoveries, off-route detours or an impromptu day off when you find a great place to stay. Trips like these are not as arduous as some expeditions but they are every bit as satisfying – and they are still adventures, for they allow for spontaneity. And if you are carrying a tent and camping gear, you're prepared for just about any eventuality because you've always got a place to spend the night.

This book examines the possibilities out there, the different styles of travelling and the basic gear and know-how that you need. We also look at some of the more exciting cycling destinations around the world, complete with suggestions as to which routes to take and what you need to plan a trip in that region. The *Adventure Cycle-Touring Handbook* does not set out to tell you exactly where to go: it's your adventure, after all. But it's good to have a general idea of a destination and what you're likely to find when you're there and this is what this book aims to do.

In the final part of this book we include stories from all around the world, not just about the biking but also about the adventures cyclists had on their journeys. It's the old idea that a bike ride isn't just about the riding but also about the places you were able to get to and the people you got to meet – and all because you decided to travel by bicycle.

PRACTICALITIES 1

Planning and preparation

WHAT KIND OF TRIP?

This book is mostly concerned with the practicalities of going on lengthy and adventurous bike trips, but before your trip takes shape, you need to ask yourself what kind of trip you want and what you hope to get out of it. One of the beauties of cycle-touring is the immense freedom and flexibility you have on a bike, and your trip can be every bit as individualistic as you are. Indulge in a bit of blue-skies thinking about dreams and goals, tempered by a realistic appraisal of your strengths and weaknesses, and from the ideas that come up, destinations, a route, what kind of bike and gear should follow.

Your motivation should be clear and give shape to the trip. Do you want a relaxing trip or are you out to challenge yourself? Many sensation-hungry cyclists look for the excitement that comes with pushing themselves physically and exploring parts of the world that can in some cases only be reached by bicycle, such as the tracks of the Tibetan plateau or remote African villages. You may not be sure you have it in you, but aim high; your abilities will surprise you. What would have seemed impossible before your trip gradually becomes reality as you become a stronger, more confident rider. One of the aims of this book is to prepare you to ride in places most people would not dream of visiting.

When people ask you why you're undertaking your trip, it could be because it doesn't sound like much of a holiday to them. It probably won't be like any other holiday you have taken, it will hopefully be much better, but think of your trip as your own Grand Tour, a bespoke personal education in all that the world has to offer. You will benefit enormously from it, and by meeting ordinary people in the remotest places, some who may never have met a foreigner in their lives, you'll

Travelling solo means you can stop where you want for as long as you wish.
© Daisuke Nakanishi

RIDING EVERY INCH OF THE WAY

Many cycle tourers set off with a vow to cycle all the way, except when absolutely unavoidable – usually ferries to cross seas or rivers. Indeed first timers often assume it ought to be done this way, that they've somehow cheated themselves and betrayed the greater cause should they take the train or a bus when a perfectly rideable road exists. On this view the ride is an act of purification or a political statement; it's just you, your bike and the world. Recognise this as a not uncommon over-adventurous reflex to the humdrum and predictable life you may be leaving behind; you're up for it and want to get your teeth into a challenge!

In the car-dominated West the environmentally affirmative activity of cycling as full-time transportation (as opposed to widely practised recreation) encourages a certain zeal which might eschew any form of engine-powered assistance. It's something that more experienced riders get over once they realise it's not necessarily about riding, it's about travelling. It doesn't mean you have to hail down a local farmer in a pickup every time a stiff climb or an annoying headwind presents itself; it merely recognises that a bicycle's great advantages includes its natural portability – and that one of the better lessons learned on the road is flexibility.

Riding it all is challenging stuff indeed; the downside of this kind of commitment is clear: a fair amount of discomfort and even danger at times – heading out of towns on busy motorways or through run-down shanty-towns, riding in extremes of heat and cold, unable to catch up with the favourable seasons for travel.

Lashed to a bus roof, in a train or on a ferry or plane, you can cut out a busy or boring stretch or have a chance to meet some locals and so enrich your experience. Refusing to consider these options is to make a rod for your own back. So you slogged your way resolutely across the endless Kazakh steppe. Was it a month well spent? Or would you have rather shot ahead to ride the alpine meadows and heavenly mountains of Kyrgyzstan before the first winter snows? Some hardy blogs conjure up contorted reasoning as to why, under their rules, it was permissible to take transport in one situation but not in others.

If your time is unlimited, you might want to ride every inch of the way. Otherwise, you'll have a lot more fun and get further if you press 'fast-forward' once in a while. This is the key: it's your ride, not someone else's.

change the world just a little bit – hopefully for the better! Don't feel guilty just because you're able to take the time out for the trip of a lifetime.

The company of strangers

People will ask you if you're going alone and, if so, quiz you if that's safe and whether you'll have a good time on your lonesome. This is understandable;

Travel with one companion and you have someone to share both good times and bad.
© Björn Josk

we are a gregarious species and solo travel does not come naturally to everyone. For most people though, the decision is already made, it's merely a matter of recognising your situation for what it is. Either you have a partner with a like-minded commitment or you don't. If you don't and you still want company, you can post on various bike-touring forums, outlining your plans and asking if anyone might be going your way, at which point you can reveal a bit more about yourself in private with prospective riding partners. The good thing about these arrangements is that they aren't set in stone, that you can go your separate ways if your riding styles or personalities clash.

Life on the road involves meeting many fellow riders who easily become temporary friends, camping companions for that evening or often longer if you're both heading in the same direction. Adventure cycle touring encourages a certain comradeship and it's unheard of for long-distance riders to

Travel with three and there'll always be someone to take the photo. © Michel Bouyssou

pass each other and not stop for a chat. The friendships you make tend to be robust but focused on cycling, and that's why they often only last the few days or weeks you ride together, but break up when your paths and plans diverge. There are people who prefer to ride alone for the most part but enjoy a week or two with other riders now and again. It's a chance to learn new things and experience different styles of travel. The challenge can be in readjusting to being with other people and the compromises required; things that aren't an issue when you're alone.

Among all the people you'll meet on your travels, you'll probably remember fellow-cyclists as the most like-minded and supportive. But friendships with origins back home don't always survive the transition to the road where old rules or loyalties are no longer relevant. Travel gives you the freedom to find your own style as a process of self-discovery, and that is often easiest done in the company of strangers where you can re invent yourself as the miles unroll. If you're riding with a friend from home, you need to talk about all these possibilities and agree that expectations may change on a long ride, and have to be accommodated.

If you're in a committed relationship with someone and you both want to take on the big trip, congratulate yourselves on your good fortune in finding someone with the same aspirations. These rides are often some of the happiest and most successful, as many blogs will attest. There's more need for compromise than the temporary arrangements discussed above, but also more support when the going gets rough. The couples that ride together most happily tend to be fairly equal in their physical abilities, but over the course of many months most couples find their endurance abilities converge. As for mental strength and determination well, it's a chance for men to catch up, but they don't always get there!

A few basics to consider are that equality involves acknowledging differences, such as body mass. When packing your bikes, aim to carry roughly the same percentage of body mass. For an 80kg man, that might mean a 15kg bike + 25kg of gear, but a 60kg woman aiming to carry the same 50% of her body weight on a similar bike should therefore carry only 15kg of gear on a 15kg bike. That's the problem: women tend to carry proportionately more weight than men. Women carrying similar weights to heavier men will have a much harder time of it, but if they stick it out, invariably end up becoming much stronger.

PLANNING SCHEDULE

With a well set-up bike and experience, riders who regularly take adventure-cycling tours can leave planning till the last minute. If it's your first big trip with a new bike and new gear, begin planning well ahead or the mistakes you make in those last weeks when you should be out having farewell drinks with friends will cost you once on the road.

One year before departure
• Think of the key gear choices that take time to get right, not least your bike.
• Take test rides, ask around, visit bike shops or manufacturers and easiest of all, trawl the internet.

Six months before departure
• The rest of your gear: camping equipment, electronics and camera have to be pinned down, bought and tested. It's time to get racks and panniers to carry it all and wear your intended choice of clothing long enough to see how you like it.
• Decide which inoculations you need (see p17); jabs such as hepatitis A should be six months apart.
• If you're taking this route, learn how to blog and update your web page on the road.

Three months before departure
• Book flights if necessary.
• If it expires less than six months after you expect your travels to end, get a new passport.
• Start applying for any necessary visas.
• Work out who's going to feed your cat, pay your mortgage and store your stuff.
• Get your financial affairs in order: addresses, credit and debit cards and a PayPal account (see p14).
• Identify gear you haven't got but think you'll need.
• Think about fitness training if you don't exercise regularly.
• Begin loaded test rides and short camping trips to test your system.

One month to go
• Start buying small food items such as tea as well as medical supplies and batteries.
• Pick up spare parts for your bike and supplies such as SD cards for your camera.
• Have your bike shop look over your bike and service it, or better still, do it yourself.

Two weeks to go
• Get a bike box or packing material from your bike shop, if flying out.
• Start packing and leave your panniers packed.

RESEARCH: ONLINE AND IN PRINT

What you'll read on cycling and travel forums is not checked for accuracy but it has a quality that books lack: it's interactive and up to date. Internet forums (see p302) are great places to correspond behind the veil of anonymity. Many are like clubs so lurk first and get a flavour of the forum's personality. Some forums stick strictly to disseminating information, others are occupied by people with perhaps more spare time on their hands than is good for them and many are dominated by a coterie who have an answer for everything, but among the half-baked opinions and waffle are real gems of information.

For the low-down on global travel Lonely Planet's Thorn Tree (⌨ www.lonelyplanet.com/thorntree) is best overall. The bike touring branch, On Your Bike, is the most international bike forum you'll find and is as useful on the road as it is when planning your trip. Other branches on Thorn Tree cover every country or region you might visit and there's a good branch on cameras and computers angled towards travel needs. Like any forum, the Thorn Tree can be inconsistent, moody and even plain wrong and if On Your Bike is not to your taste, there are other cycling forums where you might get more specialist technical expertise, though nothing beats the Thorn Tree for access to on-the-ground information about destinations and routes.

It's a good idea to read a book on cycle maintenance (see p302) before you go and possibly before you buy a bike. Haynes' *The Bike Book* is a great start though there's no need to go in too deep; there's always a 'how-to' guide for everything on the internet, often with a video too. It's rarely worth taking reference books (including this book) on a trip, so digest them before you go, or rip out the pages you think you'll need. Country or region-specific guidebooks are the only exception here, because once stripped down you dip into them often enough to make them worth the weight.

It's not worth buying guidebooks speculatively; do your most general perusing of destinations here to see what catches your interest then search on the internet for accounts from cyclists who've ridden to the places you're interested in. Once you've narrowed a route or destination down, buy the necessary guidebooks. On a long trip if you can get them sent to you en route so much the better or consider swapping them on the road. It's usually hard to buy the latest edition of a guidebook in typical adventure-cycling countries. Information on the road comes from meeting other cyclists and using old guidebooks found in guest houses while bearing in mind that some key information may well be out of date in old guidebooks.

Documentation, money and information

PASSPORTS AND VISAS

Make sure your passport has at least six months validity well after the last possible entry date of your last intended country. Plans change and you'll need all the flexibility you can get. If your country issues them, get a new passport with more pages than the standard issue. It's easier than getting extra pages afterwards, a practice allowed by some governments but which may disappear soon.

Hang on to your passport, whether it's dodgy officials who want to take your passport out of your sight, or guest houses who want to keep it overnight. Police and other officials may have no legal authority to hold your passport and even honest guest houses experience loss, theft or worse. Carrying photocopies of the photo page will save time whenever a copy is needed and may suffice in hotels or with police requests to see your passport details. As a backup, carrying high quality scans of every page of your passport, including all your visas, on a small USB flash drive is highly recommended. Back that up on a web page you can access, or as attachments to an email you send to yourself before leaving home.

Budget bikers will find that visas account for a high proportion of their overall expenses. It's become a nice little earner for many African or Central Asian countries that don't rank high as dream destinations. And then there are countries such as Turkmenistan, which usually only grants a five-day transit visa, barely enough for the 550km route from the Iranian border to Uzbekistan. Many of these countries are desperate for foreign currency and demand payment in US$, so check Thorn Tree or similar for what you'll need for your next couple of countries and scan farther ahead for countries that might have become off limits in case you need to plan an alternative route. Some countries

PART 1 – PRACTICALITIES

want new banknotes, others won't like the curtain in the background of your visa photos and Muslim countries may insist on women covering their hair in visa application photos.

Visa agents are helpful in these situations, but at a cost. For example, Brits trying to get into Iran will need to use a visa agent such as Magic Carpet (💻 www.magic-carpet-travel.com), while Stantours (💻 www.stantours.com) is well regarded for finding a way through the thickets of Central Asian bureaucracy; its stock-in-trade is to provide Letters of Introduction or invitations to the countries it covers.

Many of the tricky countries such as these have varying entry requirements for different nationalities and policies often differ between embassies of the same country, such as China, where you can only get a month's visa from some embassies but three months from others. China and and Libya are two places which tend to change the rules often and this is why checking on internet forums is more likely to be accurate than googling possibly stale advisory websites.

MONEY

In terms of money, travelling today is easier than it's ever been as foreign cash and bank cards are better understood and ever more widely accepted wherever you go. There are a number of options for how you handle money on the road and access your account back at home, but with a little planning ahead you'll always have some way of getting cash locally no matter what situation you find yourself in.

Before you leave home

Consider getting new debit and credit cards if they are a year or two old as once the magnetic stripes wear out, the cards will be almost unusable. If you don't have a credit card, consider getting one for the advantages of some protection against loss or disputes with retailers and for emergencies like buying plane tickets, as sometimes debit cards are not accepted. If you only take one credit card, Visa has the edge, particularly in ATMs. None of the other charge or credit cards come close to Visa and Mastercard's global reach. American Express can make sense as an emergency card, but not as an every day debit card, although it does have benefits, including the use of their offices around the world as places to pick up mail; useful for having gear sent on.

Set up your credit card so it's automatically paid off in full each month. Inform your card issuers where you're going and make a note of the numbers to call from abroad in emergencies and give them your own contact information, both email and phone numbers, then check that they've got it right by calling up afterwards or managing your account online. It is all but certain that your bank cards will be suspended at some point in your travels, as ATMs and internet banking are vulnerable to shoulder-surfing, keystroke-logging and card-cloning, so double-check your password and security questions and answers as well as bank contact numbers.

Internet banking is very convenient to use on the road but can never be 100% safe so don't use it any more than you have to and if possible, set your account up for telephone instructions as well as for online banking.

Carrying your own computer is considerably safer for handling banking or any internet purchases you need to do as long as you understand how to protect the computer properly with passwords and firewalls. Using USB drives and portable hard drives is more troublesome as they pick up trojans or viruses at internet cafés and are then subsequently rejected as being infected.

Lastly, a PayPal or similar account can come in handy for receiving money or making payments as it can avoid extortionate bank charges for overseas transfers and exchanges currencies at reasonable rates. You can easily transfer money you have received from others in your PayPal account to your bank account at home and so access it via an ATM.

Cash, travellers' cheques, debit and credit cards

Before ATMs began accepting foreign cards, travellers had to carry large sums of money around, mostly in travellers' cheques. The big advantage of travellers' cheques is that they can be replaced if lost or stolen, the drawback is the rates you get on cashing them are worse than for cash or using debit cards. Nearly all travellers use debit and credit cards nowadays and change cash

DAILY TRAVEL BUDGET

Bicycle touring is arguably the cheapest form of long range travel. Weeks and miles pass under your own propulsion and many nights are spent camping for free or as someone's guest, saving what is normally the biggest expense of the day: accommodation. A survey of the contributors to this book shows that the average budget for bike tourers is around €10 day (at the time of writing a euro was worth £0.89 or US$1.35), so just €5000 could see you on the road for a year and a half. That's a very tight budget in western Europe, but easily manageable in much of the Developing World, where a bed in a shared dorm in Southeast Asia might cost less than €5 a night and meals just a few euros. Prices are similar in the poorer countries of South America (such as Bolivia, a great favourite among cycle-tourers) but in the richer countries, Chile and Argentina, some costs, especially in Patagonia, will be similar to the USA or Europe. Africa is cheap for adventurous cyclists who go off the beaten track, eating only local food and cooking for themselves in the back country, but predictably rises once you reach relatively rich South Africa.

Online hospitality clubs are also a good way to overnight cheaply in towns and cities: check out:
- www.couchsurfing.org
- www.hospitalityclub.org
- www.warmshowers.org, which is specifically for cyclists.

A cheap night in a flop-house in west Tibet. © Peter Quaife

Five-star camping place at Hassankeyf in Turkey. © Peter Gostelow

PART 1 – PRACTICALITIES

FROM ASIA TO AFRICA ON A WHIM AND A ROCK-BOTTOM BUDGET

One humid day in Colombo, Sri Lanka, I found myself standing in front of a fitness equipment shop staring at a few mountain bikes hidden between the treadmills. I'd always wanted to tour on a bicycle and it seemed like a good time to start, so I bought the bicycle for $500 and returned to India immediately to start riding. I improvised some hilarious panniers from plastic boxes and began a pilgrimage from Varanasi to Jerusalem. I was woefully unprepared and came close to giving up after two days.

Fortunately at the train station I met some other travellers who talked about their dream of cycling from Manali to Leh, a famous road in the Indian Himalaya. I was inspired to make another attempt at cycle touring. I took the train to Delhi and purchased some proper cycling gear (tool set, cycling pants and pump) from Firefox Bikes (💻 www.firefoxbikes.com). I also bought a simple kerosene/paraffin Indian stove for $11 that lasted for the rest of the trip.

I bused on to Manali, went to the local trekking shop, bought some fake Cordura material and coaxed the local tailor into making me some simple front panniers (see p 58). I made a front rack out of aluminium shelving and strapped the panniers to the bicycle. It all cost me a whopping $20.

I then set off and rode for two weeks over the four high passes to Leh; the best ride of my life thus far. The improvised bicycle equipment made it over one of the toughest cycling roads in the world and that was just the start!

I was having hassles with my tyres so spent some money and bought some Schwalbe Mountain XR (see p46) from a French woman and another British woman came walking down the street ready to throw away her old ripped panniers. She gave them to me and commented that they would not last long. I patched them up, experienced more mind-blowing riding in northern India, bused over to Pakistan and headed up the Karakoram Highway. In a local cycle shop I found an old Topeak rear rack and replaced my handmade Indian rack.

I loved the riding but financially it was apparent that I had to return home to Cape Town fairly soon. I bought a plane ticket to Nairobi for $400 leaving $1800 to ride home. I rode through Kenya, Uganda, Rwanda, Tanzania, Zambia, Malawi, Zambia, Namibia and South Africa, all the way to my parents house. It was beautiful riding and extremely safe. My front racks broke a few times, so I eventually had some made out of steel instead of aluminium by a local African mechanic. They lasted all the way home. It cost almost nothing but I did not do any adventure activities or go into national parks, though I still managed to get chased by an elephant. Zambia was the most expensive and Namibia and South Africa ironically the cheapest because there are less people and I slept out in the bush 80% of the time.

During that trip I remade my front rack out of steel, patched up my rear panniers a million times and rebuilt both wheels with new hubs brought up from South Africa by a friend. I cooked my own food, slept in the bush and stayed in dodgy hotels to make the money last and arrived in Cape Town with $500 left to start my life anew.

So ended an epic adventure on a minuscule budget and improvised gear; there is no excuse not to get out there and try for yourself!

Adrian Cooke
(photo © Adrian Cooke)

only when they cannot use their cards. Debit and credit cards can also be replaced if stolen or lost and these days are used in almost every country except the most undeveloped (and therefore inexpensive) countries and a few quirky ones such as Algeria, Libya, Iran and Bhutan. Check your card issuer's policy on sending replacement cards: some will only send replacement cards to your home address or may send an emergency card that is valid for only a few months. Worldwide lists of ATMs can be found at 💻 www.mastercard.com or 💻 www.visaeurope.com/personal/travellingabroad/atmlocator.jsp for Visa and Plus cards.

How much money to carry

With cash machines becoming increasingly widespread, there's less need to carry vast amounts of cash. But you still find countries that won't take foreign cards and which are often some of the most interesting destinations. At other times, banks run out of cash or the phone networks are down and the ATMs won't work, so you need to carry a cash reserve, something to get through the hard times, and a safety margin on top of that. I start off with perhaps €1000 and $1000 and some pounds sterling if I'm heading to countries where I'm not sure how easy it is to get money. If you know you've got to pay for visas in US$ on your route, you'll have to factor that in, bringing enough small denomination notes (and in good condition for the fussier embassies). Bringing travellers' cheques would be an alternative to carrying so much cash, but as your US$ and euro stash runs down, top it up by changing money with other travellers who want to sell their dollars for local currency. The US$ still rules in South America and Asia, the euro is better accepted in North and West Africa. In the more mainstream destinations of southern and east Africa anything goes. The differences in competitiveness of exchange rates you get between currencies are generally too small to worry about.

Carrying cash

Get a purse to carry your 'day money'. This could be your fake wallet, the one with the expired credit cards that is reluctantly handed to a mugger. It's all you need show the world and the value is so low you can afford to keep it in an outside pocket. What you ought to avoid is unnecessarily flashing a main wallet with the foreign bank notes and so on.

The safest place to carry day cash and valuables is always on your person somewhere, either a chest pouch (waterproof-lined to cope with sweat) or a waist pouch. The latter is generally uncomfortable while riding so most cyclists hide the stash in a front pannier when on the bike. Emergency cash can go deep in panniers, never near the top where casual thieves will soon find it.

Bar bags look like obvious targets for thieves and only work if you're strict about taking the bar bag off the bike every time you're away from it. Ortlieb bar bags are not comfortable to carry, so get something more suited to off-the-bike use and take it out of the Ortlieb bag when you leave the bike locked up somewhere. Use bags or pouches you can wear rather than carry over your shoulder.

Health on the road

INOCULATIONS

Medical guidance can be given only by your doctor or health clinic staff and this section provides suggestions only. If you have not travelled to developing countries before, a visit to a travel health clinic can be an expensive proposition involving several repeat visits for follow-up doses of vaccines. Although many of these immunisations are good for several years and you may well be up to date on some, the first appointment at the travel clinic is the time to sort out which you have or have not had and to get them all listed on an official, multi-lingual vaccination certificate which you might have to show at some borders.

In some cases, you have choices whether to choose a large and expensive vaccination or just a small booster, as is the case with rabies. Only you can decide, based on your appetite for risk. The World Health Organization (🖥 www.who.int) and the US Centers for Disease Control and Prevention (🖥 www.cdc.gov), which bills itself as 'your online source for credible health information' is a great place to start with preparations. Much will depend on where you travel, but there are a number of immunisations that are good for all travel, no matter where you go.

The most common immunisations are:

● **Hepatitis A and B** These can now be taken together but are expensive (although the hepatitis A shot is available free in the UK on the NHS). They need to be started at least six months before you set off (as the vaccination involves two shots, six months apart). Highly effective and good for ten years.

● **Tetanus** The disease itself is omnipresent in spore form and the risk of catching it from dirty wounds can be high. Cyclists taking falls are likely candidates and the adult booster jab is one of those you can get and and forget about for a very long time.

● **Rabies** Cyclists, of course, are an 'at risk' group from infected dog bites and having this immunisation gives you a couple of days to get to a clinic for a series of big jabs. There's more at: 🖥 www.who.int/rabies/en.

● **Yellow fever** These days it's not the jab you need so much as the certificate to say you have been inoculated for those countries that require it for entry, mostly in Africa.

● **Typhoid, polio and diphtheria** These are vaccinations you may have already had. Polio has almost disappeared but is present in countries such as India. Typhoid and diphtheria are uncommon but found throughout the Developing World and typhoid is prone to appearing as an epidemic. These three should be checked off as 'up to date' on your visit to the clinic. Note that typhoid, like any other water-borne disease, is most common during the monsoon season, so make sure your plans take this into account (it's not much fun or healthy riding in a monsoon, so you might want to avoid this season altogether!).

● **Japanese B encephalitis and meningitis** These are regional diseases and not widespread, but which can be fatal and therefore are worth considering, depending on your destination.

OTHER HEALTH HAZARDS

Malaria is the biggest headache for travellers in affected areas. Carrying bulky boxes of prophylactics is a pain but if you buy locally, you risk buying counterfeits, especially in India and Thailand, so you are better off paying full price at home. The prescription is always specific to an area and despite the expense it's not a good idea to use leftover tablets from a previous trip.

Take malaria seriously, it's one of the world's biggest killers, especially in Africa where the more dangerous cerebral malaria is present. Reducing your

PART 1 – PRACTICALITIES

exposure to malarial mosquitoes is very important as malaria prophylactics are not 100% effective, they may merely slow down the onset of symptoms. Long-sleeved shirts, bandannas and particularly thick socks or other ankle-level protection are all good precautions, especially at dusk in malarial zones. Long trousers (along with socks) also have numerous other benefits, such as preventing scratches, sunburn and tick bites.

Which repellent you use is a matter of personal choice. Deet has a long shelf life and is very effective in concentrated form. If you have had no reactions to it you are probably safe using a stronger mix than the typically ineffective 10% Deet formulas common in Europe. Where possible, apply it to your clothes rather than your skin, especially socks or on a bandanna worn round your neck. Deet is nasty stuff, though, and the more you can rely on clothing instead of Deet, the better off you are. The same is true for the insecticide permethrin. You will read suggestions to dip your mozzie net in permethrin and you can buy clothing treated with it, but it is a powerful neurotoxin, the use of which should be minimised. A long-term traveller would do well to avoid it altogether and to minimise the use of Deet by dressing appropriately, using nets and avoiding going outside during peak mosquito biting hours.

SUNBURN AND SUNSTROKE

Sunburn is still under-rated as a risk by light-skinned Westerners who are most at risk from it, especially cyclists who are outside all day, every day. Skin-cancer rates are rising and the risk is much higher in tropical zones and areas in the southern hemisphere where the ozone layer has been denuded. Hats and clothing are less messy solutions than sun cream, though you need both. There's a tendency to think that once you have a

Thermonuclear protection: a Tilley hat

good suntan, you don't need to cover up or use cream; not true. Incremental doses of UV cause incremental cell damage, leading to an increased risk of skin cancer.

Sunstroke is a related risk. Riding in temperatures up to and over normal body temperature (37°C or 98.6°F) is not unusual in much of the world. Sunstroke occurs when the body's thermo-regulatory systems can't keep up and is most typically brought on by dehydration. Adequate hydration is vital, helped by not exerting yourself in the hottest time of the day when a hard-working cyclist could be losing several litres an hour.

Recent research proved the blindingly obvious truth that plain water rehydrates the body faster than anything else, including so-called rehydration drinks whose sugars and minerals slow down the body's absorption of water. Glucose drinks and oral rehydration solutions are good for recovery from dysentery and diarrhoea that bring on dehydration, but are not as helpful for otherwise healthy people who have lost fluids. Eating plenty of fresh fruit is the best way of absorbing minerals.

PART 1 – PRACTICALITIES

Drink extra water at high altitude.

ALTITUDE SICKNESS

Most long-distance riders approach their first high mountain range in a state of mild trepidation, though as they conquer their first high pass this becomes euphoria and a fair few go on to become addicted to riding among the world's highest mountains. But to reach this happy state, cyclists must first learn to respect mountains, and that means understanding how to acclimatise properly and avoid Acute Mountain Sickness (**AMS**).

The effects of high altitude can become noticeable at around 2000m (6500 feet) and sickness usually becomes a risk at around 3000m (9800 feet). Fly in to Lima or Lhasa at 3600m (11800 feet) and you can expect a headache which will continue on and off for a few days. Many riders set off soon after that but may still not be fully acclimatised, especially as they're planning on going higher. Pharmaceutical pain-relievers have little effect on high-altitude headaches, but the South American herbal tea maté is recommended for aiding acclimatisation. It can be bought cheaply in bulk from health food shops before you go. The most fundamental trick, besides ascending slowly, is to drink considerably more fluid than normal, and much more once you start tackling passes. Altitude sickness is a controllable risk; use your head and you don't have to fall victim to it and can cross the many passes of Peru, Tibet and Ladakh which exceed 5000m/16,400ft. Avoiding it is easy: acclimatise properly!

Above 3000 metres you are at risk if you sleep over 300m higher than the night before, and most cyclists can knock off a 1500m gain in elevation over a day, so plan on getting over the pass to a safer altitude: 'Climb high, sleep low' is the mantra of the high altitude biker. That means you need a good map and to find out from oncoming cyclists what's ahead of you in case the ascent leads to a plateau from which your only descent is to turn back. Have a plan to descend if you experience symptoms of strong headaches, dizziness, nausea, and breathlessness; descending is the best first defence against the symptoms of altitude sickness. Symptoms will ease if you can descend as little as 900m. Plan your ride so you have provisions and gear for camping on the way up and have a fall back position if you cannot make the pass due to exhaustion or weather.

There are several reasons why you won't want to sleep on a pass anyway, such as high winds and the lack of water, shelter or somewhere flat enough to pitch a tent. The nature of many rides in Ladakh (see p138) enable this 'climb high-sleep low' routine.

There are two types of AMS and both are deadly: High Altitude Pulmonary Oedema (**HAPE**) is a fluid build up on the lungs reducing their effectiveness in an already oxygen-depleted environment. High Altitude Cerebral Oedema (**HACE**) is a similar condition involving swelling of the brain. Visual impairment and confusion make it more dangerous for a HACE victim to ride down to safety.

Some climbers and cyclists on short trips where every day is vital try to speed up their acclimatisation by taking Diamox, a prescribed drug that encourages respiration and works partly by increasing the heart rate which won't make for a restful night's sleep. Be wary of this option as it will encourage you to go higher while masking symptoms. Don't take it without a friend to keep an eye on you. By far the best solution is to go slow and acclimatise in the first place. Once acclimatised, you can ride at 4000m as if it were sea-level, and although you'll certainly notice how 5000m-plus feels, you'll be able to enjoy these passes and be on the way to being hooked on getting high!

OTHER HYGIENE ISSUES

Cyclists do get pretty filthy sweating and riding in dust all day and it's not always easy to give your clothes a proper wash, so you need to be vigilant for the downsides of poor hygiene inherent in a camping-cycling lifestyle.

Many a cyclist develops minor skin irritations on the road due to infrequent or inadequate washing. Aspire to have a good wash either in a stream, or if privacy or downstream villages are concerns, using a folding bowl such as Ortlieb's 5-litre job.

In men or women, 'crotch rot' is endemic to cycling, all the more so in tropical climates and not helped by the skin-tight, synthetic cycling shorts and irregular washing. To keep it at bay, wash or change your shorts or underwear daily while washing and then 'airing' yourself in a sarong or other loose-fitting clothing. If water or other facilities are in short supply, antiseptic baby wipes work very well; if they dry out they can be revived with a splash of water and a bit of soap. Also consider using a mild antiseptic cream such as Germolene, Savlon or tea tree oil. A rash in your nether regions – for cyclists, anyway – can be cured with better hygiene and exposure to sunlight and fresh air, but if a fungal infection has developed it may need a cream from the pharmacy.

A HEALTHY DIET

Riding daily, your muscles have additional calorific, vitamin and mineral requirements and in places maintaining an adequate diet may not always be easy. Reducing your daily distances is the simplest answer but is not always possible. Cramming in extra nutrients or 'energy bars' is the usual 'quick-fix' solution for sporty types, but unless you have a support vehicle this is impractical once on the road. Trying local food is all part of the experience of bike touring; a chance to learn more about food and food culture and talk to people in the process, rather than relying on home-bought foods as if you were on a trip into outer space. Far better to rely on eating fresh food as a way of maintaining nutrition.

After a long day's ride, piling on the carbs or protein can overwork your body just when it should be resting. Riders often resort to junk food for quick fixes, but sugary foods cause a surge in insulin levels and are another source of fatigue and imbalance. Far better to adopt a balanced diet that allows for slow absorption of calories in line with a steady burning of those calories while riding. On the road you won't find energy bars but in poor countries chocolate bars of the 'Snickers' type are very common. When it's cold and mountainous with not much food in the shops, these are your quick energy source but where possible, choose fruits, preferably those you can peel, as well as nuts, seeds and beans, and rely on multi-vitamins only in situations where the local diet is limited or inadequate.

LEARNING TO PACE YOURSELF

Cyclists' health troubles all have something in common: the sufferers – commonly mileage-obsessed lone males or riders caught up in the initial 'must crack on' stage of a long ride – are usually overdoing the riding and underdoing the washing, proper eating and resting. Riding for long distances day after day runs down your body's reserves of energy and nutrients and makes you far more susceptible to illness. Allowing plenty of rest gives your body time to recover and, if necessary, produce extra muscle to cope with the increased work. It may take a few months to find your natural pace. The truly competent travellers are those who keep a steady, relaxed pace. They stay well within their range and so have a good reserve of stamina and health to fall back on if they really need it.

Muscle pains may subside as your body adapts but are a warning sign that should be heeded. Joint pains and soreness are indications of overuse, or postural problems; you may need to change your bike's set-up. Try to keep within a comfortable range of exertion in terms of daily duration as well as intensity. Stretched and relaxed muscles are more supple and less likely to suffer damage than weakened or exhausted muscles that are close to their elastic limit. Muscle tissue needs time to rest and recover and simple maintenance will help, such as daily stretching exercises and an occasional massage, where possible. Never forget it's good to take plenty of time off the bike, perhaps walking, sightseeing or reading and resting; all good ways to help your body stay strong and have a richer and more varied trip.

DEALING WITH DOGS

It's easy to get anxious about the threat of dog attacks on the road and you will occasionally encounter aggressive dogs on a leash that could do a lot of damage if let loose. Short of carrying a sawn-off shotgun, there's no fail-safe way to fend off big, aggressive dogs, but most encounters are with much smaller mutts who are all bark and no bite. Here are some tips:

The most effective (but least satisfying) way to deal with a barking dog hot on your tail is to stop pedalling, get off and walk; they will quickly lose interest.

If a dog is still aggressive, facing it to show you're ready and alert, while looking away is the aggression-lowering posture. Never look small or submissive.

Dog charges, usually when they're emboldened by their doggy chums, are all bluff. Run at them, stop and throw stones, shout, wave sticks and look like you mean business. The dog will always turn tail.

Slings are used by many shepherds for herding cattle and also scare the hell out of dogs but are inaccurate and dangerous to anyone standing nearby. Catapults are much more accurate and easy to find in many rural areas. Ultrasonic dazers only work against dogs that aren't really a threat to you; the Hound of the Baskervilles will only be further enraged by the irritating sound.

There is a very small chance you will meet an untethered savage dog. Watch out near flocks of sheep and especially at night when these dogs may be on the loose. You may be able to hold the dog at bay by standing still behind your bike, for hours if necessary, till the beast loses interest. In time, all dogs will calm down and walk away, so play the long game and circle the wagons if challenged by a seriously aggressive dog. If you do get attacked, don't hold back. Predators often back off if they decide it's just not worth it.

What bike?

People have pedalled across continents on all sorts of bikes: recumbents, tandems, $50 Chinese cheapies and even a home-made penny-farthing. All it takes is two pedals, as many wheels, a chain and the desire to do it. There's no guarantee you'll complete your mission even if you spend thousands on a made-to-order, expedition-ready beauty because, like all bicycles, it won't pedal itself, but starting out with a well-chosen and equipped machine stacks things massively in your favour.

Look for an adventure-touring bike with these principles in mind:

● Comfort is non-negotiable. Never be tempted by a cheap price or fancy gear into buying the wrong size bike or something that doesn't suit you.

● Strength is more important than weight. Long rides on bad roads will test your bike and every component on it and an extra kilo of weight devoted to a stronger frame, rack or wheels is not significant when you think of all the other gear you are carrying.

● Simple designs and standard, generic components are best as you will find replacement parts and tools to fix your bike far more easily than if you choose exotic kit.

● Go for good mid-range chromoly or aluminium. The high-end stuff such as 853 chromoly or titanium is invariably used to build a lighter frame rather than a stronger one and such frames will be more difficult, if anything, to repair than thicker bog-standard tubing.

● Lastly, ride a bike you love. Some bikes will take a bit more effort to convert to a world tourer but touring is a very personal, customisable thing and you should consider your own tastes and instincts. If you love your low-down recumbent or feel more comfortable on your 700c-wheeled hybrid, work through all the issues and adapt the bike to suit your own style and needs.

NARROWING DOWN YOUR CHOICES

The most likely choice will be between a mountain bike and a touring bike, two styles which emphasise strength and comfort. Mountain and touring bikes have converged and swapped ideas and technology over the last decade or so and your average adventure-touring rider will have adapted a mountain bike to be more like a touring bike, or vice versa.

Both mountain bikes and tourers are designed for strength; true mountain bikes (as opposed to the 'MTB' look) being stronger and more rigid (though possibly with full suspension) to deal with gnarly terrain. Tourers are designed for comfort and carrying capacity, which they achieve by having screw fittings (known as eyelets or braze-ons) for racks, clearance for wider tyres and a long wheelbase for loaded stability at speed and so heels don't strike the panniers and toes don't strike the front wheel as you pedal and turn. You want all these features in an adventure-touring bike.

Touring Bike Anatomy

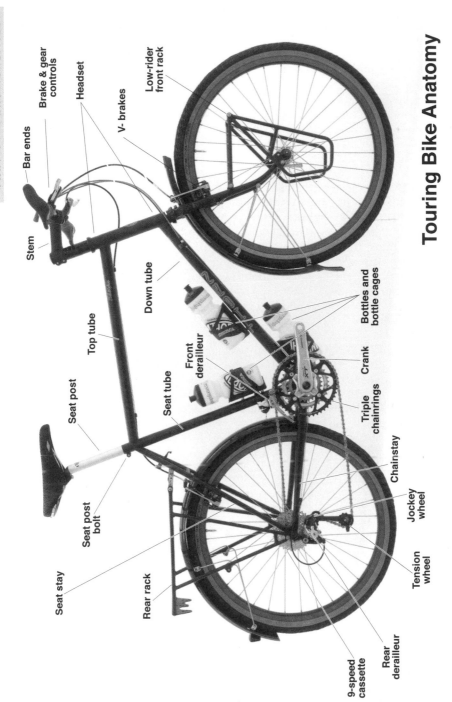

Bar ends

Brake & gear controls

Headset

Low-rider front rack

V- brakes

Stem

Top tube

Down tube

Seat post

Seat tube

Front derailleur

Bottles and bottle cages

Crank

Triple chainrings

Chainstay

Jockey wheel

Tension wheel

Rear derailleur

9-speed cassette

Rear rack

Seat post bolt

Seat stay

Touring bikes

Tourers were the traditional choice for bicycle travel and have a long history. Originally an adaptation of racing bikes, they have fairly lightweight frames and drop bars with extra clearance to fit mudguards, carry gear and a longer wheelbase to allow racks and to aid stability. Experienced cyclists who enjoy a faster ride on roads and recognise the value in travelling light prefer touring bikes, but for typical adventure tourers the frame isn't strong enough and the drop bars are impractical.

These kinds of bikes were perfect in the days when touring meant light and fast runs around Britain while staying in hostels. Nearly all touring bikes have 28" wheels, a size known as 700c (roughly the metric equivalent), and are designed to run tyres up to 1.5" wide. Touring nowadays is likely to mean carrying camping gear as well as travelling further to rougher places and touring bikes run into difficulties here as they don't handle heavy loads or have the fat tyres necessary for riding the back of beyond.

Nonetheless, if you like to tour fast and light, a well chosen and equipped touring bike will carry you in comfort and speed. It's true that you won't find tyres and wheels in most countries in the 700c size as easily as 26-inch MTB wheels, but if you can live with that risk you can buy or build wheels as strong as any mountain bike's in the larger size.

Mountain bikes

Most new riders who aren't diehard cycling enthusiasts will probably choose a mountain bike for a first tour. The handlebars and gear shifters are more usable and speed is less important than carrying capacity and day-to-day comfort. Modern hardtail (ie: front suspension fork) MTBs need a little work to make them tour-ready, but they offer many improvements over traditional tourers.

It's possible to buy a bike designed from the wheels up to take you round the world and those suggested on p32-6 are all great rides, but you can use them as inspiration to build your own adventure tourer for half the cost. There is much to be said for choosing a mid-range MTB with generic kit in standard sizes that is easier to fix or replace; good chromoly or aluminium frames will only weigh a pound or so more than exotic materials of the same strength, but are likely to be easier to repair.

Almost every mountain bike you look at will have a frame made of aluminium alloy (commonly abbreviated as 'alloy' in bike shops, although chromoly steel is also an alloy or blend of metals). A harsh ride and metal fatigue affected older aluminium frames, but modern, good quality MTB frames have massive welds, oversized tubing and suspension forks to minimise these attributes. For more on frame material, see p29.

Mountain bikes' rigid and more compact frames, due to larger diameter tubing and smaller triangles are well suited to carrying loads without flexing or cracking under the stress of prolonged riding on unpaved roads. Their wide handlebars and more upright riding position give the rider better control over rough surfaces while carrying a heavy load. MTB brakes are by far the most powerful; ideal for confidently controlling a heavy rig on steep and unpredictable mountain roads. Last but not least, the advent of mountain bikes has pushed gearing ever lower; perfect for hauling a load through the Himalayas.

Trek 3900 © Björn Josk

Marketing being what it is, mountain bikes have diverged into niche categories in recent years including racing, downhill or 'freeride': steer clear of these; you need a good all-rounder which, if it has any designation at all, will be 'trail bike' or 'XC (cross-country) hardtails'. Avoid models with rear suspension; among other reasons is the difficulty in securely fitting a stable rear rack (see p55 for the trailer alternative).

Staying in the mid-range, price-wise (around £400-600 new in the UK, $600-$750 in the USA), will avoid the pitfalls of an over-specialised machine that might have lightweight racing wheels, fussy air-suspension forks and exotic frame materials that cannot be easily repaired. High-end MTBs with plush suspension forks and hydraulic disc brakes are excellent for trips of up to a couple of months, but could become liabilities on a long trans-continental haul.

If you're looking at a good quality mountain bike it's sure to have a suspension fork and disc brakes. On smooth highways you won't often need suspension but it makes riding washboard tracks and unpaved back roads far more comfortable, saves a lot of stress on your wrists, and makes for safer and more enjoyable riding in the mountains. It's useful if a suspension fork with a disc setup also has bosses on the fork tubes to take V-brakes. Then, should your front disc fail on tour it will be fairly easy to track down some rim brakes (assuming your bike doesn't have rims designed only for disc brakes. For a fuller discussion of suspension forks, see p49).

Mountain bikes are designed to take the punishment of bad roads but they'll need a little customising for your road trip. You'll need to swap the knobblies for more efficient touring tyres, do a bit of rejigging to get a comfortable riding position and fit racks, but they are strong bikes and in the mid-price range, all the componentry (see below) should be good enough for touring. Mountain bike wheels are strong but a bit lighter and perhaps less durable than a touring biker would prefer as manufacturers specify lightweight rims and tyres that make the bike feel lively when a customer takes it for a test ride, but won't last for much more than a year of hard riding. Bone up on what to look for in bike wheels on p44.

If you're going round the shops testing mountain bikes, here are some touring-specific features to consider :
● Small adjustments notwithstanding, can you foresee day-long comfort? Is the riding position too stretched out and is the handlebar height roughly level with the saddle?
● Are there threaded eyelets or 'braze-ons' on the frame and front fork for fitting racks? (See p56 for racks that might work if there are no braze-ons on your bike.)
● Is the rear wheel so close to the seat tube (a feature of MTBs designed for steep climbs) that you may have problems with heel clearance once panniers are fitted ?

DROPPED OR STRAIGHT HANDLEBARS?

Racing and traditional touring bikes have dropped handlebars, aka 'drops' or 'drop bars'. Designed for speed and streamlined efficiency and usually paired with cantilever brakes, traditional touring riders claim drops are the most comfortable bar. Drop bars have more hand positions so you can sit more upright or tuck down in a headwind or when going downhill but for adventure touring, drop bars are simply not as good as straight bars. They aren't wide enough to give good leverage with heavily-loaded front panniers on rough mountain roads. The brake levers are all the harder to reach on steep downhills and the brakes themselves are much less powerful than MTB brakes. Ultralight riders can get away with the cantilevers usually found on drop bar touring bikes, but for most of us, it's much harder to control and stop a bike that has drop bars. There are modifications that can increase the power of drop bar brake levers, but the result is often mushy braking. Stick to proven cantilever brakes such as Avid Shortys.

Switching a setup between drops to straights can be done but be cautious here. Nearly all bikes are designed for one kind of bar or the other. Drop bar bikes are usually a bit shorter in the 'cockpit' (seat to handle-bars) and for straight bars to work, you might have to fit a very long stem to find a comfortable riding position. Fitting drops on a mountain bike is likely to be an ergonomic disaster as well as a stylistic faux-pas. The frame is usually too long and the fork geometry will resist the light steering that drops give. Bikes that work well for switching between drops and straights are either in-between tourers and off-road designs with fairly light steering – or are available in short or long frame lengths, such as Thorns.

Ergon grips with Cane Creek bar-ends. A comfortable hand position (or two) is critical on long rides.

- Is the bottom bracket so high you feel unstable when riding the bike or have problems touching the ground with the seat at the right height?
- Are the wheels, forks or the frame made of exotic materials such as carbon fibre, or a complex construction which would both be difficult to repair in the field?

Expedition touring bikes

A relatively recent development, expedition touring bikes are typically made-to-order machines incorporating the best of materials, equipment, design and technology to build a bike that can carry loads over the hardest terrain for months if not years at a time. What you get is a ready-to-ride adventure-touring bike built to your specifica-tion; the perfect blend of mountain and touring bikes with no compromis-es. Unwanted elements such as a mountain bike's high bottom bracket and short chainstays, or a touring bike's flex-prone frame under heavy loads are designed out, while all the

Roberts Roughstuff © Peter Quaife

necessary rugged braze-ons are designed in. The frame material is usually chromoly for its resilience and superior shock absorption to stiff aluminium (more on p29). Most of these bikes are complete custom builds or come in a wide range of sizes, including different frame lengths and not just heights, so you are getting a made-to-measure fit.

For the price you pay, you might wonder why some of these bikes don't have suspension forks or disc brakes, but though you can often choose these options for your expedition bike, many buyers are looking for the ultimate in simplicity and reliability and go for high quality in a conservative, traditional design. These are the ultimate adventure-touring bikes, but at a bespoke price.

Recumbents

The comfortable seat of a recumbent bike is a great place from which to see the world; the riding position is relaxed and natural with a reduced frontal area that slices through headwinds effortlessly. The low eye-level can obscure pot-

German road cruiser: Street Machine Gte

holes immediately ahead and can make you less conspicuous to other road users, but saddle sores, wrist and back trouble are rare and the more upright position of your head and neck is perfect for enjoying the scenery. Carrying their loads low, recumbents are ideally suited to fast road rides, but cope much less well off-road and on steep hills where their greater weight and the rider's inability to stand on the pedals slows them down. They're also a pig to carry up steep and narrow guest house stairs to your room. In traffic, recumbents feel less agile than conventional bikes; it's harder to see and react quickly, hop up and down kerbs or race away from traffic lights.

For comfort, they cannot be beaten and if you love yours, these criticisms will not deter you from riding a recumbent around the planet. But you have to be an extrovert to enjoy the attention a recumbent attracts or you will soon get tired of it.

Tandems

The rewards of tandem riding are a fast bike and close company, though the latter can be quite a strain on a relationship. These days tandems are built for the heavier rider to sit up front (most are sold to mixed couples) and so have a relatively smaller cockpit at the back. There's much less space for each person's gear compared to riding two single bikes, so many loaded tandems nowadays tow a trailer as well as carrying panniers, making the whole rig as long as a car and nearly as heavy.

It's clearly an eye-catching and spectacular way to go, and like a recumbent attracts attention but don't expect to save any money buying a tandem instead of two single bikes: for adventure touring on a tandem, you need the best quality you can afford. Tandems need to be very strong in every aspect to support the weight and pedalling force of two riders and fare best on flat roads. They're fast in a straight line but slower on hills as it's harder to co-ordinate pedal stroke, and they're not as nippy in traffic as a solo bike.

If you're thinking of buying a new tandem, consider having one made for you. That way the fit for each rider would be closer to ideal and you could specify S&S couplings, clamps which separate the frame midway allowing you to break the tandem down to a more manageable size; some planes and even trains won't take the length of a tandem frame.

Frame material

Most bike frames nowadays are made from aluminium rather than the more traditional material, chromoly steel. Aluminium is slightly lighter and is more easily welded by machines in a variety of shapes, whereas chromoly steel is produced in tubes of only a few different sizes, so aluminium has become virtually the only material for modern mountain bike designs. There are other exotic materials used for ultralight racing bikes, such as carbon fibre, but these are unsuitable for touring. Carbon fibre is easily damaged and not repairable, and titanium, though strong and light, is extremely expensive and certainly not repairable in the field. The argument that often flares up in the online world about whether steel or aluminium is better for a touring bike revolves around their relative repairability and questions of taste and comfort, as aluminium is a much stiffer material with no flex to it and is said to give a harder ride than resilient chromoly. Heavily loaded bikes riding on 2" wide tyres will feel fairly similar no matter which material they are made of, and saddles and suspension help to mitigate a harsh ride, so comfort is not a significant issue for adventure touring and taste is an entirely personal matter. Repairability is something touring bikers do need to consider but field repairs are generally limited to welding cracks; you'll be lucky to make even a temporary repair to a bent frame or fork.

Steel is known for flexibility, that's why springs are made from it. For cycling, this translates into a frame that has a little give to it on rough surfaces and a tapered and curved steel fork is the most simple kind of suspension. Aluminium is a stiffer material and ideal where no flex at all is wanted, such as wheel rims. Bumps and impacts are absorbed into the material and in the long term, this leads to metal fatigue. Frame fractures due to metal fatigue are very rare, however, generally involving very strong riders on large-framed heavily-loaded bikes or extreme mountain biking, and frame fatigue should not be an issue for a bike that is looked after. This is why manufacturers give long guarantees against frame failure. Aluminium frames usually have oversized tubing and extremely thick welds to increase rigidity.

The question of whether chromoly is easier to repair in the field than aluminium is largely hypothetical, as you can expect only an emergency repair on some Ugandan backstreet if you crash your bike and bend something. Aluminium can't be bent back into shape without it cracking, and if your aluminium rack takes a hit, don't be tempted to bend it back, just brace it with tent pegs and duct tape. Frames are much harder to repair and though you can try to bend chromoly back into shape, it will be much weaker and any repair will only be temporary. Both chromoly steel and aluminium can be welded and

WHAT'S IN A NUMBER?

The best known bicycle frame material is Reynolds 531, introduced in 1935. A forerunner of chromoly, Reynolds 531 can be brazed but not welded and though largely superseded by stronger chromoly, the springiness of 531 means it is still often chosen for building bicycle forks – look for the distinctive lugs on the crown of the fork. Reynolds later produced other steels that could be TIG-welded, such as 631, which is air-hardened and heat-treated. These extra treatments increased the strength and price of the material. Subsequently 725 and 853 chromoly came along and the latest is 953, said to be as strong as titanium. While it's easy to infer that a higher number is better, remember that these are brand names and not technical standards and other steels are available such as

A common place for aluminium frame cracks, but this repair has lasted 2 years+

Columbus Nivacrom that are similarly high quality but don't play the numbers game. Generically chromoly is often referred to as 4130, a code of the American Iron & Steel Institute that defines only the composition.

Aluminium has a similar range of treatments and processes that add strength and confusion to the mix. Aluminium used for any good quality bike is of 'aircraft grade', be it the common 6061 standard or 7000 series, which has numerous sub-variants. In addition to the number, there is often a designation such as T6 after the four digits that denotes the type of heat treatment the metal was subject to. While there are quality differences between the various aluminium types, the method of construction and welding is highly important in determining overall frame strength and it's too simplistic to decide from the material alone whether one frame is stronger than another.

Although high grade aluminium or chromoly is much stronger than plain vanilla grades, bike makers generally use it to make lighter frames, which means that your mid-range mountain bike is likely to be just as strong, though a kilo or so heavier than a top-end frame. For touring, a kilo is an insignificant difference and in the event of a cracked or damaged frame it may be easier to effect a field-repair on medium quality steel or aluminium where there's more material to work on than on a thin high-end frame.

you'll see aluminium being welded in many a small town in the Developing World, but these welds, if successful at all, rarely hold for long. Aluminium usually needs to be heat-treated after welding or it loses 30% of its strength.

Component groups

The biggest name in bike components is the Japanese company Shimano, who market their products in several different ranges so buyers know if they are looking at top, middle or lower-quality kit. The names of these ranges change over time, but currently Shimano's line-up is as follows: Alivio (entry-level specification for mountain bikes); Deore, the standard level; the new SLX range (replacing the long-running LX); top of the line XT and XTR for ultra-lightweight racing-grade components to suit no-expense-spared types. For adventure touring SLX is pitched as the best value level in terms of quality, with XT the highest level you should look at.

Shimano typically introduces technical innovations to the top-grade XTR and XT ranges first before allowing the masses to gain access later on. For example, Hollowtech bottom brackets (see p48) and Shadow rear derailleurs (see p40) – both introduced by Shimano in 2008 – are well suited for long-range bike touring but are currently only available at the SLX level or above. It's a similar scene with the other big cycle component manufacturer, SRAM, the US firm that owns RockShox, Avid and Truvativ.

You will definitely notice smoother or more efficient operation that comes with more expensive gear-shifting and braking componentry, but you're unlikely to notice lower-grade wheel hubs, bottom brackets and headsets. When new, these bearings will all perform as well as high-end gear but may weigh a tiny bit more and not last as long. Compared to brakes and derailleurs, hubs, bottom brackets and headsets are 'static' components which will last a long time and needn't cost the earth to replace. Hubs can be serviced easily on the road (replacement ball bearings are found everywhere) and bottom brackets are sealed systems and are replaced easily with tools found at bike shops. You'll also need shop tools to remove the ball bearing race on a headset, but nine times out of ten it's just an adjustment and grease job, or new ball bearings, either of which you can do with the tools you're carrying.

Choosing a new bike

Many cyclists, especially those on tight budgets, set off with a bog-standard mountain bike and most will do just fine. Out on the road they may realise there are many better choices, but the main thing is they got on their bike and did it. Don't assume you have to spend thousands on a custom-made bike for your first big trip; save that treat for when you come back and can appreciate something better. If you do get a chance to ride a top-range expedition bike, try it and see if you can feel the difference, but if these are out of your price range, a good mid-range mountain bike will do the job. As with many products, big bicycle manufacturers need to be seen to update models every year, even though it might add up to just a paint job. Especially in the harder-to-sell extra-small and extra-large frame sizes, you can save a great deal by buying last year's near identical model, but be cautious if tempted by a great bike that's one size too big or small as it may be difficult to achieve that all-important comfortable fit.

What separates different bikes within a given brand is often the level of components used to equip it: the brakes, suspension forks, cranks, derailleurs, hubs and so on. Very often you will find the same frame dressed at two or three different levels of componentry and it might not save you much money to go for a cheaper level only to find you have to upgrade some things later on. Here is a selection of suitable bikes:

SURLY LONG HAUL TRUCKER
The LHT is a great blend of road and mountain and equally at home with straight bars and 1.75" tyres as it is with 700c wheels and drops. You can buy a complete bike new in the US, but many riders choose to buy just the frame

Surly's versatile LHT is the most popular custom-built tourer. © Andrew Hanson

(only the frame is imported into the UK for tax reasons) and build up a dream bike or transfer gear over from an old bike. The frame is 4130 chromoly with all the braze-ons a touring cyclist could dream of: racks, mudguards, spare spokes, three bottle cage mounts, brake hangers and even mounts for gear shifters on the down tube, should all else fail. You can fit V-brakes or cantis, depending on what handlebars you choose.

Everything on the LHT is a standard easy-to-find size. It's got relaxed, stable steering and long chainstays for either size of wheel; a generous 18". The smaller frame sizes are built for 26" wheels only, while 22" and larger frames take 700c wheels with tyres up to 1.75" (about the largest you'll find in that size).

BRUCE GORDON BICYCLES

Bruce Gordon designs and builds custom lugged frames and loaded tourers in northern California. His reputation for high quality extends far beyond the

Bruce Gordon © Bill Weir

USA and his bikes have been used on many tough tours. Bruce's bikes come with flat bars or drops with reliable 'barcon' shifters at the end of the drops, though you can order both flat and drops fitted with cables that can be disconnected so the bars can be switched. Bruce's top-end model, the Rock'n'Road Tour comes with Shimano XT components all-round. Bruce Gordon builds frames and chromoly racks in-house and hand-builds wheels using Sun rims (see p45). A 26"-wheel version, the Rock'n'Road Tour EX has a high-mounted front rack and will take fat MTB tyres.

Two less expensive options are available, either the BLT (LX level componentry) and a new frame and racks-only option, the frame being built in Taiwan. Unusually for a modern bike, Bruce Gordons are fitted with old-fashioned quill stems (see p306), meaning you can raise or lower the handlebars anytime, though threadless steerers can be requested.

THORN RAVEN TOUR AND NOMAD S&S

Thorn pioneered making expedition touring bikes and in 2004 produced their first model designed specifically for the Rohloff 14-speed hub gear system (see p41), the Raven Tour. The Raven Tour is extremely versatile and ideal if you only want one bike. It's not the lightest bike in the world but it is one of the strongest, built from oversized chromoly made exclusively for Thorn. If you want a stronger frame, your only choice is another Thorn, the Nomad Mk2, which has thicker seat tubes and stays and can take a shock fork as an option. It's also available with S&S couplings, making it much easier and quicker to pack the bike down for transport in a package small enough to avoid airline surcharges.

Thorn Nomad © Kyle Archer

The advantages of designing Thorn's adventure tourers from the ground up for Rohloff are that the torque arm needed to hold the hub in place on most conversions is not needed, nor is the chain tensioning wheel. Instead, Thorn use an eccentric bottom bracket held in place by two easy-to-adjust bolts. Cable routing is designed for friction-free shifting without tight bends in the cable for more effortless gear-changing. Most buyers choose Thorn's own wide and swept riser bar, as the Rohloff shifter will not fit on drops.

Thorn offers a unique 100-day return policy, enough time to take your new bike on tour and return it if you're not happy. Better than that, they offer to support your Rohloff by shipping a loaner hub and wheel out to you wherever you are while your hub is being repaired.

KOGA-MIYATA

Dutch-made Koga-Miyatas are designed from the ground up for exactly the kind of riding this book is about, and they're fully equipped for it too. A couple of years ago Koga shocked the hardcore touring world by switching to aluminium for its trekking bike frames (the forks are still chromoly) and their top-end model, the World Traveller, weighs in at a very respectable 15.7kg (34.5 lbs) considering that it's loaded with lights, kickstands front and rear, a lock, pump, bottle cages, rack and mudguards. It's all top brand stuff too: Tubus racks, Shimano XT including the Hollowtech crankset (see p48), all rolling on in-house built double-eyeletted wheels (see p45).

A rare chromoly Koga-Miyata frame

If you want 700c wheels, the Traveller covers that need. Mark Beaumont rode a custom Koga (look for the Signature custom range) with 700c wheels for a little more speed on his round the world record run in 2008. For steely types, a chromoly-framed 700c model, the Randonneur is available, but weighs in at 1.6kg more than an aluminium World Traveller. Most Koga riders go with the butterfly bars popular in Europe. It's a comfortable, more upright stance, but less sporting than either straights or drops.

PART 1 – PRACTICALITIES

ROBERTS ROUGHSTUFF

Britain and the USA are the only two countries with an ongoing tradition of building touring bikes; if tourers are hard to find in British or American shops,

Roughing it on the Karakoram Highway

they're almost impossible to find anywhere else. Roberts is one of many small chromoly frame builders in the UK, but stands out for building not just fine racing bikes but also tourers, the toughest of which is the Roughstuff. It's true custom build; every option is up for discussion and Roberts will size you up and suggest tubing and a build-up best suited for you and your needs. Typically it involves a choice of Reynolds 853, Italian Columbus Nivacrom and 725,

but the latest 953 (regarded as strong and light as titanium), is now becoming available. The main joins are lug-free fillet-brazed (built up with brass fillets around the weld and sanded to a smooth seamless finish).

The most commonly chosen set up is drop bars, Campagnolo shifters and front derailleur and Shimano XT on the back resulting in superb shifting. Roberts usually suggest Tubus racks and then send the frame and racks off to the paint shop for a colour-coded look. As the photo shows, it's possible to switch to straight bars for mountain riding or off-roading, though this particular conversion using GripShift twist-grip controls required an expensive change of rear derailleur to match the shifters.

THORN SHERPA

The Sherpa is the entry-level derailleur bike in Thorn's adventure touring range, though in all respects it is a premium quality bike available in short and

Loaded touring on a Thorn Sherpa
© Paul Schmidt

long frames in varying sizes. The frame is made of the same oversized 4130 chromoly as the Thorn Raven in Taiwan, where most high-quality steel frames are now made. You can upgrade everything and still have a bike designed for hard touring at a lower price than the Rohloff models. The frame is the same quality as the Raven, the fork is identical, so what you have is a perfect touring set up with all the fixings for bottle cages, racks, mudguards and dynamo with very solid geometry for easy control of

a heavily-loaded bike. The Sherpa is the way to go if you want a drop-bar Thorn, as the Rohloff shifter won't fit drops. It's also a great frame-only option.

MID-RANGE MTBS

Since so many riders set out on round the world trips using 'bog-standard' mountain bikes, it's worth looking at their strengths. Cheap bikes below say $600/£400 with an 'MTB' appearance tend to be heavy, klutzy designs for absolute beginners with short-lasting wheels and crude suspension forks. At the other end of the scale expensive mountain bikes costing £800 (or around $1000 in the USA) or more are too fussy and specialised, with things you don't want for touring, such as 28-spoke lightweight racing wheels (see p44 for more on wheels) and high bottom brackets for good ground clearance. Above the Specialized Rockhopper/Giant XTC price-point, things

Specialized HR Pro on Shandur Pass,
Pakistan

you do want, like rack eyelets or rim brake mounts disappear. So look at the mid-range: the Rockhopper (disc or rim brake models), the Giant XTC, the Trek 4500. You'll need to switch the knobblies for touring tyres, but everything else is ready to go once you've fitted racks. These are cross-country designs, so the ride is fairly stable and the rider is not too stretched out, nor are the handlebars set too low for comfort. The forks have a more limited range of travel than high-end mountain bikes – 100mm is plenty – and you get good quality components such as Deore gear groups and Tektro brakes. Models like these are not as perfect as a dedicated expedition tourer, but the majority of first-time adventure riders choose mid-range MTBs and have no complaints.

HP VELOTECHNIK STREET MACHINE GTE

If you're going to tour on a recumbent, the aluminium-framed Street Machine Gte is the pick of the bunch. It's compact for a recumbent, weighs the same as a conventional tourer but has the greatest load-carrying capacity of any, and all of it is low down for added stability. Two Ortlieb motorbike panniers (48 litres combined) will fit the chromoly frame rack underneath your seat and there's room in between those for a tent. Rear panniers sit behind the rider and there's space for a cargo bag too.

The Street Machine is a great ride on good road: stable, fast and fairly responsive with its 20-inch front wheel. Recumbents give a great view of the

Customs inspection in Central Asia
© Robert Thomson

world flying by and out of the mountains you'll be more comfortable for longer reposing on a Gte than hunched over any diamond-framed dinosaur. The Street Machine has rear suspension right under the seat and would make a perfect bike for a Rohloff hub. There's a choice of a more conventional handlebar or under-seat steering, which takes a few minutes to get the hang of, but is far more comfortable in the long run. A recumbent will make your life a bit more complicated, but if you're rarely off paved roads and want to cover big mileage every day, the Street Machine will do it in style and comfort.

MARIN MUIRWOODS

The Marin Muirwoods has been chosen by numerous adventure cyclists over the years as a budget bike that works very well as an adventure tourer with

From Scotland to Surabaya via Tibet on a
Marin Muirwoods © Erika Bird

little extra investment in equipment needed. Until 2009 it was just about the last MTB-style mass-made bike with a chromoly frame. Now you have to choose the larger-wheeled 29er (see p44) if you want a chromoly Muirwoods, but you still get the rigid chromoly fork with eyelets for a front rack on either model and eyelets for a rear rack too. Other advantages are the 8-speed cassette, which takes a slightly thicker and longer-lasting chain than a 9-speed, though you would be wise to upgrade the cassette to a wider range

and to try to swap the chainrings for a smaller set to make life easier going up mountains. The 29er version has cable-operated disc brakes, another plus for adventure touring.

The componentry is so-so but good enough for touring, mostly Deore, Alivio and Acera level kit. The smooth-tread 1.4" kevlar-lined tyres are certainly worth using as your first set of tyres.

OTHER DREAM BIKES WORTH CONSIDERING

If you're prepared to look further afield, there are numerous alternatives, mostly from Germany. The Tout Terrain Silk Road is a Rohloff-based bike but has an integral stainless steel rack. It's an elegant, simple design with lots of good features and available in the US at 🖳 www.peterwhitecycles.com or in the UK at 🖳 www.bikefix.co.uk. Nöll (🖳 www.noell-fahrradbau.de) also makes Rohloff-based bikes using their own oversized racks for enormous loads and an entirely enclosed chain. Patria's Terra (🖳 www.patria.net) has the best looking chain-tensioning trick for all the Rohloff bikes I've seen, a sliding dropout rather than an eccentric BB. The Terra's frame is a traditional lugged construction for added strength. Traditionalists should head to Paris to order a Rando-Cycles Globe-Trotter (🖳 www.rando-cycles.fr). Made-to-measure elegance.

BYOB: BUILD YOUR OWN BIKE

A number of bike manufacturers offer frame-only deals. They include Surly, or Thorn's Sherpa which comes with a fork too. Mostly these are smaller outfits offering chromoly frames built in Taiwan rather than expensive made-to-order or full custom-builds. With its Inbred MTB frame, UK-based On-One (💻 www.on-one-shop.co.uk) has set the trend and is the cheapest option, but there are many others, including Merlin Cycles (💻 www.merlincycles .co.uk) with a top-end Reynolds 853 CroMo frame. Both are disc-only frames with no bosses for rim brakes.

On-One Inbred gets a workover from owner Phil Davis

Buying a frame like this is a great option if you have a mountain bike with good components but a frame that is too compact, won't take racks or just too specialised to work as a tourer. Just transfer the groupset and you're ready to roll for under around £400 ($600). Unless you have a donor bike you'll spend much more on transmission, fork, brakes, wheels and so on, but you'll have the satisfaction of your own custom-specified bike for much less than the high-end names mentioned earlier. Your local bike shop can assemble it all for you, or you can learn those skills yourself on a course (see p302).

Adapting a used mountain bike

You may be on a tight budget or perhaps you're turned off modern mountain bike designs with the near inevitability of ending up with an aluminium frame fitted with potentially fiddly suspension forks. In which case looking for an old MTB is a flash of inspiration; not only will you save money but you'll also get a bike that may be better suited to the kind of riding you have in mind: simple, reliable and easy to maintain on the back roads of the world. Out there you can still find inexpensive parts easily enough as locals still ride bikes with technology or equipment from yesteryear; it's the latest gear that can be hard to find.

Here's what to look for when checking out older bikes:
● Avoid suspension or be wary of early generation suspension systems. Don't even consider rear suspension bikes.
● Stick with chromoly frames; aluminium welding is much better nowadays; in older bikes fatigue is more likely. If you prefer aluminium, go with a bike no more than a few years old that as far as you know has led a gentle life.
● Older mountain bikes (1990s or earlier) were generally cross-country designs, so you'll find them to be good all-rounders in terms of handling. Chainstays shorter than 17" (43cm) may be too short for big feet to clear the rear panniers.
● An 8-speed cassette can be upgraded to give as wide a gear range (ie: highest and lowest gear) as today's 9-speeds. For 7-speeds it is a stretch so look for an 8-speed bike if you're heading for the hills.

● Bar-top (or 'bar-con') shifters are worth looking out for; a simple design, easy enough to use and fix. They are now hard to find, though sometimes turn up in odd places like Romania or India. Bar-top shifters however, can be built up using the bar-end (or 'bar-con') gear levers sold for touring bikes which fit in the ends of drop bars.

● Non-compact frames. Older bikes usually had full-length seat tubes and near-horizontal top tubes, giving more room inside the triangle to fit bottle cages and other essentials such as your growing flag sticker collection.

● Threaded headsets (as opposed to modern threadless systems such as Aheadsets) made it very easy to adjust your handlebar height as well as turn or remove the handlebars altogether without altering the headset adjustment. Cantilever brakes are as old as the hills and when well-adjusted, nearly all will stop you fast enough. Plus it's easy and inexpensive to upgrade these to more powerful V-brakes.

Remember it's primarily the frame you're looking out for. Assuming it's in good shape don't be put off if everything else is junk as long as the price is right; it can all be changed.

Where to find them and what to look for

A walk to my local train station finds a classic 1986 Stumpjumper, a '90s Diamond Back and an old Marin hybrid chained up every day. It's the sad fate of so many once-great MTBs to be relegated to commuter hack-bikes when they could be wheeling with the condors across the Cordillera Blanca. There's little incentive for their owners to sell them because they're virtually worthless to most people and they're becoming harder to find. Good examples often show up on eBay, Gumtree or Craigslist but are hyped in a 'they don't make them like this any more' way as if the seller knows what treasures they are. Rather than trawl eBay with separate searches for models you're interested in, check out the AuctionWatch feature, which searches eBay sites worldwide, at 🖥 www.retrobike.co.uk/auction. Bike forums are also great places to look, especially for serious old touring bikes.

Above all you need to make a close inspection of the frame, and not just aluminium frames. The most common type of damage is from a front-end crash which shows up as a bump underneath the down tube, right at the top where it joins the head tube. Look also for cracks around the welds; the bottom bracket is a likely place, especially on an old aluminium frame. Forks that appear to be bent backwards, even if a tiny amount, is not a good sign. A weakened frame may not crack up until you're hammering with a full load down the KKH, but eyeing up a bike from the front, top and side will identify anything out of alignment, as should a test ride. Try riding the bike no-handed to see if it's balanced or if it wobbles. Look for any roughness in the steering: the headset might need

1992 Rockhopper still going strong

some work. Old bikes can grind and click down in the bottom bracket, but these are cheap and easy to replace.

There are many good bikes out there but the big names like Trek, Specialized, Giant and Marin will be easiest to find. Look for chromoly Treks such as the 830 or 950 models or a MultiTrack. Specialized Rockhoppers and Stumpjumpers were classics until they went to aluminium and the frame design changed radically. Late model steel HardRocks are fine too. Marin's bikes in the 1990s were all steel (and some still are, see p36) and were versatile designs, as were Giants. GT bikes like the old Avalanche are a bit trickier to fit racks to but the oldies are good strong designs, if pitched as a little racier.

Many once great independent names have been sold to the big brands now, but a Ritchey, Ibis, Bontrager, Gary Fisher (before Trek bought them) or Breezer would be a real find. If you find oval-shaped Biopace chainrings, you've got something from the 1980s that's had very little use but will still probably need replacement. Don't go back beyond 7-speed cassettes; the axle spacing was narrower for 6-speeds. Seven-speed cassettes were the first Hyperglide models with indents and ramps cut into the sprockets to ease shifting. Later 7-speed hubs were wider: 135mm, the same as today's 8 and 9-speeds – and the ones to go for.

Gears, brakes and wheels

Now you've got your bike, new or used, you need to assess what works, and what needs upgrading. Ideally you've bought something with decent componentry (see p30) and may only need tyres (see p46), a rack or two for the panniers (see p56) and a dialled-in seating position (see p51).

GEARS

Adventure-touring bikes use mountain bike gear groups, which offer a far wider as well as lower range of gears than road bikes. The current standard gearing is a triple chainring of around 22, 32 and 42 teeth matched with a 9-speed cassette ranging with a high gear of 11 teeth and a low of 34, (although you can get 8-speed cassettes with the same ideal 11-34T range).

The reason for having so many gears is that it's easier to shift between similar sized cogs and so maintain an optimal cadence or pedalling rhythm. It's worth knowing that you don't really have 27 different speeds as there is a lot of overlap; middle chainring 4th cog may be the same as big chainring 2nd cog, but the latter selection will give a cross-over chain alignment which will

Paul Woloshansky's well-pimped Tech Pulse, with home-made racks, licence-plate fenders and army-surplus canvas bag panniers.

rattle and accelerate chain wear. In reality you only use the bottom couple of cogs when in the smallest chainring and the top few cogs when in the largest chainring so this adds up to around 15 usable speeds in all (and is why Rohloff's sequential 14-speed Speedhub is not so far off the mark; see p41).

How many speeds?

Today nearly all good quality new bikes come with 9-speed cassettes giving 27 gears on a standard triple chainring, but 8-speed cassettes (24 gears) are still very common and are possibly easier to find around the world. If you have an 8-speeder , don't see a 9-speed cassette as an essential upgrade. An 8-speed might not shift quite as slickly as a 9, but the thicker sprockets last a bit longer and the cassette is narrower so there is less dish to the wheel (see below) and so it's all a little more durable – the overall priority for adventure touring. The chain is also wider on 8-speed set ups and if regularly cleaned and maintained lasts longer too. The differences aren't huge but riders building a tourer from scratch will often choose an 8-speed system because of this durability.

Seven-speed gears are still fine for touring but the cassette's range is usually 13-30T, low enough for all but the steepest hills. Avoid the Shimano 7-speed MegaRange cassettes still found on some new bikes. MegaRange makes a big jump to a gimmicky 34T ultra-low bottom gear, but the whole point of multiple speeds is to make incremental, not big jumps between gears.

Shimano's latest designs are worth looking at. The three top-end Shimano derailleurs (SLX, XT and XTR) use the new Shadow design. It's a great improvement for touring because the old loop of gear changing cable on the derailleur that so easily snagged or kinked has been dropped and the derailleur itself sits behind the cassette and inside of the axle skewer, so the derailleur is well protected if the bike falls over or your panniers hang low. SRAM has a smaller range of gear groups but as with Shimano, go for the penultimate range (X.9) as the top-of-the range (X.0) is a huge jump in price for the dubious touring benefits of carbon-fibre construction.

Gear changers

You have three options for gear levers and it's worth trying them out to see which you prefer. On the road, it's not all about super-slick shifting which you might appreciate while racing to work; it's about simple, robust and even repairable designs that won't get easily damaged in a crash or while lashed to a bus roof and is why the old fashioned bar-con shifters (still available from SJS Cycles in the UK) are not such a retrograde step. With no vulnerable or exposed levers, twist-grip shifters are the simplest and so are well suited to touring (Rohloff hub gears – see p41 – also use a twist-grip control). The best known is SRAM's GripShift, which brought twist-grip shifters back from the dustbin of history and became the first competitive alternative to Shimano.

Thumb and forefinger trigger shifters are the most common type on flat bar bikes. The latest Shimano RapidFire shifters are great for touring because you can use either finger or thumb to push or pull the top lever, allowing a greater variety of hand positions. RapidFires also have a flexible clamp so you can position them where you want.

Less commonly seen and quite possibly an over-complex fad is the dual-control lever, a brake lever that also clicks up and down to change gears. Integrated brake/gear shifters work well on drop bars but are less useful on a mountain bike; you can't change your brakes without changing the gear levers and you can't fine tune the position of either as they're a single fixed unit.

Rohloff – the hub gear option

Hub gears are almost as old as derailleurs but until Rohloff they were not designed for the high torque needed for loaded touring or mountain biking. There are other hub gears available, but nothing strong enough for heavy-duty touring (though watch out for Shimano's new Alfine hub, currently available for MTBs but with a narrower gear range). The German Rohloff Speedhub is an ingenious 14-speed internally-geared system running a single chainring and sprocket. Operated by two cables, all the gear changing goes on inside the hub, protected from dust, grime and knocks. The Speedhub is tough and has proved to be very reliable, and compared to the adjustments and cleaning which derailleurs regularly require, it needs very little maintenance and is considered by many tourers as the ideal set up for long range travels.

Cable replacement and oil changes are a bit more complex than servicing a derailleur, but an oil change might only be necessary every 5000 kilometres or so, the suggested service interval. Replacing cables every 20-30,000km is easier than waiting till they break. The bad news is that Speedhubs cost around € 1000; that's three or four months riding to most world travellers.

A Speedhub's 14 speeds are evenly spaced and are a touch lower than the lowest possible derailleur gears while being just one gear shy of the highest gear a 9-speeder can manage (the gear a loaded touring rider hardly ever uses). The chain always runs in the same plane between the chainring and sprocket and so ought to last much longer, especially if you use Rohloff's own extra-strong chain. The single sprocket can be also reversed as it wears so giving more miles before replacement. The hub also gives a symmetrical spoke profile (no dishing with equal spoke size and tension) adding up to a much stronger wheel with less risk of broken spokes on the drive side (a common problem with derailleurs). And if you do break a drive-side spoke, it's much easier to replace.

Rohloffs can be adapted to run well on all sorts of bikes if properly installed, but UK manufacturer Thorn designs a range of touring bikes specifically for Rohloff Speedhubs. Thorn's design is the cleanest of all as it doesn't need the clumsy torque arm fitted down the left-side chainstay, nor a vulnerable chain tensioner. Fitting a Rohloff hub to a bike not designed for it can be a major conversion and is best done by a Rohloff specialist rather than your local bike shop.

Some Speedhubs shift smoothly, others (usually conversions) are a bit notchy, but it's usually down to cable installation or lubrication, the internal

Rohloff Speedhub: a black box

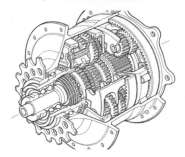

Inside a Rohloff 14-speed Speedhub –
planetary gears.

mechanism is rock-solid and in any case is not user-serviceable.

The problem for the touring cyclist is that if something should go wrong, you're on your own. Forget local bike shops who will have never seen a Rohloff. Go to ▣ www.rohloff.de and download the technical manual to troubleshoot and determine if you can diagnose the problem; chances are it's cabling or time to change the oil. In the extremely unlikely event that it's something internal, you'll have to send it back to Rohloff, although if you bought Rohloff-equipped Thorn, they'll send you a replacement wheel wherever you are in the world. You will occasionally read of Rohloff disaster stories, most commonly about the flange cracking where the spokes mount, but it's the rarity that makes it an event. People don't post messages in forums just because their derailleur broke, and Rohloffs rarely mis-shift; a derailleur will mis-shift more in an hour than a Rohloff will in a month of riding.

There are aesthetic considerations too, not unimportant for something you will notice every time you turn the pedals. Some find the simplicity of the system and the ability to change gears while the bike is stationary to be winning arguments; others find the grinding noise and slight drag in seventh gear can get irritating; it's a regrettable characteristic of the design, not something broken.

CHOOSING BRAKES

Loaded touring bikes need powerful brakes, not least when descending from mountain passes. Mountain bike brakes have become much stronger relative to the old cantilever brakes you find on traditional drop-bar touring bikes. Rim brakes, mechanical disc brakes and hydraulic disc brakes are all very different options with their own merits, but to play it safe maintenance-wise, go with the oldest and simplest setup: rim brakes, or mechanical disc brakes (also called cable-disc brakes).

Rim brakes

Most mountain bike rim brakes are the V-brake design, which is a kind of cantilever with extended direct-pull arms (meaning the brake cable pulls the arms together, rather than upwards as in older cantilever models). Cantilevers and V-brakes fit on the same brake bosses and swapping your cantis for V-brakes is about the easiest and most effective upgrade you can do. All V-brakes are powerful but the better quality V-brakes offer more refinement or useful features such as using brake pad cartridges. Worn brake pads are replaced by sliding them out of a cartridge that stays in position so you don't have to reposition the new pads. Cartridge pads are light and slim so it's easy to carry plenty of them. Rim brakes are nice and simple, easy to maintain on the road but quite fiddly in that fairly frequent tweaks are needed to keep them performing. Properly adjusted V-brakes give a lot more braking force than those that haven't been looked after. The downside of V-brakes is that they depend on a clean dry wheel rim to brake on and don't work well in rain. They also shorten the life of your wheels considerably by wearing down the side of the rim, but you can mitigate this by cleaning the rim and the brake pads to remove grit which will otherwise act like sandpaper on your rims. Ceramic-coated rims will last considerably longer but are not cheap.

Shimano XTR: the most powerful cable rim brakes.

Disc brakes

Disc brakes have been slow to gain acceptance in the touring world but have much to offer. Disc brakes require much less physical effort to keep 50 kilos of loaded bike plus rider in check. This large braking force for little effort is something you'll appreciate as biting winds and jarring potholes numb your hands dropping down from Ladakh's high passes. Discs also avoid wear on the wheel rim, greatly extending their longevity and if your wheel is knocked out of true, braking is not affected so you can re-true the wheel at the end of the day rather than at the roadside. Compared with most rim brakes, braking in the wet is as good as in dry weather and your rims won't overheat on long downhills (though the disc and pads certainly will).

'Mechanical', in other words cable-operated, disc brakes are far simpler than hydraulics and you might rightly ask: does a bicycle even need a hydraulic brake system? Disc brakes are a big improvement over rim brakes and mechanical is the ideal choice for adventure touring, offering all-weather stopping power without the fuss of fragile hydraulic couplings and seals. Popular models such as Avid BB7s are simple to install and set up, and feature tool-free pad adjustment from both sides and confidence-inspiring modulation or 'feel' as good as any hydraulic brake.

If you choose to go with the sexier hydraulic discs, recognise the risk of rare but fatal damage to the hydraulic brake lines. Maintenance of hydraulics may seem daunting but is a simple skill to learn. Bleeding mushy brakes by purging tiny air bubbles from the fluid (much as you would a domestic radiator at home) is a very infrequent and actually fairly simple task with quality units. Check out the online video tutorials by whichever company produces your brakes. As long as your hydraulic brakes use standard automotive brake fluid, you will easily find the supplies you need to maintain them. Servicing the brake pistons may be necessary too, typically involving opening, cleaning and replacing the seals in the calliper. Whenever you remove the wheel and transport the bike, **you must remember to wedge the pads open** (with a coin, for example) or they

Avid BB7 cable-operated disk brakes – powerful and easy to adjust

may lock together. The only major downside is that hydraulic setups can get damaged and leak (albeit more commonly in transit) and the thin brake hoses and couplings are not something you'll find in a Punjabi back street where brake cables hang thick as spaghetti.

Disc brakes cannot be fitted to a fork or frame that isn't designed for them because the braking forces are much more tightly concentrated than on a wheel rim. It is possible to buy a rigid fork (see p50) that will take a disc brake but callipers can make fitting a rack awkward (options for disc-friendly racks are on p58). As with suspension, rather than go through all the complications and expense of fitting something your bike was not designed for, get a bike (or at least a frame) which is disc-ready.

WHEELS

Bicycle wheels are designed to balance the competing needs of strength and speed. Because weight has a much more noticeable effect on rotating parts like wheels, bike manufacturers are tempted to fit fairly light wheels that give a bike a much livelier feel than the heavier wheels that adventure tourers need. Nonetheless, the wheels on any decent mountain or touring bike are designed to take some abuse and are likely to be good enough for a year or more of hard touring before you need to think about replacing them

It's possible to build an excellent wheel in either 26" or 28" (700c) size suitable for heavy touring, but outside of the developed world, you will only find 26" wheels and tyres. The quality won't be very good but you'll always find something that fits; not so with 700c wheels. If you're touring on a bike with 700c/28" wheels, you need to ask yourself if you can have a new wheel shipped to you in the unlikely event of serious damage to your wheels.

There is a certain lore about bicycle wheels which is partly due to the fact that handmade wheels are still much better than machine-built wheels (which are what you get on all but the most expensive expedition bikes). If you are starting out with a new mid-range bike, you can stress-relieve the spokes (instructions at 🖥 www.sheldonbrown.com/wheelbuild.html#seating) to help them become properly seated to reduce the stress on each.

Choosing a new wheel

Wheels do wear out in the normal course of things and if you're headed for the back of beyond you might want to upgrade what you've got so you're ready for the toughest roads you can find, loaded down with a month's supply of Snickers and dried noodles. Only very cheap wheels come ready made, and as you can choose hubs, rims and spokes individually, bike shops usually only build wheels when someone orders them. That's your chance to upgrade and have some great touring wheels built that will see you through thick and thin.

Hubs

Wheel hubs are one of those components we like to fit and forget, so the better a hub you get, the longer you can afford to leave it before opening it up, cleaning it out and replacing the bearings. Keep life simple by asking for something standard like Shimano Deore, SLX or XT as going for major brands always simplifies things in terms of repair, replacement, availability of parts and compatibility. If your hubs continue to run freely with no play, you might only need to service them once a year. These days you can find out what bearing sizes or parts you need for a hub service from the web (for Shimano, go to 🖳 http://techdocs .shimano.com). Ball bearings come in standard imperial sizes everywhere in the world so you don't need to bring them from home, but knowing the size helps if you've worn them down when it comes to service time.

End of the road for this rim. Though you are risking a crash on a cracked rim, most will carry you a few hundred miles from when you first notice the crack developing.

Rims

Bicycle wheel rims are made of aluminium alloy for lightness and rigidity and eyelets (small 'washers') around the spoke holes help spread the load and are a sign of good quality. Stronger rims are double-walled and are what you want for touring. It's also better if they come with eyelets on each wall (double eyelets) to help prevent the spoke nipple from pulling through.

The French brand Mavic is the biggest manufacturer of bike wheel rims but there are complaints from some tourers that Mavics are prone to cracks around the spokes. The high temperature of the hard-anodising process used on some of their rims strengthens them but also leaves them brittle. Cracks develop on the anodised surface which migrate into the rim wall. Go for a non-anodised 'silver' rim: Mavic XM719 or 717s are good bets for touring.

Mountain bike rims aren't designed specifically for touring; new MTBs are usually sold with a mid-weight rim weighing around 450g. Remember that rotating weight has a greater effect on performance than static weight, so be cautious but consider something a little heavier. Some good choices in 26" include Italian DRCs (530g), Rigida Andras (686g) and long-time heavyweight champs, Sun Rhynos (745g). These last two rims are so heavy that the makers don't bother with eyelets: the rims are thick enough not to need support. Unless you're very heavily loaded or the worrying type, you don't need a rim this heavy but could get by with a 565g-Rhyno Lite XL. It's a wider rim suited to fat tyres and sometimes recommended for downhilling but works fine for adventure touring. Lighter riders will find Sun's CR18 (500g) strong enough for touring. Even

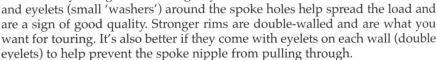

DISHING

One of the drawbacks of derailleur gears is that they weaken the rear wheel because the spokes on the cassette (righthand) side are at a very shallow angle. This is called 'dishing' and the more the wheel is dished due to wider cassettes, the weaker it is. Spoke tension on the drive side spokes has to be greater to compensate for the dished shape and you will find you break more spokes on the drive side of the rear wheel (see p62 for the tool you need to carry to replace drive-side spokes). Drive side spokes are shorter than left side spokes and you should carry a couple more of them, but with good quality hand-built wheels and moderate loads, breaking spokes should be a rare event. Beyond a certain age spokes will start to break more often; that's a sign to replace them all and probably the rim too.

if your bike has disc brakes, bear in mind that disc-specific rims are built without the thick braking surfaces on the sides. You might want the option of fitting rim brakes some day, so stick with a more traditional and solid construction.

Spokes

The ideal spoke count for a touring wheel is 36 holes but 32 is much more common on good quality mountain bikes and is good enough. Any less (the next possible figure is 28 spokes) is too light for touring. Ask for the heavier-gauge DT Swiss, Wheelsmith or Sapim spokes, the most common high quality brands.

Tyres

Fitting good tyres is probably the biggest single improvement you can make to any bike to turn it into a world tourer. Tyres are the most basic form of suspension and are the only kind you need for road riding and most unpaved roads.

Light loads allow you to ride on faster, narrower tyres. © Peter van Glabbeek

Fitting 2-inch wide tyres will protect against a multitude of sins such as an overloaded bike, weak racks and wheels or a frame unsuited to bad roads in the first place. If you go for narrower tyres – and even a 1.75" tyre will give a noticeably harsher ride – you'll pedal with less effort for sure but unless you lighten up, you're risking broken spokes and rack bolts and buckled wheels. I've watched numerous riders on 1.75" or narrower tyres descending beautiful mountain passes at a crawl because they were overloaded or their wheels weren't strong enough to risk going faster. Downhills are one of the greatest and hardest-earned pleasures of cycling and it's a shame to miss out on the fun because your bike isn't tough enough for it.

If you have a mountain bike with knobby off-road tyres, change them for something that is designed for the job; touring calls for tougher and heavier tyres than mountain biking. Whatever vehicle they're on, most users judge a tyre by its tread, but it is the quality of the carcass that defines a tyre's load-carrying and shock-absorbing parameters. The tread pattern is a secondary matter but you'll soon learn that a smooth tread rolls more efficiently, is more predictable on bends and in the wet and lasts much longer than an off-road tyre. Riding unpaved roads, having a tread pattern rather than a smooth or slick tyre becomes more important, especially on loose surfaces.

Folding tyres are more expensive than rigid bead tyres but lighter and much more convenient as spare tyres as they take up less space.

Unlike wheels, where everything in 26" size is designed for mountain bikes, there are some excellent tyres designed specifically for adventure touring. These are the best options for long, hard trips:

Schwalbe Marathon XR

The venerable XR has been the classic adventure-touring tyre for many years. Despite its hefty 790g weight in the 2" width and hefty price too, it's become a favourite for its toughness, puncture-resistance and long life. Perhaps for this latter characteristic Schwalbe have decided to discontinue the XR – stock up if you can find it. Marathon XRs have tough sidewalls which give a hard ride, but provide unrivalled protection against cuts from rocks, making them first choice for remote backcountry riding. They come in 1.6″, 2″ and 2.25″ versions for mountain bikes and 1.4″, 1.6″ and 2″ for 700c wheels.

Schwalbe Marathon Extreme
Schwalbe's Marathon Extreme is too new to have built up a long-term reputation among tourers, but all the signs are promising. Where the old technology was to throw a lot of rubber onto a kevlar lining, the Marathon Extreme and the Supreme (see below) use a new compound said to be much harder and certainly much lighter at only 570g for a 2″ tyre. Schwalbe claim the Extreme is as puncture-resistant as the XR and despite larger knobs on the shoulder, has lower rolling resistance. With its more aggressive tread pattern, it's certainly better suited to loose rock, gravel or off-roading. Extremes come in 2- and 2.25 inches for 26-inch wheels, and in 1.4 and 1.6 inches for 700c wheels.

Schwalbe Marathon Supreme
The Supreme uses the same new Triple Nano compound as the Marathon Extreme. It's a slick-tread design which is also too new for a long track record, but with Schwalbe's reputation it's likely to be good. At 595g for a 2″ tyre it's almost as heavy as the knobbier Extreme and should match or exceed it for longevity but with low rolling-resistance, which is what you want most of the time. As long as you're not riding on loose dirt or gravel, the Supreme will be a very efficient tyre and well-suited to rides round India or South East Asia while still versatile enough for diversions onto mountain tracks.

Continental Travel Contact
Less expensive than Schwalbe's Marathon range and usually sold with an inner tube thrown in, the Travel Contact comes in rigid and folding versions but is a great combination with a hard and fairly smooth centre ridge for low rolling resistance on roads, and small shoulder knobs for a bit of bite in loose bends. The result is a fairly efficient tyre,

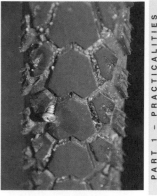
Almost puncture-proof
Marathon XR © Peter Gostelow

Schwalbe Marathon Extreme

Schwalbe Marathon Supreme

Continental Travel Contact

100g lighter than a Marathon XR but with better off-road cornering. The 26" size comes in one width – 1.75" but the 700c size is available in 37mm or 42mm, which is 1.45" or 1.65".

BOTTOM BRACKETS AND HEADSETS

Unseen and overlooked, the bottom bracket (or 'BB') is the large bearing inside the BB shell in between the cranks. It's likely to be a sealed unit and there's no servicing to be done, but if you know yours is old and you're setting off to circle the globe, replacing it is a good precaution. It takes shop tools to install a BB and any bike shop that sells MTB-style bikes should have something that will fit, though first check if tightening your old BB will solve any clicking or loose play in the cranks. Mechanics the world over will be familiar with one of the standard Shimano BB designs and have the tools for it, whereas if you've got a high-end hub made by anyone else, you could be stuck for help.

One great development in BBs in recent years has been the new outboard bearing design, the most common of which is Shimano's Hollowtech II, although Truvativ and Race Face also make them. Outboard bearings screw in from either side and sit outside the shell, meaning they are both wider and larger in diameter and much stronger than a conventional BB. The bearings themselves are cartridge types, meaning the bearings are contained in one unit and are not serviceable but are easily replaced and at a pinch you could do the job without special tools, or even carry two spare bearings. The downside of fitting outboard bearings is that you'll have to change the pedal cranks and you will need to get a shop to grind the faces of the BB shell to make sure they are absolutely parallel. Shimano's Hollowtech is currently available only on SLX or XT groupsets.

Almost every bike sold today uses a threadless headset, commonly known by the name of the most popular brand, Aheadset. It's simpler and easier to adjust than the old threaded kind and you don't have to carry a large 32mm wrench to tighten it. It's also very easy to get at the headset bearings to service them and they are always cartridge bearings so they don't spill out when you open up the headset. Although threadless headsets are nearly all $1^{1}/_{8}$", if you are replacing the cartridge bearings you must look for one of exactly the same shape as well as size. If you've got a non-standard width headset such as a Cannondale, be sure to carry spare bearings for a long trip. Other ultra-wide headsets such as Koga-Miyata's are non-standard in other ways and though a very strong design, will not be easy to service other than at a dealer.

Hollowtech II, Shimano's outboard bearing design

Comfort stations!

You've got your mechanicals sorted but comfort is just as important if you want to finish your trip still smiling. A saddle and handlebars that conform to your body and preferred posture are absolutely non-negotiable although suspension can't be considered essential.

SUSPENSION FORKS

Suspension forks are not necessary or recommended for general touring but are a lot of fun in the mountains and improve your bike's handing considerably on rough ground, besides reducing wrist and arm fatigue. The more off-road riding you're planning, the more suspension makes sense. Many riders who have bought a hardtail MTB choose to keep the suspension fork, thinking it will come in handy somewhere along the way and because it's an extra expense to replace it with a rigid fork (see p50 if you are considering this option). In typical touring conditions of high mileage mostly on roads, a good suspension fork will probably keep working for a year or longer with a minimum of maintenance and then slowly seize up as the ingress of grit and moisture causes internal corrosion and turns the oil inside to sludge. A worse outcome would be an air fork collapsing through a broken seal. All good quality forks can be locked out, meaning turned into a rigid fork at the turn of a knob, bringing your problems to an end but if that's not possible, the fork is finished and you will have to try other means of eliminating all movement in the forks, such as filling the lower legs with sand to fill the void. Fitting racks to suspension forks calls for a little ingenuity, or buying a rack designed for suspension forks (see p58).

Choosing a new fork – oil and coil

If you're actually buying a suspension fork (most probably to replace a cheap unit that came with your bike), play it safe and look at moderately priced forks from brands such as Fox, Marzocchi, Manitou, RockShox and Magura. A fork for touring should have relatively short travel, no more than 100mm and be designated for 'XC-trail' use. Research on the internet, starting somewhere like ▨ www.mtbr.com to find out what's popular and how reliable they are, while bearing in mind that reviewers could be high jumpers, weekend racers or blowhards rather than more sedate tourers. Though they're falling out of favour due to being slightly heavier, for long rides motorcycle-style oil-damped coil suspension is likely to be more reliable than the now dominant air forks. Both use oil to damp or slow down the rebound action but to save weight air forks rely on the compression or spring effect of air instead of a steel coil. As you can imagine, expecting a sliding air seal to retain pressure while hammering for weeks on Patagonian ripio is a tall order. However, this is only a general recommendation; reliability can differ greatly between particular forks of the same type or manufacturer and models change so often that it's almost impossible to make a useful generalisation, but see Tom Allen's recommendation for Magura's Odur fork on ▨ http://tom.ride-earth.org.uk.

It's harder to find good quality forks that have bosses for rim brakes, but it's a useful fallback to be able to fit some V-brakes, which can usually be found in bike shops around the world, if your disc brakes fail or, as Sebastien Demange found (see box p104) that brake fluid freezes at -30°C.

Maintenance on the road

Looking after a suspension fork on tour is largely a matter of keeping dirt and grit from the upper legs, or stanchions, so it cannot damage the seals. Oddly, modern forks no longer have the rubber boots around the exposed stanchions to keep dirt at bay, as boots also tend to keep dirt in and pressed against the stanchions as they slide up and down. The most important thing you can do is to keep those stanchions clean by giving them a good wipe with a dry cloth every day and washing the forks fairly often. Servicing requirements are unique to each fork and so are the seals but it's no business for amateurs; if you take your bike to your local bike shop at home, they will likely send it to the manufacturer rather than open it themselves. If you have an air fork, you will need to carry a small high-pressure pump to maintain the correct pressure inside the fork. The valve may have a Schrader fitting but you need the precise gauge that comes with an air fork pump.

The worse that can happen with an oil-and-coil fork is that it starts leaking; as long as the leak is at the stanchion seal and not the bottom you will only lose oil gradually and can top it up (Between 5W and 15W is the norm; about the consistency of cooking oil and not something you will find everywhere). The more common problem with suspension forks on tour is that they gradually seize up through neglect, which is no great disaster.

REMOVING SUSPENSION FORKS

Thorn's
Mt. Tura fork

The longer your trip, the less sense a suspension fork makes as it will need a proper service or repair at some point. Most of them weigh over 2kg so you will save around half that weight and have an easier time fitting racks by removing it and installing a rigid fork. It's what fellow Trailblazer author Laura Stone did when she set off for a year's riding to research *Himalaya by Bike*. What you need is a so-called suspension-corrected rigid fork that will suit a mountain bike originally designed for suspension forks.

Thorn have always sold their adventure-touring forks as separate items, but they now offer one with the extra length necessary to replace a suspension fork running around 80-100mm of travel without altering your bike's geometry and handling. You get all the braze-ons for racks and a

dynamo in a classic raked and tapered design. The curvature of a good fork helps soak up road chatter and the tapering gives a sensitivity to both smaller and larger bumps. Choosing a rigid fork, preferably a classic curved and tapered fork will let you fit a simple and reliable rim brake. If you still want to run disc brakes, you need a straight fork but you will lose the suppleness and shock absorption of a good quality touring fork. In the US, Vicious Cycles (⌨ viciouscycles.com) and Surly (⌨ www.surlybikes.com) make a range of 'straight blade' forks with optional braze-ons for low-rider racks and fenders (mudguards to Brits) and mounts for disc brakes if desired. Surly also make touring forks such as the Long Haul Trucker fork that come with rack and mudguard braze-ons.

Suspension seatposts

If you crave some sort of rear suspension, a suspension seatpost is by far the easiest way to achieve it; the many ingenious downhill-racing rear suspension designs are not suited to carrying baggage or irregular maintenance. The telescopic style suspension seatpost is the cheapest way to get some backside protection but sometimes you wonder if it has any effect. With a simple elastomer design requiring no maintenance, the Cane Creek Thudbuster offers a noticeably plusher ride with up to double the play and none of the initial 'stiction' of telescopic seatposts. The short-travel model (shown here) is all you need for touring.

Cane Creek Thudbuster

FINDING THE SWEET SPOT

A lot of research has been done on finding the ideal cycling position, but it's all in the name of increasing racing-oriented efficiency, not trans-continental comfort. It's another area where the touring cyclist has to spend a lot of time and thought adjusting their bike until it's as comfortable as possible. You'll be spending as much time perched on your saddle as you ever did on a chair in the office and it's vital to get the right saddle and in the right position for long-term happiness. More than just a sore butt, if you get your riding position wrong you could end up with back, neck or wrist trouble that jeopardises your trip, but get it right and there will be nothing stopping you.

Plan well ahead and experiment with all comfort-related issues and remember it's a top priority in choosing a bike. Most mountain bikes nowadays have the bars set level with saddle, it's an improvement on the stretched-out low handlebar style inherited from racing bikes that made downhills tricky when heavily loaded. You need to put in some long rides on your bike as well as a short shake-down tour to check it out for comfort. If you make changes to the riding position, you need to be sure they work for you: last-minute changes to a stem or saddle are often quickly regretted on tour.

One short cut to finding your ideal riding position is to go for a bike fitting at a bike shop. You can either choose a more traditional fitting where you sit on a frame and get measured up, or go for a computerised fitting service such as 💻 www.bikefitting.com. Your measurements are mostly taken in a standing position and fed into a computer that generates all the measurements needed to suit not just your body but the riding style you prefer. Make it clear that you want a touring setup and choose only the basic fit as the more in-depth programmes are designed for racers looking to maximise power output.

Here are some starting points for finding a good riding position. It's easiest if you can get a friend to help you by looking at your position while you are sitting on the bike.

You should not have to reach so far forward that your back arches, which will give you backache on tour.

Having set the saddle height, adjust your **handlebars** so they are level with the saddle. If you have drops, the top of the bar is where to measure.

Your kneecap should be above the pedal spindle. Move your **saddle** back and forth to find that position, then road-test it as you may find your riding position on the saddle is a little different to how you sit on it while stationary.

Don't hunch your shoulders; keep them relaxed and keep your spine straight as it goes up into your head.

Start with your **saddle** horizontal. If you have to tip it up or down, it may not be the right saddle for you.

It's easy to change the **stem** for one with more height or extension. Too long and you will strain to reach the bars; too close and you will be too upright and not have enough power over the steering.

Set the **saddle height** so your legs are almost fully extended when the pedals are furthest away from you. Your ankle should be relaxed, at a right angle to the leg and not pushed up or stretching down.

1. Get the saddle height right first. The right spot will probably feel higher than you think is natural. At the correct height you should be able to only just touch the ground with one foot when sitting on the saddle. With a foot on the pedal extend one leg down as far as possible: there should be a slight bend at the knee with the feet horizontal on the pedal.

2. Now fine-tune the saddle angle. Start with a level (horizontal) saddle. This spreads your weight best and allows you to move around more easily while riding.

3. Move the saddle fore and aft to find the spot where your kneecap is over the axle of the pedal when that pedal is horizontal and pointing forward.

4. Finally check your handlebar stem is the ideal length and height. Your handlebars should be roughly level with the saddle because this balances your weight between hands and seat and avoids placing excessive stress on either. A general guide for the stem length is that when sat on the bike and looking down at the front axle, the centre of the handlebar should be in line with the axle, not in front nor behind it.

Remember that these are just guidelines, it is much more important to go with what feels right and then take a long ride to confirm it. Getting the right stem is the biggest hassle because there's no adjustment and you're simultaneously looking for two measures, the angle of the stem and its length. Bike shops may have a box of used stems to loan out or swap so you can find the right one for you. Otherwise buy an adjustable cheapie to pin down your optimum position. When you've found the right spot, get a bombproof rigid stem that won't snap on you when you least want it.

Generally speaking, tall riders converting compact-framed MTBs for touring are looking to substantially increase handlebar heights, but sometimes so-called riser handlebars and the typical range of Aheadset (1^1/$_8$") stems are inadequate, partly because the modern, Aheadset-style stem merely clamps to the available steerer tube (part of the fork) which may itself be insufficiently long. A fork with an adequate length of steerer tube to spare is best but an inexpensive way of getting the same result is to fit a stem raiser clamp which adds around 70mm of height to a steerer tube.

LOVE IN THE SADDLE

The most difficult aspect in the fraught quest for comfort is finding the right saddle. Almost every touring biker will tell you a firmer saddle works best in the long run as it will support your nether regions on the hips' sit bones, rather than letting them sink in to soft foam or gel. But with saddles more than anything, advice from others is only their humble opinion, it can never be a hard or indeed 'soft' rule. You have to go entirely by your own impressions and the only way to do that is to experiment by spending plenty of time on your saddle before committing to a long ride. You may never find a saddle you'd want to take down the aisle but you ought to be able to find one where the discomfort doesn't carry over from one day to the next and builds up over time. Saddle troubles are often alleviated simply by wearing padded shorts, but look for a couple of characteristics that make a good touring saddle. A reasonably large area to sit on rather than a racing blade will spread your weight and so reduce pressure points. A larger saddle will also give you some room to move around to relieve aches or boredom or to sit forward a little when climbing. It needs to be broad enough at the tail to support your sit bones. Women are likely to need a broader saddle than men as their sit bones are typically wider.

Saddles with a groove down the middle are now very common and work by relieving pressure on the pudendal nerves and arteries which pass on the saddle side of your sit bones. It doesn't have to be a massive groove, even a faint depression and softer material along the centre will do the job. Specialized make a lot of channelled saddles; their much-imitated BG (Body Geometry) range is worth a look, particularly the less expensive all-round models rather than racing or triathlon-specific items. In saddles more than any other component, comfort has little to do with cost; that factor more commonly relates to lightness and racing needs where potential customers have money to spare. Another brand worth looking at is WTB, known for the Rocket V saddles. The characteristic dip isn't always a good sign in a saddle (it can mean too much contact and less ease moving around) but oddly it works for many riders. The Rocket Vs also have a slightly dropped nose to make it easy to climb on the front of the saddle and avoid getting jabbed in the rear if you hit a bump.

Among tourers the classic Brooks range of leather saddles may be the most popular brand. Brooks claim they made the world's first anatomic saddle in 1930, the B17 touring model. It may not feel like a classic after the first long ride, but like a good shoe, a leather saddle will wear in with age and outlast other kinds of saddle. Although incredibly durable, Brooks saddles are vulnerable to getting wet. They need waxing, either with Brooks' own Proofide or something like Nikwax. But you need to keep the saddle as dry as you can even when it's thoroughly proofed, which includes protecting it from spray from underneath. The less expensive, thinner models like the B17 break in

It's rare for the rails to break on a Brooks but the owner was still devoted to this one.

quicker but are more prone to losing their shape than the thicker hide examples such as the Team Pro or Swift. The worst situation is to have to ride on a wet Brooks saddle, as that is when it will stretch the most. Carry and use the tensioning spanner to keep the saddle taut, but take care not to over-tension a wet saddle; there's a risk of it shrinking and ripping off the rails as it dries. Lastly, like your best school shoes, a shiny leather saddle will scratch easily, but it's only cosmetic damage and can probably be polished out by the first shoe shine-wallah you come across. A smooth slippery surface has benefits in making sliding around the saddle easier, something the more common gel examples don't do so well.

Not everyone bonds with a Brooks, but those that do swear by them. If you're in the US, the best information, advice and most comprehensive stock (as well as an amazing 6-month returns policy) is at Wallingford Bicycle Parts (⌨ www.wallbike.com). If only more shops would take saddle returns!

HANDLEBARS

The other point of contact between body and bike that greatly affects comfort is the handlebars. Most MTB or straight bars nowadays have a bit of a backward sweep to reduce wrist strain. If you feel there still isn't enough curvature to the bar for a natural wrist position, look at SJS's Comfort bar or something similar. This is the bar most buyers of Thorn bikes choose for touring, with 18 degrees of sweep and an inch of rise and tight bends that don't waste space on straight sections. It's a wide bar, great for control but if you aren't broad-shouldered, it might be too wide; just saw off an inch. Ergon grips (see p27) are the most comfortable grips going, offering a flat platform for your palms that spreads the pressure and allows you to keep your wrists straighter than wrapping your hands round a circular grip. There is nothing like Ergons available for drop bars, but double-wrapping drops with tape or adding some foam padding and then a further layer of tape will make them more comfortable for long days on the bike as well as insulating your hands in cold weather.

Other handlebar types

Although they suit a few individuals, beware of butterfly, moustache, pretzel or other exotic shaped bars. These look like great touring bars but aren't really designed for it, nor are most of them strong enough. Look for Modolo's Yuma bar for a good quality example. Butterfly bars have a lot of hand positions, but what you really need is one good position, not three or four bad ones. The main problem is the brakes are too far back and not where you need them, on the ends of the bars where your hands naturally rest when controlling going downhill.

PART 1 – PRACTICALITIES

Racks and panniers

You've chosen the right bike, got gears to go, brakes to stop and a comfortable setup. Now you have to make arrangements to carry the load. If you're wondering how to do it, a perusal of the bikes posted on 💻 http://fully loadedtouring.com – currently numbering over 300 and many of them adventure tourers, including two of mine – will give you lots of ideas. You'll see that the most common setup is a pair of big panniers on the back, another pair of smaller bags on a front rack, something over the back rack, and a handlebar bag. In case you haven't guessed, touring with a backpack is a short route to

THE TRAILER ALTERNATIVE

If you cannot or do not want to fit racks on your bike, a trailer is the way to go. For serious off-road touring (see 💻 www.bike packing.net), trailers are a good option and are probably the carrier of choice for rides such as the 2000-mile Great Divide Mountain Bike Route between Canada and Mexico (see p195). Towing a trailer makes your bike lighter and more responsive on singletrack and washboard and trailers can be removed quickly unlike racks, returning your bike to its original light and racy condition for short side trips around town or into the mountains.

There are many different models out there, but look only at single-wheel models which are more efficient for touring. The well established BoB (Beast of Burden) Yak is the oldest and most popular trailer, but there are other options, the best of all being the Extrawheel Voyager. At just over 2kg it

weighs about half as much as a BoB Yak but has a couple of key design advantages. The load is carried in two 40 litre panniers either side of the wheel, placing little stress on the vulnerable connection with the bike's rear axle. The trailer wheel itself is either 26" or 28" and could be swapped with a front wheel; it's a much stronger option than a small wheel which will not last as long.

Trailers of course make for a much longer and more cumbersome rig. You have an extra bag when you take a plane and another awkward carry up rickety guest house stairs. It's trickier in crowded traffic too and you have to worry about the the hub, the connection and pivot, the extra tyre and rim. On RTW rides, trailers are rarely seen but might appeal for extended off-roading or tandem riders, where space is always very limited.

It's a dog's life in the Yukon. BoB Yak trailer.
© Matt Goodhind

55kg of food and 10 litres of fuel – Martin
Adserballe sets off for the Changtang
plateau in Tibet. © Dominique Kerhuel

posterior misery and a sweaty back. At the very least you'll need a solid rear rack, a pair of panniers and a bag on top, and as with tyres, the hard-pressed rack needs to be up to the job.

RACKS

Racks are a relatively recent invention for bike touring, the older generation squeezed everything into saddle bags or handlebar bags. Blackburn made the first modern racks for bike touring some 30 years ago from aircraft grade aluminium tubing and though strong for their weight and great for light camping trips, heavily-loaded adventure tourers nowadays pick something stronger. Luckily several manufacturers are waiting to supply your needs.

Tubus

German-made Tubus are among the best chromoly racks available. Their long-running Cargo model has a dog-leg rear strut to stabilise the load against

Tubus Logo (rear) and Tubus Duo (front)

swaying and a triangular middle strut to provide exceptional rigidity. If you want to set your panniers a little lower or need a little more heel clearance, Tubus' Logo rack should work for you. The Cargo and Logo are rated for 40kg loads, but aim for less than half of that and your rack will never break on tour.

Tubus also make four great front racks including the Swing which is designed for suspension forks and carries the panniers angled out from the crown of the fork.

Old Man Mountain

OMM make the strongest aluminium racks. To avoid any risk of flex and therefore metal fatigue to which aluminium is prone, OMM racks are exceptionally rigid. The base is made of solid CNC-milled aluminium with double bolts connecting the struts of the rack. Long welds curving round the top platforms making a solid structure; weld failures are unknown. OMM racks are

Old Man Mountain's Cold Springs rack

designed with mountain bikes in mind and work well with suspension forks or disc brakes, even if your fork has no rim-brake bosses or rack eyelets. Most OMM models are designed to carry the weight on the axle by using extra-long skewers to hold the rack mounts against the wheel dropouts. There are a couple of conventional eyelet-mounted models too. The high-mount front racks have a useful platform for carrying gear on top of the front wheel.

Jandd

Jandd make heavy-duty aluminium racks and other outdoor gear including panniers. The Extreme Front rack is a combination high or low rack, useful either for extra space or just having the ability to move the panniers up to a high position for off-roading or fording streams. The Expedition rear rack has an aircraft-carrier size platform on top and is large enough for 700c wheels.

Jandd Extreme front rack

Surly

US bike-builder Surly make chromoly racks and their front rack looks the business if you want a large capacity rack that carries panniers either high or low. It carries the load over the axle and though it weighs a hefty 1.3kg, that's nothing compared with its 32kg capacity. If you're going heavy, this is the rack for you.

Surly front rack

Thorn and Bruce Gordon

Thorn's racks are available only from the maker but will fit any bike with braze-ons. These are uncomplicated triangular 531 steel designs (easily repaired by brazing) with thick welds and an extended top for carrying tents and available with a useful plate to attach almost any rear light. The expedition-grade rack is said to be good for up to 60kg (but stick to a more normal load of 15-20kg) but there are lighter duty items as well and an excellent tandem rack. In the US,

Thorn Expedition Steel rear rack

Bruce Gordon makes chromoly racks of similar quality, with a front rack that carries its load higher and further back so as to be right on the steering axis.

Fitting, repairs and DIY racks

Make sure your rack comes with the best bolts you can buy; choose stainless steel with a little extra length so you have something to work on if the bolt shears off inside the braze-ons. Backing up with vibration-resistant Nyloc nuts is also a good idea, as is dabbing on some blue Loctite to prevent bolts working loose. A few hose clamps in your repair kit cover some possible rack disasters; your ingenuity will have to cover for the rest. Rack repairs can be like

DIY rack and panniers: €12

corporate-bonding exercises, with duct tape and sticks used to craft a bodged repair, followed by a trip to the nearest welder with fingers double-crossed.

Some travellers-turned-cyclists have designed their own racks in the absence of anything suitable in the shops, as Adrian Cooke (see box p16) did when he bought a bike in Sri Lanka. He got simple sections of aluminium shelving cut and bolted together and connected the result to his shock forks using hose clamps. If you're tempted to have a rack made for you, clamps and bolts will give the strongest join. Bending and welding tubes weakens them; this is where most home-made racks break.

Weight distribution considerations

Ultralight riders and those on short trips often make do with rear panniers only, but on a long trip, you'll be camping much of the time and a stove, pots and food won't all fit on the back without risking overloading the rear rack and the wheel. Fitting front racks allows you to carry more and balance your load. The price is much heavier steering but the result is a much safer, more stable ride.

Front racks and panniers are intended to carry less than rears; you only want about a third of the weight there. Some riders carry rear panniers on the front as well as the back, but larger panniers are prone to sway more and will interfere with the steering. It's not recommended but if you need to carry more up front, look for larger racks such as Nittos.

Fitting racks to a suspension fork

Suspension forks weren't designed with touring in mind and make no provision for racks, but a couple of well thought-out racks will do the trick or you can make your own. Old Man Mountain's racks will work on any fork but are easiest to fit on forks that have bosses for rim brakes. Suspension forks increas-

---

RACKS AND DISC BRAKES

Tubus Disco rack: a close fit round a disc brake

Until recently, if your bike had discs your only option was to buy a hub-skewer mounted Old Man Mountain rack (see p56). Excellent though it is, you might want more choices to find the best fit. Topeak have produced the Super Tourist DX, a budget aluminium rack designed to fit around disc brakes. Tubus also recently introduced a new and light design called the Disco; it's currently the only chromoly option for disc brake bikes. Like most OMM racks it mounts on an extra-long skewer, but you should check that it clears the disc brake before buying.

ingly do not have brake bosses, so OMM make band clamps (hose clamps in the UK) to fit round the forks to stablilise the rack while the weight is borne by the axle. If you want a steel option, Tubus make two different designs. The Swing rack sits on the crown and doesn't touch the forks at all, but the panniers lie at an angle inwards on each side. It's a slightly odd look and the very stout and short rack sits high up. Some riders say that at certain speeds the

The lightweight option – but no room here for cooking gear.

Swing vibrates a bit like a tuning fork but it's a secure setup. It won't fit every suspension fork, so check before you buy. If your fork does have brake bosses, Tubus now make the Smarti, a good simple option if you want chromoly.

PANNIERS

Good panniers last for years, over which time you'll appreciate their dependability and strength. Cheapies, by comparison, tend to be stitched nylon where the waterproofing wears off quickly, soon followed by the stitching. German-made Ortlieb panniers are by far the most popular panniers among long-distance cyclists (see cover photo). Ortlieb revolutionised pannier design by developing a radio-frequency welding technique for a totally waterproof stitch-free pannier with the most simple and long-lasting closure of all; a foolproof roll-up/clip-down fastening as used in canoeists' dry bags. Ortlieb was also the first to use locking clips to hold the pannier onto the rack and theirs is still the easiest to use, though they can fly off now and again. Despite many attempts at imitation, Ortlieb remain the market leaders; they will out-last any other pannier.

Other choices include Vaude Aqua Pros; some swear they're better in certain details but the older ones are more prone to minor breakages. If you like lots of pockets, and have deep pockets of your own, consider Arkel panniers. What Arkel considers a light-touring pannier adds up to 42L capacity per pair, about the same as Ortlieb while the GT-54 with its special pocket designed for Thermarest mattresses is excessive for most needs; remember, you may have to carry them too. A virtue of Arkels is the strong aluminium frame on the back of the pannier; they won't twist or flap about on your bike.

Brit traditionalists have long favoured Carradice panniers, made out of tightly woven waterproof canvas (though they may not be a match for an Indian monsoon season or a roll-up Ortlieb bag that can actually float). Carradice are known for making old-style saddle bags which would be fine for a tent-free tour of South-East Asia,

At times like this, you'll be glad your bags are 100% waterproof. © Janne Corax

PANNIER PACKING TIPS

The more you travel, the better you get at packing. Once you've got your system down, stick with it so you always know where things are or if they're missing.

Most of us get off the bike on the left hand side and lean it against a wall on its right hand side, so put the things you need most often in the left rear pannier. Changes of clothing are likely several times a day; wrapping up for an early start, stripping off for a long midday climb and then wrapping up again against the wind chill for the fol-lowing descent. In the right pannier, I put food and spares, batteries, books and a spare tyre at the bottom. The front panniers are the 'kitchen' and 'bedroom': the stove and pots are on the left side with bowls and cups (easy to get at for a quick roadside brew-up) and the right side has the Thermarest and sleeping bag. The tent is strapped on top, packed in a cheap and cheerful thin nylon daypack to provide extra UV and damage protection, but with a bit of extra space for a padlock and cable and a mat to sit on for lunchtime.

for example. They aren't hi-tech in any respect and the locking clips, though very secure, are a fiddle every time you try to get the bags off the bike. On the plus side the canvas is very hard-wearing and at 54 litres a pair the volume matches the Arkels, with extra large pockets big enough for a bottle of bur-gundy on each side.

Handlebar bags

Keeping your valuables and camera right in front of you on the bike is a lot more comfortable than wearing them and so a handlebar bag is a necessity – almost every rider has one that is easily removed and carried on the shoulder when not on the bike. Ortlieb makes the only reliably waterproof handlebar bags good enough for cameras and other electronics, especially if you get the optional padded camera insert. The medium size is perfect and will just take an SLR.

If Ortlieb's handlebar bags aren't your style, you might get on better with mounting a bag you already use and like, such as a bum-bag (lumbar pack), clipping it on the front of the handlebars, or even behind, resting it on the top tube. LowePro camera bags might also work well.

Other bike accessories and tools

Is a **bell** really necessary on a touring bicycle? Yes; it will be greatly appreciat-ed all over the world by children as something to twang and as a friendly warning to pedestrians that you are coming through. A 150db siren goes down especially well on the Indian subcontinent.

A **pump** such as Topeak's Mountain Morph is ideal; a miniature trackstand pump that can deliver much higher pressure than other compact pumps and is robust yet small enough to conceal in a pannier. Don't trust the gauge: one rider cracked his rims by over-inflating with this pump.

A cycling **multitool** is good for having most of what tools you need in one place; I find them less easy to misplace than individual Allen keys, though I carry both as you might need the short end of an L-shaped Allen key to fit into odd places. Topeak's Alien series are well-equipped but there are dozens of different multitools and you should buy whatever feels comfortable in your hand while looking for the highest quality you can find.

A **Leatherman** or similar general purpose multitool is versatile and essential. The larger Leathermans are a bit heavy but all the tools are good quality and useful, whereas lightweight tools don't always perform well. If the wire cutters on your

Get some respect with this pump-horn, found in Lahore.

Leatherman can cut brake cable without fraying it, you won't need to bring a dedicated wire-cutter, but you could either pre-cut cables and solder the ends, or leave them uncut until you find a workshop with decent wire-cutters.

A proper **spoke key** will do a better job of truing a wheel than the little one you will find on almost any cycling multitool. Spoke keys are easier on your hands and less likely to round off a spoke nipple, which will need to be replaced if that happens.

A quality 15mm **pedal wrench** that is wider than a cone wrench but still narrow enough to get round a pedal will be handier than you think although you could instead borrow one when you need it for a flight. Make sure that your pedals are tight if you have to refit them without a pedal wrench, and get them greased and tightened properly as soon as you can.

You can scrounge a dab of **oil** from any motorbike shop or bring your favourite for those occasions when you wake up to a rusty chain. A small pot of synthetic grease is useful for big cleaning jobs like headsets and for installing pedals but again, you can always find some when you need it.

A brass **tyre valve adaptor** is almost weightless and adds up to more redundancy (in the 'back up' sense), as your pump will almost certainly fit both Schrader and Presta valves.

Carry a **chain splitter** (often part of a cycling multitool) and a universal chain link such as SRAM's Powerlink. Make sure it fits your chain; either 7/8-

WHAT ABOUT A KICKSTAND?

This is very much an optional accessory, but a decidedly cool one. There's only one worth using, the Esge twin leg model which weighs 650g; it holds the bike upright as you kick the legs down, then you rock the bike back onto the stand just like a motorbike. It's much easier to load panniers on a free-standing bike and easier to work on it too. Against that, it is still an accessory rather than a must-have so that's an extra unnecessary pound you'll be hauling up the mountains.

speed or 9-speed width. A few extra links saved from your last new chain should be carried for replacing damaged links.

When it comes to a **cassette remover** the tiny NBT2 is all you need. It's essential when replacing broken spokes on the drive side of the rear wheel as you can't fit them without removing the cassette. In the UK you can get NBT2s from 🖳 www.spacycles.co.uk. Harris Cyclery in the USA (🖳 sheldon brown.com) sells a similar tool, the Stein mini lock ring tool.

Other items include **spare tubes**, a small **puncture kit**, good quality **duct tape**, **cable ties** in various sizes, various **bolts** and **nuts** and **washers**, one **spare tyre** and **hose clamps**. Carry up to five spare **spokes** for the drive side and three each for the left side, rear wheel and front wheel. Rohloff users need just a couple. A good bike shop can shorten spokes easily.

HOW MUCH STUFF?

We all think we're carrying the absolute minimum and that everything we have on our bikes is there for a good reason, but it's a strange coincidence that every biker manages to fill their panniers to the very brim before the trip and keep them full for the duration. It's noticeable from some internet travelogues how some bikers' gear seems to get larger as the trip progresses till they look like a dromedary camel with two great humps, front and rear. Here three different cyclists tell what's in their bags and why.

Ultralight: under 15kg

Cameron Smith

I once read that if you don't notice your gear or have to worry about it on a trip then it must be working well and you've made the right choice with what you have. This pretty much sums up how my equipment was for me on this six month trip across China, including Tibet, on my Mongoose 700c hybrid. I carried the following equipment: a one-man tent that was said to be three-season and which passed the Tibet wind test with flying colours; a down sleeping bag that kept me warm well below zero and a full-length Thermarest. In the spares and tools department I took only an inner tube, pump, chain lube, a few patches, spare nuts and bolts, brake pads and a multitool. I used only the chain lube and the brake pads. Toiletries added up to toothbrush and paste, toilet paper and a hand towel. I cycle in lycra shorts with a shirt, SPDs, socks, hat and sunglasses. Off the bike I've got some trousers, a spare shirt and a pair of thongs (flip-flops to Poms). When the weather turned nasty I had my rain jacket and pants, gloves, beanie, buff, a microlight fleece, and when it really got cold, a toasty down vest. Throw in a headlight, some map sections and road notes, a few medicines and that's about it, total: eight kilos including panniers, but with no cooking gear.

Ultralight in Tibet
© Sabine Leu

I chose to take most of these items because I didn't want to freeze to death or not be able to sleep comfortably. If I thought I could have travelled with only a blanket and a coat and still been smiling each day, I would have. It's amazing how much gear you can stuff into two panniers. In Tibet other cycle tourers assumed I was on a guided trip. On this trip I expected to encounter cold wet and windy conditions, all of which I did, including snow and with the above gear I was never cold or uncomfortable. I don't see lightweight travel as a hardship or challenge; it makes riding more pleasurable. I like to keep things simple and go by the thought 'less is best' which accounts for the fact that I never get flats or any breakages whatsoever. And the sheer delight of riding such a nimble bike is a plus for me.

There is only one piece of kit I will never go without again and that's a cooker. Not for making dinner so much as having a hot sweet black coffee in the early morning while sitting in my tent admiring the view. I can fit a few days worth of food in my panniers and a few water bottles on the rack and because the bike is light I can comfortably cover more than 100km a day, even in the big mountains, and could always get to a town for food or water without having to be a supermarket on wheels for several days. At the end of the day, I reckon as long as a person is well rested and well fed and is just stoked to be out on the open road then the trip is going to be fantastic, whether you have 8kgs of gear or 28kgs.

Medium weight:15–25kg

Stephen Lord

I usually carry a similar amount of gear no matter where I'm going; this photo was actually one of my lightest trips, although it was cold weather camping – Tibet in early November. Recently I've been using larger Carradice panniers with 14 litres extra capacity over Ortliebs, and somehow I still manage to fill them, which tells you something.

I go for comfort, which to me means a roomy two-person tent, a 1½" Thermarest and a sleeping bag that won't let me down. On this trip I learned the hard way that black sesame tsampa for breakfast is a bit much for my stomach, that porridge is hard to clean up from my pots when the water's frozen and that at 3800m rice only cooks to mush. Since I started taking a down jacket on trips, I've never been cold. When your energy is low at the end of the day, it's surprising how cold you can get sitting in camp waiting for dinner. I wore an Icebreaker thermal for a couple of weeks solid in Tibet and cycled in zip-offs; not especially comfortable without padded shorts. I forgot to bring rain pants; the following year I rode in much wetter east Tibet and my riding partner Dom (see South America, p209) asked me 'don't you think you're taking a big risk in the mountains without rain pants?'.

Cool days and cold nights on the Kampa La
© Laura Stone

I remembered that comment ever since, because he was dead right, especially in east Tibet; I was lucky that time. My luxury is to be able to heat some hot water for a wash in the tent and to have good moisturiser and sunscreen for my face – I've seen too many prematurely aged faces in the mountains.

I carry an NBT2 cassette remover, a couple of spokes, a spare tyre and a tube. Nowadays I don't bother with a pedal spanner; I buy or borrow one to pack the bike and haven't carried oil for the last few trips; I just cadged it or find a few drops in used oil cans at petrol stations.

For entertainment I recommend a Charles Dickens novel. One chapter a night is enough excitement and will leave you hanging till the next night. At that rate they can last for two months. Books work at altitude too, which iPods don't.

Heavyweight: over 25kg

Álvaro Neil

I believe there are two kinds of bicycle travellers and the category you choose is defined by what equipment you carry with you. There are people who make what I call short trips of less than one year, and then there are nomads who live on their bicycles. I am a nomad, travelling now for ten years and over that time I have come to prefer comfort, even if it means carrying an extra five kilos. I am a clown and magician by trade, so I must carry some stuff for my shows. I am also a writer and photographer, so I carry a laptop to update my website and write my books and articles for bike magazines. My photographic equipment alone weighs three kilos.

I carry three stoves. The well-known MSR Dragonfly, another that works with gas canisters (in some countries it is cheaper than petrol) and another one that I made from a beer can. It works with kerosene and inside a hotel room doesn't make the noise of an MSR.

I like my hammock. Even if I don't use it for months, the day I do I feel I'm in paradise. During my trip in Brazil the ants weren't able to eat the floor of my tent as I was above the ground. My tent is a four-kilo, two-man Robens Double Rock. I like to put my panniers inside if it is raining. I carry eight Ortlieb bags; some of them are multifunctional like a small backpack for shopping in the city,

Clowning around in Bhutan

or a big one for trekking in the mountains. The big pack is about 13 kilos when full and when the road is very sandy and I have to push my bicycle I put it on my back.

I always carry a spare Marathon XR and chain. Probably the part of my equipment I use least is the medical kit (including condoms), but I am happy not to use it (except the condoms). After being in Africa for three years I don't like to run out of food so now I always carry food for at least one or two days.

I never know my route in advance so I carry most of my winter clothes with me. Sometimes you apply for one visa, it's rejected; you must take another way, and then winter comes.

I always carry some books. Guidebooks if I can find them but also some novels, and maps. And of course a world map which sometimes I like to post on my hotel room wall and enjoy dreaming about my future years.

Transporting your bike by air

Regulations for checking bikes onto planes are confusing to say the least, varying between airlines and airports, as well as seemingly depending on who checks you in and what sort of mood they're in. The post-9/11 restrictions have complicated things greatly, especially in the US. Forewarned is forearmed and calling around the airlines before you book and again before you fly for airport-specific information is worthwhile. You may need to book the bike in beforehand, so it makes sense to call the airline before flying.

For flights and airports you're unfamiliar with, the prudent thing is to box the bike yourself (see p66) before setting out for the airport on public transport. That way, you won't be dependent on the check-in staff's mercy to get your bike on the plane. It may also be easier to use public transport to get to and from airports rather than cycling before and after long flights. A boxed bike makes this an option whereas a fully assembled machine may not be allowed on a bus or fit in a taxi.

Weight limits

Over the past few years airlines have gone their own ways regarding weight and bag allowances. It's hard to generalise except to say that the terms for passengers have worsened, although paying a flat fee for a bike is preferable to paying excess baggage fees of €15 per kilo or more. The rules change so often you need to check again just before flying, though 🖳 www.dp software.co.uk/airlines has a fairly up to date summary of baggage rules and allowances.

There are still some generous airlines out there that carry bikes free of charge – Emirates and Thai Airways are two of the bigger names often mentioned by touring cyclists – although nothing on their website or from phone calls will confirm this, so get confirmation from recent travellers on internet forums like the Thorn Tree (see p12) before booking.

Be prepared to argue if your flight has several legs and an airline tries to charge you for excess baggage on the shorter hop. Get your bike checked through all the way to your final destination, and even if there are months between flights, make sure (or simply bluff and bluster) that you're entitled to the larger allowance for all flight segments. You cannot be expected to shrink your bags for some flights when they were all booked together, as is the case with an RTW ticket.

PART 1 – PRACTICALITIES

Boxing the bike

To avoid additional stress at the airport, box your bike at home or have your local bike shop do it. Use zip-ties or duct tape to fix loose items. Bike shops usually do a nice job in padding and boxing your bike for a small fee and are helpful in providing boxes; just give them a few days notice. If you're flying within the US, a bike shop can box and send your bike via UPS, though it might cost almost as much as the airline would charge and may take up to five days to arrive. Ask the shop to leave the box open so you can add extra luggage before flying and use up the weight allowance.

On the return journey you will have to box the bike yourself. Any large cardboard box can be broken down and used to pack the bike. Then it can be wrapped in a tarp and tied up like a parcel. Allow about an hour to wrap or box a bike carefully. I usually cut the box down to the size of the dismantled bike so it's easier to get in a taxi or bus and in dozens of flights I have never had any serious damage, only scratches.

To prepare the bike for flight, you need to make a dense, tightly packed package so that all components reinforce each other and all vulnerable components are inside this mass.

1. Remove the pedals. You'll need a 15mm wrench, though on some pedals you need an Allen (hex) key. Note that the left pedal loosens by turning clockwise; most important! Never just throw pedals (or anything else) in your bike

Get packing materials from local market

box, they will scratch the paintwork and may fall out. Wrap them in newspaper then tape or zip-tie them to the frame or racks.

2. Remove the saddle or lower it all the way down, depending on whether you want to protect the saddle by taping it down somewhere in the middle triangle of the frame, or use it to provide padding for the bike.

3. Disconnect the brakes and release the wheels. Your brake arms will spring outwards and are safer if taped tightly together. If you have hydraulic brakes, it is vital to tape something between the brake pads to prevent them popping out if the lever is depressed.

4. Wheels and tyres. Remove the quick-release skewers from the wheel axles and tape them to the spokes. Place the wheels either side of the bike and tape them together (as in the

Remove racks etc. and arrange round frame

photo right) with some cardboard between wheel and frame to prevent scratches. Aircraft holds are only partially pressurised, so let some air out of the tyres or they could burst in flight. Check-in staff insist on full deflation; it's a waste of time arguing with them but try to keep some air in the tyres to protect the rims and tyres.

Find safe places to tuck saddle, racks and handlebars, then add the wheels on either side of the frame with extra cardboard in between wheels and frame and around pedals, gears and chainrings

5. Unscrew the derailleur where it is bolted to the drop-out. This way, you don't have to disconnect the cable; just ensure it is loose enough by pulling it out of the brazed-on frame guides on the chain stays so it will not get kinked. Wrap the derailleur in newspaper and tape it to the bike frame inside the rear triangle or between the spokes. Wrap up as much of the chain as you can in newspaper or bubblewrap and tape that to the frame.

6. Remove the handlebars. You should have enough slack in the cables to do this but disconnect cables entirely if you think they may get kinked in transit. It's best to tape or tie handlebars to the frame; your wheels may be far forward enough to position flat handlebars between them for better protection. You have a lot of important and fragile components on those handlebars, so place them where they are protected and allow for movement. Cardboard and newspaper padding will help.

7. Mudguards. The rear mudguard has to come off and is quite well protected if simply wrapped around the rear wheel. The front mudguard may be OK on the bike if it is flexible, as the best SKS brand is. Racks really depend on your bike and the box and how small you want the package to be. They are at greater risk left on the bike but if you plan on riding away from the airport, leave them on.

8. Some finishing touches. Screw all rack and mudguard bolts back on the bike. Add some extra padding around the rear stays and especially the derailleur hanger. Removing the largest chain ring removes a very sharp edge and makes the package easier to stand up. If you have a Shimano Hollowtech BB, it's easy to remove the entire chainset. Extra cardboard around the chainrings prevents them slicing their way out. Fitting plastic supports in between the rear

Now wrap it up and rope it up tight and book tuk-tuk to the airport.

stays and the forks protects against the bike being crushed. Bike shops will give you these disposable plastic blocks and they're worth keeping with you for the return trip. I put fragile items such as a helmet in the middle of the rear triangle or inside the main triangle and tape them in. A tent can go between the rear stays to add support. Above all, make sure that no small parts are loose in the box, as they will fall through the inevitable holes that will have appeared in the box when it arrives on the baggage carousel.

Ground Effect's excellent Tardis bike bag.
© Roy Hoogenraad

Bike bags

A re-usable nylon zipped bike bag greatly speeds up packing your bike and good ones such as the Ground Effect Tardis have sleeves to hold the wheels either side of the bike and pockets for sharp items like pedals and quick-release skewers, protecting the frame from scratches. If you're flying in and out of the same city you can leave it with a hotel. If you happen to be riding in Japan, bike bags can be found in Tokyu Hands stores under the catchy brand name 'The Big Bicycling'. Though costly, these are the lightest bags around and large enough for big frames.

The unpacked alternative

Some believe you're better off not boxing the bike at all, but checking it in 'as is', on the grounds that if it looks like a bike, they'll treat it like a bike. It can work

for point-to-point flights between small airports near to home. Some airlines will provide huge plastic bags to wrap the bike and check it in without a fuss; Asian airlines seem to love shrink-wrapping things. Supposedly pedal removal and handlebar turning is all that is required.

As a rule I think the non-boxing idea is a little optimistic and boxing your bike has a lot more advantages in getting to and from the airport. Besides, you cannot always be sure how airline check-in staff will react to an unpacked bike. Nonetheless, the only time we tried wheeling on the bikes at the tiny airport in Chitral, Pakistan, they got priority boarding and places at the front of the plane; see photo.

Clothing

Every trip will call for its own choice of clothing, depending on the climate, seasons and type of ride you're doing. A short summer ride around France needs different clothing from an overland trip to Australia. For short trips cycling-specific clothing is the best choice, as for sheer efficiency it cannot be beaten. On the other hand, cyclists on longer trips get tired of dressing in bikers' gear for months on end and tend to adopt cheap local clothing after their original kit has worn out.

If you're going round the world, don't expect to be able to carry clothing for every eventuality. Just buy what you need as you go and send home, send on or sell what you don't need.

Cycling shorts

Try riding in proper padded, skin-tight lycra cycling shorts and you'll soon realise why most cyclists prefer them. The reason they work is not just the padding but because they become a slippery second skin that slides over rather than snags on the saddle, so reducing friction and consequent soreness. Not all men like to walk around with their family jewels exposed in such an acutely sculpted profile (and in most Muslim and Buddhist countries close fitting clothing of any type is bad form) and so riders often wear baggy shorts on top.

No one ever tells you to wear bike shorts without underwear (also known as 'going commando'), but that is the most comfortable way to do it for both men and women, as chafing from seams on your undies is avoided. It's hard to find real chamois leather linings in bike shorts these days, except in the most expensive ones, but they're not that suitable for touring anyway because they dry so slowly. There is nothing like easing into a pair of cold, damp chamois-lined cycling shorts to wake you up in the morning! Even synthetic bike shorts can take a while to dry so you really need two pairs for touring if you want to wear them every day. A better plan over the longer term is to occasionally have a rest by riding in something else. Cycling shorts work particularly well with hard leather saddles like Brooks where a little softness makes a big difference in terms of comfort.

Three-quarter length padded baggy shorts have become very popular over the last few years. An exposed shin and calf seems to be non-controversial (at least for men) and off the bike, they hang lower while on the bike they ride up and ventilate better.

LAYERING

Layering is generally accepted as the best way to regulate body temperature. Layers keep you warmer by trapping air and can be added or taken off as you ride, depending on how warm or cold you feel. The layering system extends from your thermal underwear to the waterproof mitts over your gloves. Performance clothing is generally broken down into three levels: base, insu-

Merino wool makes a good base layer – thermally efficient and looks better than cycling-specific clothing.

lating (or mid-layer) and shell (or outer-layer). Natural materials may work best for your base layer on a long ride. Some people find certain types of synthetic base layers smell after a few hours exertion, others have no complaints after days of riding.

Base layer

For exercising at intense levels, synthetic materials are best. A synthetic shirt can be quickly hand washed and will be dry by next morning. However, when cycling at touring speeds in moderate temperatures, you don't always need the most efficient fabric and you may well feel more comfortable wearing normal clothes rather than looking like you just came from the set of Star Trek.

Merino wool is more expensive than synthetics or cotton, dries more slowly and needs a little looking after (you won't want to give your prized merino top to a dhobi-wallah to bash clean on the banks of the Ganges) but it's very comfortable over a wide temperature range, nice to sleep in and remains odourless far longer than many synthetics.

A cotton T-shirt is the most versatile clothing item for any traveller. Cotton works well for 3-season cycling, though in extreme heat or humidity it will clog up with sweat. A loose-weave baggy cotton shirt is better than a T-shirt in these situations. Like much 'specialist' travel gear, don't bother with special travel shirts, the over-designed kind with pockets and vents all over and usually a synthetic or poly-mix. The weave is too tight to breathe enough for cycling and you'll ride with a sweaty back.

Mid layer

Fleece works best for mid layers, being lighter than merino and much easier to wash and dry. Good quality fleece also lasts a very long time. Forget down or quilted designs for wearing on the bike, they are poor at venting and have to be kept dry. A windproof fleece doesn't breathe well enough for strenuous cycling and doesn't compress much so it's not great value for the space it takes in your panniers.

Outer layer

On the bike you'll never need more than a mid layer plus a rain jacket or shell on top. But for staying warm in cold climates when you're sitting around in camp, nothing beats a down jacket. It doesn't have to be top quality, in fact for the hard life it will lead, compressed in your panniers and never cleaned, it makes more sense to wait and pick up a cheap down jacket when you hit the mountains where they will be easily found – Asia is famous for cheap knock-offs of brand-name down jackets. Synthetic fillings like Primaloft and so on are catching up with down in terms of warmth to weight and are much easier to look after.

Down is useless when wet, so a good shell layer on top finishes off your clothing. Get a good quality waterproof jacket as it will be one of your most often-used pieces of clothing, providing the wind-proofing that good fleece lacks and adding instant warmth when you throw it on at the top of a windy pass for protection on the freezing descent. Gore-tex jackets are getting better every year but for cycling eVent may be a better material as it is thought to be more breathable and can be washed in ordinary detergent with the rest of your clothes, only requiring occasional reproofing. Don't forget to bring some waterproof trousers, they can be lifesavers if caught high up in a storm, enabling you to keep riding without getting hypothermia. They are also great for wearing when all your other trousers and underwear are in the wash!

A good shell jacket in bright colours keeps freezing winds at bay on long descents and is very visible.

Despite the hype, breathable waterproof fabrics cannot achieve the impossible. If you're pedalling hard in the rain, it's impossible to stay as dry inside as you would if you were standing still. Riding creates heat and moisture and waterproof breathable jackets can only vent moisture slowly, particularly when soaked in rainwater. The simple answer is to ride more slowly in the rain so that your body generates less heat and also to treat your jacket with a water-repelling spray like Nikwax TX Direct so rain drops roll off rather than soak through. Soft-shell jackets are less effective for bike touring; neither 100% waterproof nor particularly warm, although for short trips in dry mountain areas they might be more comfortable and breathe better than a hard shell jacket.

Whether you go for bright colours or dull ones is a personal matter. As a foreigner, you look like you're from outer space anyway to most locals so the colour of your jacket won't make much difference. If you prefer bright jackets for visibility when cycling, then get one; they certainly make for better photos.

Off the bike, zip-off trousers are the only way to go for most climates. They're so versatile and are now found everywhere once your first pair wears out. Lightweight zip-offs only last about six months if you cycle in them.

HELMETS

There's no doubt helmets are gaining in popularity among adventure tourers and seem to be worn just as much on the Friendship Highway between Lhasa and Kathmandu as they are back at home. Yes it's a hassle to bring one along and it's another bulky item that has to be treated with care, but how else are you going to lay your hands on a hard hat for a hairy mountain descent or the no less perilous ride into Tehran? I use mine on mountain descents and in cities or freeways, wearing a Tilley hat most of the time and a wool or fleece hat when it's cold.

Finding a good helmet while you're on the road is almost impossible; you've left it too late. Far better to bring it along, even if you only wear it occasionally. Also bear in mind there are a few countries out there, Australia and Spain being two of them, where cycling helmets are now compulsory.

Feet, hands and head

While cycling easily generates heat to warm the body core, feet and hands don't move much and will feel the chill. If you're travelling in SPD shoes rather than trekking boots, a pair of neoprene booties or Gore-Tex overshoes can make all the difference. Layering applies to the hands too. A pair of fleece gloves is ideal for cold mornings and evenings. Throw a waterproof shell over the top and you're ready to take on more severe conditions.

Heads also feel the cold. Plenty of body heat is lost through an uncovered head and the ears are real superconductors. Products like the Buff neck-warmer are light and versatile; they can be cinched up for a hat or used as a scarf and also work well as a dust mask (or full-on hejab at a pinch!). Lycra leggings and sleeves are another good way to keep warm while riding and take up next to no space in panniers.

FOOTWEAR

No one denies the greater efficiency of stiff-soled cycling shoes over conventional trainers or sandals. Nowadays there is a huge range of cycle-specific footwear on the market, ranging from sandals to light hiking boots (for example: Shimano's MT90 boot), most with a recessed Shimano SPD cleat built into the sole of the shoe. Many bike tourers choose combination pedals such as Shimano's M324 which take toe clips if you change your mind about SPDs – or the MTB-style M424, another pedal that works with or without SPD shoes. Though riding with cleats is more efficient, they aren't for everyone and a long trip is the wrong place to find out. The virtue of non-cleated pedalling is the greater freedom you have in choosing footwear, and in finding a comfortable position on the pedals; some cleated-shoe cyclists develop knee problems because their feet are fixed in one position.

Among long-distance riders, it's common to find people wearing trainers, sandals, Birkenstocks or even hiking boots instead of SPDs. You will never hear any of them fretting that their pedal stroke might not be efficient enough; footwear is a personal choice, and comfort wins over efficiency on long rides.

ALTERNATIVES TO SPDS OR TOE CLIPS

Some people have a fear of falling off the bike with their feet trapped in toe clips. Others find toe clips break too easily for long tours or they can't find them in large enough sizes. And some people have knee troubles with SPDs or fall off a few times at low speeds because their shoes were stuck in the cleats. PowerGrips, a simple alternative from the 1980s, are making a comeback. These are strips of very tough canvas which bolt diagonally to ordinary pedals. You put your foot in at an angle and when you straighten it, the straps tighten a little and your foot is secure. The idea is that if you get thrown off the bike, your feet come out easily; every rider I've asked says they've never had a problem getting out of the straps. PowerGrips are a very robust and simple system and worth checking out if you don't like SPDs or toe clips.

It's difficult to tell what will work for you over the long term. I've seen people happy with their sandals and even flip-flops, even though they appear to have developed flat 'rickshaw feet' from pressing their feet into pedals all day. My own very thick sandals split after a few months cycling. Since then, hiking boots or trail shoes have been the solution for me; stiff enough, comfortable, waterproof, warm and great for walking in.

Camping

A cyclist can't carry much more than a backpacker; a set of Ortliebs is only good for about 65 litres capacity plus the tent on the rear rack and 7 litres more in a handlebar bag. So you need to have good gear which means high quality and lightweight to make the most of the limited capacity.

TENTS

Unless you are travelling in lowland India or South-East Asia you'll want to camp, for which a tent is desirable. Sometimes you hear people saying how much lighter tarps are, but they don't work well when you need privacy or a refuge from mozzies, cold, wind and rain, which is quite a lot of the time. A good tent is the most versatile and secure solution, and a freestanding (and preferably mesh) inner tent can even be used inside a hotel room as a mosquito net.

The best and most suitable tents for bike touring are generally in the 2.5-3 kilo range; about 5½ to 6½ pounds. You can find them lighter, but the latest designs from the top US tent makers have achieved light weights by using thinner materials and smaller flysheets which means they don't stay waterproof for long. The industry measure of waterproofness; the 'hydrostatic head' figure, need only be 1000mm to be regarded as waterproof, but this is a column of water dropped from only a metre onto

Camping indoors
© Peter Quaife

the material. It's waterproof for a short amount of time, and touring is about something being dependably waterproof during an all-night storm and staying that way after months on the road. It's a tall order for which ultra-light weight is not compatible so look for a tent with a flysheet of minimum 3000mm hydrostatic head, though if you favour short ultralight trips you could get away with something lighter. The time you will be really glad you chose a tough tent is in the mountains and something solid, at the expense of a pound or two more (in money and not just weight!) will be worth it.

Features to look for in a good tent

Go for a two- to three-pole geodesic design. Single pole tents are for ultralight trips and generally too small for tall people. MacPac's excellent Microlight tent is one of the best single pole tents, but is too compact for a long trip and of course vulnerable to side winds. Should you want some company one night, you might regret not having the space for guests. Among two-pole designs, either go for a tough tunnel tent like the MacPac Minaret, or a simple crossover pole design which doesn't depend on being pegged out, but will blow away if you don't tie it down. Three-pole designs are the best at withstanding winds from any direction or even a heavy snow-storm. A tent with four poles is likely to be a four-season mountaineering tent and is overkill for most bike touring. Four-season tents have steep sides to shed snow easily and often have two doors (a nice touch) in case one end gets snowed under.

Most people will appreciate a bit more tent space on a long trip, so think in terms of a two-person tent for solo use and a three-person tent for a couple. You need space to move around and with a bit more room your tent will all the sooner become just like home and not an emergency shelter. Large vestibules over each door are useful for storing wet or dirty panniers close by as well as for sheltered cooking. A couple of tents on the market have vestibules big enough to cover your bike, but it's not needed, although at times you might feel more secure pulling your back wheel under the vestibule and tying it to something.

The strongest tent poles are made of so-called aircraft-grade aluminium, the same as a bike frame. DAC poles are the best brand, having section ends that don't need ferrules and saving weight in the process. Look for fairly short pole sections as they will be much easier to pack without overhanging off the rear rack. Most tent poles are around 8.5mm in diameter, anything thicker than that is a great plus. Poles do occasionally break, usually in high winds, so you need a short section of tube which 'splints' a broken pole. Otherwise use duct tape to strap a tent peg along the broken section.

Whether single-skin or the more common flysheet and inner, ventilation is essential for comfortable camping. Flysheets that reach all the way to the ground will keep the inner drier but make venting less effective. These tents tend to have scoop air-vents on top to encourage air-flow between the inner and outer and so purge the condensation that you produce. Pitching your tent where you can catch a breeze will reduce condensation significantly. Some tents have continuous pole sleeves on the inner tent that greatly reduce the air-flow between inner and outer, and other, cheaper designs have the pole sleeves in several short sections, which makes it maddeningly slow to set up the tent. The clip-type of pole attachment, where the flysheet is clipped on to the inner, is far and away the best way of attaching the poles. A variation is the Hilleberg system of having the tent poles threaded into sleeves on the outside of the flysheet, with the inner tent attached with toggles to the flysheet.

Look for minimal stitching; one of the virtues of expensive Hilleberg tents. However taped or sealed, stitching is always a weak spot and where a tent is most likely to tear. Many tents have tape glued over the stitching, adding a bit of weight but eliminating rain ingress and reducing wear on the seams. If your tent doesn't have taped seams, you'll need to seal them with a urethane glue such as SeamGrip, though on silicone-coated tents use Silnet.

After a few years when polyester looked set to take over as tent material, nylon is back in fashion. Polyester doesn't stretch the way nylon does when wet and is slightly more UV-resistant, but nylon is more suited to silicone coating and a nylon flysheet with silicone coating on both sides is the best tent material currently available.

The problem with tunnel tents: hammering pegs into concrete...

Although there are weight savings to be had, avoid single-skin tents unless you expect to camp very occasionally or are travelling in arid but not freezing regions. They aren't as warm as double-skin tents, are more awkward to set up and cheap versions suffer condensation problems.

Tent pegs are worth upgrading to the best you can get; it won't cost much and the strongest tent pegs with a 3-edge design are the only ones that might last the whole trip. V-shaped pegs are a good second-best, but anything else will bend or go blunt over time. Pegs with nylon loops are much easier to pull out of the ground. Take a few spares and count them back into the bag when you take the tent down so you don't lose any; brightly coloured pegs are easier to spot.

Nearly all tents are now offered with an optional 'footprint', a groundsheet cut specifically for that tent which can usually be left attached to the tent. The price is a little exorbitant when a bit of tarp will do, but footprints are very convenient and there's never a chance of their blowing away or sticking out from under the tent only to funnel rainwater underneath. Using a footprint or groundsheet inside the vestibule or porch of the tent helps reduce condensation from wet ground. Lastly, drab-coloured tents are best suited to stealth camping.

BIKE TOURING TENTS

Here is a selection of some of the best two person tents around, but if they don't quite suit you, most of the same recommended manufacturers offer alternative designs with the same materials and attention to detail. You can often find the same model in two different weights, so if you want to save weight on a Vaude tent for example, get one with the lighter, silicone-coated flysheet and save around a quarter of the heavier tent's weight. Hilleberg tents come in two different weights, the lighter of which is ideal for bike touring.

Hilleberg Nallo 2

One of Hilleberg's best sellers for backpackers and bike tourers, the Nallo 2 weighs only 2.5kg with the optional footprint. Two foolproof pole sleeves in the flysheet mean you can put it up in the dark with ease, and there's massive venting front and back to limit condensation. Like all Hillebergs, the flysheet is double-coated silicone, though very thin and needs treating with care. The inner

Hilleberg Nallo – perhaps not as roomy as a yurt but a little more portable

MacPac Minaret © Alex Prain

tent is one of the lightest of all, breathes well and is actually waterproof as long as you don't touch any moisture on the other side of the fabric. The one-metre high peak height is right above your head as you sleep, by a huge yet well-sheltered doorway. Hillebergs are pricey but everything is top quality, down to pre-curved 9mm DAC poles and many thoughtful features inside and out that make it easy to pitch and use. The vestibule is large enough but if you need more space, the GT variant offers a long pole-supported vestibule you could get most of your bike in.

MacPac Minaret and Celeste

Another design that has changed little over the years – always a good sign – the successful Minaret is a very strong two-person tunnel tent that weighs the same as the Nallo but is a little smaller. It's tough as nails with a substantially thicker floor than most tents; it doesn't really need a protective groundsheet underneath except to keep it clean. Four vents minimise condensation but are a bit noisy in the wind. The vestibule is smaller than many but can be configured to provide extra length for tall people. The door is a bit low too and headroom is not great so this tent is best for people less than 6ft tall. Think of the Minaret as a roomy solo tent; look at the Celeste for a good two-person model weighing in at around 3kg. It has big doors and vestibules on each side as well as a shape that deflects wind from any direction. Like all MacPacs, it goes up with the inner and outer together, but can be set up with either alone, a very handy feature for any tent.

Terra Nova Voyager and North Face Tadpole

Voyager © Antony Bowesman

Terra Nova's Voyager is now available in a lighter weight for ounce-counters, though go for the full-strength Voyager with a 6000mm hydrostatic head flysheet and a 7000mm floor. Like the MacPac Minaret, you pay for a more compact design to save weight and minimise wind resistance. Terra Nova uses the best materials: double-sided silicon-coated nylon in dark green. The poles are DAC 8.55mm in a strong configuration and the flysheet is low to the ground, improving rain protection but less light and airy than similar and slightly lighter tents such as North Face's classic Tadpole. Neither the Voyager nor the Tadpole tents are great for tall people; the Voyager is actually closer to 185cm long internally than the claimed 220cm. The Tadpole is made of thinner materials but the mesh inner works well in warm places and has a handy side-opening door so you don't have to stretch all the way to the front to open up every morning. Lightwave and Mountain Equipment also make tents in this highly aerodynamic style.

Exped Southern Cross

Swiss tent maker Exped produce a range of tents well-suited to bike touring and all available in a sensible shade of green. The Southern Cross comes close

to having it all; it can be set up with inner and outer together, or either one separately and the inner is free-standing as well, though you'll need to peg it out and use the guy lines as well. The headroom is a useful 105cm over a fairly wide area, not just a single point. The Southern Cross and the similar Venus II (pictured) have a door and vestibule on each side, making them very liveable for two people. The flysheet is made from old-style polyurethane-coated polyester and

Exped Venus II © Björn Josk

the Southern Cross inner is mosquito-mesh, so it's better suited to warm climates.

Vaude Odyssey and Hogan

Vaude make great tents at more affordable prices than the selection above. It's also possible to buy most of their designs in two weights, but the ultra-light-

weight models seem to sell far better than Vaude's classics which weigh up to 4kg. The Odyssey at 1.8kg is just a little larger than the popular (and also recommended) 1.5kg Hogan Ultralight, tent but with the same good quality 3000mm-rated flysheet and thick 10,000mm-rated floor. With more headroom and a larger vestibule it's overall more suited to taller people. If you need more room, look for the full-size Hogan, almost 3kg but with an ingenious external pole system and

Vaude Odyssey © Peter van Glabbeek

more generous 115cm inner height and 240cm length, with short extra poles down at the end to raise the tent over your feet; useful for size 12 footed giants. Couples should look at the Space II, two doors and vestibules, external pole sleeves and 3.5m², about 38 ft².

WILD CAMPING

After a few weeks on the road you will soon develop an eye for discreet and secure camp spots, though the kinds of places you choose will vary for each country and type of terrain. In western or eastern Europe the main priority will be to conceal yourself, as wild camping will likely be frowned upon and any attention may be unwanted. Woodlands are the best for free camping in Europe; go just a hundred metres or more from any footpath to avoid early-morning dog-walkers or mushroom-hunters and you'll be all alone. Asking for a place to camp will ensure you keep out of trouble so don't be bashful in countries or regions that are open to it. Wild camping generally gets easier as you go east in Europe: the French will point you towards the many municipal campgrounds, the Germans are more accepting of discreet overnight camping as long as you camp late and move on early, and east Europeans are most likely to suggest a place if you ask.

From the Middle East onwards, things really open up. Here one reason to pursue 'stealth' or discreet camping is that you will eventually tire of being invited into locals' homes. This tradition of hospitality is especially strong in Muslim countries, where locals feel it's an obligation. Refusal can be awkward so think ahead; you will be faced with offers of tea from many, many kind people until you reach India! On the other hand, if you are near any community or household, it's polite to ask for camping permission. Good luck in explaining your preference for camping over staying in their home where you will be expected to sing for your supper.

An ideal camping place is unseen from the road and not in the line of vehicle headlights, close to water, and with early morning sunlight to warm you and dry your tent. Pick a level spot but not in a dip that may attract water and one that is ant-free and with no signs of an impending visit from herds of sheep or goats. Among bushes is good and a place with plenty of firewood is even better, though make sure you are in a truly wild place and not farmland where locals may come and investigate. Fires are great in the mountains or remote places like western China, as long as you're not using someone's prized winter fuel.

Bridges can be great to camp under, but avoid culverts for the obvious flash-flood risk. Don't camp too close to a river; it will be cold and damp. Camp under a tree and your tent will be drier than otherwise, not because of the shelter but because the tree will absorb some of the ambient humidity overnight. And as long as it meets all the other 'health and safety' criteria, camp where there's a great view; it's why you're there! Those places can be the most memorable nights. A storm might brew up in the night so if your tent is not strong, stick to more sheltered areas, but to be at least a little in the open or slightly raised ground will place your tent in moving air, which it needs to vent properly.

Expect lots of visitors when camping near villages © Friedel Rother

All the colder for being next to this river in October in east Tibet

SLEEPING BAGS

Most bikers go for down sleeping bags, not just for the warmth but for the low bulk. The better the down you get, the more compact your sleeping bag will be. Down is delicate and as everyone knows, clogs up and loses all its loft when wet and takes ages to dry, so look after it by keeping it in your panniers, first stuffing it into a roll up dry-bag which will allow you to squeeze the air out. It's not the end of

Airing out a sleeping bag

the world if your bag does get a little wet, as long as you get some sunshine and breeze to dry it out. A tumble-drier with tennis balls or soft shoes in will help bring it back to life all the quicker, but good luck finding one in outback Irian Jaya.

The most important thing to look for in a sleeping bag is the fill power of the down. The higher the number, the better quality the down; it fluffs up more. A basic down bag will have about 550 fill power rising to 750 which is down containing the least amount of feathers. Fill power is measured a bit differently in the US and the numbers come out about 100 higher, ie: the range is around 650-850 in fill-power. Sales patter claiming to use Polish or Hungarian goose or duck means little; Chinese down is good enough as long as the fill-power is what you want. If the bag label says something like 85/15 it means 85% down and 15% feathers; a pretty good ratio as pure goose down bags are extremely expensive.

Individual needs differ but around 700g of good quality down will keep almost everyone warm down to -5°C. Don't go for too warm a bag, you'll only depend on it once or twice and it will be too bulky the rest of the time. If it's really cold, you'll be wearing everything you've got in your bag or you will find shelter, a need readily understood anywhere in the world with the appropriate shivering gestures performed on someone's doorstep. For most people, a three-season bag designed for around -5°C is warm enough until they take on mountains in late autumn or winter.

Make sure you buy a bag with a hood, though nearly all of them have one built-in. The feature that makes a bag really versatile is a full-length zip so you can unzip it into a wide duvet during warm weather. It's a rare feature as it's associated with cheap rectangular bags and not the highly efficient but not very versatile mummy bags. An ideal compromise is the so-called semi-rectangular bag which is narrower around the legs and with a zip that opens right the way round your feet. Western Mountaineering (🖳 www.backcountrygear .com) have made such bags for years using the best quality down. MacPac recently started making some great three-season sleeping bags with a full length zip too. These days almost every sleeping bag manufacturer makes a women-specific bag. It's high time they did, as having a close-fitting bag that

REPAIRING AN AIR MATTRESS

Repairing air mattresses is much like repairing a bike tyre puncture, only a patch is normally not necessary. Urethane glues such as SeamGrip will fix a puncture more easily than Thermarest's own Hotbond glue, but need four to six hours to set, so it's bad luck if you discover your puncture in the evening. Set to work immediately, use only a drop of glue and head for the local disco while it dries. Good quality duct tape might work at a pinch, but clean it all off in the morning and then glue the hole, riding with the repair exposed to the air. Delamination bubbles usually mean the beginning of the end for a mattress as they usually spread quickly as air pressure forces the nylon skin off the foam. Once you get your first bubble in an air mattress, start looking for a replacement fast.

is not unnecessarily long keeps you warmer and saves weight. A silk liner will keep your bag clean and is useful in hostels and guest houses to keep bed bugs away as well as for hot summer nights.

Sleeping pads and air mattresses

To save space most bikers choose a Thermarest-style inflatable mat, generally picking the very lightest models. Even these are at least twice as thick (1"/2.5cm) as the old 'karrimat'-style closed-cell foam mat, but with less than half the packed volume. The thinnest Thermarests, however, are also the most delicate; if you ever use them outside the tent you're risking a puncture (see box above). Thin airmats are also vulnerable to delamination due to grease and sweat migrating through the nylon. It's vital to wash off any dirt or sweat regularly to extend your mat's life. The three-quarter length is comfortable enough but won't keep the cold out from the ground and leaves you vulnerable to condensation from underneath too.

Exped make a great improvement on the traditional self-inflating air mattress, a 4" thick mat with a light down or synthetic filling to insulate the mat underneath – be wary of inflatable mats that have no foam or down inside as these will be colder to sleep on.

The puncture-proof and worry-free alternative that is suited to thorny regions like much of Africa is an old-fashioned closed-cell foam mat. These are much bulkier when packed yet thinner and less comfortable to sleep on, while being slightly lighter than air mattresses. They're handy for sitting outside the tent, which is how inflatable mats often get punctured. The cheap generic kinds are less than a centimetre thick and not too effective.

If you want a puncture-proof mat, look at Thermarest's Ridge-Rest model. It's 1.5cm (about 5/8") thick, rolls up into a fairly bulky package but is very strong and works well on sloping ground; you won't slip off it easily. Alternatively, at 1.9cm the Z-rest is thicker and more comfortable and folds into a more compact box shape, but abrades easily when tightly strapped on a bike rack.

STOVES

For short trips of up to a couple of weeks it's easiest to use a butane gas stove, a very clean fuel that's easy to find throughout the developed world. You will find the old style Camping Gaz '206' puncture-type canisters much farther afield under many different brand names, whereas Camping Gaz resealables are only made by Camping Gaz and impossible to find outside western Europe; it's the one cartridge type to avoid. The other style of threaded resealing cartridge made by Primus and many other brands is easier to find in many countries, especially in areas known for mountain climbing where expeditions leave spare cartridges behind.

On a longer trip the cost of those canisters adds up and once you leave Europe, the chances of finding them become slimmer. You need a multi-fuel stove. While it's nice to have one that will burn anything, you'll regret ever filling your tank with diesel and most types of kerosene too ('paraffin' to Brits). Realistically you only need a stove which can run on unleaded automotive gasoline petrol. Unleaded can be found almost anywhere you'd expect to find a filling station. Choose the lowest octane rating as it has less additives that block camping stove jets. Fuel coming from a pump is less likely to be adulterated than anything poured from containers.

There's a wide choice of lightweight stoves. Some favour Coleman stoves such as the 442 dual-fuel model. It's convenient because you don't have to attach the fuel tank each time you set up the stove and it's quiet too, but performance at altitude is sluggish. MSR's WhisperLite Internationale lives up to its name and burns unleaded petrol (gasoline), kerosene (paraffin) as well as more refined Coleman fuel or 'white gas' (the champagne of stove fuels and almost as expensive, but very rare outside the developed world except for South America). MSR's Dragonfly is noisier and bulkier but is the cook's choice with the very useful ability to simmer. Mountaineers go for MSR's XGK EX, a rugged no-frills flame-thrower perfect for boiling noodles to a pulp at altitude, but unable to simmer without spluttering. All MSR stoves have a plastic pump which is more likely to break than an aluminium pump, but is at least replaceable.

Swedish brands Primus and Optimus also make very good stoves. The Primus multifuel stoves have a wide base and pot supports – an important consideration as watching your dinner tip into the sand can really ruin your day. Primuses are a touch heavy but are solidly built. The top of the range Omnifuel has a simmering control but as with all these stoves, that extra valve

BOTTLE CAGES AND CARRYING LIQUID FUEL

Carrying fuel is a pain in the neck for cyclists. Petrol and especially kerosene are highly noxious and need to be kept well away from your food and clothing. The bottle with the stove fuel pump is more prone to leaking than bottles with the maker's intended stopper, but all of them are best kept outside the panniers in a bottle cage or in external pockets. The small 600ml fuel bottles fit in a standard bike bottle cage but it's not hard to find a larger cage to take a one-litre fuel bottle (try Topeak or Minoura). Despite what the stove makers say, one-litre bottles by Sigg, MSR, Optimus and Primus are interchangeable

(but make sure you're buying a fuel bottle and not the almost identical drinks bottles with a coated interior. Primus and Optimus recommend the small 600ml bottles to run their stoves, but one litre bottles will also work, which should last for up to two weeks of making quick meals and hot drinks.

A petrol stove is a nuisance too. Although they seem designed to fit inside your pots and are best protected there, they leak noxious fumes no matter how well you wrap them in plastic bags so you will need to wash out your pot every time before cooking in it.

PART 1 – PRACTICALITIES

is one more thing to go wrong, especially as the rubber gasket is close to the burner. The cheaper Primus Multifuel has only one control at the fuel bottle and it's interesting that Optimus have chosen to abandon the fine-tuning control on the updated Nova Plus stove and now have one flame adjuster at the fuel-bottle end well away from the burner. The Nova folds up into a very compact bundle but appears a little more delicate than the others and has a novel magnetic jet-cleaning trick enabling you to clean soot out while the stove is on. MSR stoves also have an excellent jet-cleaning design, the bane of these sorts of stoves, but this is one area where Primus needs to catch up as their stoves have to be cleaned the old way by poking the jet with a very fine wire (a strand of brake cable would work as well). I have broken many a stove on the road but have always managed to keep my Omnifuel going.

CARRYING WATER

Topeak and Minoura make long bottle cages that will take a 1.5-litre disposable water bottle fund all over the world. Minoura's is better in that the tough clip holding the bottle won't break, whereas the rubber band on Topeak's cage lasts about a week (but can be replaced by a zip tie). Instead of using disposable

1 litre fuel bottle in Bikebuddy bottle cage

600ml Sigg fuel bottle in standard bottle cage

water bottles that last only a week or two on your frame, look for Sigg or similar bottles that will just about fit. Nalgene bottles are ideal for bike touring and most water filters (MSR, Katadyn Hiker and Vario) fit directly on the wide-mouth types. Using 1.5 litre bottles raises your water capacity to three or even 4.5 litres on the bike frame, a huge amount for most situations, but only enough for half a day when ambient temperatures rise close

to body heat (37°C). The 1.5-litre bottles are a little unwieldy and if your bike frame is small you may not have room to mount two long bottle cages. Sigg and Profile also make bottle cages that will take one-litre bottles, or you could try an adjustable Topeak Modula cage. It's also worth bringing along a ten litre Ortlieb or MSR Dromedary water bag for occasional use; it gives you freedom to find a camping place away from water supplies. See 🖥 www.bikebuddy.co.uk for another option for carrying larger bottles securely in tough stainless steel removable bottle cages.

TREATING DRINKING WATER

Some travellers are either lucky or clever enough to get away with never treating water on very long trips, but it's best to have the option by at least carrying some pills if not a water filter because buying bottled water every day is not an option in more remote locales.

Water filters can take a bit of muscle to pump and cartridges need replacing every couple of thousand litres, depending on the model and the amount of silt that's blocking it. The cartridges aren't cheap, nor are they available where you most probably are, but you should be able to get a couple of years use out of them. Compared with carrying lots of iodine or chlorine pills, it's more weight and bulk but the water is available to drink the moment you've pumped it and there's no after taste. Pills are OK as a backup if you don't trust the water on occasions, but not for a long trip as you shouldn't take iodine or chlorine for long. Filters don't kill viruses, but unless you are in

Steripen: the latest in water purification

a cholera-infected area or near a village (in any case, be careful about agricultural run-off for possible chemical contamination) it's not a major worry. Filters work for amoeba/protozoa such as those old favourites giardia and cryptosporidium.

One filter that's relatively easy to pump and fast in delivering the goods is Katadyn's Hiker model, which uses a glass-fibre filter in place of the heavier and slower ceramic types. It's less prone to cracking if it freezes, but pump it out after using it anyway. A filter that needs a lot of force is more likely to break, which is why the best filter, Katadyn's classic Pocket filter, is made with a metal pump. It's overkill for bikers and expensive, but the mini version is well worth a look, even though it filters a fairly tedious half a litre a minute.

The compact Steripen looks like a breakthrough in water purification, being a battery-powered device that uses UV light to kill practically every bacterium and virus with no musclepower needed. But some reviews suggest the electronics may be flawed and that it hasn't yet proved itself for reliability, and of course it does not filter away sediment or foreign matter.

KITCHEN ESSENTIALS

Any cheap spoon and fork will do. They get lost easily so don't bother with the expense of titanium; stainless steel comes up cleaner than any plastic spoon and restaurants are usually happy to spare you one when you lose one. Carry a plastic fork, spoon or spatula to stir a non-stick pan. People who can live on noodles can get away with any old cooking pot and clean them easily with sand or in a stream, but slightly thicker pots designed for camping transfer the heat much better, avoiding hot spots and saving a bit of fuel; a good

COFFEE-MAKING

Having tried most of the coffee-making gadgets out there, I've concluded that the best camp coffee is made by using none of them, though it takes a little longer. You can use any type of coffee, espresso or coarse-ground. Put it in cold water in your pot and bring to the boil, reducing the heat as it warms up and take it off the heat as soon as it begins to boil. Stir once. Bring it to the boil two more times with the heat on low, taking care not to overheat the coffee. The third time it comes to the boil, the coffee grounds will have sunk to the bottom of the pot and you can pour the coffee without a filter.

non-stick surface is worth getting if you're prepared to look after it. A pot with a lid which doubles as a frying pan is great and combined with a stove that simmers, you can expand your cooking range from just noodles and boiled eggs to rice, omelettes, pancakes and even simple flat breads. There are lots of good quality nesting pot sets available, though you can get by with one pot, especially if you are cooking with another fully equipped cyclist; communal cooking happens more often than you might expect. For a single pot, Primus' EtaPower looks a good bet as it has a built-in heat exchanger to diffuse heat that adds very little weight but saves on fuel. For mugs and bowls, polycarbonate, generally marketed as Lexan, is ideal in that it is practically unbreakable and insulates well. It's good for drinks bottles too.

TOILET BAG: SOME SUGGESTIONS
- Swiss army knife with strong scissors (try Wenger)
- A good metal file for nails (should be found on your penknife or Leatherman)
- Nail clippers
- Skin moisturiser and general purpose suncream – easy to find along the way
- 50+SPF suncream – bring this from home
- Toothpaste – no problems finding toothpaste anywhere
- Dental floss – get the flat kind that can also be used for sewing repairs
- Crystal deodorant – buy from a health shop back home, even the small ones last for years
- Talcum powder – for freshening footwear, drying out fungal nasties and for puncture repairs
- A small mirror – useful for solo travellers

OTHER USEFUL CAMPING GADGETS
LED lights have taken over for all outdoors activities and are perfect for the head torches worn at night in camp. Developments in batteries and LEDs continue, but my current favourite for the last few years is the Petzl E-Lite. It's by far the lightest headlight on the market, so light I carry two of them. I can always find one and can change batteries in the other at night if necessary. The batteries are lithium CR2032s which are also used in Cateye cordless bike computers in both the transmitter and receiver. The batteries only weigh 3g

---

SUNGLASSES

You'll be wearing them most of the day for much of the trip and since we're talking about your eyes, it's worth getting a good pair or two. All sunglasses sold should meet minimum standards of protection against UV, but good ones will give a much clearer view, better colour separation and be less tiring for your eyes. Two pairs, perhaps in different shades or tints is not a bad idea, as are crush-proof cases. At altitude you need darker glasses and some bikers bring glacier goggles for use in snow or up on the salt-pans of the Andean altiplano, where a backup pair may be a life-saver. For most of us, it's brighter light on the road than it is back home, so slightly darker glasses than you wear at home are a better choice; polarised lenses are great for road glare and enhance mountain views. Oakleys have a well-deserved reputation, are very clear, give a close fit for keeping out dust and are made from tough polycarbonate, good protection if you encounter stone-throwers. Pricey, but highly recommended.

SOLAR POWER OR EXTRA BATTERIES?

Solar power appeals to many cyclists. Solar technology has improved but battery technology has improved faster, jumping from Ni-Cad to Ni-Mh to lithium in recent years. Most small gadgets are now powered by lithium batteries that last longer but are impossible to charge directly from a solar panel's very variable power output. You need something like a small motorbike battery to store the solar panel's charge and provide a steady current for your lithium batteries. The weight of the panel plus the storage battery can easily exceed a kilo.

Even in the back country of Africa you should be able to find a guest house or shop with reliable electricity at least once a month. Camera batteries weigh around 30g each and copies can be bought on the internet very cheaply. That's only 150g for a month's worth of fairly heavy use of camera batteries: far less weight and worry than carrying solar panels.

each and can be bought in bulk over the internet, and found in camera shops in most countries. The E-lite weighs only 27g – about an ounce – and should always be in your pocket for the blackouts that occur so often in rural villages and some big cities too. It's light enough to wear round your neck while sleeping if you want to be certain you can grab a light quickly in the night.

For cleaning grease from pots, get some E-cloths, the microfibre cleaning cloths. Don't get bike grease and grime on your cookware cleaning cloths; use rags for cleaning bike gear and tools. Keep cutlery separate from bike tools, using your penknife or other light knife for food or personal things, and a multitool for working on the bike.

Lastly, don't forget a good quality compass; anything by Silva, Recta or Suunto will do. A global compass will work better if you're travelling in the southern hemisphere.

GPS

Luke Skinner

Since technology has become cheaper and handsets smaller over the last ten years or so, the GPS (Global Positioning System) has become an invaluable navigational aid and one which many cycle tourists find useful.

GPS receivers work by calculating the time taken for a signal to reach the user from satellites orbiting the Earth. Since the signal travels at constant speed, the time can be used to calculate distance, and with three signals, the unit can give latitude and longitude. A fourth signal is needed to give an accurate altitude. There's a total of 24 satellites in orbit, of which 12 are visible from anywhere at any time. Most modern receivers have 12 channels, meaning that they can receive signals from all of these satellites at any one time. The signals do require a clear line of sight, so it is very rare to find all 12 available, although most receivers rarely have trouble locating the necessary four (except when indoors, under overhanging cliffs or in very dense forest).

Since the US government turned off 'Selective Availability' (the deliberate degradation of the signal for civilian use) in 2000, it has been possible to pin-

Garmin Etrex – a navigation *aid*, not an alternative.

point your location with an error of less than 5m anywhere in the world. This is obviously very, very accurate, but it must be remembered that the position given is only useful when you have something to compare it with. In most parts of the world, maps (even when they are available at a scale which would make such small measurements meaningful) are nowhere near accurate enough for a position found by GPS to be helpful. When testing out our unit in the Western Sahara, we found that the position given, when plotted on our map, often put us many kilometres to one side or other of the road we were standing on! Other users have found that their GPS showed that important features on their maps were displaced by several kilometres. All this serves to emphasise the point that GPS can only really be as accurate as the maps you use it with.

It's worth thinking carefully about what maps are needed to complement a GPS. In many European countries, a grid exists similar to the Ordnance Survey grid in Britain, and most GPS units will be able to provide a grid reference in place of a latitude/longitude (lat/long) position. However, in less well-mapped areas, you'll be relying on plotting lat/long on the map, so something with grid lines is essential. Bear in mind that if the grid is too widely spaced you can fill in the gaps with a ruler and sharp pencil, but on most projections the lines of longitude are very slightly curved. If your map is of a small scale then drawing straight lines to interpolate can be a significant source of error. In terms of scale, you need a scale of 1:250,000 or at the very least 1:500,000 to really take advantage of the accuracy offered – anyone trying to navigate in an area remote enough to make GPS worthwhile would be well advised to get hold of the most detailed maps available.

One situation where GPS is extremely helpful is when you have known waypoints for important landmarks. Obviously, if these are taken from maps suffering from the inaccuracies mentioned above, GPS can do little more than point out these errors. However, if the waypoints are known to be correct, GPS can be used to point the way with incredible accuracy and reliability. GPS waypoints are becoming more and more widely available on the internet and in guidebooks, particularly for popular overland routes. Arriving as the sun went down at a ruined French fort in southern Morocco, after a gruelling day on atrocious tracks, we were relieved when a previously stored waypoint helped us find the nearby auberge. Our guidebook simply told us it was near the fort – when in fact it was out of sight of the fort itself, over a small rise. Without the GPS we could have spent hours searching the area as darkness fell. However, a warning against relying totally on someone else's waypoints in a remote environment hardly needs to be given.

Another interesting application is the storing of your own waypoints. A routine fix stored in our GPS's memory each evening when we set up camp has provided a fascinating record of our meandering route through Africa, despite rarely using the thing for actual navigation!

Bearing all this in mind, if you decide to add a GPS to your navigational toolset then the next obvious question is: which unit? There is a bewildering range available, varying in size, complexity and price but for cycle-touring the smaller, simpler units are the obvious choice. Anything allowing you to upload digital maps will be of little use outside Europe and North America, and the size and power requirements of these units makes them unsuited to use outside a vehicle anyway. A relatively basic model, such as Garmin's excellent Etrex range, will do everything you could ask for and more and could be had for less than £100. I would forego the fancy gadgets and look for good battery life, a compact size, and a decent screen above all else. Some handhelds offer removable screens which can be replaced if damaged – a useful moneysaving feature if you scratch or damage the screen. A handlebar mount is extremely useful, enabling virtually hands-free operation.

In theory it ought to be possible to do away with bike computers altogether and use the GPS to give (far more accurate) readings for distance, speed, etc, although until battery life improves significantly it is not really feasible to leave most units on all day – my Etrex Summit, admittedly a few years old, goes through a pair of AA batteries about every 15 hours if used this way.

GPS definitely has its place on a cycling expedition in the more far-flung parts of the world but it should be seen as a useful aid to navigation rather than a magic wand. It would be extremely unwise to set out into a remote area without the best map you can get, a compass, and the knowledge to use them – apart from anything else, you never know when the electronics might fail or the batteries unexpectedly go flat!

2 ROUTE OUTLINES

Adventure touring is the opposite of guided touring – it's about independence and freedom and inevitably taking a little risk too. You can pick and mix your countries just as you can dip in and out of sections of this book. Although it highlights the most common routes for riders headed out to the Far East from western Europe, don't feel you have to follow someone else's route. Adventures often begin when you first strike out off the beaten track and onto an unknown one. With a couple of days' food in your panniers, chances are you won't go far wrong. If you need to hit the fast-forward button and beat winter or get out of somewhere before your visa expires, just do it.

Many riders are drawn to the idea of an epic RTW or transcontinental ride; it's a lifetime's dream and drawing a line across the map is easy, but don't feel you have to stick to an ambitious plan once you're on the road. You may well find greater rewards from exploring one region intimately rather than having a series of distant destinations in mind. And you may find that some parts of the route are just too tough, too dangerous or too boring to ride.

This section aims to give you a broad overview of the adventure cycling world, to show some of the possibilities out there and give a sense of what it's like to cycle in each country or region. From this you can build a plan using detailed maps and guidebooks. A number of mountain roads, such as the Great Divide Route in the USA or the Friendship Highway in Tibet, are so well known as cycling routes that each is covered in some detail but otherwise we believe that adventurers like to find their own road.

© TRACEY MAUND

Europe

Many first biking adventures start in Europe – it's the logical and easiest place for most cyclists to begin and build strength, skills and experience. You don't need a guidebook for a bike trip in Europe and if you have mechanical troubles, it's not too difficult to find parts or get your bike repaired.

Getting there is also a piece of cake. If travelling from the British Isles, the cheapest option is the ferry (Dover-Calais is the shortest crossing, though Portsmouth, Newhaven near Brighton, or Harwich are quieter and easier for many people to ride to). A dedicated bus service (💻 www.bike-express.co.uk) from the UK to four destinations in France, Spain and Italy will carry your bike fully assembled. You can take your bike on the Eurostar train to Paris, Lille or Brussels, though it has to be booked in advance and bagged. Those who have flown with their bikes to Europe frequently suggest using Europe's smaller airports if you plan on riding away from the airport. On the other hand, long-haul travellers say that Amsterdam's Schiphol Airport is one of the best: it even has a bike path leading to the city or nearby campgrounds.

WESTERN EUROPE

France has the best road network in the world for bikes. A look at a map shows you a disproportionately high number of small roads (look for D roads on French road maps) which have very little traffic on them. Indeed France hardly bothers with bicycle routes because these roads are so biker-friendly. You won't see many locals bike-touring until you hit Germany, but biking in all forms is well established in France and you'll get respect from motorists. The camping scene is the best anywhere, with good campgrounds in almost every town and many villages too. Go for the municipal two-star campgrounds – these are generally the best value, having the necessaries but no frills and fewer caravans. There's an excellent hostel network and also the private *gîtes d'étape* for cheap overnight accommodation with meals. All these options are above many budget travellers' horizons but if you're wild-camping, and need to clean up every few days, try a *camping à la ferme*, which is usually the next-

READY-MADE ROUTES

As governments have developed national cycling routes, so the EU is taking an interest in trans-European routes (though has yet to throw in some funding). The planning is being done by national cycling federations and groups like the UK's Sustrans organisation (💻 www.sustrans.org.uk; tree maps provided, some downloadable). The European organisation EuroVelo (💻 eurovelo.org) has created 12 transnational routes across Europe running as far east as Moscow, though the network may not be fully complete yet. Following a signposted route obviously makes navigating easier – as long as the signposts are easy to find and follow – and the routes keep you off busy roads and tend to avoid steep hills. The Danube route has been going for ages though it is best in Germany and Austria and harder to follow from Slovakia onwards. After Belgrade, most cyclists head south towards Montenegro, Macedonia and Greece or east through Romania.

cheapest option. Wild camping in France is a little tricky – mushroom hunters and dog-walkers are up early and won't appreciate your presence, but it's time to get up anyway. Just leave it till late before pitching your tent in the woods.

Your bike travels with you on most regional trains and will not need to be bagged. Bikes are now allowed on many TGVs (high speed trains) too, though they must be dismantled and bagged; your bike normally travels on the same train as you but this is not guaranteed. Sheldon Brown (🖳 www.sheldon brown.com) has a number of interesting pages on France, including a useful French-English bicycle dictionary. France is more a nation of cycling spectators than participants these days, and though you will be able to get repairs done easily enough, it is harder than you might expect to find specialist touring gear in France. Wait till you're in Germany for that.

Spain is less oriented than France to cycle touring but that only makes a cycle-tourist an exotic visitor. Few tourists stray more than a few miles inland from the Mediterranean coast but this is the real rural Spain, far from the 'costas' and where you'll hear little English spoken. If you're headed for Africa, consider riding there through Spain and taking the ferry from Algeciras in southern Spain to Morocco. The ferry to the tiny Spanish enclave of Ceuta is the preferred option as it takes bikes for free and the Spanish-Moroccan border at Ceuta is relatively quiet compared to the hustle of Tangier.

Mountain biking is a popular recreational activity in Spain and there are many signposted MTB routes in the Pyrenees and elsewhere, and also the Vias Verdes, the network of disused railway lines. Hopefully one day these routes will be combined to make one long off-highway route across Spain but until then the ancient pilgrimage routes to Santiago, principally the main route between France and Santiago in the far north-west of Spain, or the Via de la Plata, come the closest. The better known Camino de Santiago is set to become a recognised long-distance cycle route, but bikes don't follow the often steep and difficult

---

WHAT DID THE ROMANS EVER DO FOR US?

They built the foundations of the Via de la Plata (forward thinking Romans – it's well suited to cycling), a 1000km trail running through fairly remote country. Accommodation is in small hotels and hostels as well as pilgrim refuges and the occasional monastery. It's a simple, spartan trip with plenty of doubletrack and open spaces suitable for wild camping, though not too many streams. Starting in Seville (get a pilgrim ID card from the office at the cathedral for access to very cheap hostels) you pass through the wild, hard lands of Extremadura to Mérida, then open country till Salamanca after which the land rises to the colder, damper mountains in the north and the Celtic region of Galicia. Not to be underestimated, this ride could take over three weeks of long days but would be a great trial run for adventure touring. The town hostels can get full over public holidays, but many of the village hostels between larger towns are almost empty, and asking at the village bar will produce the key. See 🖳 www.santiago-compostela.net for more information.

The wide open spaces of
the Via de la Plata

THE NORTH SEA CYCLE ROUTE

Said to be the longest signposted cycle trail in the world and passing through seven countries, this 6000km-route follows the North Sea coast, mostly on protected cycle paths or minor roads, including unpaved roads in places. The route involves many ferries across seas and estuaries, though one flight is now necessary, from Bergen to the Shetland islands. This flight runs only twice a week and should be booked well in advance.

Expect wind and rain to be the biggest headaches and to have to camp for at least half the time, but with some excellent wild camping opportunities in Norway, the wildest stretch. You will see very little traffic except on occasional short stretches of main road in Norway. The route isn't all villages; major cities passed through are Newcastle, Aberdeen, Edinburgh, Bergen, Gothenburg, The Hague and Hamburg. The German coastline is fairly crowded but cool and breezy – beware the concentration campgrounds from the old days of East Germany, but it's hard to find a free spot to pitch your tent along Germany's small and popular coastline. The North Sea Cycle Route can be cycled in either direction but most maps, the UK's excellent Sustrans maps being an exception, assume you will cycle it anti-clockwise. See ⌨ www.northsea-cycle.com for more details.

walking path exactly. Also pedestrian pilgrims take priority over cyclists for beds in the refuges, but a biker has the luxury of carrying camping gear, and a night in the tent beats one with a hundred snoring pilgrims keen to rise at 5.30am.

Bike paths abound in **Germany**, **Austria** and **Switzerland** and are often easily found on approaches to cities. Germany is a federal state and bike trails are organised regionally, making planning a trip the length of the country a little tricky. Start at Germany's government tourism website (⌨ www.germany-tourism.de/cycling/cycling.htm/ takes you to their interactive map) and you will see a network of regional routes. Combine these and you have a ready-made route across Germany. Scenically, it can be mundane in places, but the routes are away from traffic and have amenities for cyclists along the way. Your only distractions are food, beer, villages, old churches, museums and changing backdrop along the way. To me, it's heaven and when you're along the Grand Trunk Highway in Pakistan amid thundering traffic, potholes and with no shade for miles on end, you'll remember it fondly. Berlin is one of the most bike-friendly large cities anywhere and among the cheapest – contrast that with London.

The River Danube route attracts lots of cyclists – not just long-distance tourers but day-trippers and commuters – so it can be crowded at weekends. It's now signposted as far as Budapest which gives you about 1000km of almost traffic-free riding. There are campgrounds, but you can also ask at boat clubs if you can camp on their lawns – I was never refused. The most popular section, where on weekends you'll rub shoulders with groups of orange-haired German *frauen* as old as your mum on shopping bikes, is from Ingolstadt (north of Munich) to Vienna but the most beautiful and quiet section is the far west, where the Danube begins just below the Black Forest. Wooded valleys (good for wild camping) and villages – bliss. A commonly-followed route from Britain would have you riding down the Rhine and following the Rhine-Main-Donau canal to join the Danube, all of which would be flat. Far less well-known, but equally interesting and useful as a route through Germany, is the path along the River Elbe, which runs as far as the Czech Republic and could easily be combined with the Prague-Vienna Greenway (⌨ www.pragueviennagreenways.org).

EUROPE EN VÉLO – 1929

In 1929, American graduate **Jean Bell** *worked his sea passage across 'the Pond' to Europe, bought a bike, had a rack fitted and became a true cycle-touring pioneer.*

8 July 1929 – Arrival in Antwerp
We seem to have taken an extremely long time getting here but the seaman's pay which got us to Europe puts us quite a bit ahead of the game financially; the voyage finally ended, the crew paid off.

9 July 1929 – Buying bicycles
After breakfast, we set out in search of a bicycle shop. The call of the open road is strong and we're anxious to be on our way, really to begin our vagabonding abroad.

At first glance, Belgian bicycles look just like our bikes back home. Two wheels, two pedals, one chain, one seat, all that a cyclist needs for around-town riding; our plans for making a long-distance ride, however, require a luggage rack. We also would like to have a coaster brake and a tool kit which will permit us to make emergency roadside repairs. Obviously there is a need to upgrade our vélos for long-distance traveling. The salesman calls in the mechanic and we explain why we need a rack. We will probably be cycling to Paris, we tell them. The mechanic nods, 'Oui. C'est possible.' With a rack mounted over the rear wheel we now have a place to lash our 'carry-on' luggage.

Our next request. 'Can you install coaster brakes?' Here we foul out. What in the world is the French for 'coaster brake?' Eventually we drew a 'Pas possible,' followed by a vigorous shake of the head. We gather from his response that this technology apparently has not yet crossed the Atlantic from west to east. Brakes on these bikes consisted of a lever mounted on the handlebar which, when squeezed, activated a pad on the front wheel which served to slow down progress ... more or less. But the lack of coaster brakes, at that moment at least, did not seem worth wrestling for, so we skip to our next request: single [solid] tires.

Well, 'win some, lose some'. We would get the rack but struck out everything else. And, oh yes, the price. Would you believe it, their grand total selling price per bicycle,was 1100.25 Belgian francs ... the equivalent of US$25, all of which we recaptured when we sold them in Bulgaria some four months later. I don't know why the rims on the wheels of my bike are wooden; Amos's rims are metal. Some thousand miles later, the significance of this difference will become clear.

Weight and simplicity are significant factors in long-distance cruising. Our plans for the road are to wear blue jeans, blue work shirts and tennis shoes. Our baggage includes changes of shirt, underwear, socks and pyjamas, also a blue-knit 'UC' sweater. Add maps, camera and film, a water bottle ... the list grows with astonishing speed.

Ah yes, let me not forget to mention the $300 letter of credit Mom had tucked away with my passport and seaman's papers. Incidentally, this map mentioned above, is a Rand McNally pocket map of Europe and the Near East which I had bought in a New York drug store. This funny little map guided us all the way across Bulgaria and, eventually, to Jerusalem.

13 July 1929 – Amsterdam
I have one major goal in Amsterdam: to see the Rijksmuseum and that famous painting by Rembrandt, *The Night Watch*. All by itself the sight of this memorable canvas pays off the time and effort of getting there.

We decide to make an effort to end each day in a small town ... the smaller the better for a number of reasons: 1. The prices are more subject to bargaining. 2. The prices are usually lower. 3. Probably most important, your host is not so busy with other guests and an evening with him around the fire is a heartwarming experience. Some of our most interesting nights have been spent with the host and his wife. Their questions are exceedingly interesting and, hopefully, ours are too. Perhaps the best advice a traveler gets is 'Avoid stopping in big cities.'

23 July 1929 – Amiens
Noontime found us, like Goldilocks, lost in the woods outside Amiens. We were hungry, very hungry. Eventually we reached a promising peasant dwelling. An old lady in a black apron and white lace cap was feeding the chickens as we drew near. We told her we were hungry and wonder if she could sell us something to eat. What is outstanding in my memory of these strangers whom we approached with requests for favors such as this was their almost universal smiling and obliging aquiescence. Wiping her hands she said lunch had finished but if the messieurs would care to wait? We would! And while

she podded peas and peeled potatoes for our three-course lunch we sat in her kitchen, spoke bad French and told her of our travels and of America. What a lunch!

With such experiences are the scrapbooks of vagabonds filled. Nothing stereotyped, nothing pre-arranged by a travel agency, nothing staged for its effect on tourist pocketbooks. Only a desire to please, a warm glow of friendship which steps across barriers of race and language. Such are the true joys of wandering.

16-28 September 1929 – Austria

What a lot of ground for two college boys to have covered in approximately two months!! Belgium, Holland, France, Germany! One thing about Amos and me, we are more than willing to 'dream big'.

7-14 October 1929 – Bulgaria

We expect to reach Svilengrad in three days. The map shows a 'very good road' most of the way. Seven days later we drag into Svilengrad cussing all Bulgarian road maps. We expected to find paved roads. We did! They were paved with a six-inch layer of yellow dust which concealed rocks. Bicycling is evidently not the accepted mode of transport over lonely Bulgarian roads. We nearly cause a runaway or a smash-up each time we meet or pass an animal-drawn vehicle.

By mid-afternoon we have reached the foothills and begin what promises to be a long, steep climb. Suddenly there is a very loud bang and I find myself sprawling over the handlebars into the gravel. My wooden rim has shattered when my tire exploded and the inner tube is tangled in the chain. So ... here is our very first accident in all those long miles from Antwerp.

Have you ever tried pushing a loaded bicycle backwards **and** on one wheel? It seems that I have been pushing forever when we finally reach the small village of Razgrad. We eat our first meal since dining on bread and sausage the night before. That accomplished, we show the waiter our bike. He is all smiles and indicates that we should follow him. About a block up the street we come upon a bicycle shop. To our great surprise we are greeted in very passable English. Here, in the middle of the Balkan Mountains, we have found a bike shop owner who had put in some 15 years as a waiter in Chicago and only recently returned home to retire. Our needs

When moving from one major metropolis to the next, we simply posted our city clothes on to await our arrival.

do not faze him. 'Of course I can get you a new wheel'. He will phone in the order and we should be ready to roll in two days. 'Two days?' I am very dubious. I had seen no phone lines; nor had we encountered either a UPS or Fed Ex van on the road.

Believe it or not, my damaged wheel is replaced and as good as new. We bid goodbye to all our friends (by this time it seems that we have become old friends with everybody in the village) and after three hours of steep hill climbing, we reach the pass. Some 3000ft below lies a broad valley through which the Maritza River flows gently, reminiscent of the Los Angeles River in late summer.

My nine-month trip around Europe, Asia and Africa cost a total of $265.67, almost all of which I managed to cover in various jobs along the way. Not as tourists, or statesmen, or students but as *wandervogel* we 'did' the Old World on a minimum of cash and a maximum of exuberance.

Jean Bell continued to travel into his nineties, frequently visiting his son, Ross, and his wife, Vicki, in France. He died in California in 2009, aged 101. His autobiography, 'A 90-Year Journey through the 20th Century' is available from 🖥 www.amazon.com.

PART 2 – ROUTE OUTLINES

T R I P   R E P O R T
AROUND THE WORLD

Name	Friedel Rother & Andrew Grant
Year of birth	1978 & 1974
Occupation	Travel writer / IT
Nationality	Canadian
Other bike travels	None before this trip
This trip	Canada, UK, France, Spain, Germany, Holland, Portugal, Morocco, Italy, Greece, Hungary, Slovenia, Slovakia, Austria, Turkey, Syria, Iran, Turkmenistan, Uzbekistan, Kazakhstan, Kyrgyzstan, Thailand, Cambodia, Laos, Malaysia, Singapore, Australia, New Zealand, USA
Trip duration	3 years
Number in group	Two
Total distance	About 40,000km so far
Cost of trip	About 40 euro cents per kilometre

Longest day	144km, through the flat, flat rice fields of Cambodia
Best day	Climbing to 3600m pass then descending to stunning alpine Lake Song Kol in Kyrgyzstan.
Worst day	Being stranded 40km outside Istanbul after misjudging the distance into the city.
Favourite ride	Anything remote with high mountain views
Biggest headache	Getting our Central Asian visas
Biggest mistake	Trying to camp in Thailand – tent invaded by ants
Pleasant surprise	The kindness of people all over the world, particularly in countries like Iran and Syria
Any illness	Tendonitis in ankles (Friedel); typical bugs in Syria

Bike model	Robin Mather custom-built both bikes
New/used	Bought in 2006 for this trip
Modifications	None
Wish you'd fitted	An air horn for scaring pesky drivers
Tyres used	Vredestein Spiders, two sets of Marathon XRs
Punctures	Very few
Baggage Setup	Ortlieb panniers all the way, four each
Wish you'd brought	A pillow
Wish you hadn't brought	Teva sandals. Cheap flip-flops would have done.
Bike problems	Broken rim, cracked rack mount, rusted back dropouts
Accidents	None
Same bike again	Yes, definitely
Recommendations	Invest in the best gear you can afford (particularly tent and rain gear) but don't let lack of money hold you back from adventure.
Any advice?	Just do it. At some point you just have to take that leap into the unknown and trust the universe to support you.

EASTERN EUROPE AND THE BALKANS

Travelling east puts some of the excitement back into border crossings, where they still exist. The EU now extends considerably further east and use of the euro will soon extend beyond Slovakia, which adopted it in 2009. Countries like Poland, Hungary and Slovenia are now relatively Westernised in the cities but the countryside remains slow-paced and far cheaper. It's still a sharp contrast to cross from Germany into Poland – but the unexpected thing is that Poland is much more lively than Eastern Germany.

Slovenia is a great touring destination; Ljubljana is a manageable size for cycling with an excellent campground on its northern side. The Julian Alps, which border Italy and Austria, are highly recommended. Road passes reach as high as 2100m and there are good free-camping possibilities everywhere except Triglav National Park. In the park itself there are more quality campsites per kilometre than anywhere else in the country. A circuit of the northwest takes you through Soca, good for hiking, kayaking and rafting trips as well as cycling. To the south, the karst formations of the Kras region offer laid-back villages, forests good for camping, vineyards and rolling hills. And in the far south of the country you have Slovenia's small but attractive coastline, while the south-east has rolling hills with spas, campsites on farms and easier riding.

Travellers in a hurry to make tracks east or down the Dalmatian coast of Croatia may well avoid the Istrian Peninsula, but it would be a pity, for this area is full of towns built in the Venetian style during the Middle Ages. It's a popular holiday area, not particularly cheap although there are campgrounds, mostly built in the communist era on a grand scale. Some are now for nudists only; a revealing experience for a night or two. As a cyclist you will probably be in better shape than anyone else there!

You could take a ferry from Pula on the Istrian Peninsula to Losinj, one of the chains of islands off the Croatian coast. Going this way via the islands you avoid the traffic on the busy but beautiful coastal road. If you're riding down the coast to the historic Croatian city of Dubrovnik you'll ride through a 20km stretch of Bosnian territory, though you won't need a visa for the transit section. EU citizens get a three-month visa for Croatia or Bosnia-Herzegovina at the border. Travel south of Dubrovnik is either by ferry to Italy, and then again to Greece, or by cycling through Albania.

Mostly Muslim but a secular state, **Albania** is considered a safe but certainly an adventurous destination, though gun ownership is widespread and organised crime and corruption are still major problems.

Serbia and **Montenegro** also have much to offer bikers. The hilly areas of the south are free of tourists, with quiet villages where traditional farming techniques are still practised. Luka Romih (see p96) found local people very hospitable, offering food and places to stay. This was also the case in Bulgaria and Romania.

Bulgaria and **Romania** are less expensive than Serbia but with little traffic and offer superb touring, mountains and a long coastline on the Black Sea. Horse-drawn carts are still a common form of transport across much of the countryside. The range of food in these countries is relatively meagre but there is an abundance of home-grown produce that villagers or farmers will happily sell you. Accommodation is often in private rooms (around €6 per room), people's gardens, farmland (farmers are easily found, so ask permission) or even in churches. Hot springs may cost only €0.50.

SLAVS REUNITED

Even though Serbia used to be a part of our own country – the old Yugoslavia, that is – we'd never been there. We found ourselves cycling through the northern part of Croatia and wondered what it would be like in Serbia. After hearing so much about how friendly they are and the recent Serbian-Croatian-Bosnian war, we really had no idea what to expect.

Vojvodina, the northern part of Serbia, is almost completely flat and is home to some two dozen nationalities or ethnic groups, though only the major ones are represented by a number larger than that of a small village. This makes the whole province a fascinating place if you're interested in people though the landscape appeals only to those who are not looking for obstacles to cross.

Straight after our arrival in Serbia we noticed a radical change from Croatia; everybody was a lot more relaxed, easy-going, always thinking (as we say) the Balkan way: no worries! Yet they have a lot to worry about: the country's economy is devastated, people are lucky to have a job and even if they do, they can make only a part of what they need to see them through a month. Everyone has to make some extra effort to make enough money and they laugh sadly when they tell you 'funny' stories about the regime's godfathers and their way of doing business.

We were continually surprised by the hospitality we received in Serbia. Though we had problems finding a secure place to pitch a tent in Croatia, we never had that problem in Serbia. In Croatia, people warned us about warmongering lunatics wandering around and how dangerous it might be to camp freely. Instead, everyone in Serbia reassured us that the worst we would encounter even if we slept in the middle of a village would be noisy and curious drunks coming home in the middle of the night.

As Slovenians, we could speak the language and were welcomed as former brothers from Yugoslavian times, but we're not sure how much of that hospitality would be extended to a stranger who couldn't communicate with the locals. Then again, Serbia was once part of a prosperous country, so the people don't see you as a Space Viking coming from another planet, as is often the case in parts of Asia. On the other hand, they are often quite angry with English-speaking people because they see them as part of the 'willing coalition' of countries that supported the USA during their bombing of Serbia. So some caution when expressing one's view of world politics is quite important. As with all Mediterranean people, you're either their friend or their enemy.

For scenery, Serbia south of the Danube (and especially the Djerdap Canyon cutting through the Carpathians and through which the Danube flows) is much more interesting. Hills and mountains and forests are abundant all the way through southern Bulgaria and would be a real shame to miss.

We found the people in Bulgaria much more reserved than those in Serbia. They rarely approached us even when we waited to see if anyone would ask us if we needed help with something. In the end, we gave up and had to make an effort to find someone who would be willing to do so. On the contrary, when we came to the first Turkish settlements (there are about 600,000 Turkish people living in Bulgaria since Ottoman times) we found the people much more open and approachable. We could recognise each Turkish village by its mosque, whose minarets were positioned to be seen from a distance. We were really happy to find such villages at camping time; after a day in the saddle Bulgarian kebabs were much more delicious than the 'original' Turkish variety and came with chips.

Luka Romih and **Manca Ravnikar**

(Opposite) Top: The 1300km Pamir Highway (see pp124-6) runs from Dushanbe in Tajikistan to Osh in Kyrgyzstan through spectacular mountain scenery. (Photo © Peter Gostelow).
Bottom: Lunar landscape high in the Pamirs, Tajikistan (see p123). (Photo © Holm Rautenberg).

Russia

Edward Genochio

Russia covers an immense territory but much of it is devoid of roads and inaccessible to cyclists. The road network in European Russia (west of the Urals) is relatively well developed, leaving you plenty of choice for touring, but in Siberia (east of the Urals), roads are few and far between: if you're planning to ride to Vladivostok on the Pacific coast, there's basically just one east-west road, the Trans-Siberian highway, although there are unsealed chunks between Chita and Blagoveschensk (halfway to Vladivostok). In theory the whole route should be paved within the next few years but don't count on it.

Russian road maps

Decent road maps suitable for cycle touring are hard to come by outside Russia (though specialist map shops can help), but once you're in the country you should be able to pick up a comprehensive atlas. A good one to look out for is *Atlas Avtodorog Rossii* (Atlas of Russian Roads), jointly published by Astrel and AST. This covers the whole of Russia in 150 pages but it's light-weight and easily portable, with the area around Moscow shown at 1:500,000, the rest of European Russia at 1:1m and Siberia at 1:2.5m. Since there are so few roads in Siberia anyway, that scale is adequate for all touring unless you plan to follow hunters' trails in the back-country, in which case you might be able to pick up maps locally.

In fact, virtually all mapping of Russia is based on the same cartographic style so whichever atlas you have, the mapping will be the same. If your tour is limited to a small part of Russia, smaller atlases are also available, extracting the same mapping for a particular region.

In the atlas referred to above and on most other road maps 'federal roads' are shown in red; they should be sealed and of reasonable quality. Many red roads are designated 'M' roads, for example the M53 from Krasnoyarsk to Irkutsk; though technically motorways, there's no restriction preventing bikes being ridden on them. Federal roads are now quite well signposted but this is not so on other roads, so trust your map, compass and judgement, or ask a local.

All other roads shown on the map are unpredictable and occasionally don't exist at all. Roads shown in yellow with black edges should be sealed, but you can't always count on this, especially in Siberia. Sometimes 'yellow' roads are very good though; ask locally. Roads shown in green on the map are never sealed, though in dry weather they can be fine to ride and will have very little traffic. If it's been raining, green roads are a write-off – just one passing tractor will turn them into quagmires.

(Opposite) Mosquitoes are a problem in many countries. A mosquito net or an all-mesh inner tent is essential and makes camping a breeze in hot climates, whether by the Nile or in this Egyptian guesthouse. (Photos © Tom Allen).

Asia MAIN TRANS-CONTINENTAL ROUTES

NORTHERN ROUTE

The least commonly taken route goes across Russia and Siberia, dropping down south to Mongolia or China when you run out of warm weather (or get carried out by horse-flies). It's probably the least-populated, shortest and fastest route, a fact often overlooked because maps exaggerate the size of polar regions. Not always good roads, but fairly direct and less visa hassle than any other route.

Border/visa issues Russia is the biggest problem, especially for Brits. You need an invitation and have to register (see p101) with OVIR (a government agency) within three days, often by staying in an expensive hotel. Mongolian visas are obtainable in Russia and extendible in Ulaan Baator, likewise China visas can be obtained in Mongolia, then extended in China.

Arctic Ocean

Alaska

Magadan

TRAILBLAZER

North America

JAPAN

Toyama
Tokyo

Khabarovsk

Vladivostok

N. KOREA
Pyongyang
Seoul
S. KOREA

Harbin

Beijing

Skovorodino

Chita

Ulan Ude
Ulaan Baator

MONGOLIA

Lake Baikal

Irkutsk

Urumqi

R U S S I A

Novosibirsk

Semipalatinsk

Almaty

KAZAKHSTAN

KYRG.
Bishkek

UZBEKISTAN
Tashkent

Aral Sea

Caspian Sea

TURKMENISTAN
Turkmenbash
Ashgabat

AZERBAIJAN
Baku

GEORGIA
Tbilisi
ARMENIA

Tehran

St Petersburg

Moscow

SWEDEN
NORWAY
FINLAND

Copenhagen

London

E U R O P E

Sochi

Black Sea

Sinop
Trabzon
Istanbul

TURKEY

LEBANON
ISRAEL
SYRIA
Damascus
Amman
JORDAN

IRAQ
Baghdad

0   500   1000 miles
0   500   1000   1500km

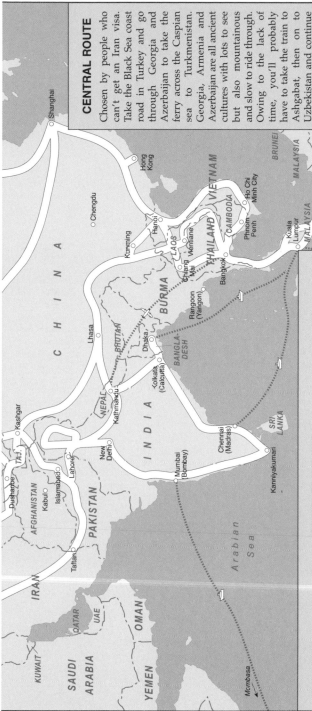

CENTRAL ROUTE

Chosen by people who can't get an Iran visa. Take the Black Sea coast road in Turkey and go through Georgia and Azerbaijan to take the ferry across the Caspian sea to Turkmenistan. Georgia, Armenia and Azerbaijan are all ancient cultures with lots to see but also mountainous and slow to ride through. Owing to the lack of time, you'll probably have to take the train to Ashgabat, then on to Uzbekistan and continue east. Alternatively, try for a ferry heading to Aktau in Kazakhstan, from where it's about 1500km of desolate land past the Aral sea to Almaty.
Border/visa issues:
Getting any kind of Turkmen visa is tricky; there is border guard corruption.

SOUTHERN ROUTE

The most common route. Turkey to Iran then either up into Central Asia or through into Pakistan. The latter route is direct but not much of a pleasure – neither the Iranian nor the Pakistani authorities want tourists in the Baluchi cross-border region, and you will likely have police supervision pushing you on until Quetta and probably end up taking the bus too. The Central Asia visa hunt begins in Tehran. Continue to China over Irkeshtam pass then down the KKH (get Pakistan transit visa on entering) or choose between the long slog through west Tibet or the much easier road route via Ürümqi.
Border/visa issues Assuming you can get an Iran visa, getting a long China visa is the biggest headache – you can't extend it in Tibet, but you can exit to Nepal if you're short of time on your visa.

THIS IS HARD-CORE

Tent. Stove. Wild camping, rock-bottom budget. You think you're doing it the hard way?

Okay, now halve your budget. And then halve it again. Ditch your tent. And the stove. Knacker your bike. And bring your mum along.

When I saw Zhenya on the road out of Saratov, I at first took him for a local: clunky old Soviet one-speed bicycle (peeling sky-blue paint job), wobbly rear wheel (half the spokes missing), fishing rod (lashed to top tube), bundle wrapped in a plastic sheet (tied on the back with string), soot-blackened cooking pot (perched on top). Tattered floppy sun-hat. No shirt. Flip-flops. His mum following not far behind, with a kettle.

But Zhenya and his mother Tanya were far from local. They had already come 2000km. We were all heading west, so we rode the next 1000km together, and as we went, they told me their story.

Zhenya and Tanya were ethnic-Russian Kazakhs from Leninogorsk, in Kazakhstan's far north-eastern corner, a day's ride from China. They had set out in search of Tanya's long-lost brother Sasha who lived, as best they knew, somewhere in the town of Korocha on the Russian-Ukrainian border. No address, no telephone number – just the name of a town, 3000km from their own.

They didn't have the money for the train fare, but then Zhenya had remembered the two old bikes rusting in the shed. With a bit of oil and a few well-aimed hammer-blows (every Russian, from taxi driver to cosmonaut, can fix anything mechanical with a hammer) he had got the pedals turning, and Zhenya (twenty-five) and his mother (almost fifty) had hit the road. By the time our paths crossed, the deserts of Kazakhstan were behind them; there was just Russia to go.

They were fuelled by tea, mostly, which they brewed every couple of hours on a road-side camp fire. To my mind this took a lot of time, but to theirs it was essential. About my Primus stove they were ambivalent: they saw something in its convenience, but mistrusted its fiddliness, and the cost of its petrol.

Their chains slipped so badly that they couldn't pedal into the wind, let alone uphill. But it was midsummer and we rode or walked until the very last of the light,

and this way we managed to make over 100km a day.

For food we stole potatoes and dill from the fields and boiled them with macaroni to make soup. Tanya stole sugarbeet and boiled it to make a dessert she called Russian pineapple. We ate a lot of it and it tasted pretty bad. We stole peas and with them filled our pockets, eating them from the pod like sweets as we went, throwing the wrappers on the roadside. For a treat we bought blocks of margarine, rated at 544 kcal/100g, good for road fuel and thrombosis, and washed it down with penny-priced ice creams. One tea-stop we found a good hedgerow and spent all day harvesting it for berries. Zhenya and I collected, and Tanya boiled them up to make a cauldronful of jam, which we ate long into the night, spoonful after sweet, dripping spoonful.

Tanya and Zhenya slept out under a polythene sheet; I crept into my tent, safe from the mosquitoes and a little ashamed.

Unprotected from the sun, Tanya's flip-flopped feet developed sores and boils that made pedalling agony, but still she made her 100km days. In the evening she made soothing poultices from wildflowers and tied them on her toes with grass. For directions they had a photocopied page from a world atlas, and kept west by the setting sun. Zhenya had a camera and once a day directed a photoshoot with great seriousness, making marks on the road where each of us should stand.

A week's riding like this and we reach Korocha. It turns out to be a big town. We go door to door asking, street after street. Late in the evening we find someone who thinks they know someone who might know Tanya's brother. We are led across town, the three of us: Tanya the sister, Zhenya the nephew, and me the stray Englishman. They want me to knock on the door and make up some cock-and-bull story. There's good wind-up potential: you don't get many Englishmen knocking on your door in Korocha.

But when Sasha opens the door Tanya can't wait and rushes past me, into the arms of her brother whom she hasn't seen for fifteen years.

Edward Genochio

Visa registration

A headache for cycle tourists in Russia is the system of visa registration. In theory you are supposed to have your visa 'registered', either at an official tourist hotel or at an OVIR office (effectively a branch of the police – the police can always direct you there) within 72 hours of arrival. That is fine for tourists on package tours of Moscow but causes problems for cyclists who may not even reach a town big enough to have a tourist hotel or OVIR office for several days after entering the country.

The rules about visa registration are subject to local interpretation and this 'flexibility' can either work for you or against you. The safest and simplest option is to try to spend one night in a tourist hotel (you'll need to find a decent-sized town) as soon as feasibly possible after entering the country. Registering directly at OVIR is usually more of a hassle.

Camping and other accommodation

Camping is possible virtually everywhere in Russia outside the big cities. You won't find organised campsites except in very touristy areas like Lake Baikal, but there's plenty of space for your tent everywhere you go and nobody will mind so long as you're not trampling their tomato plants.

If you're really out in the wilds of Siberia, you should be careful about bears – seek local advice – though local people on the Trans-Siberian highway claim that bears don't wander near the main road anyway. In Ussuriya, in the Russian Far East, there is a theoretical risk from tigers but you'd be very lucky to see one. The real threats come from smaller creatures. Mosquitoes and horseflies will drive you to distraction but are not serious hazards; ticks, on the other hand, are and they are widespread across much of Russia. They carry serious diseases including tick-borne encephalitis and Lyme disease, so make sure you are inoculated in advance and take precautions against tick bites. Wear long trousers tucked into your socks when walking in the woods or in long grass; locals recommend wearing a hat as well. Check your clothing before getting into your tent. Show no mercy to any ticks that you find – they look like little spiders but have hard bodies and are very difficult to crush. Fancifully painted signs by the roadside warn you of the tick danger and what the local species look like.

On major trucking routes you will find motel-type accommodation for around US$10 per night – but it's not always at conveniently spaced day-ride intervals. In most of Russia you really do need to carry a tent or at least a bivvy bag. If you chat to locals in towns and villages you will often find yourself invited to stay the night but you can't count on that every night.

Shops and provisions

You can ride a long way in Russia without going near a town but even in Siberia you'll probably pass through or close by a village at least once a day. Almost all villages have a shop that will sell a few basic provisions, though the shop is not always easily recognised – it may be in someone's front room. Ask around for *magazin* and you'll quickly be pointed to the right house. In the morning you'll probably get bread, and there's always pasta in various guises (all called 'macaroni'), rice, biscuits, and tins of fish and meat. You'll often find a few oranges, apples or bananas, too.

For fresh local produce, you're better off asking at private houses. Most village people cultivate a vegetable plot and are usually more than happy to sell you whatever is in season. Potatoes are ubiquitous, and you'll also find cabbages, cucumbers, carrots and tomatoes. Eggs and fresh-from-the-cow milk are available too, just ask around the village for *moloko* (milk) and *yaiytsy* (eggs). Meat can be harder to find, though shops will often sell a variety of salamis (*kolbasa*). Where there's reliable electricity, many shops will sell ice-creams which are cheap, tasty and morale-boosting. Several varieties of refreshing yoghurts are sometimes available too, along with cheese and chocolate-flavoured butter.

Every village will have a pump or well from which you can draw water. Generally it is alright to drink, though in some places it can be rather salty. Residents will quickly tell you if the local water is contaminated. Finding the village pump-house or well is not always easy – they come in a variety of well-camouflaged (pun intended) guises. Ask around for the *kolonka* (water-pump) or *kolodyets* (well).

If you prefer someone else to do the cooking, you'll find regular truck-stop cafés along major routes where you can eat hearty, though repetitive, fare for a few dollars. Expect to slurp your way through a lot of *borsch* (beetroot consommé), mashed potato and goulash. Off the main routes, you may struggle to find eateries, though it's worth asking in villages for the *stolovaya*, or canteen. Set up to feed workers on the collective farms, many have now closed and not all will serve 'outsiders', but it's worth asking: sometimes you'll get lucky and score a hearty meal for a bargain price.

GIVING YOURSELF A DAMN GOOD THRASHING

If you're riding in Russia, there's a good chance that someone will invite you in for a *banya* – a traditional Russian sauna. Never mind that at home you might think twice before accepting an offer to work up a sweat over a few beers and a spot of light sadomasochism with a burly Russian woodcutter, out here you should not turn down a banya invitation. These things have magical restorative properties.

I had been flogging into the wind all day somewhere in the southern Urals. Eight hours in the saddle and I was all but spent, ready to find a camp-spot and call it a day. I stopped in a village seeking bananas for a quick carb' fix, too tired to contemplate cooking dinner. Instead I found Aleksey, who insisted that he fire up his banya for me. An hour later when I emerged, I'd sweated out all the day's tiredness and aches and felt ready to ride another eight hours. It was like getting two days for the price of one!

It's standard practice in a Russian banya to give your fellow bathers vigorous beatings with bundles of birch branches. This is supposed to encourage the pores to open and ensure a deeper cleansing. It's also fun, some people think.

Siberians, though, who enjoy living up to their reputation as Russia's hard men, think birch branches are for wimps. Real men – or real Siberians, anyway – like to be beaten with giant Siberian stinging nettles. The odd thing is that it feels so good. The nettles do their stinging stuff, but within a few minutes the pain soothes into an all-over body tingling that lasts for several days. I'll never go back to boring old birch.

Of course, if you visit Siberia in winter, there may not be any stinging nettles available. Real men just have to make do with a dip in Lake Baikal instead – hopping into swimming holes cut through the ice.

Edward Genochio

Police, the 'GAI', and bureaucracy

Russian drivers love to complain about the cops, who have a bad reputation for shaking down motorists for trivial or fabricated offences. Still widely known by their Soviet-era acronym of GAI, the armed traffic police are now formally known as the DPS. Their regular checkpoints can look intimidating but in fact they rarely cause trouble for cyclists.

Beware of roads near borders – particularly the borders with former Soviet republics which, until recently, were pretty porous. There is a 'restricted zone' stretching several miles inland from most Russian borders, though these are not always clearly marked. If you stray into such a zone you run the risk of being picked up by the local border guards and potentially subject to a fine. If you are planning to cross the border legitimately via a recognised route, you should have no trouble; problems arise on small local roads that run parallel to the border. I was arrested on one such road near the Kazakh border and held and interrogated for 24 hours.

ROADS AND ROUTES IN RUSSIA

If you're heading east on a Trans-Siberian route, you have a few choices as far as Omsk. Thereafter, there is only one road, though there are a few side-trips to the north and south that you could consider along the way. Many people enter the country in the north around St Petersburg but this means that you have to get through or around Moscow before heading further east, so consider entering from further south, between Kursk and Rostov-on-Don – traffic in the south, away from Moscow and the main roads to Europe, is generally lighter.

If you're riding through European Russia, you'll cover a lot of very flat miles, so reaching the Urals may come as something of a relief. Don't expect towering peaks, though – the Urals are more rolling hills than serious mountains.

Many people assume that Siberia is a frozen wasteland but in fact its southern half enjoys a warm, if short, summer, from late May to September, during which you're more likely to feel too hot rather than too cold. (In spite of this, Siberians, with their characteristic dark humour, enjoy saying that 'In June summer hasn't quite started, but by July it's already over'.) Once you've encountered Siberia's insect life, though, you may seriously want to consider Arctic conditions. Between Chelyabinsk and Novosibirsk, in particular, you're basically riding through an uninterrupted swamp inhabited by a few unfortunate people and a vast number of extremely hungry mosquitoes and giant horseflies. Repellent (available locally, or try vodka – drinking it, that is) helps a bit against the mozzies, but the horseflies seem impervious. These guys are big, and when they bite it hurts (they've got teeth). There's not much you can do to escape – they'll be with you all day, and they have no difficulty maintaining a touring bike's pace. Take comfort from the fact that the worst of it lasts only about 2000km; once you're past Novosibirsk the swamp gives way to hillier terrain and the flying tormentors become fewer.

Heading east, you can break the monotony of the Trans-Siberian route by branching off south of the highway. Good options include:

A THREE MONTH RIDE ACROSS SIBERIA – IN WINTER

Bastien Demange spent three months cycling through Siberia in winter. He rode some 4200km before the approaching expiry of his visa forced him to take a train to Vladivostok. Bastien wanted to see Siberia in winter to learn how people live in such harsh conditions, having to cooperate more just to survive, and to learn how he might cope on a three-month solo ride in one of the toughest regions on the planet.

Bastien offers the following tips to anyone considering a midwinter ride:

'Sweat means death' is a well-known saying but governs everything you do, from dressing to riding to camping. Wear too many clothes and you are hot and will sweat. Water at -20°C freezes quickly so your jacket and clothes freeze too. Be very careful regulating your heat by riding at a steady pace and adjusting your clothing. Most important: clothes must be highly breathable. You will spend much of your time keeping them dry and worrying about moisture. Using a vapour barrier liner (VBL) inside your sleeping bag will ensure your bag stays dry and reduces humidity inside the tent. Camping at -40°C, everything in the tent will freeze, including the tent itself and the zips on the doors. It is hard to camp for more than a few

nights like this. Don't treat a Siberian winter ride as if it's a polar expedition by camping when there are villages nearby. Camping is very hard and you should take advantage of the hospitality you will inevitably be offered at every village along the way. Meeting people is one of the best and most memorable parts of the trip and you will learn a lot and have a great time if you stop at the villages, which are often a few kilometres away from the main road and not visible from it.

At around -30°C your bicycle begins to freeze up and riding is very slow, around 8km/h even on the flat, though Siberia is rarely flat. Much of it is undulating land with ascents and descents of around 2-3km, meaning you warm up on the ascents and feel cold on the downhills. The oil in my hydraulic brakes froze when the temperature fell below -30°C and I had to take a bus back to where I was eight days before to buy some V-brakes to fit on my bike. Spiked tyres (Schwalbe and others make these) work well in a Siberian winter, but you will fall off the bike now and again in any event.

Biscuits are the only food that does not freeze. Take a thermos flask and fill it with tea for hourly warmups.

Everywhere, I was asked why I was doing this ride in winter, and it was not easy to answer. Never ask yourself this question during such a tough ride, leave that question till later. At one point I considered taking the train to Chita, but I told myself I didn't come to Russia to ride the train and continued until my visa ran out.

Thanks to **Bastien Demange**
⌨ http://bastiendemange.com
(photo © Bastien Demange)

● **The M52 south from Novosibirsk.** This will take you down to the Altay Republic, with some fine scenery and a back-door route into western Mongolia via Tashanta (see p159). An alternative, adventurous option is to ride the track from Kosh-Agach north-west into Tuva, rejoining a decent road at Ak-Dovurak. Seek local advice about this route. You'll need to take food for several days, be prepared to ford some sizeable rivers and carry good local maps and a compass.

● **Turn south at Achinsk** (west of Krasnoyarsk) and head for Abakan. From there you can ride the 1200-km 'Sayan Loop' through the Sayan Mountains. Take the M54 south-east to Kyzyl in Tuva, then turn west to Ak-Dovurak. From there you can attempt the track crossing to Altay Republic, or complete the loop by turning north back towards Abakan, through more spectacular scenery on the border between Tuva and Khakasia. This loop route includes a few sections of unpaved road and a couple of serious passes. A variant would be to turn south halfway between Kyzyl and Ak-Dovurak and head for the Mongolian border at Khandagayty. There is a Mongolian consulate in Kyzyl that will issue tourist visas (see also p159).

● **To the Mongolian border.** From the south-western tip of Lake Baikal, the A164 heads west along a broad valley towards the Mongolian border at Mondy. It's a scenic route with a couple of short side-spurs on the northern side of the valley that you can explore. One day they may open the border, creating a fantastic route linking Baikal and Lake Hovsgol in Mongolia, but at present that border is firmly shut.

Turkey

With Europe behind you at last, and minarets and those huge bridges over the Bosphorus beckoning, your trip takes off in Turkey. Sadly you can't ride over either bridge as they're both motorways, but have a good rest and look round Istanbul – off the bike – while you plan your route east. All but the most committed will take a bus or ferry out of the city, it's a cyclist's nightmare.

Broadly, you're going to take either coast or go inland. The Black Sea coast route is the fastest, with a couple of weeks of dual carriageway (divided highway) with lots of tunnels to save you the hills, but bring reflective road-crew jackets and lights for the tunnels. Expect lots of trucks, but a wide shoulder to ride on. Trabzon in the east is a highlight – a city with ancient routes, a side-trip south to see the monastery at Sumela, and a chance to pick up a Georgian visa. Inland, you could pick any number of small roads. There's no way to avoid hills in this mountainous country but there are a lot of warm and friendly farming villages along the way, great fresh food and plenty of touristy diversions – Cappadocia might be the place to while away visa-processing time otherwise spent in Ankara. The southern route is the longest as it's a dog-leg south, then east. The spectacular coast has short and sometimes very steep hills with amazing views over the sea. The flat sections have good wide roads but are busy.

TURKISH BATHS

Some of the most authentic travel experiences are some of the cheapest and one that cyclists will appreciate after a hard day's ride is a good steam bath. Hammams are common throughout the Middle East and Iran. In touristy parts of Turkey (eg Istanbul) they are overpriced and expect tips but in small towns and villages they cost next to nothing and some are many hundreds of years old.

The attendants will guide you through the process but you can't go far wrong as long as you keep your towel on. Ask for the full works and you'll get a massage after working up a sweat sitting in the steam room. You can spend as long as you like relaxing in the hammam, it's a great way to unwind. Men and women bathe separately except in the tourist places.

TRIP REPORT
EUROPE TO NORTH AFRICA

Name	Tom Allen
Year of birth	1983
Occupation	Web developer
Nationality	British
Other bike travels	1 week mountain-biking in Scotland
This trip	England, Netherlands, Belgium, France, Switzerland, Germany, Austria, Slovakia, Hungary, Romania, Bulgaria, Turkey, Georgia, Armenia, Iran, Syria, Jordan, Egypt, Sudan, Ethiopia, Djibouti, Yemen, Oman, UAE, Iran, Armenia
Trip duration	2 years
Number in group	Three, then two, then one
Total distance	17,000km
Cost of trip	about £4500
Longest day	170km in Sudan
Best day	Dirt tracks in the Fagaras mountains of Romania
Worst day	The day I left
Favourite ride	The Ethiopian Highlands – tough, raw, spectacular
Biggest headache	56-degree heat and sandy headwind in Oman
Biggest mistake	Making a big, restrictive plan before leaving
Pleasant surprise	Everybody wants to help you
Any illness	Knee problems in Europe, bowel trouble in Turkey, malaria in Sudan
Bike model	Kona Explosif cromoly frame, custom self-build
New/used	New
Modifications	Magura Odur forks, Rhyno Lite rims, Magura disc brakes, Shimano XT drivetrain, Brooks saddle, rear-view mirror
Tyres used	Schwalbe Marathon XR 2.0"
Punctures	None in Europe, about 10 thereafter
Baggage Setup	Bar-bag, Tubus Logo rear carrier, Carradice Super C rear panniers, drybag on top, Extrawheel Classic single-wheel trailer
Wish you'd brought	Free-standing tent, lightweight cooking pots, inflatable cameraman
Wish you hadn't brought	Wok
Accidents	Fell down a hole in an unlit Turkish road tunnel – four stitches in face
Same bike again	Definitely
Recommendations	A trailer takes a lot of strain off your bike. Prevention is better than cure but in a pickle you'll find that everything can be fixed somehow.
Any advice?	Don't build an institution around your trip – no-one's giving out medals. Find out what you need to know, then go and see the world your way.

THE DOGS OF EASTERN TURKEY

It will take more than a Dog Dazer to scare off the dogs used to protect sheep in eastern Turkey. These are hounds of the Baskervilles and should be tied up by day, but may be loose protecting a flock of sheep, the sight of which is your tipoff. Tom Hermansson Snickars was stopped on his bike by a dog that bit his pannier and pulled it clean off the rack. Throwing rocks as big as you can is the best way to keep them at bay.

Turkey's eastern region is home to the Kurdish people. If by any chance you hadn't noticed that easy-going Turkey was Muslim, you will in Kurdistan. More devout, poorer, very friendly, this politically troubled region will show Muslim hospitality to a visitor, as will the Turkish army whose checkpoints dot the roadside. For contrast, we spent the night at some Syrian Orthodox monasteries in the mountains near the Syrian border – the services are in Aramaic, the language of Christ's time.

At the Iran border there are three options but most people take the first and well known crossing at Doğubayazit, aka 'Dog-biscuit' to travellers. The route passes 5000m Mt Ararat, with predictably extreme weather – it's all above 2000m in the east. The central crossing at Kapiköy is by train only. You can pick it up at night-time (not daily) and travel as far as Tabriz in Iran unless you want to get off the train at the first stop in the middle of the night. The train starts in Istanbul and crosses Lake Van on a ferry. The southern crossing at Sero in Hakkâri province is least commonly used. It's the most hotly contested region between the PKK and Turkish army, and though you are not a target, the atmosphere is tense. One rider told of the sound of artillery as his lullaby while camping. It's also far less populated on the Iranian side if you enter there.

Lebanon, Syria and Jordan

Philip Davis

With its easy accessibility from Europe, wonderful climate, amazing archaeological ruins and beautiful scenery, why isn't this part of the world thronging with tourists? Politics and history are two obvious answers. But these issues aside, it's a fine region to cycle in. The people are immensely friendly, the roads are good for cycling and the food is great. What more could you want?!

Visas and practicalities

Only Syria requires visas in advance of arrival for those nationals whose country has a Syrian embassy, though many travellers report getting visas on arrival even though their countries have Syrian representation. Entry is at the whim of border guards who may act like bouncers at a night club – not everyone gets in, but you may also be invited in to the boss's office for a cup of tea. Neither Lebanon nor Syria allow people who have visited Israel to enter their countries and you may still be denied entry at the border even though you have a Syrian visa. Jordan and Lebanon issue visas at the border.

Most basics can be bought in the region but you won't find parts for modern bikes, so bring a basic toolkit and spare spokes and chain links. Note that the inland areas of Syria are largely desert and there can be long stretches without villages or shops: on the route to Palmyra, for example. Although primarily Islamic countries, Jordan, Syria and the Lebanon are quite liberal and cosmopolitan so there is no great problem with wearing shorts and T-shirts on the bike but you will need to cover yourself when visiting holy places. You should try to bring a respectable clean set of clothes for visiting people's homes.

Camping is possible in some parts of the region, especially in the grounds of some hotels, but not really a viable option in many areas. As this region is not on the backpacker trail there can be a shortage of good-quality budget accommodation. Most towns will have a hotel but expect to have to bargain to get a room at a reasonable price. As wealthier local people like to holiday in the cool-

MUSLIM HOSPITALITY

Whether it's a religious obligation or just plain friendliness, people in the Muslim world are noticeably more generous than those outside it. It started for us in Turkey where we found every petrol station served free tea and had a table and chair to sit at. In Syria we wouldn't have got very far if we had stopped for every tea invitation and our money was often refused when we stopped for a snack or sugary Middle-Eastern sweets. Sometimes it was lunch or ice-creams, you never knew when someone might insist on treating you.

When we were stuck for a place to spend the night, as can often happen in crowded countries with few tourists, we had only to ask someone – anyone – with gestures even, and a process would begin of asking around, the police sometimes being consulted, and finally a place being found for us. Once in a while it seemed okay to offer some money but we had to be careful not to offend. In tourist areas, of course, it's quite different and the friendliness you get is just sales patter – this is business, and you have no obligation to accept a cup of tea from a carpet shop owner. But what was astonishing was the generosity of the poorest people. In a village some way off the road in Iran, we were allowed to camp in a field, given water and brought dinner on a silver tray, the finest honeycomb ever, bread and jams to rival any in Europe, home-made cheese and a pot of tea.

It is almost impossible to give anything in return in these situations. Almost as hard is explaining that you would rather spend the night in your tent than in someone's house. If you ask for permission to camp near a village, you're almost certain to be asked in by someone. Evenings in homes become wonderful memories, but after a few of them you may prefer a bit of privacy. That's another reason why the most prudent thing is often to camp in a secluded spot where you aren't imposing on anyone and can get an early night, which you certainly won't if you have to entertain your hosts.

Stephen Lord (photo © Friedel Rother)

er uplands, there are many attractive hotels and small resorts in the mountain areas of all three countries. These can be very reasonably priced out of season.

Safety

All three countries are relatively safe with low crime rates. There is a low hassle factor in comparison with some other countries in the region. Local people can be immensely friendly and helpful, although they will usually be puzzled as to why anyone would choose a bike as a means of travel (especially in Lebanon). People will cheerily invite you to join them for a meal or a hubbly-bubbly, or casually offer to lead you to wherever you want to go. A driver in Beirut led me to my hotel by allowing me to slipstream behind him! Many women travel the area solo with few problems.

Driving standards are appalling: sometimes cars will go round roundabouts the wrong way or even along a motorway the wrong way – disconcerting if you're riding on the hard shoulder and a car comes at you.

SOME ROUTES

From Amman in Jordan, there is a road north to the border and Damascus. This road is busy but has a generous hard shoulder which is perfect for cycling. An unmissable stop one day's ride north of Amman is the Roman City of Jerash. This is one of those places that make the region special – an ancient site that would be buzzing with tourists all year round if located in Europe. But here you can explore it in relative isolation. There are some guesthouses around but a good bet is to cycle up into the hills to the west to the peaceful Olive Branch Resort, which has good deals out of season and camping is allowed in its grounds. It is an excellent base to explore the area.

From Jerash you can cycle direct to the border, but it's much better to bear north-west into the uplands towards the university city of Irbid, a town with no shortage of fast food outlets to satisfy the hunger that will hit you after tackling your first big climbs. Around Irbid there are rarely-visited Roman remains and beautiful countryside. The roads are generally in very good condition with light traffic but gradients are steep.

It's a nice, flat day ride from Irbid to the Syrian border town of Deraa, best known as the place where T.E. Lawrence had a painful encounter with a Turkish police officer. It's a dull place but train buffs will find the local rail yard fascinating, with its collection of ancient steam engines rotting away on sidings. There are also some very interesting Roman remains in the area.

Then from Deraa it's a straight, 100km ride to Damascus. But be careful to take the old Damascus road, not the new motorway. It's an easy ride that will be a perfect introduction to this region.

South of Amman in Jordan is very cyclable and includes some memorable destinations, most famously the desert landscapes of Wadi Rum and the magnificent ruins at Petra. The Kings Highway runs through the heart of the country linking these sites and others. The views are fantastic but it's hard work crossing the wadis – the road crosses three dry river canyons (the Wadis) and drops and climbs 6-800m each time. Taking the Desert Highway would be flatter but you'd miss the views. The wadis themselves are sandy – leave your bike somewhere safe and hike into them. These two areas are somewhat

PART 2 – ROUTE OUTLINES

touristy so be careful of your belongings. Note that central and south Jordan is very hot in the summer months with temperatures often reaching 40°C. The Dead Sea features many attractive resorts but most of these are on the Israel side. Don't forget it's well below sea level so expect a long, hard slog to get out of there. In winter the Dead Sea Highway and the road along the Dead Sea are a really refreshing ride, though.

Damascus

Entering Damascus is a little bewildering but no more difficult than any other large city. Don't be surprised if a local cyclist (and there are many on the road using big old bikes, locally called 'donkeys') comes up to you and offers to lead you to where you are going. This is typical of the casual generosity of Syrians. Most tourist and backpacker accommodation is in the central Martyrs' Square area or alleyways a few hundred metres to the north. A couple of tiny shops on the south side of Martyrs' Square sell beer. There are few tourists in Syria and most are on bus tours but the benefit to you is a constant refrain of 'Welcome to Syria' and tea invitations wherever you go. Damascus has a couple of first-rate museums and an easy walk to the huge walled Old City (the oldest continually inhabited site in the world, with streets that are mentioned in the Bible) and the world-famous Ummayad Mosque, converted from a Byzantine cathedral. The Old City has several excellent, authentic and very cheap hammams.

Lebanon and northern Syria

It takes just a day to get into Lebanon from Damascus, and a lovely day's cycling it is. There are longer routes on minor roads to the north, but the border crossings can't be guaranteed. The main road leading to the vast Bekaa Valley is relatively quiet and despite its name it's more of an upland plain, penned in by two parallel mountain ridges. After cycling through barren desert areas your eyes will be dazzled by the iridescent irrigated fields of wheat that carpet the ground in spring.

The northern part of the Bekaa is primarily Shi'ite so don't be too surprised to find yourself at a Hizbollah checkpoint. But don't worry, they are welcoming to the occasional tourist who braves it this far north. The biggest attraction by far is the amazing Roman temple complex at Baalbek. The scale of these ruins has to be seen to be believed, dwarfing even the finest temples of Italy and Greece.

The south of the Bekaa features some less impressive ruins, but offers pleasant cycling. It gradually gives way to the hilly countryside of south Lebanon. This area is under the control of the UN but it's a relatively safe area in which to travel.

ENTERING ISRAEL FROM JORDAN

From Amman, it's only 90km to Jerusalem and you won't need a visa to enter Israel – they catch you going out with a €35 exit tax. Remember to ask the Israelis not to stamp your passport so you can enter Syria with a clean passport and deny having ever been to Israel. Jordan will allow you back in on the same visa.

Beirut and the coast of Lebanon are a hostile environment for cyclists. Traffic is thunderous and there are few refuges. Nobody cycles. Take the bus north to Tripoli, then continue into Syria. The road is along a beach, which sadly is also a huge Palestinian refugee camp. It's safe, but a grim reminder of the history of the region.

North of Lebanon, it's easy to get into the north-western highlands of Syria. This is a great place for cycling with good quiet roads. The rolling

Camping is allowed in several archaeological sites in Syria © Peter Gostelow

hills, olive groves and upland forests of the area are reminiscent of the south of France or northern Italy yet it is almost totally unexplored by tourists.

Culturally it is very distinctive, inhabited by a mixture of Orthodox Christians and Alawis (a somewhat mysterious offshoot of Shi'ite Islam with many Christian and even pagan elements), from whom comes the ruling family in Syria, the Assads. And most of all, it has one of the true wonders of the world, the Krak de Chevaliers (signposted as 'Citadel'), probably the finest intact mediaeval castle in the world. Although by Syrian standards it's a major attraction, it is quiet for much of the day. You can camp outside the restaurant behind the Krak, less than a hundred metres away. And it's not the only castle in the area – the whole region is dotted with crusader remains, sometimes in spectacular locations.

A day's ride east of Krak de Chevaliers, Hama is an atmospheric town with French colonial architecture and water wheels that the guidebooks send people to. It's on the freeway between Aleppo and Damascus or you could plan a trip to Palmyra from here or ride from Homs to the south. A ride from Damascus to Palmyra would be hard, busy near Damascus and dry and without shelter the rest of the way.

Aleppo has much to offer travellers and if you enter Syria from Turkey, you are bound to visit. It's a mix of religions and cultures, is great for food, has a spectacular Citadel and one of the largest and probably the longest covered souks in the world. Rooftop camping at guesthouse Al-Gawahar is highly recommended.

Georgia, Armenia and Azerbaijan

Mark Elliott

The fascinating Caucasus is a cradle of human civilisation. Arguably the historical location of the Biblical Garden of Eden, nowhere in the world has so much history, scenic variety, passion and political complexity crammed into such a tiny area. Since the collapse of the USSR in 1991 there are officially three independent countries in the south Caucasus: Georgia and Armenia are both ancient, Christian nations recovering from years of turmoil while Azerbaijan is a low-key Islamic-Turkic nation whose capital Baku is undergoing a remarkable oil boom.

Since Armenia and Azerbaijan fought an unresolved war in the 1990s the borders between their territories have been firmly closed. The Armenian puppet state of Nagorno Karabagh still occupies over 15% of Azerbaijan's land and is a de-facto country of its own (you can pick up NK visas in Yerevan). Landmines and ruined cities fill the no-man's land between Armenia/Nagorno-Karabagh and Azerbaijan so there's no earthly way to cycle across the borders whatever a map may suggest.

Similarly there's no way to cross overland from the Caucasus republics to Russia. Tensions are still high between Russia and Georgia following their summer war of 2008 which resulted in Russia recognising the independence of South Ossetia and Abkhazia, both of which had broken away from Georgia in the early 1990s. The road from Azerbaijan to Makhachkala in Dagestan, Russia is open to locals but not to foreigners.

Georgia

Glorious Georgia, with its fabulous castles, Caucasian mountain tower villages, superb food and passion for wine (that many claim originated in Georgia 5000 years ago) is the obvious starting point when cycling east from Turkey. Mikhail Saakashvili's Rose Revolution has rooted out Georgia's once-infamous corruption and insecurity and visas are no longer required for most western nationals.

Turkey to Tbilisi

There are two main routes from Turkey to Tbilisi, Georgia's delightful capital. The main route is from Trabzon via Sarp, sub-tropical Batumi and historic Kutaisi. However, an alternative option that's also paved and much less heavily trafficked runs from the little alpine town of Posof via Akhaltsikhe (visit Sapara and the Vardzia cave churches near here) and Borjomi (a famous little spa town). Either route passes close to Gori, Stalin's home town where a Stalin museum and statue still stand.

Tbilisi

Tbilisi itself is one of the most appealing cities in Eastern Europe and well worth a few days' exploration. There are several popular (but totally unmarked) down-market homestays around Marjanishvili metro, one of which, Green Stairs (🖳 vazha@lycos.com, 53 Tsinamdzghvrishvili, ☎ 941552, mob 893-331236), has a place to store bicycles safely. Dodo's Homestay (🖳 dodogeorgia@gmail.com, 18 Marjanishvili; ☎ 954213) has more space but less privacy.

Tbilisi to Azerbaijan

Crossing from Georgia to Azerbaijan is straightforward though you'll need an Azerbaijani visa in advance (this will take about five days in Tbilisi). There are two main route options. The main road is from Tbilisi to Ganja via Red Bridge (Krasny Most) but the scenery is somewhat desolate and you'll end up in Azerbaijan's dreary central steppe.

Far nicer is to start off towards Georgia's wine-paradise region (Kaheti). The map shows two main ways to do this. The quietest starts out across a mountain pass via Gombori to Telavi. Beware, however, as that road has some pretty rough pot-holed and un-surfaced stretches (repairs are due for 2009-2011). The main Kaheti road is busier but has the advantage of passing close to Sighnaghi, a charming little hill town with fortress walls, pretty old houses, a tourist office, ATMs and a rash of new accommodation options and homestays. David Zandarashvili's (11 Georgitsminda, ☎ 31029, mob 899-750 510) is the most popular backpacker homestay owing to David's good English and good-humoured 'real' family.

Whether you go via Telavi or Signaghi, you'll cross into Azerbaijan at Lagodeghi where there's now a decent little guesthouse at the far end of town. The low-key border crossing is a few kilometres further and from there the road via Balakan and Sheki is beautiful and very varied for most of the way to Baku.

Azerbaijan

As you cross Azerbaijan the landscapes evolve from thick deciduous forests via rolling grasslands to deserts outside the cosmopolitan capital Baku. Curving round a bay on the Caspian Sea, Baku has many splendid century-old buildings and a UNESCO-listed walled old city. With a plethora of expat bars and Anglo-Irish pubs for all those oil executives, Baku makes a great place to recharge the batteries (if you can afford £4 for a cappuccino!) but Azerbaijan isn't as well set up for travellers as Georgia, and the amazing oil boom of 2006-2008 has sent Baku prices into orbit.

You're likely to find fellow cyclists discussing the Caspian Ferry conundrum (see p114) if you stay at Baku's small but brilliantly central 1000 Camels Hostel (mob ☎ 055-677 8175). However, many cyclists prefer to stay at Baku's much less central Hotel Velotrek (☎ 012-4315187, AZN15 per person) near metro 20th Jan. While it's rather impersonal and you might get kicked out should a visiting sports team need your room, the hotel is attached to Baku Cycling Club which can offer useful help with bicycle maintenance.

Crossing Azerbaijan

The obvious cross-country route between Balakan and Baku is magnificently varied and well asphalted yet graciously quiet west of Qabala. You'll follow the base of Azerbaijan's stunning high Caucasus foothills on oak-lined avenues and there are appealing side trips, most notably to Sheki where there's a delightful old town, a renovated khan's palace and a sensibly-priced hotel in a superbly atmospheric old caravanserai.

Heading east

With the Azerbaijan-Russia border closed, you have two main options from Baku. The best choice is to cycle south into Iran along an attractive but often busy and very rainy route through Iran's lush, rice-growing Caspian provinces. Visas for Iran are hard to arrange in Baku so it's better to come prepared. (See 🖳 www.tandemtoturkestan.com for Cass Gilbert's report of his ride on this route.)

The alternative is taking one of the 'floating vomitorium' ferries across the Caspian. A good proportion of travellers get stranded in Baku for days or even weeks waiting for one of the 11 spaces on this highly irregular train-ferry to Turkmenistan. Even once on board the ferry can be delayed for days waiting for a berth at Turkmenbashi (so take loads of food and water aboard) such that your Turkmen visa could expire before you get off the ferry. There's an even less frequent ferry to Aktau in Kazakhstan, sailing just a few times a month.

Whether from menacing Aktau or surreal Turkmenbashi, cycling onwards across Central Asia will not be too visually exciting: there's endless dull steppe (treeless plains) or the raging Karakum Desert to cross. However, both cities are railheads so you could zip across to more appealing parts of Central Asia fairly conveniently if you are not fixated on a punishing long-distance slog. The added complication is the annoying visa details: Kazakhstan visas tend to have fixed starting dates. Given the uncertainty of the ferry schedules you are quite likely to end up wasting a fair amount of your valuable visa validity waiting around and westbound you could end up overstaying (which would be very unpleasant indeed). There's a similar problem for Turkmenistan compounded by the fact that Turkmen transit visas are already very short for anyone planning to cycle. Neither is easily available in Baku. However, things look set to improve in Turkmenistan as the new regime gains in confidence and starts opening up to tourism.

Nakhchivan

A little-tested trans-Caucasus alternative is to swing past Agri Dag (Mount Ararat) in eastern Turkey, cross into Nakhchivan and continue into Iran from Culfa/Jolfa.

Magnificently stark Nakhchivan is a historically fascinating enclave of Azerbaijan (entirely disconnected from the rest of that country by Armenia and remember that Armenian-Azeri borders are completely closed). So you'll need an Azerbaijan visa, available in Istanbul but not on the border. But beware: while corruption at the notorious Sadarak (Nakhchivan-Turkey) border has reduced recently, travellers are still viewed with considerable suspicion by Nakhchivan's KGB, especially around Culfa.

Armenia

If for some reason you can't get an Azerbaijani visa, it's possible to transit from Tbilisi to Iran via Armenia. Armenian visas are issued on the land borders (though if you're heading to Iran you'll need to have prepared the Iran visa way ahead as usual). The route crosses some high mountain roads. See 🖥 www.cilicia.com for oodles of travel advice about Armenia.

Iran

If Syria is slightly eccentric, Iran is stranger still, at least in towns and cities where the government's influence is all the stronger. Iran would be a unique country even if it weren't for the Islamic Revolution, but since 1979 it has dropped out of the orbit the rest of the planet is on and has become all the more worth seeing for that uniqueness.

Notoriously difficult for Americans and not much easier for Brits to get a visa, you need to see a visa agent if you are from either of these countries – try 🖳 www.magic-carpet-travel.com in the UK, you'll pay about double an already-pricey visa fee but can collect your visa at the Iranian embassy of your choice, which is essential if you're already on the road. Extending a visa when you're in Iran is easily done at police stations in large towns. Women should not be put off by Iran's image either – it's more liberal for women than other Muslim nations, and the full-monty chador isn't necessary, just long (and not tight) sleeves and legs down to the feet and a headscarf. Most Iranian women wear a garment that looks like a mid-length fitted black raincoat and headscarf and the young ones are always trying to push the boundaries. People in the cities are well-educated compared to other Muslim nations and foreign women are treated respectfully.

Tehran has some of the worst traffic anywhere – say your prayers, cycle in but then give the bike a rest and take buses or the excellent but limited subway system, which runs a good way up north (followed by a bus) to the 'stan embassies. Once your Central Asian visa applications are in, it's either chill out higher up the mountainside out of the smog, or take a bus or train to Esfehan – or ride it. Closer to Esfehan lie ancient villages and quiet countryside away from the freeways. North-west Iran, with a majority Azeri population, is great for cooling off and finding small back roads in the mountains. It's possibly even more friendly than the rest of the country, but you will be welcome everywhere, though watch out if you go through the troubled Balochi tribal region en route to Pakistan or the evangelical holy city of Mashhad in the

PART 2 – ROUTE OUTLINES

LOCAL DANGERS AND ANNOYANCES

Iran has precious few of these, thankfully, though the police can be a nuisance. It seems their bureaucracy often requires that they keep tabs on foreigners passing through and we were asked several times for our passports, which they wanted to photocopy and fax to Tehran. This resulted in a pretty heated argument at one point as we realised the limits of their authority – the police aren't supposed to take your passport away. This may be because of a scam in Tehran where fake policemen steal tourists' passports. We also heard of a couple of pickpocketings and muggings in Tehran, and the formal advice to tourists from the Tehran police is to leave your passport at the hotel to guard against its loss. Normally it's a bad idea but in Tehran, I was persuaded. If a policeman asks you for your passport in Tehran, just show them the receipt or business card for the hotel. Carrying copies of your passport to give the police should defuse this situation.

DRESS CODE ALERT!

It's not just women, it's men too; men in shorts. Iranians don't expect their national football team to compete wearing long trousers, so when you're riding in the country and not stopping (and it's hot), baggy shorts are fine, ¾ length is better. The moment you stop in a village or town and want to speak to people, you should zip on – this is where zip-offs are ideal for a speedy cover-up. In the country people are no more religious than in the cities, but they are more conservative and your efforts will show respect. You never see tight clothing in Iran either, and dressing to local sensibilities will ensure you get the full friendly treatment for which Iran is famous among travellers.

---

north-east. The Caspian Sea route is direct and has a shoulder to ride on, but you'll need earplugs for the traffic. It is a temperate zone, however, quite unlike the rest of Iran, with forested mountains and rice-growing. There's little free land and you'll have to ask around for camping or hosting.

Central Asia

Friedel Rother

For sheer diversity and adventure, it's hard to beat Central Asia's mix of history and terrain. This mysterious land, wedged between the Caspian Sea and China, has been home over the centuries to Turkic tribes, Mongols and Russian imperialists. Today's traveller is greeted by everything from ancient Silk Road cities to fine Islamic architecture. Then there's the chance to sip tea with nomads as you cross mountains so high they'll take your breath away – literally. Passes over 3000m are routine. Add in scorching deserts, fertile valleys, spectacular lakes, glacial views and rugged wilderness and you'll start to get a hint of what attracts touring cyclists to this region.

© Friedel Rother

Getting visas for the ex-Soviet states of Turkmenistan, Uzbekistan, Kazakhstan, Kyrgyzstan and Tajikistan entails mounds of paperwork, patience and money. Once through the door, a hard day of pedalling won't always finish with a hot shower. Crumbling infrastructure is a lingering legacy from the breakup of the Soviet Union. Facilities are often rudimentary and power cuts can be frequent. Take solace instead in the hearty food dished up by roadside cafés. Retreat after supper to the local *banya* (public bathhouse) where a few pennies buy the right to dump buckets of hot water over your head, sit in the sauna and even whip yourself with a few birch sticks, should you feel the need.

Of the five 'stans, Kyrgyzstan is the easiest to visit and best overall for cycling. It's light on red tape and corruption and heavy on scenery with plenty of remote tracks for the truly adventurous. A network of homestays offers a unique chance to see traditional family life and be spoiled with spreads of jam, cream and freshly baked bread. If you have more time, a circuit taking in the Silk Road cities of Bukhara and Samarkand and Tajikistan's Pamir Highway is the way to go. Turkmenistan is little more than a desert dash because of the restrictive visa system but, if you can manage it, a trip to Merv (an archaeological wonder) or the bizarre capital Ashgabat isn't soon forgotten. Vast Kazakhstan is largely overlooked but is not without its merits. Check out the Tien Shan mountains and Charyn Canyon, easy to take in if you are headed east to China.

Food and drink

Central Asians like their meat – or rather, their fat. Main staples include *shash-lyk*, skewers of kebab chequered with lumps of grisly fat. *Plov* is pilaf, a but-tery rice dish accented with chopped carrot, sultanas and chunks of mutton, soaked in the fat of the sheep's tail. *Laghman* is another popular dish: fresh thick noodles in a meat and vegetable soup, dunked with frisbee-shaped bread and washed down with green tea. *Manty* are steamed dumplings stuffed with meat, a lighter alternative to heavy meals. You can always request a salad of tomatoes or cucumbers or a side of *grechka* – buckwheat – to accompany the main course. *Bishparmak* (literally 'five fingers') – a delicacy of horse meat served over large noodles – may greet you in Kazakh family homes. It's a favourite at banquets. The boiled head of a sheep is also considered delicious eating. Vegetarians could struggle: the concept isn't well understood by most locals. Your best chance of finding a meat-free meal is in the few hotels designed for Westerners but don't be surprised to see them simply pulling the mutton out of the soup. Stock up when you're in large towns as the choice in smaller towns is limited unless there's a market. You can usually count on finding the basics like flatbread, pasta, rice, eggs and some vegetables but rarely fruit or nuts. In tiny villages, the store may be in someone's home so ask around for the *magazin*.

Ice-cream is available on every street corner and bowling-ball sized water-melons make great summer thirst quenchers. *Gazli su* is carbonated local tap water, sweetened with shots of syrup to mask the rust. *Kymys* is a beverage with a kick (in the stomach, and often out the other end) – fermented mare's milk that's pungent, slightly alcoholic and considered a boost for strength and virility. It's sold by the road by farmers and nomads.

Last but not least, thanks to the Russians, vodka is every Central Asian's favourite tipple. Combining Islamic hospitality and a Russian fondness for alcohol can have lethal results for inexperienced bikers who have been 'on the wagon' in Iran before arriving in the 'stans. Forced invitations are plentiful and often extended with a hand gesture that, to the uninitiated, looks like someone threatening decapitation. Don't be alarmed. To the locals, it's simply an invitation to come drink. A lot.

Weather

Late spring to early autumn is the ideal time to visit Central Asia. Winter's harshness begins to fade in March. By April, temperatures are pleasantly

TRIP REPORT
THAILAND TO TURKEY

Name	Even 'Tomato Sister' Verrelst & Björn 'Tomsom' Josk
Year of birth	1980 / 1974
Occupation	Primary School teacher / social worker
Nationality	Both Belgian
Other bike travels	Guatemala to Costa-Rica, France, Helsinki to Antwerp
This trip	Thailand, Cambodia, Vietnam, Laos, Yunnan, Burma, Sikkim, Nepal, Ladakh, Kashmir, Pakistan, Iran, Turkey
Trip duration	498 beautiful days
Number in group	Just the two lovebirds
Total distance	15,367km
Cost of trip	€7500 each, everything included
Longest day	151km from Dalat to Na Thrang, Vietnam
Best day	Every cycling day in Indian Himalaya
Worst day	Off-road trip in Bokor NP, Cambodia (lack of water)
Favourite ride	65 km in Shimsal-Valley, Northern-Pakistan
Biggest headache	Obtaining Iranian visa
Biggest mistake	Not responding to stone-throwing kids, now we chase them down
Pleasant surprise	Sharing-mood all over the world but especially in Pakistan
Any illness	Home-sick, 5 seconds every 3 months
Bike model	Disposable Trek 3900, MTB, €200 (photo p26; no fun anymore? = we sell it)
New/used	New from Probike near Lumbini Park, Bangkok
Modifications	€0.70 truck horn (see p61), bought in Lahore, Pakistan (best idea ever)
Wish you'd fitted	More flowers like on the Pakistani trucks
Tyres used	Knobbly ones that came on the bike
Punctures	Even: 18, Björn: 15, they're welcome breaks
Baggage Setup	Added a Chinese front rack, €10, lasted whole trip
Bike problems	Front suspension nearly finished
Accidents	Björn hit a Vietnamese guy who was just standing next to the road while watching the roadmap
Same bike again	Björn recently bought a recumbent, we'll see.
Recommendations	Steripen: waterpurifier, it saved us tons of plastic bottles along the way. Take a tent – it gives you the opportunity to stop everywhere
Road philosophy	Cycle-touring can be hard, travelling can be demanding, but in the end, everything works out fine.

warm across the desert and dry grasslands of Turkmenistan and Kazakhstan. In Uzbekistan, farmers will be busy tending their fields and it's nice enough to sit outside as you drink a cup of tea. Trips into the mountains of Kyrgyzstan and Tajikistan are best put off at least until June. Any earlier and you risk arriving at a pass that's still covered in snow.

Kazakhstan's Tien Shan mountain range
© Friedel Rother

As summer progresses, the lowlands swelter in temperatures that frequently exceed 40°C. Bazaars are overloaded with seasonal fruit but this is not the time to be crossing the isolated steppe, where shade and water are at a premium. Instead, follow the nomads to the Jailoos, or high summer pastures, where the months of July and August are marked by an endless carpet of green grass and flowers.

Cooler temperatures return in September. Nights become noticeably chilly and the first snow can appear in October. Autumn cycling remains comfortable in the valleys and you can feast on the recent harvest. By November it's time to head home before the severe cold sets in.

Visas

The hardest part of cycling in Central Asia is arguably getting in the door. The minefield of bureaucracy has, if anything, become worse since the break-up of the Soviet Union. Regulations seem to change at the drop of a hat. Embassies frequently move without notice, open late or not at all. 'Big party last night. Too much vodka. Not open,' one diplomat mumbled to us over a crackly intercom. Double check addresses and requirements before setting out.

Get visas in advance if you have time – allow a couple of months for it, saving time traipsing around embassies when you're there. Only Kyrgyzstan grants visas on arrival, and only at Bishkek airport, which is usually the cheapest flight in from Europe. Once you're in the region, ask other travellers for the latest advice. What takes 24 hours in one city could require a week of shoving through a queue in another. In any case, bring immaculate US$ bills, issued after 1996. The smallest mark can mean a second trip to the bank.

Whether at home or on the road, have a clear idea of when you hope to reach each destination. All visas have a fixed validity. Enter late and you lose the days. Extensions are difficult or impossible to obtain except in easy-going Kyrgyzstan. Consider overlapping visas by a few days. This adds the possibility to move on early. Double-entry permits can be handy, especially for Uzbekistan – a transport hub with enclaves and jigsaw borders.

You'll also want a fat wallet – budget at least $100 per country – and the help of a specialist travel agent to do some of the work like issuing letters of invitation (🖳 www.stantours.com is recommended). This unremarkable piece of paper can be faxed ahead to embassies en route, ready for your arrival, for a charge of around $30-40. It's money well spent, though visas always depend on where you are from and where you apply. A good agent can also secure permits to ride remote roads along the Chinese border in Kazakhstan and Kyrgyzstan. The GBAO permit for Tajikistan's Pamir Highway (see p124) is easily obtained along with your visa.

TURKMENISTAN

Turkmenistan is a main gateway to Central Asia for overland travellers going east, lying between the Caspian Sea and Afghanistan. The government is an authoritarian ex-communist regime that excels at erecting gold statues of the president and impressive marble buildings but seems less attentive to keeping towns and roads in good repair.

A cyclist's view of the country is a fleeting one. Five-day transit permits are standard, unless you hire a costly guide. This makes the 550km dash between Iran and Uzbekistan just possible if you get through customs reasonably quickly (allow 2 hours), pedal hard and avoid severe sandstorms crossing the Karakum desert. Arriving from Azerbaijan, the ferry has to arrive on time for you to stand any chance of crossing the country, and you'd still need to take the train for most of the way.

The barren landscape and weary infrastructure can be numbing but smiling Turkmen people more than compensate. Passing tourists are a rarity, greeted with gifts of juicy watermelon, bread or even money. Have a few trinkets handy to reciprocate. In the evening, roadside cafés make an ideal stop. Tuck into a bowl of mutton soup. Wash it down with tea and then ask if there's a place to sleep. Often it's free but the cafés can be filled with boisterous truckers. You may prefer to camp. When the distance seems overwhelming, hitch a lift from one of the many passing trucks, hire a taxi or take the painfully slow train between cities. Just don't overstay your visa. That would cause untold misery at the border.

The ancient city of Merv, once destroyed by the son of Genghis Khan, is an excellent justification to skip at least some of the cycling. A visit to the capital Ashgabat (literally 'city of love'), with its gleaming marble buildings, is also not to be missed if you get the chance, although many transit visas won't allow you to go there. The second-city of Mary, flanked by wide boulevards, offers a similar glimpse of the opulence favoured by the current rulers.

UZBEKISTAN

No tour of Central Asia is complete without including Uzbekistan. Just the names Samarkand, Bukhara and Khiva – a trio of beautifully restored Silk Road cities – evoke romance. Their stunning tiled mosques never fail to impress and the markets are just the place to haggle over a souvenir Uzbek skullcap or stuff your panniers full of dried fruits and nuts for the travels ahead.

The capital Tashkent is less of a jaw-dropper in terms of sights but its leafy streets and parks are pleasant enough spots to linger while you await onward visas. Cycling around the city is an easy way to reach spread-out embassies, with the added advantage of minimising harmless but time-consuming ID checks. Policemen focus in on tourists using public transport or walking. Their green uniforms are such a regular sight that locals joke they are planted on street corners in place of trees. Tashkent is also Central Asia's main transport hub, with the best choice of regional and long-haul flights.

Monotonous scenery dominates between the towns. Aside from the mountains that separate Tashkent from the silk-weaving factories of the Fergana

Valley, flat agricultural fields are the norm. They are fertile only because of the canals that channel water from the dying Aral Sea to farmers trying to grow cotton and vegetables on the dry plains.

Teahouses along the road are a bright spot. Pull out your wads of Uzbek Soms (the highest note is worth less than $1), get stuck into hot and savoury pastries, chat with the locals and perhaps even spend the night. Beware, however, the Soviet-era requirement that tourists be registered in hotels and carry papers issued by these hotels to prove where they've slept. Wild camping or accepting local hospitality means you'll have a gap in your record and could theoretically face a hefty fine for your unorthodox resting places. In practice, many cyclists have a few holes in their hotel registration and leave the country without issue. Still, any night spent outside formal accommodation does pose a minor risk. AROSTR travel agency (🖳 www.arostr.uz, ☎ +998 90 186 86 48) in Tashkent is a reliable source of information on registration.

More bureaucratic hassle can arise if you take more money out of Uzbekistan than you declare on the way in. Customs officials have the right to confiscate the difference unless you can produce receipts proving you withdrew cash from your own accounts as opposed to selling things in the country.

KAZAKHSTAN

It's the world's ninth largest country by area, with vast oil and natural gas wealth, but Kazakhstan is very much overlooked when it comes to tourism. At first glance this is understandable. Many cyclists find the relatively high prices off-putting. Camping is essential for those on slim budgets. As for dream cycling, the vast, arid and treeless plains of the steppe can't compare to the alpine lakes of Kyrgyzstan. Rusting ships on the dry bed of the Aral Sea form a perverse tourist attraction but there's a lot of riding through nothingness to reach them.

Despite this, there are reasons to add Kazakhstan to your itinerary. Visas are cheap and usually easy to obtain. With your passport in order, you can take the shortest route between Tashkent and the Kyrgyz capital Bishkek via Kazakh territory. It's a welcome escape from the regis-

Tien Shan village © Friedel Rother

tration hassles of Uzbekistan, with almost constant mountain views en route.

Kazakhstan is also the most modern of the 'stans, which means getting a hot shower is easier here than most places. The roads are in better shape and the major city Almaty is just about the only place in the whole region where you can reliably track down good quality bike parts. This saves getting things sent from home and incurring costly import fees.

Off-road cyclists are well catered for in Kazakhstan's far east and south. The Tien Shan mountains that border China are rarely visited (special permits are sometimes required). In this area we were regularly hauled inside by locals, eager to feed wayward cyclists a cup of tea or a second breakfast.

PART 2 – ROUTE OUTLINES

Close to the Kyrgyz border, Charyn Canyon is a popular weekend getaway for Kazakhs and the surrounding hills are full of tracks that alternate between high plateaus and green valleys. Out here, far from all but the occasional shepherd, you're more likely to spot eagles soaring above or a herd of horses thundering across the fields than another tourist. Good maps are essential for navigating such remote corners. Firma Geo in Almaty (Satpaev Akademik 30 «В», near Manasa Street, ☎ 3272 453435) has plenty of high-detail Soviet survey maps.

Only super-keen cyclists cross Kazakhstan in its entirety, linking the Chinese border with Russia in the west or the port of Aktau, where an erratic ferry sails across the Caspian Sea down to Azerbaijan. It's a long and lonely slog. Unless you have weeks to spare and relish isolation, use buses and trains to link the highlights together.

KYRGYZSTAN

Alpine peaks, high mountain lakes and a large and friendly nomad population are the highlights of Kyrgyzstan. Winding roads lead to passes that regularly top 3000m. The lush flower-filled pastures of summer and the shores of alpine lakes make ideal landing spots for your tent. Nomads grazing their flocks often invite the passing cyclist to stop and rest. You may even be invited to spend a night in the yurt, their traditional round shelter. Initial feelings of good fortune may fade as you're served up bowls of *kymys* (pronounced 'koomiss') – mare's milk made sharp and fizzy through fermentation – but it's the thought that counts!

Added to this natural treasure trove is a growing tourism industry and a government that's done a lot to cut red tape. Visas are delivered quickly, without fuss, and even on arrival at the airport (for most nationalities, only at Bishkek). It's the perfect antidote to the endless forms and registration frustrations that complicate travel elsewhere in Central Asia. Most people will visit the capital Bishkek for a few days, more out of necessity than anything, but at least see the State Museum and get a good square meal for peanuts in the basement café. Onward visas can be sourced here from the various embassies and you can find 1:200,000-scale sheet maps at the Kyrgyz Cartographic Institute (Kiev St 107, 3rd floor, room 4). There are a few bike shops, but don't count on a wide range of parts. Take care on the crumbling and poorly-lit streets, particularly hazardous if you're cycling after dark. As with any city or town in the region, watch out for drunks, on the streets and in cars.

Where to go

The best riding is undoubtedly in the countryside and to take full advantage you should be entirely self-supporting. There are few paved roads, but not much traffic. Some roads are mountain-biking heaven, though at times on washboarded roads in headwinds, it can be a grind.

Lake Song-Kol is one of the prime destinations to hit. Set in the mountains between Naryn and Bishkek, it's a favourite place for nomadic families to spend the summer. The lake is attracting increasing numbers of tourists but the rough piste that leads around the shore should allow you to find a quiet spot, even in high season. Take plenty of food and fuel and spend a few days watching traditional life unfold. A chat with the locals will likely result in an invitation to stay in a yurt, but you might prefer camping near one. Alternatively, there's a CBT yurt camp which serves good food and has toilets (nomads don't appear to do toilets and there are no trees to hide behind...).

Four unpaved roads lead to the shores of Song-Kol. The most popular leaves the Kochkor-Naryn road at Sari Bulak and crosses over a pass at 3600m. It may not be clear of snow until mid-June. Ask at the CBT office in Kochkor or Naryn. Here you can also pick up

Camping with nomads by Song-Kul Lake at 3000m

good Russian maps of the area – essential if you plan to use the less travelled routes, which may be little more than a faint outline of a track in the grass.

Lake Issyk-Kol is a less strenuous alternative to Song-Kol. It's the world's second largest alpine lake (Titicaca, Bolivia is the largest) and a popular holiday spot for Kyrgyz and Kazakh families. At 3000m, the water is surprisingly warm. A paved road circles the lake, with more hotels and amenities on the north side but quieter cycling to the south. Sandy beaches make ideal rest stops and for a taste of the mountains, divert to Svetov Dolina, just outside Karakol. It's a gentle uphill ride to this pasture, which fills with yurts and shepherds from May onwards. The name means 'Valley of Flowers' and in summer the grass is covered in blooms.

Aside from specific destinations, a night spent in a homestay is another experience not to be missed and is easily arranged through organisations like CBT (🖳 www.cbtkyrgyzstan.kg) and Shepherd's Life. Around €10 per person will secure you a comfortable bed in a family home, where you can clean up in a traditional banya and be stuffed to the gills with homemade jam, potfuls of tea and hearty meals. With a little Russian or Kyrgyz, you can ask around in villages for a homestay for considerably less, but in Kyrgyzstan, whenever you are offered a place to stay, it's expected that you'll pay something.

For full-on adventure, try some truly remote cycling near the Chinese and Tajik borders. This is where guided bike groups go, so you might be able to get information or transport at hotels like Asia Mountains Hotel in Bishkek. One possibility is the road that leads east and north from tourism-magnet Karakol, to Engilchek and Kara Say before descending back to Tamga beside Lake Issyk-Kol. Special permits may be needed for anything near the borders.

TAJIKISTAN

The smallest and poorest of the 'stans, Tajikistan has one huge draw card: The Pamir Highway, one of the world's greatest mountain roads. Flying directly into the capital Dushanbe entails changing planes somewhere (there are few direct flights to destinations outside Central Asia) or coming overland from Kyrgyzstan or Uzbekistan. The border with Afghanistan attracts travellers but there is inevitably heightened security and risks in travelling through this region. An open border with China has been rumoured for years but it's still not an option for tourists.

PART 2 – ROUTE OUTLINES

The Pamir Highway – Dushanbe, Tajikistan to Osh, Kyrgyzstan

Tim Barnes 🖳 www.adventure-cycling-guide.co.uk

Built in the 1930s to supply the furthest outposts of the Soviet empire, the 1300km Pamir Highway is a high-altitude adventure in one of the most remote and mountainous corners of Central Asia. With several climbs to over 4000m, on disintegrating roads and washboard tracks, it is a strenuous but hugely enjoyable undertaking. The spectacular mountain scenery is more than matched by the amazing hospitality of the Tajik people.

Access
The route starts in Dushanbe, the sleepy capital of Tajikistan. It's possible to fly from here to the start of the Pamir Highway at Khorog, but that would miss 500km of great cycling. A GBAO permit is required, which can be obtained at the same time as your Tajik visa.

The ride
The first 200km to Tavildera isn't easy. The road is in an appalling condition and there are some stiff climbs. From Tavildera it's a long ascent through pretty

AFGHANISTAN

At the time of writing, only the north of Afghanistan is safe, but for many cyclists trapped by China's visa clampdown in the summer of 2008 it was the only way to continue east – if you could pick up a Pakistan visa. Afghanistan's consulate at Khorog on the western part of the Pamir Highway in Tajikistan issues visas for $30 the same morning for a 1 month stay with 3 months validity. It is said that obtaining a visa is difficult at the embassy in Dushanbe but easier at the consulate in Mashhad (Iran).

I crossed the border coming from Khorog -Kuliab-Pyang road (very bad road for last 30km, but normal in Tajikistan). No questions, no hassle. Taybad in Iran is another possible entry point, or Termez in Uzbekistan. The Afghan side was slower but friendly. I was invited for lunch by the officials, and ended up sleeping at their house: very generous and friendly people. Also unexpected on my first night in the Islamic Republic of Afghanistan: vodka and marijuana!

To Kunduz is 60km through desert with nothing but sand and ISAF convoys patrolling. It is said to be very safe. I had lunch in the outskirts which later I was strongly advised not to do (four people had been killed two days before), but it seemed safe and most people were very kind to me. A few people looked at me with dagger-glances but there is a small percentage of Afghans who do not like foreigners at all. I experienced the same eight years ago, in Kohistan (Pakistan KKH), and they just look at you fiercely but will do nothing against you.

Every hotel asked for $20 so I had to look for another kind of accommodation, but people never invited me in and I guess they are afraid of hosting a foreigner. Eventually I got permission for free camping in an expensive hotel but on the way, surprisingly, an English teacher invited me and I spent two nights with him. It was very interesting because I could speak a lot with him and the students.

On the road to Salang tunnel and later Kabul, I slept in police stations or restaurants; they were friendly people. Some checkpoints were worried about what I carried in my bags, but I was always treated with great respect and usually they checked one bag. Most times they asked 'why are you cycling here? Are you not afraid?' and so on. It is strongly advised not to camp (landmine or bandit risk) or cycle at night. Daytime looks like normal life.

Salang tunnel is a hard climb (from 1100m to 3400m in 40km). The tunnel itself is a trap of 3-4 km with no light or ventilation; soldiers will stop a truck for the bike and the cyclist. Still, it is not a nice experience. Roads are always paved but very narrow and drivers do not mind cyclists but are not used to them.

alpine scenery to the top of the 3252m Saghirdasht Pass. The long climb to the pass is rewarded by one of the most precipitous and spectacular descents in Central Asia. There is a complete absence of crash barriers as the road plunges down a huge, steep-sided gorge to the small town of Kalaikhum.

At Kalaikhum the road enters the deep rocky valley of the Pyanj River. There is never a dull moment in this valley – one minute the road is clinging to a cliff edge over the river, the next it's passing through pretty villages and apricot orchards. Afghanistan is just across the river and most of the heroin that ends up in Western Europe is smuggled across this border. Consequently, security is tight with frequent checkpoints and regular army patrols. If these aren't entertaining enough, the road also passes through a number of mine-fields left over from the civil war in the 1990s.

Two hundred kilometres up the valley the road reaches Khorog, capital of the Gorno Badakhshan region. This isolated town offers a welcome return to semi-civilisation. There are comfortable guesthouses, internet cafés and even a couple of restaurants. It's important to stock up at the town's bazaar as there is a distinct lack of shops on the next stretch.

The Pamir Highway proper starts at Khorog, climbing the pretty Gunt Valley to the summit of the 4,217m Koi-Tezek Pass, gateway to the Pamir

Afghan food is much better than Tajikistan's, but sometimes only pilau (rice, carrots, raisins, and meat: $1.50); bread is always fresh and excellent. Water is safe, mostly from water pumps, and pastries are delicious.

From 2000m altitude, it was quite cold at the end of October, and forget about cycling after November. People are generally surprised but friendly with no English spoken except for a few youngsters in towns. Often they did not accept my money for food or meals. They always approached me asking 'kuja meri?' (Where are you going?), but sometimes they asked how they can help me.

Kabul is not safe but as I look like a poor Afghan, I have felt safe walking everywhere. In my opinion, for a humble tourist a bad experience (like being kidnapped or killed) would only happen in the case of very bad luck. At the city checkpoint they tried to scare me and checked all my luggage, but a week before, a British woman was shot from a motorbike. I have been walking even after sunset, and my Belgian friends often go running with no problems, but things happen and kidnapping is frequent, I was told, mostly in the morning.

Indian visas are issued here in only 3 days ($65, for 6 months starting the date they issue). Pakistan visas are almost impossible to get (I was told 'perhaps you will be refused');

I got only 15 days and it is not valid to go by road because the Khyber Pass is forbidden and in a war situation right now. Of course, the southern crossing points are out of the question. The staff at my embassy (Spanish) gave looks of shock and panic when I told them I was cycling here and were no help in getting a Pakistan visa; a letter of introduction from one's own embassy is asked for by Pakistan – I lied and said we had no representation in Kabul. Friends got me onto a Red Cross flight to Peshawar, and my bike came by land with a refugee. Pakistan was not allowing any foreigner into the so-called Tribal Areas on their side of the Khyber Pass.

Adam Chalupski and **Salva Rodriguez**

Stowing a bike to take through Salang tunnel. © Adam Chalupski

Much of the Pamir Highway is paved.
© Tim Barnes

plateau. Alternatively, it is possible to continue up the Pyanj valley into the fabled Wakhan corridor. This is a beautiful, remote valley with spectacular views of giant 7,000m peaks in the Hindu Kush. From Wakhan it's possible to return to the Pamir Highway via a tough climb over the 4344m Khargush Pass.

Back on the Highway, the ride across the Pamir plateau is a hugely enjoyable experience. It is a wonderfully remote landscape of high peaks and turquoise salt lakes. There is very little habitation and virtually no traffic. In the middle of this empty quarter is the tiny back-of-beyond settlement of Alichur with one very small, very well-hidden shop. From here it is another 120km to the small town of Murgab that offers a few comfortable homestays and the chance to re-supply in the small bazaar.

After leaving Murgab the road skirts the Chinese border before climbing to the summit of the Ak-Baital Pass, at 4655m the highest point of the route. A rough descent from the pass drops down to a remote valley and miles of washboard track leading to lake Kara-Kul. With a backdrop of high snowy mountains and the ever-changing colours of the sky and water, this eerie lake is one of the most hauntingly beautiful sights of the trip. In contrast, the tiny village that clings to the lake shore looks as if it has been blasted by a small nuclear weapon.

From Kara-Kul the road climbs up to the Kyrgyz border at the summit of the 4,336m Kyzl Art Pass. The most bone-shattering descent so far leads down to the wide grasslands of the Kyrgyz Alay valley. In summer, the prairie-like valley is studded with the grey-white yurts of very hospitable Kyrgyz shepherds. On the far side of the valley is the village of Sary-Tash and the first cafés and shops since Murgab.

A right turn at Sary-Tash leads over the Irkeshtam crossing into China and the Silk Road city of Kashgar. Straight on, the road to Osh climbs over the double-headed Taldyk Pass (3615m) and descends into the beautiful Gulcho valley. After the wilds of the Pamir Plateau the valley seems wonderfully civilised. There are trees and grass, houses and cars and even the odd café. The final climb up the 2400m Chyrchyk Pass is rewarded by a 50km racing descent to the finishing post in the bustling city of Osh.

NORTHERN PAKISTAN AND THE KARAKORAM HIGHWAY

Although tourism in northern Pakistan has collapsed since 9/11, it's still a great area for trekking and bike touring and though less colourful than Nepal, is similarly hospitable. The infrastructure is there for guided climbing and uncrowded treks, with plenty of cheap accommodation if you don't want to camp – though camping in the garden of a guesthouse is sometimes a great and indeed preferable alternative if the rooms look dodgy. Northern Pakistan is quiet, calm and peaceful everywhere. The North-West Frontier Province gets a bad write-up for the troubles concentrated in lawless Waziristan far to the west on the Afghan border, but those troubles stay put in valleys the armed

PAKISTAN VISAS

Most easily obtained at home, you have six months from issue to enter Pakistan but this may still not be long enough. It becomes harder to get a Pakistan visa the closer you get if coming from the west, very hard from Turkey onwards. It's said to be difficult from the Indian side, but easier from the Pakistan embassy in Kathmandu. If entering on the bus over the Khunjerab pass on the KKH you can get a 15-day transit visa at Sost, giving you just enough time to ride to Islamabad to get an extension.

forces will not enter, and the rest of the area, while religiously conservative in Shia and Sunni areas, welcomes visitors. It's a different region to the rest of Pakistan, far less crowded and mostly cooler than the lowlands.

Before you arrive in Pakistan, you will almost certainly have the impression that it's collapsing but it doesn't seem that way when you're there. Trains still run, post offices are open and people get by. There are occasional terrorist bombs in cities or on trains, but this is true of India also and both are very large countries. The north is very peaceful and not to be confused with the tribal areas in Waziristan on the Afghan border which the Pakistani government does not attempt to administer. You won't run into these areas by accident, the roads are well-guarded by the Pakistani police and army.

Karakoram Highway (KKH)

One of the highlights of any Asia trip or indeed the wide world of adventure touring, the Karakoram Highway, or KKH, was practically made for cyclists, not that they'll admit it. It's 1300km of mostly sealed roads between Kashgar in China and Islamabad in Pakistan with fairly gentle gradients in valleys lined with some of the highest peaks in the world, giving dramatic views at every turn of peaks sometimes 5000m or more above you. Planned as a trade route linking China to Pakistan, traffic levels are not bad, especially up north and there are plenty of guesthouses along the way. There is an excellent online map at 💻 www.johnthemap.co.uk.

KKH – what to expect

Allow a month for a ride along the KKH, giving time for rest stops, side trips (Skardu, see box p128, and Chitral, see box p129) or perhaps a trek. Flying in to Islamabad you have the option of going native and staying in Rawalpindi or meeting Pakistani culture halfway by staying in Islamabad, a leafy-green and relatively quiet city. You won't need to stock up on much food, just some flavourings to liven up the basics found en route. A choice of either the official hot and dusty KKH route or a hilly but more scenic route beckons, but two days later in Abbottabad, these routes reunite. The road climbs, as do your hopes but the potential ordeal of Kohistan approaches, famous for stone-throwing kids. They don't always do it and it may be just to attract attention,

Baltit fort, Hunza, by the KKH © Chris Scott

RAMADAN IN PAKISTAN

Ramadan in Pakistan is pronounced 'Ramzan'. Mostly conservative Muslims themselves, Pakistanis understand that infidels don't practise fasting during Ramadan

Covering up on the KKH

and in any case travellers can be an exception according to Islam. Tourist businesses will serve you as usual, but many villages have no tourist businesses and simple cafés will be closed during daytime, though you can buy food and move on. We had picnic lunches a little way off the road, not hiding, but trying to be discreet; someone will always see you. No one begrudged us this.

It's obviously disrespectful (and perhaps not just during Ramadan) to walk around town eating in daylight. As evening approaches, you will see people buying food or waiting for the call of the Muezzin announcing the end of the day's fast and inevitably, some can't wait, but you should turn a blind eye to that. In the Ishmaeli north, things are more relaxed for all religious rules and fasting is more a personal decision.

but this may not be the friendliest area on the route – that comes later, in the Ishmaeli north. Around Chilas is a pretty conservative Sunni area, not recommended for foreign women solo riders and not far to the west is the Swat valley. Don't be put off, you may never get to ride through another area like this, which has resisted so much of the modern world and yet which is open to you. If the

A SIDE TRIP TO SKARDU

Skardu, lying about 220km to the east of Gilgit up the Indus valley, is actually in Pakistani-administered Kashmir and lies not far from the line of control with India. It was the scene of some fighting between Pakistan and India in 1947-8. It's a typically noisy, dusty town but with incredible views in all directions and is a base for climbing expeditions and treks. South of Skardu a road takes you up to the Deosai Plains. The pass is at 4000m and the plains are unpaved, wild National Park land at around 3500m. The road from the KKH to Skardu is a narrow, winding, cliff-hugging road high above the roaring Indus river. There are few places flat enough to camp that aren't right next to the road, but just enough small villages along the way where you can ask for a camping place. There are plenty of side streams to fill your bottles and fruit can be bought at the villages.

Skardu isn't the most beautiful town but the views are and it makes a good base for a

few days of side trips – Karpochu fort is one, Sadpara lake to the south is another and the Shangri La Hotel is good if you're in the mood to celebrate with a lunch overlooking great views, but there's a lot more riding beyond Skardu on small roads to tiny villages if you want to explore further. The village of Khaplu is a great but long day's ride to the east of Skardu and has a few hotels and a famous mosque that may have once been a Buddhist temple. Climbers used to stay at the Indus Motel in Skardu and it has atmosphere and reasonable value, but the K2 Motel, a PTDC property, now has the climbing group trade. If you're pushed for time, take the bus up to Skardu and ride back down. It's down to luck whether you get a sensible driver or a Wacky Races Driving School graduate. You can arrange and pick up a bus to Skardu outside Madina's Guesthouse in Gilgit. There is an airport at Skardu, with 737s flying to Islamabad.

(Opposite) The Karakoram Highway. Top: Posing on the Khunjerab Pass, China-Pakistan border. At 4695m this is the world's highest paved international frontier. (Photo © Peter Gostelow). **Bottom**: The Cathedral peaks are among the many spectacular views along the KKH. (Photo © Chris Scott).

SHANDUR PASS AND THE ROAD TO CHITRAL

West of Gilgit a road runs over Shandur Pass, home to the famous annual polo match between Gilgit and Chitral. The Gilgit river lies in a beautiful valley rising slowly to the pass amid Sunni villages where women work the fields and men sit around playing with catapults, though fortunately for you, they're too polite to practise on cyclists. There's a fair choice of guesthouses on the way including a few of the more expensive government PTDC chain with good food. About 150km of the route over the 3800m pass is unpaved – you keep hearing how it's paved on the other side, but this is an old joke for adventure tourers – the paving starts 80km or more beyond the pass, at Buni. You'll find excellent camping at the flat pass at an altitude that shouldn't give first-timers much problem. At times you'll curse the hard rock and wish you had full suspension, at others, such as the last day's ride into Buni, it's dream mountain biking – banked hard-pack with dramatic views changing round every corner, steep dropoffs and good long downhill runs. It's certainly steeper on the west side and probably easier going from Gilgit to Chitral as you shouldn't have to push uphill on the eastern side much, if at all, and the switchback section is only about 500m of ascent, done in a few legs. As soon as you rejoin the road for the last day's ride into Chitral, you realise what was so great about the tough times you just had – the remoteness, the achievement in having pedalled or pushed all the way up, and the lack of traffic.

Allow a week for this ride. From Chitral there are some great treks to see the tribal villages of the Kalasha people, who are non-Muslim. It may or may not be safe to ride south of Chitral, but there are flights to Peshawar and Islamabad, saving you 12 hours on a bus to the capital and costing around €40 and a little extra for the bike, which only needs handlebars turning to get on the plane. Foreigners pay more than locals for the flight but one suspects that locals get bumped off the flight to make room for rich infidels, so it's not all bad. Peshawar may be okay to visit but anywhere to the west is likely to be off-limits.

Kohistan section does not appeal, you can fly from Islamabad to Chitral cheaply with your bike assembled and begin your ride there (see box above).

The valley is broad and as it turns north, has little shade but usually has tailwinds. At Mansehra you have a chance of taking a nominally more direct and shorter jeep road up the Kaghan valley over Babusar pass (4145m) to Chilas further up the KKH. This used to be the route before the KKH opened. It's high mountain scenery and glaciers and might appeal more if you were heading south, acclimatised and tired of the main road, but you won't escape the stone-throwers going this way. To the east at Talechi runs a road to Astore and then on to the Deosai Plains National Park and thence to Skardu (see box p128). If you have time, take it, though it's very much a detour. It's mostly paved backcountry.

Gilgit is the only town of any size on this route, and it's not big at all. It has one of the best backpackers in Pakistan: Madina Guesthouse where you can rest, organise a trek or plan for either the Shandur Pass route or a side trip to Skardu.

North of Gilgit

The Indus river peels off to the east up to Skardu but its tributary, the Hunza, takes over; it's almost as massive. The mountains lining the valley become higher and more exciting, though you're now past distant Nanga Parbat. The

(Opposite) Top: Manali to Leh (see p138), descending from Baralacha La (4918m). (Photo © Chris Scott). Bottom: The '72 switchbacks' below Gama La (4618m), east Tibet, on the road between Lhasa and Markham. (Photo © Stephen Lord).

(Previous pages) Wild open country: the road to Chicham, Spiti (see p140). (Photo © Stephen Lord).

road is flat and easy with a parallel side-road to avoid the Tata trucks rolling by. In two days you get to Karimabad, aka Hunza, after a night at the quiet off-road village of Chalt, the inhabitants of which seem strangely unaware of the marijuana forest growing around them. Fabulous views of Rakaposhi (7788m) begin here. The Dirhan guest house at Minapin is another traveller hangout, then at Aliabad the turnoff to a back road up to Hunza gives you a long gentle winding climb rather than a flat road and a brutal 2km climb at the end. Hunza has fantastic views, good food and laid-back Ishmaelis. It's a great place to plan a trek in the northern region, possibly up to the Baltoro glacier, though this could be done from Passu too.

A couple more days of staggering mountain views, such as the long and ever-improving vistas of the Cathedral peaks, will get you to the small and friendly villages of Gulmit and Passu with barely a day's more riding to Sost and your fast-forward to China. Sost has no great charms but the proper village a few kilometres before the necessary bus and customs business (neither is any great hassle, though) is the better place to stay. North of Sost you will probably be on the bus, but should you try to ride up to the border and back, it is a steep and quite hard two-day ride with the steepest and worst road right at the end. It's a big climb – 2000m in 84km, but you won't be at that 4700m pass for long.

The Chinese side – Khunjerab to Kashgar

Expect a couple too many passport checks on the road to Tashkurgan but it's a lovely broad valley with Tajik villages along the way. Tashkurgan is all Tajik and has improved over the last few years from the seedy border town it used to be. The interesting streets are a few blocks east of the main road where the decent hotels are. Heading north out of town the road is fairly flat for some time till you pass through a narrow gorge and get your first views of 7500m Muztagh Ata. The gentle, flat side of it looks tempting to a cyclist and in 2002 Martin Adserballe and friends reached 7000m carrying bikes and rode enough at that altitude to make it into the Guinness Book of World Records before carrying the bikes back down.

About 10km further there is a turnoff leading to some hot springs not far up a track. Look for these characters, meaning 'hot spring': 温泉. It's a 30km haul up to the pass at Ulugh Rabat with one permanent checkpoint en route. Here there are shopping possibilities and before and after, excellent camping spots. Past Ulugh Rabat (3955m) it's a slight descent to picturesque (mentally

---

THE SOST-TASHKURGAN BUS SHUFFLE

From 2001 the Chinese closed a section of the highway near the Afghan border to individual cyclists, and it's only possible now by bus, though it's no problem to take your bike with you. The bus has to be boarded in Sost if you're going north, making the last 80km of the Pakistan side (the steepest part, wild and rugged; upper section badly sealed or not paved at all) rideable only if you come back down to Sost afterwards. For those coming from China on the bus, which you must board in Tashkurgan, you can plead with the bus driver to let you off on the Pakistani side of the pass, but they won't buy it. Otherwise you'll be bouncing down the switchbacks looking out of the bus windows for Marco Polo sheep with hardly a moment to get dizzy at being up at almost 4700m. If Afghanistan ever settles down, the rationale for the bus would collapse but it will likely survive just as the overpriced taxi on the Torugart pass has become institutionalised.

airbrush out the Chinese concrete yurts and cell mast) Karakul Lake at 3752m, but not much further descent for a further 35km, when the road drops steadily to Ghez Canyon and another permanent checkpoint. It's a barely noticeable decline of 1100m more over the 128km to Kashgar. As you leave the canyon, views open up of the Pamirs to the west and it's an easy run into the fleshpots of Kashgar and the travellers' favourite, the dorm at Seman Hotel.

India

Bill Weir

Exotic, enticing, though sometimes exasperating, India will entertain you like no other country – and cycling provides the best way to experience it! While backpackers get pushed and shoved at dirty bus and train stations as they climb into metal boxes, you'll enjoy the freedom of the open road while listening to bird song and admiring nature's colours.

India has many advantages for cyclists. Indians tend to be friendly and curious, eager to chat or patiently help with directions. India probably has more ancient sites than any other country, and many monuments have exceptional beauty. Tourist visas typically allow a generous six months with multiple entries. English is a national language, especially popular in the Himalaya, the South and big cities. You can almost always find someone who speaks it. Travel costs are low. For the same price as a camping trip in a developed country, you can savour restaurant meals and stretch out in hotel rooms that have an attached bath. You can usually bring your bicycle into your hotel room; if not, you'll probably find a nearby safe storage place. Accommodation and food are nearly always easy to locate; the only place you may need a tent is in the Himalaya or North-East. Indian cuisine may be the world's tastiest, but you'll often have the option of Western or Chinese food, or approximations of them. Indians tend to be honest. The most common overcharging is by the government's two-tiered pricing system (tourists vs. citizens). Dogs are generally mild-mannered and have better things to do than chase cyclists; if dogs do threaten, just pick up a bunch of stones. Money is easy to get from ATMs in most sizable towns.

The toughest part of an Indian ride is getting started – the country is immense, a sub-continent more than a country. Parts of India are far better for cycling than others, and certain seasons are far better than others; planning will be essential to assure a great trip.

Where to go
I recommend the Himalaya in the north for scenic grandeur, Rajasthan in the west for romantic castles and forts spread across a desert landscape, and the South for ancient cultures, temple cities and long sandy coastlines. All three regions have much colour and character along with many sights. You could spend months touring in just one of these!

Varanasi © Robb Maciag

Where to avoid
You've heard the horror stories about cyclists getting trapped in horrendous traffic, pollution, dust, heat, and flies, then burning out and quitting their trip. You can be almost sure that those cyclists were riding the northern plains, basically the Ganges Valley. This is the most densely populated part of the country with the heaviest traffic. Long-haul cyclists may wish to cross it, and riding is certainly possible, but it's neither easy nor the best that India offers. The northern plains do contain outstanding destinations, such as Agra's Taj Mahal, Varanasi's sacred riverside ghats, and Bodhgaya's profusion of Buddhist temples, but these are best visited by public transport.

When to go
Winter: Nearly the entire country enjoys a very sunny and dry cool season from the end of the rains in September until February or March when the hot season kicks in. It's great to get up every morning and know that the day will be one of sunshine and pleasant temperatures! High valleys of Ladakh and surrounding areas will be snowbound, but the Himalayan foothills have pleasant weather early and late in this season. The northern plains tend to get chilly at night during December and January, while the South has a more even tropical climate and never gets cold except in the hills. Tamil Nadu and southern Kerala catch clouds and rain of the north-east monsoon around October to early December; rains are often light and not every day during this time, so cycling is still possible.

Spring: The hot season peaks in late spring, when the plains bake in temperatures often exceeding 40°C; the Himalayan foothills are the best place to go. Snow blocks the high passes on the way to Ladakh until about mid-June.

Summer: The monsoon sweeps over India beginning in the month of June, bringing daily rains and high humidity on top of high temperatures left behind by the hot season. This is the time to head for Ladakh and other areas of the far north where the Himalayan ranges wring out most of the rain from the clouds before they reach these high places.

Autumn: September and October can still be on the warm side at low elevations, but this is an excellent time to be in the Himalaya, though the season will fast be winding down in Ladakh and other high regions of the far north. November and December often have the clearest mountain views in the Himalayan foothills as well as fine weather on the plains.

Route planning
Maps, especially the red-cover TTK state and city series, can be purchased at most Indian bookstores. Nest & Wings maps and guidebooks cover Himalayan

regions. Map accuracy can be appalling with road segments shown that don't exist or not shown when they do. Pick up some maps before you come to India; Nelles, for example, offers regional maps that use shading to give an idea of the terrain; they tend to be more accurate than Indian-produced maps, but still have many errors. Roads shown as state highways are usually best to ride, but national highways will be your only option in places and may be fine in less populated regions such as Rajasthan.

The Himalayan foothills
The foothills have great scenery and are a good way to traverse India from the Pakistan border through to Nepal or Bangladesh. You could ride all the way across in about a month from the hill station of Dalhousie in the west to the Nepal border, stopping at other hill towns on the way such as Dharamsala/McLeod Ganj, Shimla, Mussoorie, Almora, and Nainital. This route can also take in the sacred towns of Rishikesh and Haridwar where the Ganges River emerges onto the plains. A side trip to Chamba and up the valleys to Bharmour leads through splendid scenery and to beautiful stone temples. Overnight buses go to many of these towns from New Delhi – preferable if you'd rather skip the traffic and dust of the plains, or this route could be used to connect rides in Pakistan and Nepal. For higher adventure, consider visiting the four Char Dam sacred sites near the headwaters of the Ganges north-east of New Delhi – Yamunotri, Gangotri, Kedarnath, and Badrinath. Interesting rides abound further east toward Nepal: you can get close to Tibet on the wildly scenic road around the north side of Nanda Devi to Malari, or you can head over the hills to Munsiyari and follow a valley down to the Kali River on the border with Nepal; no crossings for foreigners here, but you can cycle up the valley past Dharchula on the Indian side.

Sikkim and Darjeeling
A much smaller, but still appealing, section of the Indian Himalaya lies sandwiched between Nepal and Bhutan. You can make an enjoyable loop here in about a month. Tibetan and Nepali cultures here have very colourful temples and picturesque villages. Entry to Sikkim requires a permit, easily available at

COPING WITH TRAFFIC
First, forget about how things are done elsewhere! In India the road rules are Might equals Right. That means that cars give way to trucks and buses, three-wheelers give way to four-wheelers, motorbikers give way to three- and four-wheelers, and cyclists give way to all of the above. That leaves us near the bottom of the pecking order, just above pedestrians and dogs. Actually, vehicles are quite willing to pull over if there's room. The problem is that there probably won't be enough room if two large vehicles are passing each other. Then it's necessary to quickly pull off the pavement onto the (usually unpaved) shoulder. So you need to keep an eye on traffic both ahead and behind. The easiest way to do this is with a rear-view mirror; the best are the eyeglass-mounted ones because you can 'scan' behind you by turning your head. Best are the plastic mirrors on metal frames (plastic mounts fatigue and break); you can get them from 🖥 www.rei.com. Many national highways now have sections of four lanes with paved shoulders, making cycling quick and easy, if less scenic.

the Rangpo border, Siliguri, and other towns. The eastern Himalaya tends to get more monsoon rains than the west, so you'll probably wish to hit the hills in the driest months. Laura Stone's *Himalaya by Bike* (Trailblazer) covers this region well.

Lastly, there's a long section of the Himalaya in Arunachal Pradesh in the far north-east. This is pioneering territory for cyclists. You'll need to form a group of four or more (couples may be okay), obtain a permit, and probably seek help from a travel agency that specialises in this region. A ride to the Tibetan area surrounding Tawang monastery is the 'holy grail' of cycling here, but tribal areas in the lower hills and plains also merit visiting.

Rajasthan and the West

Rajasthan is the most romantic part of India and the state to travel if you like tales of chivalry, clambering up impregnable hilltop forts, and admiring grandiose palaces and mansions. It's a big state; you could easily spend months looping around to all the sights. Rajasthan is close to New Delhi, just a day or two biking south-west, or you could take a bus or train. Jaipur is the capital with lots of grand buildings and streets encumbered with heavy and chaotic traffic. Wildlife parks in Rajasthan's east are worth seeking out if you'd like to see birds and maybe a tiger. Few travellers make it to the Shekhawati region in the north, but it's full of atmospheric little towns with ornate mansions (havelis). Pushkar near the centre is famed for its sacred lake and temple; try to visit during the amazing Camel Fair (usually in November) when you'll see camels stretching to the horizon in every direction, as well as ongoing tribal life, and varied entertainment. Way out west, you'll get a thrill on seeing remote Jaisalmer Fort; this is also a good place for camel treks or cycling out to Sam to commune with giant sand dunes. Down south, Udaipur's lake and palaces will entrance you. Also in the south, you'll get a workout climbing Mt Abu, the only hill station in the state, but worth it for the fantastically decorated white marble Jain temples.

Punjab, north of Rajasthan, has only one major tourist site – the Golden Temple in the Sikh town of Amritsar. It's a very holy spot and one of India's most memorable places. The daily flag-lowering ceremony at the Pakistan border is also a must-see. From here it's as little as two days north to the Himalaya via Pathankot. Heading south, cycling takes a week or so to Bikaner, the first town of interest in Rajasthan, but the riding is pleasant enough and it's interesting to get off the guidebook track for a spell. You'll pass through Amritsar if cycling to or from Pakistan. Gujarat, south of Rajasthan, has fine architecture in its capital Ahmedabad, but the highway south toward Mumbai carries a very heavy load of traffic. Cycling is a good way to explore the western part of this state.

Mumbai and the west coast of Maharashtra have interesting bits of cycling that you might consider. The city is surprisingly easy and pleasant to enter or leave if you take a ferry from the Gateway of India south across the bay to Mandwa. From Mandwa a very pretty coastal road runs south past the fortress island of Janjira, a worthwhile side trip. Eventually you will have to head inland and join the main highway, which is rideable but clogged by traffic and has few sights or scenic diversions. Still farther south, Goa has delightful coastal sections. Then in Karnataka it's back to traffic and dull scenery, but you can make a short detour to the picturesque beaches at Gokarna or inland to mountains and waterfalls. Overall, I think an inland route through Maharashtra and Karnataka offers better scenery and more places of interest than the west coast, though you may wish to dip down for Mumbai and Goa. Things do get interesting as you move south to coastal Kerala.

The South

For culture, ancient cities, mountain scenery, and palm-fringed beaches, consider a ride in the southern states of Kerala, Tamil Nadu, and Karnataka. All sorts of loops are possible; it just depends on your time and interests. The coastal plains have easy riding past beaches and many temples, but it's worth swinging into the mountains for the views, tea plantations, and wildlife parks. Hindu religion remains strong in this region, as its relative isolation in ancient times prevented Muslim invaders from making major inroads. Kerala has a distinctive language and culture, along with some of India's best beaches. Canoes and motorboats will take you into the backwaters if you'd like time off the bike. The great temple cities in Tamil Nadu's Madurai and Chidambaram have amazing interior stonework and entrancing ceremonies. Also in Tamil Nadu, Kanyakumari at India's extreme southern tip and Rameswaram on an island 'stepping stone' to Sri Lanka have major temples with an end-of-the-world feeling.

Life on India's back roads © Peter Gostelow

Moving north into Karnataka, the opulent Maharaja's Palace in Mysore is truly grand. As you move north through places such as Hampi and Badami, you will pass through a series of impressive ancient cities. In the northern Karnataka, Bijapur's 15-17th century architecture marks the boundary of major Islamic influence.

The Interior

Madhya Pradesh and Maharashtra include vast rolling expanses of the Deccan Plateau. Sights tend to be widely spaced, so this region is better for the long-haul cyclist. Madhya Pradesh has bumpy roads, but it offers the visitor memorable places such as the hilltop Afghan fortress of Mandu, sacred riverside temples in Maheswar and Omkareshwar, palaces in Orchha, and the famously erotic temples of Khajuraho. Maharashtra contains many ancient cave and rock-cut temples, including Buddhist Ajanta and the multi-faith Ellora.

The East Coast

Few cyclists choose the dull, long grind on National Highway 5 from Chennai in Tamil Nadu up to Bhubaneswar in Orissa. A better option might be to swing inland and visit Andhra Pradesh's interesting capital Hyderabad and nearby sights. In Orissa, aim for Bhubaneswar with many temples and other sights in town, the Sun Temple at Konark, the temple/beach town of Puri, and the large lagoon of Chilika Lake. The delightful road between Konark and Puri passes a stretch of sandy beach and runs through a wildlife sanctuary.

The North-East

West Bengal contains incredible variety – from the tiger-infested mangroves of the south to lofty Himalayan foothills. You may wish to avoid cycling into or out of the capital Kolkata (Calcutta), but the city centre is surprisingly tranquil on Sunday and makes a great ride to admire the architecture. You can ride the length of West Bengal, bypassing Kolkata, and visit the terracotta-temple town of Bishnupur, Tagore's university at Shantiniketan, the palaces and mosques of the old capital Murshidabad, and the mosques and tombs at the even older capitals of Gaur and Pandua.

You'll definitely be off the beaten track if heading into any of the seven states of the North-East proper. Three of these can be visited without permits, but the whole region is unstable to varying degrees. Much of the population is tribal with cultures closer to those of people in Tibet or Myanmar than India.

Assam, bisected by the immense Brahmaputra river, is the most easily visited and has temples, palaces, wildlife parks, and the world's largest river island to explore. Turn south from Assam to reach Meghalaya's hill town of Shillong and the famously rainy area around Cherrapunji; you could continue south into Bangladesh. Cycling into the third open state, Tripura, is tricky because the north-central part is so dangerous that you're likely to be forced to travel by bus in an escorted convoy. Tripura's capital Argatala is just 4km from the Bangladesh border crossing and most easily visited from that country, providing you have the required visas. Arunachal Pradesh is the largest and most stable of the north-eastern states, but China invaded it in 1962 and although Chinese troops later withdrew, China still claims the Tibetan region; easternmost Arunachal Pradesh also borders no-go Myanmar (see p173). India is very touchy about foreign tourists in the state; check with a travel agency specialising in this area and good luck! Parts of Nagaland and Mizoram might be open to cycling, but you may need travel agency help as well as permits. Manipur is so dangerous owing to armed rebels and drug runners that there's no chance of cycling there.

Onward travels

It's easy to combine an India ride with neighbouring countries, especially Nepal, which has a long border with India; visas can be purchased at the border crossings. Despite India's long borders with Tibet, the only open route at the time of writing is via Nepal; this is tricky because if riding from Nepal to Tibet, cyclists need to join tours with a group visa. The ride from Tibet to Nepal is less restricted because you can use a regular Chinese visa and go on your own. *Himalaya by Bike* by Laura Stone describes the lofty Friendship Highway route between Lhasa and Kathmandu. Bhutan is possible, but only if paying a huge daily fee of more than $200 and going on a tour; if you're interested, again see *Himalaya by Bike*. Pakistan's great cultural city of Lahore is an easy day's ride from India's Amritsar; the Karakoram Highway (see p127) in Pakistan's north is a classic Himalayan ride; again, *Himalaya by Bike* has a detailed description of cycling it. Bangladesh has several border crossings with India, and you could make an interesting loop ride with West Bengal and the north-east states. Lastly, although you cannot cycle or take a boat to Sri Lanka, it's easy to arrange a stopover if flying SriLankan Airlines.

TAKING YOUR BICYCLE ON AN INDIAN TRAIN

You can cover vast distances by train fairly comfortably and even in luxury for a good price. You'll need your train ticket to book the bicycle as luggage, and the bicycle must go in a baggage van; there's a small fee and quite a bit of paperwork, so it's a good idea to do this four hours or so before your departure. Hang on to your receipts – you may need them to exit the station, as security is generally pretty tight. Not all trains have a baggage van and not all stops have baggage service, so it's a good idea to check with the station's parcel office for advice – they are invariably more helpful to foreigners. It's best to take a train from the originating point to the terminus as your bicycle can go in a sealed van that's not opened until the terminus; this will be more secure and reduce the chance of damage. You may need your paperwork to claim the bike at your destination and some major stations will not allow you to take your bike out of the station without the railway receipts to show it's yours.

How the bicycle is packed will likely be left up to you but they prefer it partly covered to protect against scratches. Remove bags, water bottles and anything that could go missing, then just wheel the bicycle up to the parcel office and check it in. A parcel wrapping service may be available nearby that will use padding and jute bags. Try to arrange to have the bicycle travel on the same train as you, but don't fret if the bicycle takes longer; sometimes there's a delay in opening a sealed baggage car, or the bicycle may go on a later train and arrive days later (five days when I travelled New Delhi-Puri). On arrival there's more paperwork; check baggage cars for your bicycle, and if not there, head for the Parcel Office – the bicycle may already be there. If you're not going to

the final stop and the bike isn't in a sealed car, you may want to follow it onto the train so you know exactly where it will be when you get off. Head straight for the luggage van and make sure it comes off at your stop.

Don't forget buses for where the train doesn't run, or when you're in a hurry, as they leave all the time and there's no paperwork needed, just a small fee and tips for the lads who will put the bike on the roof of the bus (climb up and check their work before paying...). Go for the deluxe 2x2 buses if possible as they are more comfortable and usually have enough interior baggage space for your bicycle. Very easy, but expect to pay a baggage fee.

© Cass Gilbert

LADAKH, SPITI AND KINNAUR

Based on *Himalaya by Bike* by Laura Stone (🖥 www.himalayabybike.com)

Widely regarded as one of the best bike touring regions in the world, Ladakh has it all if you enjoy climbing 5000m+ passes on a fully loaded bike. It has Tibetan Buddhist culture without the weight of oppression and Indian food without the heat – temperature heat, that is. And it's paved, to a degree. You could do it on a touring bike with strong wheels and spare tyres – rocks can rip sidewalls in a second. Spiti and Kinnaur are a bit more prone to landslides and hence the piste is a bit rougher. Without breaks, you could ride all this in about a month, but a more sensible proposition if you don't have teachers' holidays is to do the classic Manali-Leh ride in around three weeks vacation, giving you time to acclimatise and some time in Leh at the end of the ride. If you are a teacher or happen to have six weeks free in summer, you could do the lot, starting in Shimla and finishing in Srinagar – 1588km plus any side trips you might do.

What has kept Ladakh free from the rampant development seen in much of India is the difficulty in getting there – it's snowed in for nine months of the year. Many riders have to make a special trip to get there as it's hard to line up the timing with a long ride through the region. It's easier to hit Ladakh in summer and then go to Pakistan for the KKH than it is to arrive late in the season for Ladakh and risk being cut off for the winter in Leh (which can be snowbound in early October). Only an Indian visa is needed, though an Inner Line Permit is needed if you go for some side trips and that is easily obtained in Manali or Leh.

Parachute tents provide hot meals, shelter and accommodation along the Manali-Leh road. © Chris Scott

If you're flying into the region, it's possible to travel the major routes without camping gear thanks to a good traveller infrastructure, though sometimes you may have to rough it at roadside truck stops known as dhabas (bring a sleeping bag, mat and ear plugs for a good night's sleep). But camping enables you to get away from the road and enjoy sleeping out under star-studded skies. In summer, camping is the way to go but in autumn, you will be glad to huddle round a stove in a parachute tent.

Manali to Leh

Manali is reached by bus from Delhi or by riding from the Raj-era summer capital, Shimla, a worthwhile tourist destination in itself and an overnight train journey from Delhi and morning steam train up to Shimla at 2132m. Only 500km of road separates Manali and Leh but there are two 5000m passes and the road climbs 2000m out of Manali to the Rohtang La in just 51km, so it pays to get fit before starting and acclimatise as best you can. Once over Rohtang La you can camp around 3000m but the road heads quickly up to more danger-

T R I P   R E P O R T
LADAKH, SPITI & KINNAUR

Name	Stephen Lord
Year of birth	1959
Occupation	Author
Nationality	British
Other bike travels	Asia, Europe and the USA
This trip	Ladakh and Spiti in northern India
Trip duration	5 weeks
Number in group	Two
Total distance	Only 800km, but it was all great riding – we took a few buses and hitched a lift up some passes
Cost of trip	£400 for flights and £350 spent
Longest day	100km – but it was nearly all downhill.
Best day	The descent from Baralacha La, from snowy peaks through grand views to a fabulous dinner in Keylong.
Worst day	25km crawl up from Sarchu to a tent-dhaba at 4750m
Favourite ride	The whole Spiti valley really – it's mostly downhill
Biggest headache	Worrying about being cut off at the pass by snow
Pleasant surprise	After a 50km stretch of roadworks, there was a hose provided for washing cars – and our bikes
Any illness	Short bouts of diarrhoea but no sickness
Bike model	Roberts Roughstuff
New/used	Used, 4 years old
Modifications	Switched from drops to straight bars with Ergon grips, Gripshift twisters & lowest possible MTB gear setup.
Wish you'd fitted	Disc brakes, though they don't fit on my bike
Tyres used	Schwalbe Marathon XR, but Chris's much lighter Schwalbe Supremes coped really well, even in mud
Punctures	None
Baggage Setup	Four panniers and tent
Wish you'd brought	More snack food for maintaining energy while riding.
Wish you hadn't brought	Camping gear. Homestays were much more interesting and weight saved would have helped on the hills.
Bike problems	Gears got caked with dust and mud now and again
Accidents	I nearly got hit once by not paying attention, but most drivers were pretty good.
Same bike again	Yes
Next trip will be	Anywhere low! I'd like to find some endless Indian backroads
Recommendations	Spiti's bad roads are now a thing of the past and there's little traffic in most of the valley. It's all very beautiful with lots of side trips for athletic riders.
Any advice?	Allow a week to acclimatise and take more days off as you ascend. A lot of people overdo it, so don't try to cram too much into your trip.

ous altitudes, so take it easy and enjoy the culture and the views along the way. The second pass heading up to Leh, Baralacha La, is at 4918m so you will be panting at the top and not much more comfortable camping near the tented camps at Sarchu at 4408m. The highest pass on the Manali-Leh run is Taglang La at 5300m, one of the highest paved roads in the world. Cyclists used to rest in Leh before riding off to bag the Khardung La (Inner Line permit needed) but it's no higher than Taglang La although it has the famous 'World's highest motorable road' sign at the top.

Leh is another travellers' haven – good food, including spirited attempts at German bakeries, and cosy guesthouses await. It's a great place to put a bit of weight back on, take side trips to see monasteries, spend hours watching a web page load or just sit and take it all in.

Leh is also around halfway to Srinagar. If you are coming back to Leh after a ride down to Srinagar, consider leaving your camping gear in Leh as there is sufficient accommodation en route and camping is not recommended after Kargil, after which the people are mostly Muslim: it's Kashmir after all. Kargil gives access to some much more ambitious riding than the main highway. To the south lies the region of Zanskar, reached by unpaved and rough roads. Road-building works over the next few years may push through from the south into this region, but for now it's still relatively remote.

Srinagar has lost its lustre since the outbreak of separatist and insurgent violence over the past couple of decades, but the natural beauty is still there and the famous houseboats await and are as hungry as ever for business. Srinagar has an airport though the nearest railhead is in Jammu, 293km away on a busy road, and itself only 219km from Amritsar and the Pakistani border.

Spiti and Kinnaur

Far less well known are the valleys of Spiti and Kinnaur which make either a fantastic circuit ride from Manali (about three weeks riding) or a horseshoe ride of around a fortnight between Shimla to the south up to Manali further north. The passes are a touch lower than on the road to Leh but no easier, save for the lower altitude, and no less spectacular. Spiti, to the north, is Tibetan Buddhist and the terrain is dry and exposed, whereas Kinnaur is Hindu and the route follows the Sutlej river (the Sutlej rises near Mt Kailash in Tibet), with dramatic tight valleys which funnel winds – mostly from the west.

Because of this, it's probably better to go clockwise and have tailwinds on the very rough roads of Spiti and ride into the wind on the better roads of Kinnaur. Although the road is not too steep in the south, the towns are all well above the river, and there aren't many wild camping spots in the narrow valley, so be prepared for a climb at the end of most days. Kinnaur is definitely Indian – expect noise, traffic, colourfully-dressed women and flies, even at 2000m.

Spiti is nearly all downhill when ridden north to south

Shimla makes a great start or end to the ride. It's the old summer capital of the British Raj and there are enough buildings from that era, around the famous Mall where memsahibs would stroll, to bring back a sense of it, though it's now smoky, noisy and overrun with monkeys. There are top-notch places to eat and stay as well as a steam train to Khalka from where fast trains run to Delhi.

The route runs very close to the Line of Control, ie the de facto border with China and you need an Inner Line Permit, best obtained on the way as you pass through the towns of Kaza or Recong Peo, or in Manali or Shimla.

China

Bill Weir (China section except Tibet)
with contributions from Peter Snow Cao & Janne Corax

China offers a vast range of touring opportunities, from historic city-hopping in the east to village-to-village explorations in the interior, to hard-core mountain and desert traverses in the west. A staggering 94% of the country's population lives in eastern China. It is crowded, intensively cultivated and relatively low-lying. Western China is virtually empty with vast ranges of grassland, desert, high mountains and plateaux.

If you want to see villages and teeming cities, ride on good roads and find decent food and accommodation every day, head east. Camping in the east is usually difficult because nearly all flat land is either under intensive cultivation, built on or flooded. In any case it is hard to find a spot away from prying eyes and it's much easier learning how to find cheap places to stay than to live like a fugitive as you cycle through the east. If you're more into adventure/expedition cycle touring, go west, but be prepared for unpaved roads, more extreme conditions and long stretches with zero facilities – in other words, classic adventure-touring.

The road network in southern and eastern China is extensive and in most parts good. Things thin out considerably as you head towards the wilder west. China is divided roughly 50-50 between endless plains and plateaux (which can get dull to ride) and steep and rugged mountains, so start your route planning with a good topographical map. For detailed route planning and on-the-bike navigation, though, you'll want to get hold of a Chinese road atlas.

Incidentally, most roads in China have regular toll-booths but as a cyclist you are exempt from paying and can slip round the side. Some river crossings marked as bridges on the map are in fact served by ferries, on which you can take your bike for a couple of Yuan.

CYCLING ACROSS CHINA

China, so vast as to be a world unto itself, offers amazingly varied experiences to those who cycle across this country. You have two options – either the very tough ride across Tibet in the south or a much easier route north of Tibet. Unfortunately most of the Tibetan ride goes through closed areas. Even in years where there is a clampdown, some cyclists still make it through, but it depends on the attitude of the PSB (Public Security Bureau); sometimes officers ignore cyclists, but you have to get through every time you're stopped, hence the nocturnal checkpoint-hopping you sometimes hear of on the internet. If in a closed area, do not stay in a hotel because the owner must register you with the police, who may fine you and expel you on a bus.

You'll have an easier time with terrain and officialdom if you stay north of Tibet. Furthermore, you can enjoy Tibetan culture and scenery without actually entering Tibet in southern Qinghai, south-western Gansu, and western Sichuan. These regions were once part of Tibet and still have thriving Tibetan villages and monastery complexes amidst high-altitude splendour.

Beginning or ending your trans-China journey in the Beijing area is not recommended because you would have to cycle through dirty industrial areas. Try to swing south through the very scenic provinces of Sichuan, Yunnan, Chongqing, Guizhou, and Guangxi. Yunnan has border crossings with Laos and Vietnam. Guangxi offers two crossings with Vietnam. Laos visas are available at the border, but you must get Vietnamese visas in advance at consulates in Kunming or Nanning.

BASICS FOR BIKERS

In mainland China, traffic uses the right-hand side of the road, but Hong Kong and Macao use the left-hand side. Major roads outside the cities are mostly asphalt; they're concrete pavement in the cities. Note that in remote areas some national highways are not paved. Also, China is rapidly upgrading the highway system, so there may be long stretches under construction. Many major urban roads have separate bike paths. Expect to encounter a variety of people, vehicles, bicycles, tractors and animals using the roads, even in remote areas.

Cycling in China is significantly different from cycling in most Western countries. Cyclists must never assume they have the right of way. Drivers of motorised vehicles (including motorcycles, cars, trucks and especially buses) generally assume that cyclists will yield right of way to them, regardless of the situation. If a vehicle honks frantically behind you, it is best to move off the road as soon as possible. One of China's traffic laws requires that drivers warn pedestrians, cyclists and other drivers that they intend to

Wangba – Chinese for Internet Café

pass by using their horn, which can be deafening at times. Often they'll honk at you even when approaching.

Most drivers are fairly competent, if slightly aggressive. They also tend to pass closer to cyclists than drivers in the West. With the recent rapid increase in the number of private vehicles, it is best for cyclists to keep a respectable distance and give way rather than stand their ground because they think they have right of way. Bear in mind that China has more than 100,000 road deaths annually.

Finding spares for your bicycle can be difficult. Standard 26" mountain-bike tyres are available virtually everywhere but 700c will be found only in a few specialist shops in major cities such as Beijing, Shanghai, Chengdu and Kunming. In better shops Shimano components (or copies) are the norm. Guangzhou has the greatest selection and offers the best prices on new bikes.

Peter Snow Cao

Peter Snow Cao lives in Chengdu and runs bike tours in China (🖳 www.bikechina.com)

In western China you'll probably follow one of the Silk Routes, passing ancient grotto temples, watchtowers, and fortifications. Most cyclists visit the old town and markets of Kashgar in the far west of China. From Kashgar many continue west to the Irkeshtam crossing into mountainous Kyrgyzstan; others turn south over the Khunjerab Pass to Pakistan. Ürümqi in the northwest has a desert and mountain route west to Korgas and Kazakhstan. You can obtain visas for Kazakhstan and Kyrgyzstan at consulates in Ürümqi. In this part of China you'll have headwinds no matter which direction you travel, but you'll also benefit from tailwinds.

You may find it difficult to get a visa with enough time for the cross-China ride. You will need 3-6 months, depending on the time you'll spend sightseeing and meandering. Find out which Chinese embassies and consulates give the longest visas by asking other travellers and by checking internet forums. Once in China, you can usually extend your visa twice, a month at a time. Travel agencies can sometimes wangle longer visas than you can obtain on your own.

Accommodation
Hotels for budget travellers are plentiful and inexpensive. China uses a five-star system to rate hotels with the five-star hotels charging Western prices. Getting into inexpensive digs is a matter of learning what to look for and then bargaining hard. Prices for hotel rooms are always negotiable, sometimes as much as 50-60% off posted prices, with 20-30% off a more common discount except during the May 1 and October 1 holiday periods in popular tourist destinations.

The quality of the hotel is mostly dependent on its age; the older it is, the worse condition it will be in. The cost of a budget hotel room in the big cities will be US$20-40. Dormitory beds for Western travellers are available in some big city hotels for US$3 10. Outside the big cities, cheap hotel rooms can be had for US$8-20 and there are guesthouses used by long-distance truckers with dormitory beds for US$2-5. In some places the local police will require Westerners to stay in 'approved' tourist hotels, despite the central government's mandate to the contrary.

The traveller hotels and guesthouses are most useful to the budget traveller, although many owners will not have any experience in dealing with foreigners. In the back-country it's possible to stay with local families if you're able to establish a good rapport with the family. An experience like this can be a very interesting way to learn about how the local people live but it can also be very draining: you will definitely earn your keep by providing entertainment for the family and friends for the duration of your stay! The men will always want to drink alcohol with the male traveller and a refusal can be seen as a huge snub.

Camping and food
Camping is relatively unknown in China. Nevertheless, wild camping is possible in some mountain and desert areas but be prepared for inquisitive visitors regardless of how remote you may think the location is.

For the touring cyclist, Chinese food is cheap and delicious. Breakfast in southern China usually consists of noodles, while in the north, dumplings are the mainstay. Lunch can be with rice, noodles or dumplings. Vegetarians will have to be persistent in their no-meat requirement; stating that you don't eat meat is like saying you don't breathe air. Even if there is no visible meat, vegetables are often cooked in meat fat with pork fat being ubiquitous. Average daily costs for food in inexpensive restaurants will be US$5-10. All running water in China must be filtered or boiled before consumption. Boiled water will always be provided in large thermos flasks in any hotel or guesthouse free of charge. Bottled water is readily available from shops everywhere for US$0.15-0.40 per 500ml bottle.

TIBET

Tibet is many cyclists' view of the ultimate in adventure touring – long, self-supported travels high on the roof of the world, the kind of freedom that only cycling provides, all at high altitudes and sometimes on the roughest of roads. Where others fear to go, or might drive through with the windows of their Landcruisers shut tight to keep dust out, cyclists thrive. It's not just about riding at 5000m either. Tibet's traditional culture is like no other. Tibetan Buddhism is possibly even more colourful than the Buddhism you will see in the rest of Asia and it's very much a living religion among the vast majority of the population. Despite the harsh climate, Tibetans are some of the friendliest people you could hope to meet and have a great sense of humour. Much of the attraction of a trip to Tibet lies in meeting local people

BORDER CROSSINGS IN WESTERN CHINA

Adventurous cyclists have the options of crossing between China and three of the 'Stans – Pakistan, Kyrgyzstan and Kazakhstan. There's also a road into Tajikistan, but so far it has been restricted to locals only for trade purposes.

The spectacular (and paved) Karakoram Highway links Pakistan and China via the Khunjerab Pass – see p127.

The Irkeshtam crossing connects China with southern Kyrgyzstan. You can cycle all the way and no permits are needed; roads in China are paved, the Kyrgyz side is extremely bad with football-sized rocks, but is not a major effort if you're heading east (downhill on the worst of it). From Sary Tash through the border takes a day. The Chinese border town at Irkeshtam has an abundance of dust, brothels, basic restaurants and filthy guesthouses; the Kyrgyz side has a village a few kilometres away. The Irkeshtam crossing provides a quick way to Tajikistan's fabulous Pamirs, the highlight of cycling in Central Asia—but the closest places to get the visa and GBAO permit are Bishkek and Almaty.

Torugart Pass offers a shorter route between Kashgar and Kyrgyzstan's capital Bishkek, but requires advance transport arrangements on the Chinese side through a travel agency in Kashgar; this will be costly and you probably won't be able to cycle all the way. Unfortunately Kashgar lacks consulates. Ürümqi, in China's north-west, offers Kyrgyz and Kazazkh consulates, as well as flights to both countries (most people can obtain visas on arrival at Bishkek if flying in).

You can cycle to Kazakhstan by heading west from Ürümqi to Korgas, fairly dull desert country most of the way, though you might spot herds of Bactrian camels here, and climbing to beautiful Sayram Lake with vistas of snow-capped mountains. From here it's just a day's ride to Korgas with plenty of hotels, restaurants, and shops on the Chinese side. You may have to pay for a vehicle to carry you the silly kilometre between Chinese and Kazakh posts. The Kazakh side has no facilities, but you'll find an ATM, bank, hotel, and food in Zharkent, the first sizeable town to the west. Two other border crossings farther north between China and Kazakhstan have occasionally been used by cyclists transiting Kazakhstan between Russia and China – Tacheng and Jimunai. Be warned that bicycle theft is a major problem in Central Asia, so camp away from villages and always lock the bicycle to something solid.   **Bill Weir**

MY FAVOURITE PLACES IN TIBET AND WESTERN CHINA

- The transition from the Taklamakan Desert to the first big mountain ranges in the west
- The desolation and emptiness of the Aksai Chin plateau
- The Mt Kailash, Lake Manasarovar and Mt Gorla Mandhata areas
- Crossing the Trans-Himalaya/Gangdise mountain range
- The multiple passes where Tibet and Xinjiang provinces meet

- Views close to the Tanggula Pass
- The transition from the high plateau to the lowlands of sub-tropical Nepal
- The views of the high Himalayas, particularly the Big Four (Makalu, Everest, Lhotse and Cho Oyu)
- Rawu Valley
- Namche Barwa region
- Riwoqe Pass area
- The entire Yunnan Highway

Janne Corax

on the road or visiting monasteries (known as gompas), all more easily done outside of towns and away from the watchful eyes of the police. Tibet's fortunes go up and down and this is true for the possibilities of visiting too. The riots of 2008 were a great setback in the general trend of easing travel restrictions for foreigners in Tibet, but it should still be possible to travel through the many Tibetan communities in Sichuan and northern Yunnan (Tibet's borders once extended significantly beyond the current provincial boundaries). If you're planning to ride through Tibet on a longer trans-Asian ride, your alternatives are discussed on p98-9.

Getting there is not easy in terms of visas (see p146), it's physically hard and that's what keeps most travellers away. Flying in is the best option if you are going to Tibet to ride the Friendship Highway (see p147) or the road east to Markham and on to Sichuan or south to Yunnan (see p153). Taking the train from Qinghai is an exciting option but expect extra bureaucracy and foreigner pricing. The ultimate way is to ride in, most commonly from Kashgar in the Chinese province of Xinjiang to the west of Tibet, or from the mountainous east, or from the north via Golmud.

Visas

The Chinese government regard Tibet as just another autonomous province and therefore there are no borders as such. Entering from other Chinese provinces you will not even notice that you've passed into a new province while in some other places there is just a border marker or a sign showing the geographical border. Here are some Tibet visa tips:

- A visa for China is also valid for Tibet.
- You will need a Tibet Travel Permit – the travel agent who books your flight or train into Tibet will arrange this and you'll probably never even see it but your name will be on a list shown at check-in time.
- The permit and access situation is fluid – it pays to stay updated and to be persistent.

Nomad camp in West Tibet
© Dominique Kerhuel

● Outside of Lhasa and Shigatse you will need an Alien Travel Permit for travel in officially 'closed' areas, but this situation is particularly vague and there are many inconsistencies.

● Never state 'Lhasa' or any other destination in Tibet on your visa application.

● You might find your nearest Chinese embassy usually only gives out 30 day visas. You may need to provide more information such as a flight itinerary to get a longer visa. Using a travel agent to get your visa tends to help – your application will get less scrutiny if it's submitted with 20 others that the travel agent has checked beforehand.

● If you still have a problem getting a three-month visa (or longer), go to your embassy and ask them to write a letter of introduction, stating that you need a long-term visa. Otherwise go to China via Hong Kong, where longer visas are easier to obtain.

● Visa extensions in Tibet are very hard to get. Of the major cities in central Tibet, Shigatse might give you a seven-day extension. In the outback, some of the major cities can extend your visa, but the catch with that is that you're probably not allowed to be there in the first place, so you'll probably have to pay a fine and risk bicycle confiscation before you can apply for an extension. In Kathmandu you can get a Chinese visa without any hassles but to enter Tibet from Nepal by air is another story; you have to book an expensive tour. The Chinese embassy here has different rules from any other embassy and the rules for getting a visa usually include booking a tour to Tibet.

● Forget about cycling in to Tibet from Nepal, the Chinese almost never allow it, especially for individuals and the climb of over 4000m rules it out for most.

The Friendship Highway – Lhasa to Kathmandu

One of the three great cycling routes in the Himalaya, the Friendship Highway stands alongside the Manali-Leh road and the Karakoram Highway as a fantastic adventure through different cultures and among high peaks, and possible within a four-week time span. It's a bit of a hassle and not cheap to fly in but it's possible and many people ride this route every summer and autumn. It is the hardest of those three rides too, with high altitude, some tough

---

TIBET HEALTH WARNINGS

Altitude Most of Tibet is over 4000m. Acclimatise properly before heading for the first high passes. Hospital facilities are poor and far apart.

Sun Use strong suncream on exposed parts of your body.

Weather A blizzard can trap you in a bad spot if you are not careful.

River During the monsoon, there may be some very wild rivers to cross.

Flash floods Be careful not to camp too close to river beds: during heavy weather they can rise by several metres in a very short period of time.

Landslides and rock falls Sounds crazy, but in the east, this is a very nasty hazard.

Truck convoys Visibility can drop to zero when large numbers of trucks whip up clouds of dust.

Dogs Crazed from starvation, huge Tibetan mastiffs sometimes attack without cause.

Stone throwers Violent beggars who sometimes bombard you with rocks unless you hand over what they want. Blame the package tourists in the Landcruisers for this.

High passes Plan ahead in order not to have to stop in a switchback section where you can't pitch your tent.   **Janne Corax**

HOTELS AND HANGOUTS IN LHASA

Lhasa's Chinese side has expanded so much that the old Tibetan city is now referred to as the Tibetan Quarter, and that's where you want to stay. It's almost impossible to make a reservation at the old classic traveller hotels in the centre, but take a chance and head there. The *Yak Hotel* is the best quality and has a good clean dorm and some Tibetan style rooms at the back. The courtyard is a good place to work on your bike. The *Snowlands* is cheaper and closest to the Jokhang, the very centre of Lhasa and the place to go for the short kora (ritual walking circuit), around the Barkhor, every evening. The *Snowlands Restaurant* is the best in town and has great curries. *Banak Shol Hotel* (my favourite) is a little further away but half the guests are Tibetan and the excellent rooftop restaurant is run by a Nepali who brings in gruyère-like Nepali cheese (it keeps well in your panniers). If all these are full, head to the north side of Beijing road east of the Yak to find *Pilgrim's Hotel* in the backstreets, cheaper than all of these and very atmospheric.

Spinn Café, just off the south side of Beijing Ave, is the cyclists' hangout, founded by two adventure-touring bikers who rode up from Bangkok and decided to settle in Lhasa. Spinn is an all-day restaurant that also sells spare parts for Western mountain bikes and gives a lot of free advice not just on cycling but also on the present situation for visas and permits. Check out 💻 www.spinn.cn/en.

Spinn Café's cyclist owners, Kong and Oat

unpaved passes and fierce storms and headwinds possible and the uncertainty of political or bureaucratic troubles too – it's never an entirely legal thing but most years, all goes well.

The Friendship Highway is best savoured slowly just as the other rides are. There's Lhasa itself to see while you acclimatise, visiting not just the Jokhang and Potala palace (reserve timed-entry tickets as soon as you arrive) but also riding out to the local monasteries, Sera, Drepung and Nechung just a few kilometres uphill. A great one-nighter acclimatisation ride is to go east to Ganden monastery, sitting on a spur some 500m of switchback dirt road above the main road. You can camp, walk a little higher for the views and head back the next day. Ganden was once the scene of a revolt and is sure to have a police presence.

Access

Fly in via Chengdu, Kunming or by train from Qinghai in central China. Get your Tibet Travel Permit in one of these places. At the time of writing, cycling into Tibet required a guide, but the rules will ease again in time.

The ride

It's 957km to Kathmandu, or 1158km including Everest Base Camp (EBC). There are five major passes, three are over 5000m and there's easy Pang La at 5162m on the EBC turnoff. It also has the world's longest downhill: a 4000m drop into Nepal. Allow at least 18 cycling days, including EBC side-trip. No

TRIP REPORT
CHINA TO PAKISTAN

Name	Chris Scott
Year of birth	1960
Occupation	Travel writer
Nationality	British
Other bike travels	None, just day rides

This trip	China, Pakistan
Trip duration	4 weeks
Number in group	Two
Total distance	800km
Cost of trip	About £1000 with flights

Longest day	90kms, much of it downhill
Best day	Riding out of Kashgar and all the days that followed
Worst day	None on this trip

Favourite ride	Karakoram Highway!
Biggest headache	Being forced to take the bus on the Chinese section
Biggest mistake	For a beginner I did OK
Pleasant surprise	How easy and what fun it was
Any illness	Amazingly, none, but we were careful with water

Bike model	Specialized HR Pro
New/used	Worn ex-rental picked up in Kashgar
Modifications	Brought my own tyres, seat, rack & panniers
Wish you'd had	Fatter tyres, bigger bike

Tyres used	Old Schwalbe City Jets – fast but thin for the load
Punctures	One

Baggage Setup	OMM rack with Ortliebs and holdall on top, nothing on the front
Wish you'd brought	Less bulky sleeping mat (I had an Exped mat)
Wish you'd left	Sooner

Bike problems	Cracking rim, broke spokes, crappy gear change, seized-up forks, worn pads
Accidents	None
Same bike again	As it happens yes, but only the frame remains
Next trip will be...	Ladakh, Spiti & Kinnaur
Recommendations	Don't wait till you're 50!

Any advice?	Maybe in a few years...

special precautions are needed, there is plenty of fresh water and camping is easy. There are no regular buses along most of the way.

The road is mostly paved nowadays, though it won't be on the toughest parts – the tops of the passes. The ride out of Lhasa is easy enough and the entire first day is flat. Kampa La, many riders' first high pass, is 1100m of climbing but it's well paved and simply a matter of bringing enough Snickers bars to keep you going. The dropoff is not much, you stay high and break through the 5000m mark at Karo La. Gyantse is a worthy rest day though there are no good traveller hotels and it's a flat, fast ride to Shigatse. Shalu gompa, 7 or 8km on a dirt road to the south of the main road, is worth a visit. As with all monasteries, those less visited are often the most rewarding, if only because there is usually less interference from the Chinese authorities.

Shigatse is becoming a Chinese town, but the Tenzin Guesthouse is a classic traveller budget hangout in the Tibetan quarter where you will feel at home. Take a rest day to visit the Tashilunpo, home of the Chinese-favoured Panchen Lama, check on progress at the reconstruction of the fort and possibly get a travel permit (ask at Tenzin Guesthouse) for onward travel – it's debatable if you really need it. I bought it and was never asked, the French riders I was with didn't buy it and said 'See!' in that teasing way every time we got through checkpoints together.

Two days later and you arrive at Lhatse. Sakya gompa, a turn-off south of the main highway, is a high profile and imposing monastery and should be visited if you aren't gompa-ed out by now. Lhatse itself is a fairly scruffy and windy Chinese-dominated town but the friendly courtyard-style Tibetan Farmers Hotel, with atmospheric short-drop toilets, is welcoming and serves simple but good food. It's a great place to start the long haul up Gyatso La, the toughest pass. At the top it's fairly flat for some 20km and there's little shelter if a storm or high winds kick up, which means the potential for a cold and headachey night at 4800m if not planned well... The next day is a 50km ride down to the cosy and friendly Tibetan village of Baipa, just 12km short of the turnoff to EBC. Pang La blocks your view of Everest from Baipa.

These last few days in Tibet are magical, the villages are small and largely free from Chinese influence and by asking (or Tibetans very obviously offering) you will find great guesthouse accommodation for next to nothing. Tibetan restaurants can be poor and filthy, but the homes can be much better and it's a non-tourist experience. The passes are easy now, the land becomes colder and more barren around Everest and it's usually windy. The great downhill begins after what is really a double pass you can do in a few hours – Lalung La and Yarle Shalung La. It's exciting at first but beware the headwinds that are so strong they are marked on some maps as if a permanent feature. But on a good day it won't blow and you'll fly. Lots of villagers on the way would

Gyantse

EVEREST BASE CAMP

If you've got the time and the energy, then go for it. You can certainly get close to EBC or at least to Rongbuk, if necessary hitching or hiring a vehicle to get you up there. Pang La (5160m) is crossed by a gentle switchback of

© Joff Summerfield

900m – on the other side of the pass, once you've taken your photos with Mt Everest behind you, it's a fine mountain bike ride down, leaving the switchbacks altogether and flying down the mountainside. There is a wonderful guesthouse and bar in Tashi Dzom where the village gathers every evening and half of them sleep over. The road to EBC becomes washboarded after this point thanks to Landcruisers in a hurry. You'll spend the night with the Landcruiser crowd at Rongbuk, or camp. It's worth taking the shortcut to Tingri described in *Himalaya by Bike* – you will see Tibetans from time to time to check the direction, but all roads eventually run into the vast and beautiful Tingri Plain and lead to the main road and the town itself where there are more guesthouses serving thukpa (stew with handmade noodles) around a burning fire.

love to host you and will try to wave you down, but if you don't have headwinds, it's best to keep riding. Milarepa's Cave is one good last option for a Tibetan-style homestay if the gompa is closed. Soon after is the Chinese army town of Nyalam (checkpoint hidden round a corner just before entering) after which the hard-core descent begins. You will soon see trees as the climate changes dramatically, almost certainly ending the day in short sleeves and if you want, shorts too. But it's a stony road in places that will shake you and your bike to pieces so use your rest stops to check the bike over for anything loose. Zhangmu, the Chinese border town, has good Chinese food – savour it as you won't find anything better until Kathmandu. Nepal is lush and green, the sights and smells too much to take in. You will soon roll past the seedy border scene and on into heavenly Nepal. After so much high-altitude training, the 900m climb to Kathmandu, all paved, should be no problem, with plenty of refreshment and mountain-viewing stops along the way.

The Tibetan epic – Kashgar to Lhasa

One of the longest, highest and hardest routes in the world, the ride across west Tibet from Kashgar to Lhasa continues to attract a handful of determined cyclists every summer. A west Tibet ride is all about the human spirit and whether you've got what it takes. Don't undertake this ride lightly, there are other, more pleasant routes in the region for carefree riding – the KKH is a cakewalk by comparison. But the rewards of travelling to such a remote place under your own steam, self-supported and entirely exposed to nature, are immense. Cameron Smith (see p62) told me that after battling through west Tibet, riding into Lhasa and seeing the Potala was one of the greatest days of his life.

The ride

Easier than it used to be but can still be difficult if the rivers are running high and tracks are scattered as trucks look for alternative crossing places. Nearly all the road is unpaved, however and washboarded or rocky in many places. The first 265km is flat and straightforward, ending at the large town of Yecheng (all amenities). The hard stuff begins when you turn onto Highway 219 – note the zero KM marker and breathe the last rich air (1340m in altitude) for a few months. Just over 200km later, you'll be brushing the 5000m mark on the Chiragsaldi pass. The descent only takes you down to 3800m – you may not be properly acclimatised even to that altitude, so it's vital that you go as slowly as you can on the ascent to Chiragsaldi. The next 300km never go lower than around 3600m and mark the end of Uighur settlements, few though there are, and you'll see more army camps and grotty truck stops.

Aksai Chin is a sensitive region in that China surreptitiously annexed it in 1962, but it remains more or less uninhabited, except for army bases. The army won't want the hassle of dealing with you as they'd have to take you to the nearest police station; it's easier for them to ignore you and let you ride on to Ali or another checkpoint. Nonetheless cyclists occasionally get a welcome, food, tea or hospitality from the Chinese army in such remote places. It's all high plateau which is mostly around 5000m for the next 250km, then rarely dips below 4000m until the home stretch into Lhasa. The thirty-one passes on this route, nine of which are over 5000m, are not long climbs compared with the

---

KASHGAR TO LHASA: IT'S ALL IN THE PREPARATION

1: Training. This is not a beginner's ride, so train to build fitness and stamina and if possible add a few extra kilos of fat which you will surely lose, and more, during the ride. The road is at high altitude almost the entire distance. Don't race up to altitude just because you're fit enough to do so. Expect the first week at altitude to be painful no matter how hard you've trained.

2: The bike. Make sure your bike is rock-solid with no weak points. It's no place to say 'I knew I should have fixed that before...'. You can get through on a touring bike but it will be far less comfortable on thin tyres than on thick mountain bike tyres. Everyone who has a choice rides on Marathon XRs (see p47).

3: Food and water. Take sufficient water-carrying capacity for 15L, the most you might need for some sections, and five days' food. It won't be high quality nutrition along the way, a combination of instant noodles fortified with whatever you can find – tinned fish, eggs or dried veg with Chinese Army biscuits if you're lucky. Any kind of Dove

chocolate is pretty good: buy all you can find. Forget rice and oats – they make a big mess because of the low boiling point of water at altitude. Take some multivitamins – one rider told me her hair began to fall out towards the end of the ride and her eyes were weak for some time afterwards.

4: Visa. You'll need a 3-month Chinese visa, easy to get in Hong Kong. If you can't fly there and can only get a 2-month visa, alternatively you could turn off the road at Saga and cut across past Shishapangma (highest peak entirely inside China at 8012m) base camp and join the Friendship Highway. It's a rough road but you'd have only a short climb on the Friendship Highway before the long descent into Nepal. You would need to be a strong rider and perhaps would not have time to do the Kailash kora, but you'd make it. You might also obtain a 3-month China visa in Almaty in Kazakhstan or in Islamabad. Assume you cannot extend a China visa anywhere in Tibet, though you can elsewhere east of Tibet. You can get a Nepal visa either in Lhasa or at the border.

Inside a Tibetan guesthouse.

Friendship Highway or east Tibet, but they're all at altitude and it's unlikely you'll be racing over any of them.

Around 120km before Ali there is the first tarmac you've seen in a long time, and it runs all the way into Ali, which looks like a mirage, a totally misplaced small Chinese city in Tibet. In Ali, either you 'fess up to being in Tibet illegally or they come and find you, but the fine'n'permit for ¥350, about € 40, is a rite of passage and few avoid it. You might be risking your bike getting confiscated if you don't get the permit, but you might also never be asked for it. Ali is where you find hot showers (use the public showers if you can't afford a hotel with them) and a place to rest up, wash and catch up on email.

From Ali eastwards, the intervals between settlements and supplies is generally shorter (apart from one 231km shop-free stretch) and it's a bit lower too, though the state of the roads is no better. A side trip to the Guge Kingdom south of the main road is an option, but it's a bad road ploughed up by Landcruisers and with two passes higher than 5300m. Mt Kailash is on the route and few resist the urge, indeed the duty, to make a circuit of the mountain on foot – even if you're not a Tibetan Buddhist, Bon or Hindu, it can't hurt in Karmic terms! Take food and a mat but leave the tent with your bike. That spiritual high and the prayer flags will carry you through the temporal low and swirling plastic bag garbage town of Darchen that feeds on the tourist trade to Kailash. If you have time and energy, the 100km kora around Lake Manasarovar is also good for the soul.

Saga has internet and a chance to stock up on food. The big checkpoint is on the road going to Lhasa, so if you're heading to Nepal, you avoid it. This latter route is fairly hard and less travelled but passes close to Shishapang-ma and the holy Paiku Lake before joining the Friendship Highway just before the big drop. If you're headed to the Far East and want to visit Everest Base Camp (see box p150), this is the way to go without serious backtracking and saves

Aksai Chin camping
© Peter Quaife

you a pretty big pass (Gyatso-La). If you're short on time or want to head down to Nepal, this is the quick way.

If you stay on the main road to Lhasa, you join the Friendship Highway just before Lhatse (Tibetan Farmers Hotel recommended for atmosphere, food and other travellers' company) and are only a day or two away from the bright lights of Shigatse. Most of the Friendship Highway is now paved, but don't race; on the way to Shigatse, make sure you take the short turnoff to Sakya gompa and spend a little time in Gyantse too for its sights, which are the old town, the giant Kumbum stupa and the fort. Consider a short stop at the gompa at Nam on your last day riding into Lhasa. It's by the road and often overlooked, and hence more welcoming to those who take the time to visit.

Eastern Tibet – Lhasa to Markham

Open-closed-open: that's the way the eastern route between Lhasa and the rest of China has been for many years for foreigners. Generally it's easier to get out of Tibet than into it though there have been cases where cyclists were sent back the way they came, which then led to cyclists saying they'd actually come from Lhasa in order to be allowed to ride there! It's in Eastern Tibet that you hear of cyclists doing the midnight shuffle around checkpoints whereas the situation in west Tibet

This Chinese cyclist rode a single-speed bike from Guangzhou to Kashgar.
© Peter Quaife

tends to be more open (the terrain itself deters all but the most determined). More than all the other routes, the road east changes from year to year and the best you can do is to find reliable but anecdotal evidence on the internet and then from cyclists coming the other way as you ride.

Eastern Tibet is unlike western or central Tibet in terms of terrain and people. It's a land of roller-coaster passes with huge climbs and descents – both directions are equally hard. It's farmland and relatively wealthy; you'll see new housebuilding in the Tibetan style, and seemingly every valley has its own unique style. Nomads are uncommon, but in the autumn, every day you will pass pilgrims walking to Lhasa, prostrating every step, and now and again a few cycling pilgrims even. The eastern road passes through the only part of Tibet that lies below (just) 2000m, where you will see bamboo trees and might actually get a mosquito bite in summer. It's humid and can be uncomfortably so in that region but the whole of eastern Tibet is considerably less dry than the west, with far more tree cover. That's good for wild camping, but usually you will be spotted unless you are far from villages. Depending on the level of police vigilance, you might avoid staying overnight in any town that has a permanent police presence as hotel owners are supposed to report foreign guests every night to the police. A couple of times we stayed in fairly basic Tibetan guesthouses where we were certain the owners wouldn't report us. Chinese hoteliers are far more likely to do so.

The passes on the eastern route will exhaust any cyclist. Three of the world's great rivers are crossed in their upper reaches – the Yarlung Tsangpo/Brahmaputra, the Salween and the Mekong, and if you turn south at Markham, you will cross the Yangtze close to Zhongdian/Shangri-la. The passes are huge, up to 2000m and the longest of them should be tackled in two days. Yes, someone's probably done them in one day, but forget that person, they are hard enough to do in two days without rest!

The ride

The road out of Lhasa is paved for 500km or more and it's a beautiful ride through mountainous valleys. Ganden monastery, about 50km into the ride, is a nice side-trip if you fancy a 500m climb, but there's good camping by the road if you want to stop there anyway. It might be wiser to go further and camp higher to acclimatise if you started riding in Lhasa. The first pass is high at 5013m but the climb isn't too hard. The descent the other side is only to 4300m. Many of the early towns have PSB offices; it's not a good idea to linger in internet cafés but you can probably shop if you tuck the bikes out of sight. Bayi (the first of the three 'Bs', with Bomi and Baxoi further east) is the first large army town with a big PSB office, but with a sizable covered market. It's a climb to Sekye La followed by a long (80km) descent on good road to the subtropical part of Tibet. Beautiful scenery, big wooden barns and exotic trees and bushes. The road turns to dirt at the bottom and can be muddy and dan-

---

A SOUTHERN VARIATION VIA TSETANG

A slightly longer but flatter route that rejoins the main road at Bayi is to go via Tsetang, an interesting destination in itself for access to numerous monasteries and the Valley of the Kings to the south of Tsetang. It's an open area until after Tsetang and cyclists are sometimes turned back in the towns along the route – watch out in Nang.

Leave Lhasa heading west for the airport and take the airport turnoff, through the tunnel and left again. There are hotels just outside the airport and camping after that. There are also some cheap hotels in Tsetang itself and tourist restaurants, including a branch of Tashi, the popular Lhasa restaurant. Tsetang and the surrounding area is the cradle of Tibetan civilisation – one of three caves in the mountainside to the east of the town is said to be the birthplace of the Tibetan people, who resulted from the mating of a monkey and a beautiful cannibal ogress. There are many monasteries in the valley and the famous Samye monastery 30km to the east. An easy day ride is to the Valley of Kings to the south, all well paved. There are burial mounds of the Tibetan kings and more monasteries to visit though the spirit is flagging in a few which have a strong Chinese plain-clothes police presence. Generally it seems that where the admission price is raised to ¥100, the gompa is a tourist attraction and the police are collecting the money. Often the less distinguished gompas are therefore a more natural experience, particularly as far as interaction with the monks

goes. We camped with permission inside Tsetang gompa in the old town, but in times of tension this would have put the monks in some danger. The abbot is bound to refuse any money you offer, but drop it in a box inside the gompa as a donation. Take a boat across the Yarlung Tsanpo to visit Samye. There's a trek from Samye to Ganden described in Trailblazer's Tibet Overland.

After Samye there is one more town then a 1100m climb over a dusty pass that is rocky on the eastern side. From here to Bayi, you are in a valley riding next to the river on unpaved road, camping unless you feel comfortable there are no police around. Some villages have small Muslim communities – their restaurants are clean and serve good food. This valley is probably closed and the reaction of villagers – shyness – suggests that they see few foreigners. Just keep moving, especially through larger towns, and hopefully you'll pass through without incident. As you approach the end of the valley there is Lamaling gompa built in the Chinese style in the last village you pass through. It's a short detour 7km or so uphill but well worth it. As the valley opens up, you need to cross the river, if you can, before the road crosses over to Bayi west of the town. It's a wide braided river and it may be possible to cross further south and thus avoid a large part of the town and the army base. Bayi has a large market but there's no shortage of food in this region and if you don't feel you can stop, you won't starve.

gerous, with rockfalls from the high-sided gorge. There are hot springs next to the road, but it's a bit of a scramble down to get to them. At this low point of 1950m you cross the Yarlung Tsangpo, the same river that runs east-west across Tibet, now turning south to become the Brahmaputra. There's no avoiding the army checkpoints in this narrow valley, not even at night, as one is over a high bridge, but you'll probably get through with smiles; the towns are the places they might collar you.

East Tibet: forested and lush

Now begins a long 250km climb but it's so gentle you will hardly notice it, distracted by alpine-looking peaks in the region known as Little Switzerland. Ride through Bomi (another good covered market) on to Rawok at the end of this section, with excellent camping near the lake. An easy pass is followed by drier terrain and more deep valleys and passes. Baxoi is another big army town but we found an atmospheric Tibetan guesthouse on the edge of town, good food and public showers. This is your last shopping opportunity before the giant Gama La, the 72-switchback pass (we tried to check but lost count), which begins as you cross the enormous Salween river. There are villages with small shops on the western side of the pass but you can always ask for a good place to camp if you can't find one. The drop on the eastern side is only 600m to a significant junction (and better shops). The road left leads to Chamdo, but take the right, leading down another long and gentle farming valley leading to a quite big town, Dzogong, with all the facilities you need and the unwanted ones too – police and PSB. It's a good place to stay as it sets you up for the next day, an easy dirt road climb of 1200m followed by a massive 1400m descent towards the Mekong. There's an overpriced Chinese-run guest house in Deng Ba village at the bottom of the hill, but it has a very tempting fireplace and good food.

After seeing the Mekong for the first time, another small pass leads to breathtaking views and another big drop down to 2800m. It's a long climb out through dusty red rocks but still beautiful farmland and friendly villagers who will help if you can't see an obvious camping place. The switchback section of the last pass before Markham is not bad at all and after that, it's a short run into town and all the amenities. The hotels are on the entry into town, the police and internet are further down in the centre, which features a combination of some new Chinese and old Tibetan architecture.

Camping in Little Switzerland

PART 2 – ROUTE OUTLINES

THE DOGS OF MARKHAM

We had both heard of the dogs of Markham from reports on the internet and seen hand-written remarks about them drawn on a map we looked at in Lhasa before leaving. Said to live in a farm just west of town, the beasts wreak havoc on cyclists slipping out of town in the wee hours. Having run the gauntlet of army checkpoints and prowling police cars, we were now on the last pass, wondering whether there would be a checkpoint and how bad the dogs might be. Dominique, my French riding partner, pulled out a secret weapon – some firecrackers. Fantastic idea! We tried to light one to test our firepower, but in the high winds it kept blowing out. Unreliable – no good. We gathered stones, a stick and an old fan belt and started down the mountain. 'When the dogs come out, we've got to stick together, no running away...' I shouted to my French friend, a little Anglo-French jibe that got blown away in the wind as we gathered speed. We flew past a long line of army trucks parked on the hill, another empty convoy whose purpose seemed to be a show of strength rather than transporting anyone or anything. C.W.

McCall's trucker song Convoy played in my head.... 'we crashed the gate doing 98...' as we hit asphalt and raised the pace a bit. Dom's been carrying only a left-side front pannier for weeks due to a broken rack, but it doesn't seem to slow him on corners.

We can see the army base, the barrier's up, only the dogs to worry about now. Over there, on the left, we see a couple of huskies in front of a farmhouse – tied up. Yes, they're pleased to see us too. They would love to make our closer acquaintance, for sure, and are letting us know they're hungry for blood, but they're definitely tied up. We laugh and realise immediately that these dogs are only unleashed to guard the farm at night – when cyclists ride by. In the day, they're no threat.

We celebrate our ride over a bottle of Chinese red wine and wander down to the wangba (internet café). The police chief is there, he has a Darth Vader look, a long black cape or coat over his shoulders, and though he scowls at us, he's more interested in his game of Dungeons and Dragons than in nabbing two cyclists. We've made it.

Leaving Tibet – south to Zhongdian & Dali on the Yunnan Highway

Tibetan culture extends into northern Yunnan and the large town of Zhongdian, now known as Shangri-la, is a bit of a tourist trap focussed on various colourful ethnic groups living in the area. After Tibet, it feels a luxurious, wealthy place with all the amenities you might need or want and comfortable places to stay. You'll feel welcome rather than a fugitive as you are in some parts of Tibet.

From Markham a fairly flat farming valley runs to the south. It's good riding but the 800m pass, not too difficult, takes you to stunning mountain views of sharply pointed peaks opposite and the Mekong valley 1800m below. It's a beautiful 40km further to the large town of Yenjing, which boasts perhaps the most remote Christian church in China. Along the way to Yenjing, look out for unique ethnic villages on the almost unreachable far side of the river. The border with Yunnan is only a little way further. It's palpably different from Tibet though still majority Tibetan for some way yet. The road drops further, down to the Mekong before winding round a tributary and beginning a long climb, with very distracting views across the river and a good surface at the top. The tourist resort of Meilixueshan at the top has a faux-European look to it and fantastic views of Mt Kawa Karpo across the Mekong, a peak so steep no one has yet bagged it though it has two koras (pilgrim circuits) of four and ten days each.

A short ride downhill leads to Deqin (pronounced Dechen), with an old town and a few traveller guesthouses. It's still almost 200km to Zhongdian, with few villages and little development along frequently forested roads, some paved, though some with cobblestones, which might make you wish you were back on dirt.

From Zhongdian, a trip down Tiger Leaping Gorge is a must and the small city of Dali is good for an extended rest stop, with some Tibetan-style guesthouses for those who miss the high life, in the middle of a fairly large backpacker and travellers' oasis of cheap guesthouses and excellent food, including pizzas as good as you'll find anywhere.

CYCLING IN CHINA'S SOUTH-WEST

Bill Weir

Centuries ago, the Chinese lived mainly along the east coast and called the wild and mountainous territory to their south-west, the 'South-West'. Today the name lives on even though China has pushed its borders far to the west and this region is geographically in the south-east. It comprises the five provinces hemmed in by Tibet and Myanmar on the west, Laos and Vietnam on the south, and the coastal plain provinces of Guangdong, Hunan, and Hubei on the east. For cyclists, the South-West offers incredible cultural diversity and scenic splendour. In Yunnan, for example, you can start in the tropical south inhabited by peoples of South-East Asian cultures, move north through regions populated by ancient highland cultures, then reach Tibetan areas amongst glacier-clad summits in the north-west – all in just one province! Each province has its own distinctive landscapes and peoples – there's much to discover. You can also drop into provincial capitals for good museums, spacious parks, and cultural life. Try to get a regional guidebook for South-West China because the all-China guidebooks omit many interesting out-of-the-way places. Spring (Mar-May) and autumn (Sep-Oct) generally have the best weather in the region. Summer has the highest rainfall and can be very hot except at high elevations. Winter sees much of the region freezing, but southern Yunnan can be very pleasant; Guangxi is damp with 'rain dust' in March – rideable, but with little sun. Good flight and rail connections make it easy to reach your starting and ending points; all of the provincial capitals have flights to neighbouring countries and Chengdu offers flights to Europe.

Yunnan

It's been said that if you only have time to see one province in China, then head for Yunnan. It's extremely scenic from the rice terraces in the south to the icy Himalaya in the north. There's a price for this splendour – the province is overwhelmingly hilly. So slap on the low gearing and enjoy. Ethnic minorities comprise about half the population, and you'll find nearly half of China's minority groups here. Many of those in the south practise the same Theravadan Buddhism as neighbouring Laos, Thailand, and Myanmar. Five of Asia's major rivers cut deeply into rugged landscapes – the Nujiang (Salween), Mekong, Yangzi, and Red. Yunnan's most exciting ride is a grand tour the length of the province, taking one to two months. This could include a ride through rugged mountains in the far south near the Laos and Vietnam borders, connecting Laos or Jinghong with Kunming via Jiangsheng, Luchun, Yuanyang, Gejiu, Jianshui, and Tonghai.

Central Yunnan has many traditional villages surrounding Dali that can inspire loop rides. A few days farther north, you'll see icy peaks of the Himalaya from the extremely picturesque town of Lijiang. It gets even better as you continue north to Tiger Leaping Gorge, which you can cycle all the way through. From the east end of Tiger Leaping Gorge a very scenic road climbs into Tibetan country and leads to Shangri La (Zhongdian), which has a large Tibetan temple complex. Further into the north-west you can cross the Yangzi River, make a stiff climb over a triple pass to Deqin, ride down and across the Mekong River, then hike alongside Mingyong Glacier. If you wish to get away from the backpacker hordes, head for the far west and follow roads that roughly parallel the Myanmar border all the way from Laos to the edge of Tibet, the last part up the increasingly spectacular Nujiang Valley. The Boten (Laos)-Mohan (China) border crossing in the far south is very popular with cyclists, and you can reach it from Thailand in just four cycling days now that the Huay Xai-Boten road is fully paved. Further east, the Lao Cai (Vietnam)-Hekou (China) crossing is another popular option. Yunnan also has the only available China-Myanmar border crossing, located near Ruili in the west; you'll need a special visa from the Myanmar consulate in Kunming and help from a travel agent to do this, which seems possible only from China to Myanmar.

Sichuan

This vast province includes expanses of Tibetan plateau in the west and the fertile Sichuan Basin in the east where even bananas grow. For high adventures, head west into the Tibetan areas, perhaps as an extension of a ride from Yunnan in the south or Qinghai or Gansu in the north—all Tibetan areas as well. Or just head west from Chengdu; you can be in the mountains within a day's ride, but take care to go slowly enough to acclimatise. Southern Sichuan includes challenging mountain terrain as well, but here populated by many minority groups as well as Han Chinese. You'll also experience rugged mountains north of Chengdu. Both south and north contain major cultural sites and important parks renowned for scenery. Other than the large and lively provincial capital of Chengdu, the Sichuan Basin gets little attention from cyclists, but Langzhong, north-east of Chengdu, is famed for its traditional architecture.

Chongqing

Technically a municipality, Chongqing straddles a section of the Yangzi east of Sichuan. The hilly terrain in the city of Chongqing deters most cyclists, but you'll find many historic sites and museums here. Boat tours cruise the Yangzi River downstream if you'd like a few days off the bicycle. The Dazu area, 125km north-west of Chongqing, has dazzling Buddhist grotto art; worth a detour if you're in the area.

Guizhou

Picturesque minority villages spread across wildly scenic hills in the eastern part of this province. It's nearly all good riding, and if you enjoy cycling in the hills, there's even a road to the top of Leigong Mountain (2178m). The scenery keeps on going in the west with some of China's best caves and waterfalls. Longgong Caves make a great daytrip from Anshun; trails and boat trips link a long series of large and small caves. Zhijin Cave will amaze you for its vast chambers filled with ornate and highly varied cave features; it's near the town of Zhijin, a day's ride north of Anshun. Huangguoshu Falls, a day's ride south-west of Anshun, rank among Asia's largest.

Guangxi
Come here to experience those impossibly steep limestone pinnacles so often pictured on Chinese landscape paintings. The scenery is for real, and you can experience it by cycling on backroads near Yangshuo or on a Li River boat cruise. Minority villages just north of Guilin have spectacular rice terraces and intriguing wind-and-rain bridges; from here you might continue into eastern Guizhou to experience additional minority culture. Many other parts of the province offer fine landscapes, with hardly a Western tourist in sight. The south has a bit of seacoast with beaches on the Gulf of Tonkin. Two border crossings connect the province with Vietnam—on the coast at Dongxing and north-east of Hanoi at Pingxiang (Friendship Pass). You could also reach Guangxi by cycling west across Guangdong Province from Hong Kong or, more easily, from Macau.

Mongolia

Edward Genochio

Like Timbuktu in Africa, the very name Mongolia invokes images of extreme remoteness but in Mongolia's case the image is still accurate. Today, thanks to the fall of the Soviet empire which used the country as a buffer state against China, you can find out for yourself. This is a country which has yet to shake off its nomadic origins. Outside the capital Ulaan Baator (UB), most of the population lives in gers (yurts or felt tents) and there is no evidence of even the most rudimentary infrastructure. There is only one road, north from Russia to China via Ulaan Baator. Elsewhere intermittent tracks wind across the grassy plains from one settlement to another. If you can't get your adventure cycling rocks off in Mongolia it's time to try another planet.

If you're making that haul between Russia and China, the simplest route takes you from the northern border at Kyakhta (Russia)/Altanbulag (Mongolia) to Zamyn Uud (Mongolia)/Erlian (aka Eren, or Erlianhaote, in China). This way will take you through Ulaan Baator where it's easy to pick up a Chinese visa from the embassy there.

Crossing into Mongolia from Russia at Kyakhta/Altanbulag is straightforward: the border is open every day and assuming your visas are in order you can ride across with minimal hassle. There are other border crossings from Russia into Mongolia, further west from Tashanta (Altay Republic, Russia) to

Tsagaanuur (in the far west of Mongolia) but this would be a seriously remote cross-country ride requiring very long range and stamina. An attractive option due to open soon is the crossing from Khandagayty in Tuva (Russia) to near Lake Uvs-Nuur in north-western Mongolia. The crossing from Mondy (Russia) to Khankh (Mongolia) would connect up a fine route between Lake Baikal (Siberia) and Lake Hövsgöl (northern Mongolia), if it were ever to open.

For now, the simplest route into Mongolia from the north takes you on the road from Altanbulag to UB; a stretch of about 340km is on high-quality paved road, and you can't get lost so long as you stay on the metalled surface. If you are planning side trips on other roads, you'll need good gesticulatory communication skills or a GPS and a good map (try the American, half-million TPC series) because signposts are virtually unknown. But then, so are roads as we know them.

FROM MONGOLIA TO CHINA

If you're coming to China from Mongolia, the border crossing is a little more complicated. The Mongolian authorities may allow you to ride across their 5km section of No-Man's Land, but they'd rather you put your bike in the back of one of the many vans that shuttle between the border posts every day. Even if you do succeed in riding to the Chinese side, you'll be thwarted in your attempt to ride 'the whole way' from Mongolia to China by the border guards who will insist you load your bike into a vehicle, at least for the 200 metres or so between the two gates of their customs compound. Alternatively, it's easy enough to take your bike on the trains that run from UB to Erlian over the Chinese border.

CROSSING THE GOBI

At the time of writing the road and rail crossing at Zamyn Uud/Erlian is the only one on the long Mongolian-Chinese border open to foreigners. A brand new road is being built across the Gobi to connect the border to the Mongolian capital. When I rode the route in the autumn of 2004, 140km of road had been completed, leaving 550 roadless kilometres across the desert. Sometimes there are decent tracks; the trick is to work out which one heads for the border and which goes off to someone's ger behind the sand dune on the horizon.

GPS – GER POSITIONING SYSTEM

If you find yourself disoriented and out of batteries while out on the steppe, an alternative to conventional satellite-based GPS navigation in Mongolia is the local variant: the Ger Positioning System. Low-tech but reliable, this: Mongolian gers (yurts) always have their doorways pointing south. Keep following the doorways, and you'll reach the Chinese border; head in the opposite direction, and it's only a matter of time before you're in Russia.

(Opposite) The Friendship Highway (see p146). This well-known cycling route runs 957km from Lhasa to Kathmandu, or 1158km including the side trip to Everest Base Camp. **Top**: Yak beside part of the world's longest downhill, a drop of more than 4000m over 160kms. (Photo © Peter Gostelow). **Bottom**: Ultra-light tourer surveys the Potala Palace, Lhasa. (Photo © Sabine Leu).

(Overleaf) Yamdrok Lake, one of the three holiest (and bluest) lakes in Tibet, seen from Kampa La on the Friendship Highway. (Photo © Peter Gostelow).

Sometimes the tracks become faint or disappear altogether for long stretches; get used to it, this is Mongolia. Unfortunately, where the tracks are clear and well-used, they're usually badly corrugated by passing traffic, so a bit of suspension makes riding more comfortable. Be rigorous about tightening your bolts out here when riding long distances on washboard surfaces. I lost a rack half way across the Gobi as a result of failing to do this.

It would be unwise to attempt the crossing without a compass or GPS – at least until the road is completed. Much of the way you can ride within sight of the railway line, so you can use that as your guide. Maps show the 'road' crossing back and forth across the railway, but in reality there are tracks on both sides and it is simply a matter of picking which track seems least bad. Invariably, the better track is on the other side of the railway. Storm channels running under the railway every few kilometres allow you to cross from one side of the tracks to the other when you feel the urge. Around 150km of the route goes through extremely arid dry desert with virtually no vegetation at all. For the most part it's stony desert, some of it not bad for riding on, but there are long sandy stretches where pushing is required, and lots of hidden sandy patches which will stop your bike dead and send you flying over the handlebars – to a soft sandy landing.

If you stick close to the railway, you'll find settlements of some sort every 50km or so, so carrying huge quantities of water may not be necessary, though given the high probability of getting lost for a while, it'd be wise to carry at least a couple of days' supply of water at all times. Plastic jerry cans can be bought at the 'Black Market' in Ulaan Baator. The piped water in the Gobi towns is pretty foul – it certainly needs sterilising – but bottled water is also available.

Look out for half-buried lengths of barbed wire which seem to stretch across the Gobi and could put a nice hole in your tyre if you go over them. Keep an eye on the horizon, too, for approaching sandstorms. They are most common in the spring but can strike at any time – one descended on me in mid-September and lasted all day. There's not a lot you can do to avoid them but they can cut visibility to just a few metres and the airborne grit will shred your eyeballs in any case if you try to open your eyes. Your only defence is to lie low and wait for the worst to blow over. On the plus side, you'll find your bike is spotlessly clean the next day – all the accumulated dirt and grime is sand-blasted away.

At time of writing, the road heading north from Zamyn Uud extends only about 100 metres beyond the edge of town, so if you're coming from China you've either got to plunge straight into desert riding or you can put your bike on the train as far as Choyr to skip the toughest stretch of the Gobi.

Other than the road from Ulaan Baator north to the Russian border at Altanbulag, and the beginnings of the road south to the Chinese border, there's precious little tarmac in Mongolia. All maps show a generous network of roads covering the whole country, even distinguishing between 'highways', primary and secondary roads, but 95% of these are unsealed tracks and paths, not all of them bikeable.

(Opposite) Top: Well off the beaten track in the Cardamom Hills, Cambodia (see p166). (Photo © Salva Rodriguez). **Bottom**: Another memorable day on the trip – sunrise on Christmas Day, Nepal. (Photo © Peter Gostelow).

South-East Asia offers much more than just tourist attractions though. A bicycle makes it possible to escape the tourist trail and experience some of the things that make this region special. For me it was the warmth and friendliness of people in the countryside, the bustling markets that no guidebooks ever wrote about and the colourful roadside festivals. It was also the smiles and waves of children as I cycled by that have lingered in my memory long after leaving.

The other great appeal is that the region is one of the cheapest places in the world to tour. A freshly-cooked meal from a street vendor can be bought for as little as $1, and $5-$10 will often get you a comfortable room for the night. As accommodation can be found in many small towns, camping equipment is less of a necessity. During six months in Vietnam, Cambodia, Thailand and Laos I pitched my tent less than half a dozen times.

The ease of securing visas and crossing borders adds to the appeal. Apart from Myanmar, there are very few restrictions on where you can go. Look at a map and start planning – there is an endless choice of roads to take and no-one will stop you from cycling them. The stories you have from the road are sure to impress many a bored backpacker when you arrive heroically in that guest-house only to hear them moan about the discomfort of a bus journey.

Planning

Choosing what time of year to tour here is important, particularly if you don't like rain. During the monsoon season (Jun-Sep) be prepared to get very wet at times. Non-surfaced roads can be twice as challenging to pedal and you'll be cleaning that chain more than you'd probably like to. It doesn't make a tour impossible. Mornings are often dry and rain clouds build up during the day before dumping their load in the afternoon. If you're carrying a lot of electrical equipment then make sure you've got some silica gel – cameras don't take kindly to high humidity.

October through to February is ideal for most of the region (Malaysia's east coast receives a lot of rain during this time though) after which the temperature begins to rise. Cycling in high heat and humidity is one of the greatest

challenges in the area. Fortunately bottled water is cheap and available to buy in most places.

If your tour is confined to just South-East Asia then two panniers and a handlebar bag will suffice. The simplicity of travelling light combined with the general safety of the region mean that a bicycle tour can be enjoyed by people with all levels of riding experience. Most major towns now have ATMs so withdrawing money is also relatively easy.

Even if your time is short in each country, it is worth learning the basics of the language. Away from major tourist hubs it can be hard to find many English speakers. I've always found having a pocket phrasebook to be as invaluable as a puncture repair kit, particularly when it comes to ordering food.

© Peter Gostelow

Good maps can be found in large cities like Bangkok, Kuala Lumpur and Singapore. In other places you'll have to make do with local maps or tourist ones – both can be out of date and inaccurate. Asking people for directions never hurts, but don't always assume you're getting the right answer.

Although South-East Asia may not provide the extreme adventure, empty roads and opportunities for wild camping that exist in, say, Tibet or Patagonia, it does offer the possibility of combining a moderately challenging tour with the security of good food and accommodation never far away.

Access

Unless you're arriving overland from China, Bangkok or Singapore is likely to be your first port of entry. Both provide a decent base from which to make a circular tour of several countries, although neither is very enjoyable to cycle out of. Transporting your bicycle on a bus or train may be a safer start to your tour.

Cycling in Myanmar involves flying into and out of the country, though there's an access point in China – the catch is it's the only overland exit. As appealing as it looks there is no overland route through the country to India or China and this is unlikely to change for the foreseeable future.

VIETNAM

Some love it and others hate it – Vietnam usually provokes mixed opinions from cyclists. If your experience is solely limited to travelling on Highway 1, the country's main road that connects Hanoi in the north with Ho Chi Minh City in the south, then you might quickly come to hate the traffic. Motorbikes rule the roads in Vietnam and their drivers need no encouragement in sounding the horn. Truck drivers are the same. Many cyclists end up on Highway 1 at least some of their time in Vietnam as it passes by historically interesting towns like Hue and Hoi An.

Cycling in Hanoi is not for the faint-hearted. © Peter Gostelow

Don't write Vietnam off because of its traffic though. In fact not all of Highway 1 is busy and there are minor roads branching off along parts of it that hug the coast. Here the deserted beaches and fishing bays have yet to witness the tourist influx and development that other parts of the coastline have seen, notably Nha Trang and Mui Ne. It's good news for cyclists as these beaches aren't accessible for the tour buses that ply the main roads.

The alternative to riding along the coast if heading north or south through the country is to use the

Having the coastal road to myself. Southern Vietnam. © Peter Gostelow

Inland Vietnam: mountain paradise
© Peter Gostelow

newly-paved Ho Chi Minh Highway, which runs inland through the Central Highlands and climbs up to the scenic hill station of Dalat. Traffic on this road is much quieter and the route offers an experience of Vietnam very different from that seen by the tourist herd clutching their guidebooks down by the coast. It's a more challenging and adventurous route, not least for the climbing, but also because of the long stretches between places.

North-west Vietnam is where the real mountains lie. A challenging but very rewarding ride is to head from Hanoi up the Red River valley towards Sapa and the Tram Ton pass (1900m) before looping round to Dien Bien Phu. From here there is the choice of either staying in Vietnam and returning towards Hanoi, or pushing on into the mountains of northern Laos. This region of Vietnam is usually a highlight for anyone cycling in the country as it passes through ethnically diverse villages where the modern world has yet to intrude. If your legs aren't in shape before you begin, they certainly will be afterwards. Accommodation can be found in small towns along the way.

The Mekong delta in the far south feels a world away from the mountains of the north and the central highlands. This heavily populated region is full of small roads that criss-cross the tributaries of this colossal river. Fruit abounds in the bustling town markets and it's a wonderfully colourful part of the country. You're unlikely to see another western face so join the locals for a glass of 'Bia Hoi' (surely the cheapest beer in the world at $0.20 a glass!) and a freshly-filled baguette (the best French influence in my opinion) before heading towards the Cambodian border.

CAMBODIA

It was once dubbed the Wild-West of South-East Asia, yet while Cambodia is still less developed than neighbouring Thailand and Vietnam, much has improved in the last decade. Road surfaces between most major towns are no longer of the pot-holed variety, and it's almost possible to traverse the country from east to west without leaving the asphalt. Even the famous Siem Reap-Poipet stretch, once the scourge of all who travelled it, has now been paved. Dirt roads do still exist, but unless you're heading off the beaten track

---

CULINARY ADVENTURE

Food in Cambodia is far less exciting than in neighbouring Thailand and Vietnam, unless you have a palate for fried bugs and spiders. Large towns such as Phnom Penh and Siem Reap offer more variety to cater for the tourist industry, but in smaller places it may only be some simple roadside shacks serving Chinese-style noodles or hard-to-identify dishes from several metal pots. It's all part of the adventure so be brave and tuck in – deep fried crickets reminded me of prawn-cocktail flavoured crisps.

Cambodia won't leave you and your bike too badly bruised.

Few people choose Cambodia as a touring destination in itself, but cross the border from Vietnam, Thailand or Laos. Mountain lovers will be disappointed as the country is mostly flat, as will those looking for great beaches. What coastline there is doesn't compare with the options available in Vietnam, Thailand, Malaysia and Indonesia.

The raw Cambodia is still there in the back country. © Peter Gostelow

It's the temples of Ankor that are the country's main draw and a bicycle is the perfect way to explore them. Set the alarm early and cycle from your guest house to watch the sunrise over Ankor Wat – it will be one of the most magical moments of your trip. Cambodia also offers a sense of adventure that its neighbours don't. The Khmer Rouge atrocities have left a tangible presence here, be it in the land mines that still litter the country (don't wander off the road into thick bush looking for somewhere to pitch a tent or go to the toilet) or the sight of foreign NGO vehicles speeding past you. Whilst you might be stopping in a 7-Eleven in Thailand for a dose of air-con and a choice of refrigerated beverages, here it will be a simple shack offering delicious cane sugar juice, a swinging hammock and a friendly smile.

There is a wide choice of land crossings between neighbouring countries. The north-east of the country offers a great route into Laos (check if you need a visa in advance) by following the Mekong river through the provinces of Kratie and Stung Treng. There are some long stretches here so if you tire, just hop on a boat and continue to the border. If Vietnam is next then heading south to the coast is recommended. Kampot, Kep and the ghostly hill station of Bokor are all worth visiting, but you might want to leave your bicycle in a guest house to climb up to the latter. The little-used and recently opened border crossing at Ha Tien offers a new coastal exit from the country.

Many tourists coming from Thailand use the busy Poipet route, but the lesser used border crossing further south near Paillin is a more adventurous option. It avoids the crowds and connects with the city of Battambang, where French colonial architecture, a large central market, and a handful of decent places to stay make it worth exploring for a day or two.

THAILAND

The 'Land of Smiles' is often a starting point for a tour in South-East Asia. Walk down the Khao San Road, Bangkok's backpacker ghetto, and you'll be glad you've got a bicycle to escape from the tourist masses. I know a number of people who came to

Khao San Road, Bangkok's backpacker ghetto. © Peter Gostelow

TRIP REPORT
THAILAND

Name	Simon Hill
Year of birth	1953
Occupation	Retired (Computer Operations Manager)
Nationality	British (English, Essex)
Other bike travels	UK, Europe, S & SE Asia, Australia & New Zealand

This trip	Thailand, Laos, Thailand
Trip duration	(nearly) 3 months
Number in group	One
Total distance	2686 kms
Cost of trip	Approx £1200 including flight

Longest day	116kms (Luang Nam Tha to Udom Xai)
Best day	Getting a 2 month Cambodia visa at the border with Thailand
Worst day	Too wet and cold to ride in Udom Xai
Favourite ride	Remote road from Nong Khiaw to Nam Noen (4 days)

Biggest headache	Beer Lao
Biggest mistake	Riding dirt road to Kong Lor after rainstorm
Pleasant surprise	The good quality of many roads in Laos
Any illness	None

Bike model	Cro-Mo Steel GT Outpost 26" MTB
New/used	New in 2000
Modifications	Only the frame remains! Solid forks, Sun CR18 rims, XT hubs, the rest Deore and LX. Brooks sprung saddle and Blackburn rack pre-date the bike
Wish you'd fitted	Nothing really – I like to keep it simple
Tyres used	Schwalbe Marathon HS368s 1.75" or sometimes 1.5s. These tyres have never let me down.
Punctures	One – mended by garage for 20p
Baggage Setup	Two rear Carradice Super C panniers, small saddlebag
Wish you'd brought	Good quality long underwear (my Lifas)
Wish you hadn't brought	The washbag freebies I got from the airline upgrade

Bike problems	None
Accidents	Saw a few but none happened to me
Same bike again	Yes – it's the only one I've got
Recommendations	SE Asia is a perfect balance of scenery, culture, good food and it's cheap and easy. India is fascinating, but a bit more manic.

Any advice?	Don't try to do too much – it's not the trip of a lifetime, there's plenty of time for another (and another).

South-East Asia with a backpack and ended up buying a bicycle here to do just that. Once you've got used to the heat, Thailand is a comfortable country to tour in. Roads are in excellent condition and good bike shops exist in Bangkok (⌨ www.probike.co.th), as well as Chiang Mai in the north. Accommodation options cater to all budgets and many consider the food the best in the region. It's no surprise the Thais eat 4-5 times a day. Bangkok's a good place to begin and end a tour owing to its central position in the region and cheap non-stop flights home, although it's far from cycle-friendly. In my opinion if you can cycle around Bangkok you can cycle in any city.

To test those legs try heading north from Bangkok towards Mae Sot and along the Myanmar border to Mae Hon Son and Chiang Mai. You might now wish you'd packed lighter or had fewer bottles of Singha beer the night before. These climbs in the north-west of Thailand can be punishing, not least because of 30°C+ temperatures and high humidity, but also steep gradients. A week or two of cycling here and your legs will be prepared for equally spectacular mountain scenery across the border in Laos. Chiang Khong has been a popular border crossing from Thailand to Laos for years. Another option is to leave Thailand over the Friendship Bridge at Nong Khai, 20km from Laos's capital, Vientiane. In both instances you should be able to get a visa at the border, but check in advance.

The north-eastern province of Isan offers fewer mountains, but is also practically unvisited by tourists. There's less in the way of attractions, although the Mekong flowing beside you through relaxed and traditional towns is a highlight in itself, as is not seeing another foreigner. Cycling south from Nong Khai towards Ubon is a recommended route and provides a number of border crossings into southern Laos.

The attractions of southern Thailand are its beaches and islands, which can make for a great break at the start or end of a tour, or even as you make onward plans within or beyond the region. I spent a number of happy days in a hammock on the island of Ko Tao – map of Tibet, journal, a good book and a bottle of Singha beer never far away. After several months in Vietnam and Cambodia it felt well deserved and had me recharged and ready to tackle the roads ahead. Taking a break on a small island meant it was more sensible to leave my bicycle locked up in a guesthouse in Bangkok. Many of Thailand's beaches and islands are over-developed, but it's still possible to escape the crowds if you want.

It's worth noting that the southern provinces of Songkhla, Yala and Narathiwat occasionally witness Muslim unrest and bombings. These are unlikely to affect cyclists, but seek information before travelling through.

LAOS

Most people are won over by the charms of sleepy land-locked Laos – I definitely was. Roads are at their quietest in the region, locals are amongst the friendliest and the scenery is some of the most varied and beautiful. If Thailand seems all too modern and developed then entering Laos will make for a refreshing change. As will the beer – Beer Lao is one of the best in South-East Asia.

Green heaven in northern Laos
© Peter Gostelow

The south is mainly flat, with Highway 13 running alongside the Mekong providing the main artery into Cambodia. This road passes through French-feeling Savannakhet and Pakse, with the option of detouring to climb up onto the Bolaven plateau.

In contrast the north of Laos presents a challenging array of lush mountains that continue to grow in size towards the Chinese border – cycling in South-East Asia doesn't get any better than this. Laos's capital, Vientiane, is more like a small town and it isn't far north from here before the climbing begins. This road takes you through green paddy fields, sleepy villages and spectacular limestone scenery before arriving in the country's World Heritage city of Luang Prabang.

Most main roads are now surfaced, but there are plenty of smaller and more adventurous routes to take. Highway 4, which runs from Muang Xay towards the recently-opened northern border with Vietnam, is a case in point. Such roads will be seriously challenging to cycle during the rainy season.

The northern provinces bordering Myanmar, China and Vietnam are home to many ethnic minorities. Although tourism is fast growing in Laos, a bicycle will take you through villages here where western faces are still quite rare. I arrived by boat in Phongsali after a long boat trip from Nongkhiaw up the Nam On – a tributary of the Mekong. Travelling to this little-visited part of Laos was a highlight of my time in the country, even if the road south was bone-achingly slow.

Up the Nam On river © Peter Gostelow

Like Cambodia, accommodation and food options deteriorate the further you venture from the main routes. Whilst tourist hubs can serve up baguettes, pancakes and fruit shakes, small villages may offer little more than simple bowls of noodle soup or sticky rice – a local staple. At least they usually have beer – whether it's cold or not is another matter.

MALAYSIA

Many people arrive in Malaysia with fairly modest expectations of what it will offer as a cycle touring destination only to discover it becomes one of their favourite countries in South-East Asia. Off the beaten track adventures might be harder to seek out, but this is a country that offers both physically challenging terrain and a number of other things that may extend your stay here. Firstly the food is excellent – a result of the cultural diversity that exists among Malay, Indian and Chinese influences. The smell of satay on the street, Indian dosai for breakfast, mee goreng from a roadside stall – and you thought it was only Thai food that was great. Secondly, English is much more widely spoken, which means it's easier to make more meaningful contact with the country and its people. A good case in point is David Munusamy, a keen local cyclist who's welcomed foreign tourers into his house on Penang for years. Check out the Warm Showers website for details (🖳 www.warmshowers.org). Malaysia also has excellent roads and there are challenging mountain climbs to divide two very interesting and scenic coastlines. You might find you end up staying in this country longer than planned.

Quieter roads run along the eastern coast, which is also more scenic and less developed than the western side. Confining yourself just to the east coast, however, means missing Malacca, Georgetown and Penang – worth a visit for anyone interested in the history and culture of the country. It is also possible to take a ferry from either Penang or Malacca to the Indonesian island of Sumatra.

Kuala Lumpur is no more enjoyable than Bangkok to cycle into. Beginners or those who value their life might choose to use public transport to enter or leave the city.

Travelling between coasts is a serious challenge in all that humidity and heat. The good news is that some of Malaysia's quietest roads are found in the mountainous interior. More than a cup of tea will be needed to quench your thirst after climbing up to the tea plantations around the Cameron Highlands though. Rest for a few days around Tanah Ratah and enjoy the cool air before some more climbing, but also some well-earned freewheeling towards the opposite coast.

East Malaysia, on the island of Borneo, is equally mountainous, but much less visited than peninsular Malaysia. Prices are a little more expensive and getting here will involve flying, unless you're crossing from Kalimantan (Indonesian Borneo).

SINGAPORE

This island city-state is so small that you can cycle across it in several hours. Singapore is really only a rest stop or a place to fly into or out of. After seeing some of the historical sites and perhaps the botanical gardens most people move on quite quickly, though it's good for electronics shops and has excellent and cheap food at the hawker stalls. There are several good bike shops here should you be in need of spares or a box for flying out. The Trek Bike shop at 91 Tanglin Place stocks a wide range of components and also has bike boxes.

INDONESIA

There is a greater diversity of places to cycle through in Indonesia than any other country in the region. In fact it's only your visa that's likely to prevent you from exploring more of the many islands (60 days is usually the maximum stay) and you'd have to return many times to discover all that Indonesia has to offer. Sumatra (see box p172) is vast and its volcanoes, lakes, empty beaches, friendly locals and quiet roads are perfect for cyclists. It would be quite easy to use up an entire visa exploring this island, which sees far fewer tourists than many other islands in Indonesia. Medan in the north has a ferry connection with Malaysia. From here you can head north to Aceh along the stunning north-west coast, or go south towards Lake Toba and on through the mountains to Padang. Neighbouring Java is much more densely populated and its heavy traffic makes cycling less enjoyable. Further east, Bali is great if you love beaches and tourist crowds, although the interior provides a scenic and mountainous getaway. Continuing east, the islands of Lombok, Sumbawa and Flores present more mountains and quieter roads. Looking north, Borneo and Sulawesi require more effort to reach and far fewer cyclists make it out here.

All islands in Indonesia are accessible by ferry, but it's important to be aware of which days in the week they run, and from where. There may only

YOU CANNOT BE SAD IN SUMATRA

After a comfortable week in the Malaysian peninsula, camping in hot springs and enjoying the beautiful Cameron Highlands (including by chance a good night with the aboriginal people in the jungle), I crossed to Sumatra by ferry from George Town and had five very good weeks there. In fact Sumatra was a highlight of my travel so far. Sumatra has everything: volcanoes, lakes, mountains, jungle and beaches, but best of all are the wonderful smiling people. I believe they are very happy, living in a blessed land; you cannot be sad in Sumatra!

There are not many cyclists here, perhaps because it is remote or the news is only of disasters, but it is a paradise. Every corner of the land is green and lush with exotic flowers and birds. It's also very cheap, but mostly we stayed with locals who are really friendly.

Java was indeed crowded and polluted but people were friendly everywhere I went; I always felt as though I was among family. I went to Kalimantan (Indonesian Borneo), and cycled in the west. It is undeveloped with strong sun and humidity, very steep hills and clay roads. But no traffic or tourism at all, just nice jungle, rivers and birds. Best again, the Dayak tribal people were extremely friendly. Some evenings I had no time to ask where I could hang my mosquito net, they had already organised everything. There is no public transport, electricity, bike shops and the villages are not always close, so you need to be self-reliant.

Once you cross Kapuas River, asphalt and civilisation are there, and very soon, Malaysian Borneo (Sabah), which is much more developed. I reached Kuching and took a short rest. I went to see orangutans (€0.70) and camped in Baku national park with proboscis monkeys for neighbours (€2 entrance,

€1 to camp anywhere). On the way to Brunei I saw many traditional longhouses and was sometimes invited to stay, but I felt it was just politeness so I refused and they never insisted. The Malays were generally not as warm as Indonesians, but still very helpful. You can sleep in very good *rekreasi* parks, camp by rivers, or in churches or youth centres. The Chinese community is very interesting here. They keep their traditions and I enjoyed being with them very much. In a Taoist temple, the caretaker performed a ceremony just for me and told me my future.

In Bandar Seri, Brunei's capital, there are 30,000 inhabitants living in a kampong, or village on stilts over the water. There is no tourism, so it is very pleasant to walk around there. You hear only your steps on the wooden planks and the sound of waves slapping the stilts.

The rest of Sabah was hard going since 50% of the land is now oil palm farms and it has become very hot and humid.

From the north-east tip (Sandakan) you can cross by ferry to the Philippines for €50. I got a new Indonesian visa in Tawau (very easy and took only 20 minutes) and crossed to Sulawesi island.

The mountains of central Sulawesi are stunning. The road is good and scenic with no traffic at all until Lake Poso. From there the road deteriorates as it passes through rainforest and mountains but it is fantastic cycling, thick jungle and uninhabited. The very best part is the 60km through Linde national park. The road is just a 30cm-wide path in the jungle, and we jumped over huge, broken trees, crossed rivers, pushed a lot in steep muddy areas, and yet although exhausted, we felt ourselves the luckiest men in the world.

Salva Rodriguez

be a weekly service, so it's worth planning ahead. Check Indonesia's main ferry service, Pelni (🖳 www.pelni.com).

Leaving Indonesia in the direction of Australia will usually involve taking to the air, unless you're lucky enough to hitch a ride on a boat. There are no ferry services. Like other countries in South-East Asia, accommodation is never more than a day's cycle ride away, unless heading off the beaten track. If you're after more adventure before heading to Australia there's always East Timor and Papua New Guinea.

MYANMAR (BURMA)

Myanmar is culturally and historically one of the most fascinating countries of the region to visit. Stunning gold-covered pagodas, bustling markets and a Buddhist religion very much apparent in every day life greet those who come here. Unfortunately cycling in Myanmar brings with it some restrictions. Whilst visas aren't difficult to obtain, and it's by no means dangerous to cycle here, a number of parts of the country are off-limits to foreigners. This means a cycle tour will almost certainly involve flying into and out of Yangon (which can easily be done from neighbouring Thailand) and you won't have much freedom in terms of where you can cycle. Many people look at the map and think it would be great to cross from Myanmar into India and China – in a perfect world it would. This hasn't been possible for many years, although some cyclists have arranged a visa for Myanmar in China and crossed the border from Yunnan.

Some people consider visiting and spending money in a country ruled by a military junta as unethical, but it's possible to support local economies here by cycle-touring and the Burmese people are as friendly as anywhere else in the region. In fact cycling here is a bit like visiting the South-East Asia of old. Roads have more potholes and local people are more likely to want to stop and greet you like a long-lost family member. It's something you won't find across the border in Thailand.

The areas in and around Yangon, Mandalay, Bagan and Inle Lake are those most likely to be visited. Accommodation is cheap and easy to find in these areas, as is street-food. Elsewhere in the country finding accommodation is more of an adventure and a number of hotels may prevent foreigners from staying there. There's little doubt that touring in Myanmar will provide some of the most memorable experiences of your time in the region, just don't expect to come here and seek out the lesser travelled road – you won't be allowed on it.

Thanks to Jill Lundmark for information.

DIG DEEPER INTO SOUTH-EAST ASIA

For further information see:
🖳 www.silkwheels.com
🖳 www.travellingtwo.com
🖳 www.vwvagabonds.com
🖳 www.biketouringtips.com
🖳 www.bicycle-adventures.com

Also worth reading:
Catfish and Mandala by Andrew X. Pham
One Foot in Laos by Dervla Murphy

TRIP REPORT
JAPAN TO ENGLAND

Name	Peter Gostelow
Year of birth	1979
Occupation	Teacher
Nationality	British
Other bike travels	Kyushu, Japan, 2000km
This trip	Japan, Korea, China, Vietnam, Cambodia, Thailand, Laos, Tibet, Nepal, India, Pakistan, Kyrgyzstan, Tajikistan, Uzbekistan, Turkmenistan, Iran, Turkey, Syria, Jordan, Egypt, Libya, Tunisia, Italy, Austria, Germany, Switzerland, France, Belgium, England
Trip duration	3 years
Number in group	One
Total distance	48,000km
Cost of trip	£6-6500
Longest day	210km (Libya with a tailwind)
Best day	First day of KKH in China. Good company and amazing campsite beside Lake Karakul.
Worst day	Losing pannier with photos and journal in river in Tajikistan
Favourite ride	All of Tibet
Biggest headache	Getting a Libyan visa and then an extension
Biggest mistake	Walking across a landslide and giving my pannier to a local man who dropped it.
Pleasant surprise	Getting my bike back in Nepal after it had been stolen and sold for $20
Any illness	Usual suspects (diarrhoea, dehydration, sunburn)
Bike model	Cannondale Badboy
New/used	3 years old when trip started
Modifications	Blackburn racks, butterfly bars, mavic rims
Wish you'd fitted	Waterproof handlebar bag
Tyres used	Schwalbe Marathon then Marathon XR
Punctures	Less than 20
Baggage Setup	Front panniers (20L) Rear Panniers (40L) Rackpack and Handlebar bag
Wish you'd brought	Long wave radio, multifuel stove from start of trip
Wish you hadn't brought	Nothing
Bike problems	Rear hub bearing seal broke twice
Accidents	No serious ones
Same bike again	No, upgrading to a Thorn Raven for peace of mind
Recommendations	Schwalbe tyres, Ortlieb panniers
Any advice?	The most memorable experiences are found on small roads. Stay clear of highways whenever possible.

Japan

Peter Gostelow

Japan is like no other Asian country. As an island nation its people and culture are distinctly different from anywhere else on the continent. It may be one of the most developed countries in the world, but it's also one that holds onto its old customs and traditions more than many others.

Cycling in Japan is rewarding for all the reasons that it isn't on many parts of the Asian mainland. The environment is clean, the roads are safe, nobody will charge you extra and traffic doesn't deafen you with horns blaring. There can't be many other countries as populated as Japan that are as peaceful and pleasant to cycle in.

Several thousand miles and as many islands separate Okinawa in the south from Hokkaido in the north. Between the two lies a mountainous country of smoking volcanoes and steaming onsens, ancient shrines and western idiosyncrasies that are sure to both confuse and amuse. Between them all is a network of roads very little explored beyond the main tourist sites.

Many people consider Japan an expensive place to visit. It's a myth. The truth is that Japan is no more costly than Europe, and by taking a tent and being prepared to self-cater half the time it is possible to tour here for as little as $20 per day or even less.

Before coming to Japan it is wise to invest in a phrasebook and learn some of the basics. Your efforts in attempting to speak this difficult language will go a long way. Japanese people are generally reserved and finding English speakers outside of major cities can be challenging.

Access

Most people arrive in Japan by plane. Transporting your bike in its box to the centre of Tokyo or Osaka is certainly more sensible than trying to cycle there. If coming from mainland Asia the cheaper and more exciting option is to arrive by ferry. Osaka and Kobe both operate a service to Shanghai, and Pusan in South Korea can be reached by ferry from the southern cities of Shimonoseki and Fukuoka. Vladivostok can also be reached from either Niigata or Yokohama, and Wakkanai, Japan's northern-most town in Hokkaido, runs a service to Sakhalin in Siberia.

Visas

Most foreigners receive a 90-day visa on arrival in Japan. This is a sufficient length of time to see the best of what the country has to offer and also explore more of the less well-known.

When to go

Japan's climate is temperate, but there are wide variations between the island of Hokkaido in the north and Kyushu in the south. Northern Honshu and

Is there light at the end of the tunnel?
© Peter Gostelow

Hokkaido are best visited in the summer months between June and October. From November to March it can be very cold if cycling in the mountains and there will be lots of snow, so camping is only for the masochistic. Further south, temperatures and humidity are very high during the summer months. June and early July is also the rainy season here. The months of April and May would be ideal for touring the southern islands of Kyushu and Shikoku. It is worth noting that typhoon season lasts from July to October, affecting the southern islands worst of all.

Road maps and route planning

Japan's road maps are highly detailed and frequently updated. The best ones, however, are in Japanese. Shobunsha produce a series of maps called 'Touring Mapple'. These are easily available in Japan and mark the location of campsites, public baths (*sentos*) and the most scenic roads. You don't have to read Japanese to follow them, but it's worth picking up an international map before arriving.

Any route in Japan will usually involve some climbing. Smaller roads carry less traffic but are often steeper. You'd really have to get off the beaten track to find a road that wasn't surfaced, so wide tyres are unnecessary. Following the coast will minimise the climbs but these roads are often the busiest. Japan's answer to coping with all its mountains is to build tunnels through many of them. Some tunnels can be several miles long and it's worth having lights as not all are well lit. My most frightening cycling experiences in Japan were hearing the echoing sounds of a truck approaching me in a darkened tunnel from a few kilometres away. There are even spiral tunnels in the mountains.

In cities and towns a cyclist is quite a common sight. Cycle lanes exist, but they are usually part of the pavement. Whereas a cycle bell might be ignored in other Asian countries, it is a must when riding through towns in Japan – watch out for the *Obasans* (old ladies) though.

Hokkaido is the least populated of Japan's four main islands and offers some of the quietest roads to cycle. The stunning volcanic lakes of Akan and Shikotsu are definitely worth including in a tour here, as is the Shiretoko Peninsula – one of Japan's least developed regions. Hokkaido is seen as a wild frontier by many Japanese, which, if you live in Tokyo or Osaka, it certainly is.

Beach camping is free
in Hokkaido. © Peter Gostelow

The island of Shikoku is also something of a rural backwater and would make a good destination after visiting the must-see cities of Kyoto and Nara. The Pacific coastline is jagged, wild and stunning here and you might cross paths with a few pilgrims making the famous 88-temple pilgrimage. You could do the pilgrimage by road on your bike, as the walking route has a lot of steps. Pilgrim accommodation is cheaper than normal tourist inns and is traditional in style and often vege-

Way down south on Tanegashima.
© Peter Gostelow

tarian. Cycling in the central regions of Honshu offers plenty of culture and history, but little in the way of quiet rural roads. It will also be much harder to camp here than in, say, Hokkaido or rural parts of Kyushu.

Transporting your bicycle on a ferry is a simple procedure, for which you will pay a small fee. Taking lots of ferries will increase your daily budget, but it's worth getting out to at least a few of the islands other than the main four. Yakushima and Tanegashima to the south of Kyushu make for some stunning coastal scenery. You might even continue all the way south to tropical Okinawa – a different Japan altogether. Taking a bicycle on a train requires you to put it in a bike bag (see p68). The same will apply on most buses.

Expenses

The only way to tour Japan on a low budget is by camping. Campsites are often less than £3 per night and many are free. The 'Touring Mapple' lists these. In a country as safe as Japan there is little risk in wild camping. Pitching your tent in a public park as the light begins to fade is unlikely to draw unwanted attention as long as you are discreet. I even felt safe enough to leave my tent in a park or field and wander to a nearby shop (something I couldn't imagine doing in any other Asian country).

Washing and relaxing in a public bath (sento) at the end of a day is also a cheap way to stay clean and experience Japanese culture. Sentos (£2-3) tradi-

tionally use geothermal heat (there are over 100 active volcanoes in Japan) and exist in nearly all Japanese towns. A number of naturally occurring sentos in rural areas are free to use. You might even be lucky and stumble across a mixed-sex one!

Youth hostels are the next cheapest form of accommodation and during the summer months many Japanese students and motorcyclists stay in 'rider houses'. These are simple guesthouses charging about £6 per night for dormitory-style accommodation.

The gaijin spaceship has landed:
City park camping in Kagoshima.
© Peter Gostelow

Staying in a traditional Japanese Inn (Ryokan) is highly recommended if you're not on a tight budget. This memorable experience will enable you to better appreciate the refinements of Japanese culture. See ⌨ www.japancycling.org for useful information on home-stay families and other aspects of cycling here.

Shopping in supermarkets and self-catering will also keep your costs down in Japan. Many supermarkets discount sushi, sashimi and other freshly made boxed-lunches at the end of the day and there is a variety of cheap interesting foods to buy here that you won't easily find anywhere else in the world, such as dried squid. It is possible, however, to eat good noodles, ramen and sushi in a restaurant for less than £6. If the menu is all too confusing just look for a restaurant with pictures or plastic models of food in the window.

For further information, start your research at The Japan Cycling site listed above. Also worth reading are *The Sun in My Eyes* and *A Ride in the Neon Sun*, both by Josie Dew.

Australia

Chris Scott

Despite being the flattest continent, the sheer size of Australia makes it a daunting prospect for those hoping to ride a large chunk of the country. Away from the 'bitumen' (as they call sealed roads out there) the great outback remains a tough and dangerous proposition despite the obvious appeal of thousands of kilometres of desert tracks. The distances are so great, the summer temperatures so high and the water supplies so limited that cyclists are bound to have a safer time riding in the south-east and south-west corners of the country. Here the temperate climate and short distances between settlements are much more forgiving for cyclists. Head for the southern coastline such as Victoria's Great Ocean Road (see Trailblazer's *Australia's Great Ocean Road* by Richard Everist for more information), leaving plenty of time to travel inland on tracks such as the Mawson Trail (⌨ www.southaustralian trails.com/pdf/mawson.pdf) or, in Western Australia, the ancient karri forests and the developing Munda Biddi Trail (⌨ www.mundabiddi.org.au) running from near Perth to Albany on the Southern Ocean.

Basics

Most Australian states have a compulsory helmet law for cyclists, which means this is a two-hat country – the other one is for sun protection when not riding. Visas need to be obtained outside the country but North Americans and most Europeans can get an Electronic Travel Authority (ETA) online which does the job. A standard visa is for three months but you can apply for extensions of up to one year within Australia.

Australia has an excellent camping scene, with caravan parks in most small towns around the country. The selection of bike parts is not great outside the big cities, especially if you need something touring related. The website Bicycle Fish (⌨ http://members.iinet.net.au/~bikefish/) is one of the best

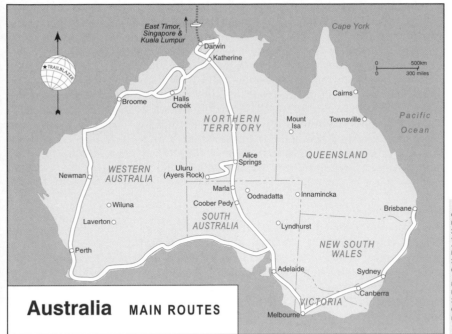

Australia MAIN ROUTES

resources for touring Australia and for a good read try Roff Smith's *Cold Beer and Crocodiles: A Bicycle Journey into Australia*, all the better for not being written by a hardened world tourer. As for which guidebook, well, in Australia you barely need one. That said, most lemmings drop onto the Lonely Planet at terminal velocity, but the Rough Guide is as good and has much better jokes.

THE NULLARBOR PLAIN

Tim Mulliner

The Nullarbor crosses a vast limestone plateau stretching 1200km across the southern Australian outback, between Norseman in the west and Ceduna in the east. Even then, these two settlements are little more than remote one-horse towns – in fact Norseman happened to be named after a horse that kicked up a gold nugget. Either way, depending on winds and your single-mindedness, it takes about 7-12 days to ride the Nullarbor.

A major misconception about this road crossing is that it's nothing but an empty desert that stretches as far as the eye can see. While this may be true of the plateau further to the north, the scenery and landscapes viewed from the road are spectacular and the sealed section is far from tree-less, despite the Latin origins of its name. Eucalyptus forests give way to scrub land where salt-bush, spinifex and bluebush dominate and for several hundred kilometres the road parallels the high cliffs of the Southern Ocean before heading inland.

Besides the superb scenery the Nullarbor is full of wildlife. Flocks of parakeets move from tree to tree with much commotion, their flashes of bright feathers and loud chattering a lovely alarm call after the silence of a quiet night's camp. In the distance a couple of kangaroos are gently gliding over the ground and you watch them in amazement before being startled by a violent shaking of bushes on the opposite side of the road: an emu's wobbling backside is all you can see as it crashes through the bushes.

As the day warms up, the aptly named 'blue-tongue' lizard stands its ground in the middle of the road poking its tongue at you. It's one of the many weird and wonderful reptiles to be seen on the Nullarbor. Giant wedge-tailed eagles are a common sight too, circling around waiting to swoop on the latest truck-mashed roadkill. At night by the campfire, the noise of those trucks muffled by the trees and shrubs around you, the howl of a distant dingo sends a shiver down your spine, compelling you to edge slightly closer to the flames.

Food and drink

Food between Norseman and Ceduna consists solely of roadhouse mush: burgers, chips and cooked breakfasts all thawed from frozen in a deep fryer or a microwave. For a ravenous touring cyclist this is seldom a thing to complain about (look on the bright side; the high oil content will help lubricate your joints) but the distances between the roadhouses, the longest being 200km, mean additional provisions are needed. At some of the roadhouses you can buy overpriced supplies and at Eucla, on the WA/SA border there's even a shop but it pays to stock up at Norseman or Ceduna. Note the meat and veg quarantine when crossing the state borders and remember that there are no banks though 'EFTPOS' card facilities are common at roadhouses.

Water can be a problem. Some friendly people at the roadhouses will take pity on cyclists and fill water bottles for free. At the ones that don't, you can

---

SOUTH-WESTERN AUSTRALIA

If you're crossing the Nullarbor towards WA, or even if you've landed there in a spaceship, at Norseman turn south, away from the thundering road train route and towards Esperence where the storm-swept beaches of Cape Le Grand and the Southern Ocean await. Westward from Esperance is an exposed and mildly hilly inland ride to Albany, usually against the wind and offering little beach access or much else of interest. Nevertheless, unless you're pining for Kansas and Oklahoma, avoid venturing further inland hereabouts – it's nothing more than an interminable man-made prairie of cross-grid byways linking wheat farming towns that time and most other things have forgotten.

West of Albany is where the real pedalling treats await. Alternatives to the main coastal highway (including the Munda Biddi Trail; see p178) begin to proliferate and on the way past Denmark to Walpole there are more lovely granite-fringed bays matching Cape Le Grand.

Walpole marks the eastern edge of WA's famous Tall Timber country – at least what the loggers have not turned to pulp. Even in the heat of summer the shady byways towards Northcliff, Pemberton and Nannup offer idyllic riding on or off the bitumen, though by the time you near Collie or Bunbury the party's over and you'll do best to seek out the quietest routes to Perth or hop on a train.

No matter how much you may be attracted to the hardcore romance of riding the sunburned outback further north, it is these temperate corners of Australia – including the more populated equivalents in South Australia, Victoria and Tasmania – that offer the most agreeable riding down under.

Chris Scott

try the water from the taps in the toilets. Despite signs saying that it's not safe to drink I never had a problem though it was rather salty at times. The only other option is to buy bottled water at the roadhouses, as long as you don't mind paying nearly three times more per litre than you'd pay for petrol!

Cycling the Nullarbor accounts for only about a third of the distance between Perth and Adelaide. It's a long grind with a lot of empty stretches, but there are some highlights along the way that are worth the slog. Apart from water shortages the biggest danger is from road trains – multiple-trailer trucks up to 50 metres long whose drivers may not share your alertness for the scenery until it's too late. Give them plenty of room and if necessary get out of their way – they are much less manoeuverable than you are.

SOUTH AUSTRALIA AND VICTORIA

When you enter South Australia opportunities open up. The state is home to much of the country's best wine and has the 900-km Mawson Trail, a network of minor roads, unpaved tracks and forest trails linking various points of inter-est and suitable for sturdy touring bikes or mountain bikes. It's one of the easiest and most interesting ways to get a flavour of the great interior of Australia without undertaking some of the long desert tracks which are beyond the touring range of human-powered vehicles.

In neighbouring Victoria, Melbourne is one of Australia's great attractions and is considered to be its most cycle-friendly city with almost 1000km of bike paths. It's therefore an excellent city to pick up bike parts and

Lush greenery in Tarra-Bulga rainforest, Victoria. © Tim Travis

camping gear and the stepping-off point for the ferry to Tasmania and the Great Ocean Road. At only 284km, the latter is perhaps not satisfying enough for some, but given the size of the country, it's an excellent way to sample its delights as few people have time to see it at a bicycling pace.

AN OUTBACK TOUR

Like it or not, Australia is defined not by its shady forests where squirrels gather their nuts, but by the gritty, lip-cracking outback, populated by laconic individuals whose self-worth stems from being a big fish in a nearly empty bowl, or where young families convince themselves that life in an isolated mining town has its perks.

With limited dawdling – or better still, lifts across the really boring sections so as to enjoy some quality time off – a 7000-km tour from Perth to Adelaide via Darwin could be done in three months, which is just about the length of the cool season in the far north and the interior, as well as the duration of the average tourist visa. During this time you're unlikely to experience any rain or even see a cloud. There are no gradients to speak of and – excluding wet season cyclones – little wind in the tropics, but obviously plan your water supplies judiciously and avoid riding at night; drunk, drugged or just plain dozy drivers are a menace and, anyway, there's nothing to see.

Riding up here away from the busier eastern states is the only true way of experiencing Australia's mind-boggling spaces. Try to set out at the end of the summer and ride into the cool season to give yourself the best chance of not 'going troppo'.

Costs and food

With just about everything coming up by road train or ocean barge from the south, the under-populated north is expensive and roadhouses are notorious for their limited range of overpriced and poor-quality fare. This is where your taste buds will hark back to Asia where you were never far from a wholesome, freshly-cooked snack for the price of a box of matches. Make the most of the fresh produce found in the supermarkets of the big towns; there are no more than a dozen along the entire route. If you make it to Darwin, check out the sizzling oriental take-aways at Mindil Beach Market on a Thursday night.

Apart from tourists on day-rentals, few locals cycle in the far north; it's just too hot at any time of year and too awkward to carry more than a slab or two of beer. Don't expect a useful stock of essential cycle spares anywhere other than Darwin and maybe Alice.

Bush camping

Obviously you'll end up camping out in the bush and not through choice. A tent's waterproof qualities will be wasted up here but the light mesh of an inner tent – effectively a free-standing mozzie net – is very useful. It gives you the peace of mind to sleep without being tormented – literally or psychologically – by insects, reptiles and other things that bounce around the bush at night. Most of the world's species of venomous snakes are found in Australia and all reptiles are more active in the heat of summer. However, it's worth remembering that they have little to gain by sidling over and biting you as you're too big to eat. They will only do so when threatened but it is worth acquainting yourself with the difference between harmless but sometimes huge pythons (usually broader headed) and venomous snakes.

As anywhere else in the world, do yourself a favour and make sure you camp out of sight of the highway, particularly when you're near towns as bored and drunken idiots may be on the prowl for something or someone to harass.

To the Top End

It's 4000km from Perth to Darwin and, of the two sealed routes, the inland Great Northern Highway rejoining the coast near industrial Port Hedland will give you as much outback as you can stomach – even if you're still only halfway to Darwin, let alone Adelaide. Mile for mile, the attractions of the longer and busier North West Coastal Highway are just too insignificant at pedalling velocities and, apart from the Shark Bay area and the North-West Cape and the Ningaloo Reef, beach life is less alluring than you'd expect.

By now firmly in the cloudless tropics, Port Hedland to Broome is a 700-km legendarily monotonous stretch, with up to 300km between roadhouses (150 to 200km being the norm up here) and with no other services of any kind. Get used to these kinds of distances and make sure your brain is in good shape because, unless you've mastered the art of velo-meditation, you'll be doing a lot of thinking. Typical wintertime temperatures

© Tim Travis

up here are in the low to mid-thirties centigrade, more further away from the humid coasts. You'll find Broome expensive but an unusually charming town (considering what's come before and what lies ahead) with a cosmopolitan pearling history. If you don't mind communing with regular tourists, it's well worth a break.

From nearby Derby to the Northern Territory border many travellers, two-wheeled or otherwise, mistake the Gibb River Road – slicing across the Kimberley Plateau – as a short cut. A short cut it is: to a sack-full of broken bicycle parts. However, the Gibb River Express bus service (💻 www.check-in.com.au) does the mostly-corrugated 700-km Derby-Kununurra run most days and will carry your gear or even you and your bike as far or as near as you like. With short excursions off the Gibb to some lovely croc-free gorges and waterfalls, and a good (if expensive) range of homestead accommodation, it's more interesting than the highway to the south but would be a very tough ride without support.

Even in the coldest months the so-called Top End of the Northern Territory, through Timber Creek to Katherine and Darwin, is never less than hot, though humidity keeps temperatures in the low thirties in Darwin itself. If heading up to Darwin and coming back via Kakadu, take a chance to ride the 120-km stretch along the quieter Old Darwin Road between Hayes Creek roadhouse and Adelaide River.

The menace of crocs and a large tidal range make the beaches around Darwin nothing special but Kakadu National Park is nearby, and an all-sealed 450-km excursion east to Jabiru and back out south-west to Pine Creek takes you past many of the park's natural and cultural highlights. Alternatively Litchfield Park is nearer the main southbound highway, offers fewer expectations and plenty of croc-free swimming holes.

Down the Track – Darwin to Adelaide

With 4000 clicks already under your belt, it's only another 3000 down to Adelaide along the Stuart Highway, aka 'the Track'. You'll want to get moving and make the most of the cool season in the interior because it's here that the frame-cracking, brain-melting summer temperatures will soon cause problems. Scenically, distances are galling when measured on a scale of 'things to see and do', but this is the nature (and to some, the wonder) of outback Australia. If it all gets too much you have a chance to leapfrog down the road a bit on the daily buses and twice-weekly trains now running between Darwin and Adelaide.

Excursion to the Rock

If you get there before October when the hot season returns, the Central Deserts around Alice Springs offer one of the few worthwhile excursions along the Track – the 750-km detour to Uluru/Ayers Rock. If your bike can handle a 200-km section of corrugated track, the best route takes you out along the rolling West MacDonnell Ranges with many inviting waterholes, and past the mysterious crater of Gosses Bluff by which time the dirt section is well under way. At the junction for Hermansburg to the east, set your sights west on Kings Canyon where the bitumen resumes – it's about 150km of rim-cracking washboard along the Mereenie Loop Road with daily traffic but no services whatsoever.

From Kings Canyon Resort, you're back in tour bus country, but even then the road passes through lovely stands of desert oak as well as a couple of road-house/cattle stations in the 300km it takes you to reach the Rock. Sure it's an expensive tourist trap but be prepared to plop your world-weary cynicism into the special bins provided at the park entrance: the elemental brooding mass of Uluru will mesmerise you, not least because you've pedalled here the long way from Perth.

The Rock is a dead end (although 4x4-supported cycle tours do run along the all-dirt Great Central Road south-west back to WA). Mere unsupported mortals must backtrack 250km along the at-times unnervingly narrow Lasseter Highway to the Stuart Highway. From here it's a ride through the most arid parts of northern South Australia for another fortnight or so, all the way to Adelaide, a cup of tea, a biscuit and maybe a haircut.

New Zealand

Roy Hoogenraad

Despite some wind and rain that come from being in the 'Roaring Forties', New Zealand is popular with bikers, especially the west coast of the South Island – which happens to be the area most affected by showers rolling off the Tasman Sea. The scenery here is spectacular; snow-clad alps, glittering fjords, steaming volcanoes and humming sub-tropical forest. Travellers arriving from overseas get a three-month visa on arrival and many of them find it barely enough to cover just one of the two main islands.

If you have a month or less, visit the South Island. You can take your bike on the few passenger train services, though it's easier to use one of the many private-bus services. This gives you the flexibility to choose a region, do the ride you want in the time you have, and take the bus back to where you fly out.

A circuit of the South Island is what many long-haul bikers go for, and they're likely to spend three months doing that. You could get round in less time, but there is a lot more to see than just main roads. New Zealand's greatest treasures are off-road and if you like hiking, try to do some of the famous 'tramps' as you make your way up, down or around the coast; the national parks are far too good to miss.

New Zealand © Friedel Rother

New Zealand's roads are narrow and in places crowded, especially so on the main road around the South Island. Buses and trucks can pass by faster than any cyclist would like, and there are also a lot of old cars well past their scrap-by date which look none too safe from a cyclist's point of view. So, as in most places, you'll be aiming for the minor roads and including some unpaved roads if your bike doesn't mind. As elsewhere, the jewels are mostly off-road and the closer you can get to that, the more you will enjoy the country.

Don't rule out the North Island, which cyclists find quieter and less touristy than the South Island. Although not mountainous, it is hilly in the north and not much easier riding. It is less windy than Fiordland but anywhere near Wellington gets blasts of winds coming from the west. There are so many good places to discover that there is no point in worrying about missing something, or following a specific route. Travelling at a bike's pace, you will have time to stop and ask local people along the way.

North America

It's tempting to overlook North America as an adventure cycling destination; many riders are looking to sample the culture so familiar to them from films and TV. But there are some meaty long-distance challenges, including the world's longest mapped off-road route. Canada itself is the world's second largest country and one of the emptiest; ninety per cent of the population live within 100 miles of the US border. North of that you have all the forests, rivers, distances (and insects) of Siberia, but without the checkpoints.

There are as many routes across the continent as there are roads, the smallest of which are traffic-free. The best of these have been mapped by the Adventure Cycling Association (🖥 www.adventurecycling.org), who supply route guides for all of them. Here we focus on the Great Divide Route, the toughest and probably the most satisfying trail on the continent for adventure riders, and the Pacific Coast Highway, the most commonly taken route for riders coming down from Alaska to Mexico or beyond. Other ideas include the ride up to the Arctic Ocean, either to Inuvik up the Dempster Highway in Canada, or up the Dalton Highway in Alaska from Fairbanks to Prudhoe Bay.

TRIP REPORT
AROUND THE WORLD

Name Peter van Glabbeek
Year of birth 1978
Occupation Bicycle touring
Nationality Dutch
Other bike travels Utrecht-Istanbul, New Zealand, Utrecht-Norway

This trip Across Europe, Asia (incl. Tibet), Australia, South America & USA
Trip duration 4 years
Number in group One
Total distance 60,000km
Cost of trip €10,000 including flights and insurance

Longest day 285km (Australia)
Best day Many days with unexplainable, complete happiness
Worst day Thailand coast, between Cambodia and Bangkok
Favourite ride Tibet, Sur Lipez (Bolivia), Andean passes
Biggest headache Destruction of developing world by powerful multi-nationals
Biggest mistake Going too fast in the first year. I have slowed down.
Pleasant surprise Hospitality & friendly people absolutely everywhere
Any illness Mostly giardiasis in Turkey, Pakistan & Tibet

Bike model First a Trek Navigator X600, now an Oxford Emerald (Chilean)
New/used Both new
Modifications Racks on Oxford Emerald
Wish you'd fitted A good steel rear rack, not aluminium
Tyres used Schwalbe Marathon XR on my Trek, Kenda Kwest on my Oxford, now some $5 tyres from Colombia. All good.
Punctures About 30
Baggage Setup Small Ortlieb front panniers on low rider, big rear Ortliebs, 20kg
Wish you'd brought Music, more pictures from home
Wish you hadn't brought Nothing

Bike problems Broken rear rack, lost rear derailleur & chain
Accidents Big crash in China, left skin on pavement
Same bike again Yes, with Tubus rear rack
Recommendations I believe the best trips are unprepared, open ended. Be open to surprises, change plans, be creative, go with the flow.

Any advice? Go light: less strain on bike and body. All you own owns you.

CANADA

Paul Woloshansky

Canada's stunning northern wilderness is almost entirely empty of human inhabitants and a magnet for those in search of adventure. A tour to Canada's lonely places requires careful planning and enough equipment to compensate for widely scattered services, so it's not unusual to see tourists on heavily-laden bicycles. Aside from the usual tent, sleeping bag and cooking gear, it's necessary to have a wider range of clothing options to deal with climatic extremes.

A good practice is to anticipate all types of weather: Alberta, for instance, has more days of sunshine than any other province, but in the past has received snowfalls in every month of the year (thankfully, not the same year!). This variation in climate might be difficult to comprehend while you're eating fresh peaches at a road-side fruit stand in British Columbia's Okanagan Valley, with the temperature hovering around 35°C; yet a week later the breezes off the Athabaska Glacier between Lake Louise and Jasper in Alberta's Columbia Icefield may chill you to the bone.

A cyclist touring the breadth of Canada will also have to deal with prevailing westerly winds and therefore the usual and easiest route is from west to east.

Terrain

British Columbia is mountainous, and an eastward tour originating in Vancouver will soon have you climbing over the spine of the Rocky Mountains, whichever route you take. Low gearing is a necessity as the hardest cycling on a west-to-east tour will occur right at the beginning, before your legs have had a chance to harden up.

Roughly speaking, Canada's prairie region stretches from the BC-Alberta border to the Manitoba-Ontario border; any hills you encounter will be mere bumps compared to what you've already ridden over. Ontario's Pre-Cambrian Shield is an older range than the Rockies and doesn't present the same challenge to a cyclist. Touring Canada's east coast presents obstacles that are common to coastal tours everywhere: plenty of short, steep climbs and descents that mark drainages to the ocean.

Camping in bear country

Wild camping can be a pleasurable feature of bicycle touring in Canada, although campgrounds are common. Wherever you choose as a stop for the night, you have to be cautious about food storage. Campgrounds in bear country will often have bear-proof food lockers available; food caches accomplish the same thing for wild campers. This necessitates hauling food bags on a line up over a tree branch, ideally a hundred metres or so from a campsite. Eating away from where you sleep is another good idea.

Forest fires regularly devastate the Canadian wilderness so fire bans must be respected – use a stove for all cooked meals; they are mandatory for some of Canada's backcountry.

Yukon Territory

The Yukon plays a large part in Canada's mythology: its gold rush of 1896 was a catalyst for the development of the west and for Canada as a nation. Read the poems of Robert Service to get a sense of those times and ride the only tour in Canada that ends above the Arctic Circle, in summer's perpetual daylight.

It's possible to take a ferry up from Vancouver through the spectacular inland passage to Skagway and then ride to Whitehorse in two days. Otherwise, the ride from Vancouver will take several weeks (approximately 20-24 days of cycling) and passes through forested mountains with settlements up to 150km apart. Most road traffic goes on the Alcan Highway and cyclists prefer the much less busy, part-gravel 1200km Cassiar Highway. The winds are generally from the south in the short summer riding season, but are not necessarily so strong as to prevent anyone riding south. Whitehorse is the starting point for canoe trips on the Yukon river to Dawson City (you can rent canoes in Whitehorse), or ride your bike up the Klondike Highway. Dawson City is considered a must-see, famous for the Klondike Gold Rush.

The Dempster Highway begins just east of Dawson City, ending 736km further north in Inuvik on the Arctic Ocean. It's remote, all-gravel, and a spectacular ride, first passing through forest and leading to bare mountains as you reach the Arctic. Along with bears, caribou and muskox there are provincial campgrounds along the way (complete with bearproof lockers) and a hotel at the halfway point – just the bare minimum to get you through.

USA

Sonja Spry and Aaldrik Mulder

The USA has an amazing amount of unspoiled natural scenery – almost a third of the country is publicly-owned land – and is a great place for camping. In fact, given the cost of most hostels, you will want to camp as much as possible. Planning your route through these areas is easy if you visit the National Park Service's website at 🖳 www.nps.gov; the State Park's information site at 🖳 www.stateparks.com; and the US National Forest Campground Guide at 🖳 www.forestcamping.com. However, be warned: free-camping is pretty well limited to extremely remote areas in the US and officials will think nothing of giving you a hefty fine should you try to pitch your tent outside designated areas.

If you are entering from Canada, then probably the most well-known route is the Pacific Coast Route, which will lead you directly to the Mexican border town of Tijuana. Alternatively, if you want to feast your eyes on something other than ocean for the first leg of the journey, you could cross at any of the small border towns in the east of Washington State and cut your way across to later join up with Highway 101 at Astoria in Oregon. The Pacific Coast Highway has a lot of facilities for cyclists and is one of the cheapest ways of crossing the USA from north to south.

Another option for getting to Mexico is to make your way along the Continental Divide via the Great Divide Mountain Bike Route: more or less the crest of the Rockies. Riding the spine is a complete adventure in itself and

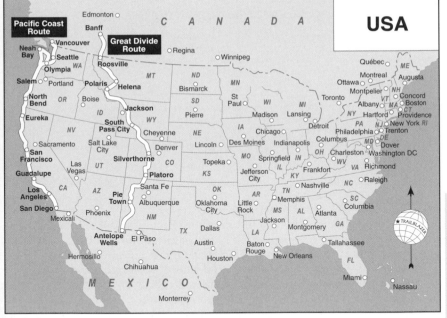

you'll need to allow the whole summer for the experience. It's wild enough and certainly remote but with excellent free-camping possibilities the whole way, and much easier logistically than a similar ride anywhere else in the world.

Visas

Immigration procedures the world over have tightened in recent years and the USA is no exception, though as a cyclist you can expect little more than a thorough questioning. Regulations are constantly changing, so it pays to do some research before standing in line at any one of the USA's border posts.

As of January 2009, the US Department of Homeland Security requires travellers from Visa Waiver Program (VWP) countries to obtain approval through the Electronic System for Travel Authorisation (ESTA) prior to travelling to the United States. VWP enables eligible citizens or nationals of certain countries to travel to the United States for tourism or business for stays of 90 days or less without obtaining a visa. Gone are the days when potential visitors to the USA could just turn up at a border control: you must first apply for travel authorisation via the ESTA website at 🖥 https://esta.cbp.dhs.gov. If you are planning to stay for longer than 90 days, it would be wise to apply for a six-month visa prior to entry, as the VWP permit cannot be extended and the 90 days also includes any time spent in Canada, Mexico and adjacent islands. You can only ask for a re-entry on the VWP if you leave the continent altogether. The same rule applies for the six-month visa as well. So, if you are considering anything other than a single entry it pays to do a bit of planning first and check all details with the appropriate officials.

HASSLE-FREE RETURN TO THE USA?

It is paramount that you hand in your I-94 Arrival-Departure Card, usually stapled to a page in your passport, when you leave the country, otherwise they might think you've overstayed your visa. While this might sound like a simple procedure, at many of the Mexican border towns it is unclear just where you should perform this duty. Quite often, you'll find yourself off American soil, smelling the barbecue chicken and preparing yourself for the entourage of taxi touts, when you realise you are still in possession of this official piece of paper that must be handed in before you leave. If in doubt, ask one of the US immigration authorities to point you in the right direction. Sometimes handing it in through the wired gate is sufficient to get it into the right hands.

If you are passing through Canada between Alaska and Seattle, it may not be necessary to part with your I-94 card, but to be on the safe side check all your documents with officials before leaving.

You cannot take citrus fruits into the USA.

PACIFIC COAST HIGHWAY

Through spring, summer and autumn the Pacific Coast Highway from Vancouver to San Diego is one of the most beautiful and laid-back cycle trips you could embark upon. It's physically challenging and rarely flat but almost anyone can do it and you'll be able to find a hot shower most nights.

You'll be entertained for the 1875-odd miles of ever-changing terrain as you wind your way past historic milestones, through charming little towns, over legendary rivers with dramatic bridges and along some of the most picturesque coastal panoramas you will ever feast your eyes on. And if the promise of perfectly stunning views of pristine beaches, foam-capped surf, contorted cliff faces and curious rocky protrusions is not enough to tempt you to pannier up the bike straight away, then the notion that at the end of the day you'll be relaxing by the campfire, beer in hand, with several other cyclists at one of the hiker-biker campsites, should be.

The only downfall is that the road is not always as cycle-friendly as you might expect for such a renowned cycle route. In a few parts there is little or no shoulder and in places the route is heavily used by logging and transport trucks who have little mercy when it comes to overtaking two-wheeled, non-motorised transport. Wearing bright clothing and travelling in a group increases your chances of being seen and gaining just a bit of road respect. Though not enforced by law, a helmet is essential.

Maps and route

In general, the route is clearly signposted and therefore the free state highway road map is adequate. It's obtainable from the many tourist offices you'll pass as you enter the states of Washington, Oregon and California. Oregon goes one step further to make the bike enthusiast's life easier by printing a version with not only details of the hiker-biker sites and other camping facilities, but elevation charts, interesting snippets of information and alternative routes avoiding the high traffic areas. For initial planning, you can download this map from the Oregon State Transportation website at 🖥 www.oregon.gov/ODOT/HWY/BIKEPED/docs/oregon_coast_bike_route_map.pdf, but for touring purposes, it is better to pick up your free waterproof copy from the first Oregon Visitors Centre you come to.

The Adventure Cycling Association also produces a five-map set with a lot of useful information and handy tips, also including elevation charts. You can buy this online at 🖳 www.adventurecycling.org/routes/pacificcoast.cfm.

Other maps and sites that may be of interest when planning your route or side trips are: 🖳 www.oregon.gov/ODOT/HWY/BIKEPED/maps.shtml for great cycle maps and the latest up-to-date information about the bicycle routes in Oregon; and 🖳 www.wsdot.wa.gov/Publications/HighwayMap/view.htm which is the official Washington State Highways website.

When to go

Most riders tackle this route between April and November. During spring and summer, southerly winds give you considerable help along the sections right on the coast, particularly in California. Spring is the most beautiful time to ride as the grass is greenest and the wildflowers are out. When the air is still in the summertime, fog can build up on the coast. Though its novelty will wear off, fog is part of the coastal microclimate in which redwood trees and many wildflowers flourish, and it's not around every day, so enjoy it. July and August are not only the hottest months, but the traffic and campgrounds are at peak capacity.

Autumn is less foggy, but the land has a burned look to it after the dry summer. In winter the wind can blow

Summer sees hordes of cyclists on the Pacific coast © Sonja Spry & Aaldrik Mulder

up the coast and in any case is far stormier, with Big Sur prone to landslides. If you're riding through in wintertime, you might be better off heading inland to avoid storms, though it will be appreciably cooler. Numerous state parks in forested areas are closed in winter owing to the risk of falling branches during storms.

Camping and shopping

When it comes to camping facilities, the Pacific Coast is a cyclist's dream come true. There's no stress about where you'll be camping for the night here, because the State Parks conveniently dot the entire length of coastline and offer a specially set-aside camp area for hikers and bikers. A complete list of hiker-biker sites along the Pacific Coast Highway can be found on the country information page at 🖳 www.tour.tk/country-information/usa.htm.

Unfortunately, as of 2008, Washington State charges a colossal $14 per tent, which makes pitching in these facilities no cheaper than most private affairs. Californian and Oregon State Parks, however, are a lot less penny-pinching and for as little as $3 and $4 respectively, you get to share a secluded area with other touring cyclists. A five-minute hot shower will set you back 50 cents in California and is included in the camping fee in Oregon.

The set-up in each State Park does vary greatly, but considering the price you pay, the amenities are usually very good. Even when the hiker-biker site

---

A BLAST FROM THE PAST

On May 18, 1980, Mount St Helens erupted causing an earthquake of 5.1 on the Richter Scale. The explosion lasted a total of 9 hours and a surge of ash rose 15 miles high above the crater. Mount St Helens' height dropped 1312ft during the catastrophe, leaving a mile-wide crater. Probably the most destructive statistics came from the lateral blasts of hot rock and ash which killed trees up to 17 miles north of the volcano: during the first 10 minutes of the disaster, close to 230 square miles of pristine forest was destroyed or concealed under volcanic debris.

Mount St Helens and the surrounding nature reserve is open for a multitude of outdoor activities. At certain times of year, the dirt road leading to Windy Ridge Viewpoint can be accessed with your bike. To find out more about permits and camping possibilities check out the Mount St Helens website: 🖳 www.mountsthelens.com/.

A detailed map of the area can also be downloaded from the forest service site via 🖳 www.fs.fed.us/gpnf/04maps/documents/MonumentTearmapFinalweb-2007.pdf

---

is full, park officials will not turn you away. Instead, you will most likely end up in a normal site for the same price. Shopping is also a breeze. Most days you'll come across decent-sized supermarkets to stock up on carbs for the evening's meal and following morning's breakfast.

Alternative routes
An inland detour (666 miles; 32,032ft total climb)
Instead of travelling the Washington State section of the coastal route you could add a bit of variety to your USA trip by traversing diagonally through the state to meet up with the Pacific Coast Highway at Fort Stevens in Oregon. The landscape is amazingly diverse, though north-westerly winds could hamper your journey somewhat in sections.

There are a number of border posts to cross at, but Waneta is the most direct path from Nelson in Canada. You'll find yourself winding up and down along the road hugging close to Lake Roosevelt. The attention-grabbing wetlands are surrounded by rolling mountains on either side of the National Park. Cross over into Colville Indian Reservation for some great camping opportunities, peaceful surroundings and starry, starry nights. It is undulating territory with a few passes around the 1000 metre mark and although some of the roads are gravel, they are generally well maintained.

Steamboat Rock State Park has a multitude of camping possibilities and the views of the spectacular red, flat-topped basalt range that runs the entire length of the Columbia basin are simply awesome. The Vantage Highway will test your patience with its vastness and potentially energy-zapping headwinds, but all will be forgotten as you fly through the Yakima Valley Canyon: one of the world's largest lava fields and best day-trips ever.

Wenatchee National Forest, Mount Ranier, Gifford Pinchot National Forest and Mount St Helens are just a few of the dramatic displays nature will have in store for you, before you meet once again with the mighty Columbia River. Getting to the coast from here is nothing short of a two-day, hair-raising,

---

(Opposite) South America In Patagonia – Lago del Desierto and Monte Fitz Roy (3375m) on the Chile-Argentina border, after riding the Carretera Austral (see p210). (Photo © Dominique Kerhuel).

(Overleaf, double page) World map.

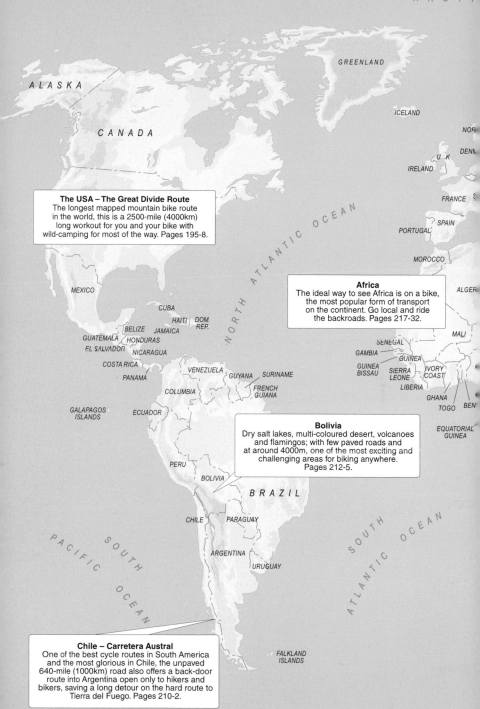

The USA – The Great Divide Route
The longest mapped mountain bike route in the world, this is a 2500-mile (4000km) long workout for you and your bike with wild-camping for most of the way. Pages 195-8.

Africa
The ideal way to see Africa is on a bike, the most popular form of transport on the continent. Go local and ride the backroads. Pages 217-32.

Bolivia
Dry salt lakes, multi-coloured desert, volcanoes and flamingos; with few paved roads and at around 4000m, one of the most exciting and challenging areas for biking anywhere. Pages 212-5.

Chile – Carretera Austral
One of the best cycle routes in South America and the most glorious in Chile, the unpaved 640-mile (1000km) road also offers a back-door route into Argentina open only to hikers and bikers, saving a long detour on the hard route to Tierra del Fuego. Pages 210-2.

Tajikistan – The Pamir Highway
Remote and little travelled but with awesome mountains bordering Afghanistan. One of the highlights on a journey through Central Asia to China, or a destination in itself. Pages 124-6.

Japan
Mountainous, exotic, surprisingly unspoilt and cycle friendly. One of the new frontiers of adventure touring. Pages 175-8.

Tibet
Lhasa–Kathmandu
(625 miles/1000km)
is the best known route but options abound here. Not for the faint-hearted! Pages 147-50.

South East Asia
More cultural variety than anywhere else – and the best food. Ideal first timer's destination. Pages 163-73.

Manali–Leh Highway
Spectacular 300 mile (475km), 7-10-day route with five high-altitude passes, two over 5000m. Pages 138-41.

Karakoram Highway
Classic 800 mile (1300km) route linking Islamabad (Pakistan) with Kashgar (China). Pages 127-31.

Outback Tour
Some like it hot – 4400 miles (7000 kms) from Perth to Adelaide via Darwin. Pages 181-4.

RUSSIA · KAZAKHSTAN · MONGOLIA · N KOREA · S KOREA · JAPAN · CHINA

UKRAINE · GEORGIA · ARMENIA · AZERBAIJAN · UZBEKISTAN · KYRGYZSTAN · TURKMENISTAN · TAJIKISTAN

TURKEY · SYRIA · LBANON · ISRAEL · JORDAN · IRAQ · IRAN · AFGHANISTAN · BHUTAN · NEPAL
EGYPT · KUWAIT · QATAR · UAE · PAKISTAN · INDIA · BURMA
SAUDI ARABIA · OMAN · BANGLADESH · LAOS
SUDAN · ERITREA · YEMEN · DJIBOUTI · SRI LANKA · THAILAND · VIETNAM · CAMBODIA · PHILIPPINES
ETHIOPIA · SOMALIA

UGANDA · KENYA · BRUNEI · MALAYSIA
NDA · NDI · TANZANIA · INDONESIA · PAPUA NEW GUINEA
MALAWI · MOZAMBIQUE
MBIA · ZIMBABWE · MADAGASCAR · INDIAN OCEAN
ANA · SWAZILAND · LESOTHO

AUSTRALIA

TASMANIA · NEW ZEALAND

trailblazer

The Adventure Cycle-Touring World
Selected Highlights

knuckle-gripping ride along busy highways, but once in the comfortable confines of Fort Stevens' Hiker-Biker Campsite, you'll be impressed with your two weeks of solid cycling. Not only that, you'll also be ready for some great ocean views.

Side trip to Las Vegas (1061 miles; 48,793 feet total climb)

Although you will miss Big Sur (an 80-mile section of cliffs where Jack Kerouac famously flipped out), you can also side-step around LA by heading out to Las Vegas via Yosemite NP and Death Valley and returning to the coast via Lake Mead NP, Cottonwood Cove at Lake Mojave and Route 66. At Amboy you turn off Hwy 95 and head over the Sheep Hole mountain range and into Twentynine Palms, then past Joshua Tree NP before hitting the coast again at Laguna Beach, just south of LA and close to the first hiker-biker camping past LA at Dana Point.

AAA has maps which will suffice for the journey and you can always pick up local information at any one of the many Visitors Centres along the way. Don't rely on the NPS's version of the Yosemite area for distances or an accurate scale, however it does identify all prominent landmarks, campsites and roads. A copy of this is given to you when you hand over the $10 park entrance fee which is good for exactly one week. At Death Valley the charge is the same per person for anyone arriving on foot, horseback, bicycle, motorcycle or on a non-commercial bus.

For the entire journey, allow around 20 cycling days with a few rest days here and there to relax and enjoy the amazingly diverse natural surroundings.

HOMAGE TO REPACK ROAD

If you fancy some dirt riding, Marin County, north of San Francisco Bay, is the birthplace of mountain biking and many early brands and models were named after local features. It was here in the late 1970s that Gary Fisher and Joe Breeze tested their fat-tyred hybrids down the famous Repack Road (a turn-off on the Pine Mountain loop) – so-called because they had to repack the wheel bearings of their old hub-braked bikes after each descent. Local bike shops have info and maps, or go to ⌨ www.marintrails.com/biking.

Other dirt excursions

There are many easier but just as scenic off-highway routes in the area. Generally, only doubletracks are open to bikes and they are serious about enforcing their 15mph speed limits; rangers patrol with radar guns, fining cyclists on the spot.

Mt Tamalpais (2500ft) is another great ride. Don't be put off by fog – ride through it to win fantastic views of the clouds below, perhaps punctured by the top of the Golden Gate Bridge or the skyscrapers in downtown San Francisco.

Samuel P Taylor State Park is hidden away amongst redwood trees, and to the south of 'Mt Tam' is the Marin Headlands Hostel, set in a rugged location far from towns (stock up on food first, you'll want a couple of days here). It's the kind of scenery and location our friend Kerouac wrote about in Dharma Bums, isolated and surrounded by hills. A tunnel saves you some legwork if you want to get through the hills to Sausalito, or to the bike trail that runs from Mill Valley into San Francisco.

South of San Francisco and less than five miles short of Santa Cruz, Wilder Ranch State Park is well worth a stop for mountain biking on the thirty-odd miles of mixed-use trails in and out of forest overlooking the Pacific. The website ⌨ www.virtualparks.org has some mouth-watering pictures for bikers as well as excellent maps.

(Opposite) **South America** **Top**: Salar de Uyuni (see p213), the world's largest salt flats, at 4082m on the Bolivian altiplano. (Photo © Daisuke Nakanishi). **Bottom**: High in the remote Pissis massif, Argentina. (Photo © Janne Corax).

Death Valley – on the way to Towne Pass © Sonja Spry & Aaldrik Mulder

When to go

Going up to the heights of Tioga Pass (9945ft) and then dropping below sea level in Death Valley, just a few days later, means you are restricted as to when you can do this trip. Tioga Pass generally closes anytime between October and November, so you won't get very far in Yosemite National Park and while low-angled daylight in the winter lends itself to exploring the lowest, driest, and hottest location in North America, there is the chance of sub-zero temperatures at night.

The spring months of late March to early April are the most popular times to visit Death Valley. Especially if the previous winter had brought rain: the desert can bloom in full glory after such a soaking. Summer starts early here and by the end of May it is getting rather hot for anything strenuous. Tioga Pass is highly unlikely to open before mid to late May. But if you don't mind pushing the physical limits, then there is a slight chance you could make this time of year work for you.

That leaves autumn as a slightly more reliable time to plan this route. Death Valley's temperatures will be warm but pleasant and the clear night skies will give you spectacular views of the Milky Way. The camping season will also have started though it will still be relatively quiet at this time of year.

Usually, all the areas in Yosemite NP remain open in October and November and there are fewer people than in the earlier months. However, short-term closures may occur due to snow, so it is a good idea to stock up on food while down in the valley, just in case you get stuck for a couple of cold nights on top. There are enough rangers around for assistance if needed.

Camping and shopping

Finding a campsite is relatively easy, though you will need to do a bit of planning prior to your departure. Visit 🖥 www.parks.ca.gov for more details

---

BEING IN THE RIGHT PLACE AT THE RIGHT TIME

The Yosemite National Park Service usually opens Tioga Pass sometime between mid May and mid June. One week before, after they've finished ploughing the road and right before it officially opens for through traffic, the NPS allows cyclists on Highway 120 (Tioga Road). They are reluctant to make any efforts to advertise it and not all rangers will receive the memo, so occasionally you will get hassled on the road. You only have to point out that the sign you just passed on the closed road gate mentioned that cyclists are permitted. You can never know the exact date when the road will

open as it varies from year to year. It depends partly on the snow pack and partly on the efforts of NPS to plough. Generally, they make a valiant effort to have it open by the end of May and by late April they usually have a pretty good idea of when it might open. So if you are planning a trip there in the spring, then it would pay to keep your eye on their website (🖥 www.nps.gov/yose/ and click on 'current conditions'). You don't want to miss out on the chance of a lifetime to ride this stretch of breathtaking countryside vehicle-free.

on camping possibilities. Much of the land outside the National Parks belongs to the Bureau of Land Management (BLM) and technically, if you can find a suitable spot on this public land, you can camp wild. Stumbling upon something appropriate is generally the problem.

There are plenty of supermarkets to choose from, however if you intend to spend some time up around Tuolumne Meadows, then you'll need to stock up at the grocery-cum-souvenir store in Yosemite Valley. It pays to fill your bags with supplies before you hit the Mojave Desert as well. Gas stations sell limited produce at prices that'll rapidly eat into your daily budget.

Depending on whether you decide to go to Badwater or not, having enough water in Death Valley in the autumn is not so much of a problem. You do need to stock up at every available water stop, of which there are quite a few, and begin each day with at least 1 gallon (4 litres) on board. The road to Badwater, on the other hand, has no available water supplies. You'll need to take sufficient liquid for two days of hot cycling.

Route 66 and Highway 95 through the Mojave Desert are a completely different story. This stretch of arid vastness makes Death Valley seem like an oasis. There aren't any water bores here, so there is no chance of filling up from any tap outlet. The only place to purchase water between Fenner and Twentynine Palms is at Amboy where they sell six 500ml designer bottles for $5. At those prices it should be called liquid gold.

RIDING THE GREAT DIVIDE

with Scott Morris

Created in 1994 by the Adventure Cycling Association (ACA), the Great Divide Mountain Bike Route (GDMBR) is the world's longest mapped off-road route, a 2500-mile network of unpaved tracks following the Rockies from Roosville on the Canadian border in Montana, through a corner of Idaho, then Wyoming, Colorado and New Mexico, ending at Antelope Wells on the Mexican border. Over that distance you'll clock up over 200,000ft of total elevation – nearly seven Everests – and now 215 miles have been added up to Banff in Canada. Few riders from the USA cycle the Canadian section, though it's probably easier to get to Banff using public transport than Roosville, especially for world travellers who don't have a car.

The Great Divide is a fabulous unending treat of mountain-bike riding that will take three months – a blissful summer of riding and camping each night in a remote, off-highway setting. It's usually possible to ride from town to town, but perhaps the greatest appeal of this route is the chance it gives you to camp for free on public lands, passing through towns only for lunch and provisions.

The ACA sells the maps and a book that make this trip a doddle, though the latter is not strictly necessary. You can also download GPS data for the trip. The route itself is unmarked, it's the map that shows the way so you'll need an accurately calibrated bike computer so that when the map says 'turn left at 3.5 miles', you hit the mark.

Terrain

The scenery is mostly 'Big Sky country' rather than closed-in valleys and you'll be continuously exposed to the power of nature and mountain weather on the Great Divide. It's a mix of ranchland and forest. The route passes no more than 60 miles either side of the Continental Divide, and gradients are not so bad, with only one or two short sections where everyone will have to push their bikes for a half mile or less.

Scott Morris's website (🖥 topofusion.com/divide) breaks down the route as 870 miles of climbing average 5.4% grade (gradient), 951 miles of descent at an average 4.9% grade and 735 miles on the flat. This is almost perfect mountain-biking country, giving you long, easy downhills. The average elevation is around 6000ft or 1800m.

Although there's almost no traffic there's plenty of washboard, rocks and loose gravel and you'll easily get through two sets of tyres. The weather is typical of the high country: snow is always possible, high winds from any direction, thunderstorms are a certainty towards the south, but more often than not it will be brilliantly sunny and very dry.

When to go
The best season for riding the Great Divide depends on which direction you ride. Most riders go south where the earliest possible start dates are typically mid-June. Snow can linger on the high passes in northern Montana until July, but the route itself is usually clear earlier. Another consideration is the seasonal rainstorms in New Mexico; several portions of the route become impassable after hard rain, so it is best to travel through New Mexico in late August or early September. Northbound riders should start in late May to avoid the heat, but it's not advisable to start too early or you'll encounter snowed-over passes in southern Colorado.

Gear considerations
You will see a lot of BoB Yak trailers (see p55) on this ride, towed behind full-suss bikes. Glacier Cyclery in Whitefish sell and rent them. A BoB makes for less rattling than a pannier set-up – if you go with panniers, use the strongest you can get and check bolts daily. Front suspension will greatly reduce fatigue; it's practically a must, and your spine will thank you for a suspension seatpost too.

A petrol stove would be the best choice. If you cannot find small cans of white gas, outdoors shops will often refill your fuel bottles cheaply. Outside towns mobile phone coverage is poor throughout the route. Carrying a bear spray (easily bought there) will give some peace of mind in Montana.

ALL CHARGED UP

Fifteen miles after crossing into Wyoming from Idaho, the trail meets a main road (north to Yellowstone, south to Lake Jackson) with gas station, shop and ranger station. There is a natural hot spring a few miles north of here identified by detailed maps in the rangers' office.

They'll warn you that the water has a high level of radioactivity and is not good for bathing, but I met a bike tourer who'd just spent two nights camping next to the pool and soaking in the hot water. Now able to ride at night without flashlights, his rationale was that it saved on batteries.

Route highlights

Starting from the north, the route begins in beautiful forested mountain and lake scenery and the lowest elevation of the entire route. Whitefish is the first decent-sized town with a bike shop and camping shops. Well worth a stopover. At Holland Lake, a simple US Forest Service campground backs on to Holland Lake Lodge, which has a bar, restaurant and sauna that is usually open to non-residents. Lincoln is your next stop with a campground, then a long ride across country to Montana state capital Helena where the museum is a must-see. The old copper-mining city of Butte is a few days south and is also worth a tour. The route moves into more open country, briefly crossing a deserted corner of Idaho into Wyoming.

The trail runs into strikingly beautiful country near the Grand Teton mountains. This is a good spot for a detour to the town of Jackson for some R&R, cunningly avoiding the first major pass in the process. Towards the Great Basin, an enormous bowl in the Continental Divide from which no water escapes, the land becomes more barren and treeless. The ACA advises carrying three gallons of water for the Great Basin, but that seems excessive for an overnight bivouac. Take a chance on one and a half gallons and you'll easily make it to the town of Rawlins the next day. The one water source marked on the map, where most people camp, is not water you'd want to drink except in an emergency.

From Rawlins you begin climbing into Colorado. The landscape changes drastically from wind blown deserts to cool pine forests. If you aren't a climber, you'll sure be one after riding through Colorado. Fortunately, most of the climbs are on firm, non-technical dirt roads. After crossing the Colorado river at the ghost town of Radium, you'll climb several more high passes before reaching the most urbanised area of the route, Silverthorne. The hordes of bustling tourists and shoppers will seem out of place, but the area is host to world-class mountain biking trails, and is worth the stop.

From Del Norte, Colorado, the route begins its longest and highest climb to Indiana Pass, just shy of 12,000 feet. The reward for the climb is sweet; on the far side lies a wonderland of high-alpine scenery that'll have you reaching for your camera. Not long after the tundra and alpine meadows the route travels through the Superfund cleanup site and Summitville.

In New Mexico the climbs are as big as Colorado, but the riding turns more challenging. However, by the time you're there you'll be ready for it. The route in New Mexico is more remote, less travelled, and easily as beautiful as any other portion of the route. Be ready for some rough riding and lack of services. Towns are further apart and water becomes a serious concern.

After descending out of the pine- and fir-covered Jemez mountains into the town of Cuba, the route traverses a remote stretch of desert BLM land featuring deeply eroded arroyos, tall cliffs and interesting rock formations. You're unlikely to see another person, apart from another Great Divide rider, on this section. Eventually, after climbing back into the ponderosa pine forests of Mt Taylor (10,200 feet), you'll have a blast of a descent into the town of Grants on the historic Route 66.

PART 2 – ROUTE OUTLINES

Grants was once a booming mine town, but as with many towns on the Trail, it has metamorphosed into a service-based economy after the bust that inevitably followed the boom. You'll find more than enough services to stock up on supplies for a long stretch of service-less riding. The next major city is Silver City, some 250 miles away.

The route now traverses El Malpais (the badlands) south of Grants. Cinder cones erupted in this area, covering the plains with black volcanic rock. It's rather beautiful, and makes for some pleasant cycling. Before reaching Silver City you will run into a place whose name says it all: Pie Town. Eat as much as you can.

The Geronimo Trail follows a narrow corridor between the Aldo Leopold and Gila wilderness areas. An off-route hike (no bikes in the wilderness) here leads to some stunning vistas. After riding on the Continental Divide itself for a few miles, the route drops to the Mimbres river valley where a hefty off-route climb leads to the impressive Gila cliff dwelling national monument.

Silver City is another large mining town long since bust and picking up the pieces. But it offers everything the touring cyclist needs after a few days in the wilderness. The 120 miles from Silver City to the Mexican border at Antelope Wells features typical Chihuahuan desert terrain, treeless and desolate with a unique, quiet beauty. If there isn't a headwind, you'll glide the last miles of road to the border station with ease.

CYCLING CUBA – AN OVERVIEW

Viva la revolucion! Cuba is one of the most bicycle friendly destinations on earth thanks to a number of factors. If Cubans aren't walking, they're on a bike no matter how poor the condition and vehicles give all cyclists a wide berth. I've seen mountain bikes without gear changers or brakes and out in the countryside that seems to be the norm. There's also a good supply of Chinese-made Flying Pigeons left over from when Cuba imported over a million of them almost two decades ago. Thanks to Cuban ingenuity, they still work! If you go, consider donating your bike (see 🖥 bikestocuba.org/).

In 2009 my route through Cuba took me along the southern coast from Santiago to Playa Los Colorados and then up to Holguin before heading across the plains to the world heritage city of Trinidad. On the southern coast the night skies are full of stars because this area is far from the bustling all-inclusive resorts and there's little in the way of light pollution. If you like hills, you can have them in Cuba and if you like it flat, you can have that as well. Other cyclists warned of thorns in the road but I didn't have a single puncture.

The highlights of cycling in Cuba include: a lack of automobile traffic; the ubiquitous music; stunning beaches; the generosity and hospitality of the Cuban people (once you get past the hustlers in the tourist areas); the amazing art and colonial architecture; and believe it or not – the food! Typically accommodations are private homes, Cuban holiday camps, two-star hotels or even five-star all-inclusive resorts. Independent bicycle touring is catching on in Cuba and there's no better way to experience this unique country.
Dave Wodchis
(photo © Dave Wodchis)

Baja California and Central America

Sonja Spry and Aaldrik Mulder

BAJA CALIFORNIA

The 1600km trek from Tijuana to La Paz is another section of the classic Alaska to Cape Horn bike route. As winter looms in North America it's the perfect place to keep warm and experience the stark contrast of culture as well as enjoy a colourful change of pace. From La Paz, it is then easy to continue onto mainland Mexico by taking the ferry to Los Mochis or further south to Mazatlan, the latter being by far the most popular choice. Either trip will set you back around US$100 per person plus the newly-introduced bicycle-carrying fee of 200 pesos.

The peninsula journey will not only take you through a unique desert with bizarre-looking cacti and flowers endemic to Baja, but along winding coastal rides and over some small mountain passes as well. Before you leave you will also have had the chance to sample a fish taco, whale watch, admire ancient rock art, learn to surf, snorkel, kayak and learn a bit of Spanish too, though English is widely spoken.

Between the major towns the road is definitely quieter but it is also narrow and sections snake their way up and over gradients that are difficult for the larger vehicles to manoeuvre through. Most of the time, the traffic is surprisingly respectful of your presence on the road, truck drivers included, and provided you make yourself seen you shouldn't have too many hairy situations to contend with.

Visa

Immigration personnel are very relaxed at the Tijuana Border, though it is a little confusing as to where you actually need to show your passports since the six month visa (US$22) is only needed if you are travelling further south than Ensenada – get it at the border as there are checkpoints later on. Once you have wheeled yourself and the bike through the metal cage turnstile, don't forget to cross the grey concrete bridge on your left and make the 200m trek back to US immigration. Hand your I-94 departure card through the gate to the guard on duty.

When to go

If you are doing the monumental Prudhoe Bay to Ushuaia trip, then you will most likely be in Baja in the mid to late autumn or early winter. This is a great time to visit as the weather is cool in Baja just as it's starting to get uncomfortably cold in the USA. Late December is the beginning of the whale watching season, but don't worry if you are too early to visit Scammon's Lagoon just south of Guerrero Negro, because you may be able to see these gentle giants of the ocean from somewhere off the west coast of Mexico once you have crossed over to the mainland.

TRIP REPORT
ONGOING WORLD TOUR

Name	Tim and Cindie Travis
Year of birth	1966 / 1961
Occupation	Drifters, Authors, Publishers
Nationality	American
Other bike travels	USA, San Juan Islands, Yucatan
This trip	N & S America, SE Asia, Australasia
Trip duration	Seven years and counting – no plans to stop
Number in group	Two
Total distance	About 10,000km/year
Cost of trip	US$10,000 – US$12,000/year
Longest day	130km but usually less – we are not in a rush
Best day	Every day that goes well
Worst day	Getting arrested in China
Favourite ride	Oregon Coast, USA but it's all good
Biggest headache	Tourist visas
Biggest mistake	Not doing this sooner
Pleasant surprise	Malaysia
Any illness	Strep throat, giardia, parasites, bacteria, sore butt, sunburn, culture shock
Bike model	Custom
New/used	New – at one time
Modifications	Just replacing moving parts
Wish you'd fitted	We have everything we need and avoid 'want'
Tyres used	You name it – we buy them as we go
Punctures	We try not to count
Baggage Setup	Front and rear panniers and stuff on rear rack
Wish you'd brought	More common sense
Wish you hadn't brought	Preconceptions and misconceptions
Bike problems	Not much – we replace parts before problems arise
Accidents	Crashed in Peru – ground knee to the bone
Recommendations	Halve the kilometres and double your budget
Any advice?	Do not let fear kill your dreams

Summers are hot in the Baja, often above body temperature. April is the last comfortable month, though the water in the sea of Cortez is still fairly cool at this time. Spring is a great time to see cacti and other desert exotics flowering.

Maps and route

Sticking to bitumen will basically mean you have one path to follow to La Paz: the 1600km of Highway 1. You can literally use the road signs to get you to the ferry terminal without the aid of a guidebook or map, though it is nice to have something to gauge distances on when bang in the middle of nowhere: and on Baja you'll definitely find yourself in that place more than once.

Remember to carry lots of water in the desert. © Sonja Spry & Aaldrik Mulder

The AAA Baja map is widely used, though is not the only one available. To its credit, all the villages, distances and scale are extremely accurate, so there are no nasty little surprises when planning those well-earned breaks. The only disadvantage is the lack of elevations outside of towns and the use of miles when Mexican signposting is in kilometres.

After Tijuana the road quietens somewhat. Follow the signs to Rosarito and the toll-free highway (*carretera libre*). You basically follow the coast through to Ensenada and there are plenty of blue ocean views during this ride. Less exciting, and with a few unanticipated climbs requiring plenty of pedal power, is the journey to El Rosario. They say that Baja actually begins from here and you'll get your first chance to experience camping out among the cacti in the central desert. This inland turn sees you saying goodbye to the ocean and unless you count the salt flats at Guerrero Negro or take a side trip to go whale watching, you won't really see it up close until you hit the other side of the peninsula at Santa Rosalia.

The Sea of Cortez side is notorious for high winds which can blow up at anytime and from any direction in the winter months. Bahia Concepcion is a stunning piece of coastline and well worth a planned break for beach camping. Loreto to La Paz is a three-day inland desert ride and, depending on your luck with the winds, can either be just hard work or utter hell.

Most cyclists take the ferry from La Paz across to the mainland (daily, 6 hours crossing to Los Mochis or an 18hr daily ferry further south to Mazatlan). La Paz has good camping and other activities such as dive trips. While it's a beautiful ride down to Cabo San Lucas and a round trip can be made through the mountains, Cabo is strictly for cruise-ship and package tourists.

Road conditions

When you have Highway 1 to yourself, more often than not, it is a very good ride: the government has been working hard to improve the road the last few years. Very few potholed sections remain and the road has been widened, though still not sufficiently for a cyclist's liking. Consequently, when the highway is busy, it is awfully tempting to seek an alternative route and even

A TRUCKER'S THUMBS UP

From a cyclists point of view, truckers are tarnished world-wide for their bike-bullying ways. From Tijuana to La Paz however, credit must be given where credit is due. The Baja long-haul drivers infamously turn tables and are praised for giving the widest berth possible, tooting very softly and even tunefully to say hello or simply let you know they are approaching, waving like crazy with a big thumbs-up and cheshire-cat smiles from their air-con cabins.

possibly discover a few of those stunning beaches everyone talks about. However, the most frustrating problem you will face on Baja is not being able to get to the remote ocean spots with anything less than a four-wheel drive and several days supply of food and water. The road passes by stunning desert or ocean scenery, but when busy with traffic, you'll be concentrating on staying as far to the edge as you can. Buses can be the most aggressive, American RVs cautious but huge, and Mexican truckers, surprisingly courteous.

The quietest time to pedal is before noon: after that the day starts for peninsular Mexicans and the road get busier. Traffic peaks between 4pm and 5pm.

Camping and shopping

Camping wild in a Baja-cultured cacti garden will be, without doubt, one of the most memorable star-gazing experiences you'll ever have. Baja used to have a bandit problem but you will be safe as long as you camp out of sight. This is standard wild camping practice anywhere but in the desert it's harder to find somewhere to hide and you have to scout a path to your intended spot that avoids cacti and broken glass. There is a slight chance that scorpions, spiders or snakes are also going to find your temporary home a cosy spot to rest for the night: make noise when you walk, don't leave bags or your tent open and bang out the shoes before you poke your toes in the next morning. Not so obviously threatening are all the spikes around you, but in the middle of the night it can turn nasty: memorise your path to the toilet before nightfall.

Hotels in Baja are not particularly good value and hostels don't really exist, so camping will definitely be your best option. By and large, the bigger towns have at least one campground facility, though amenities and price vary considerably. Don't be afraid to barter the price down. You can also ask to pitch your tent in small villages, at ranches and truck stops throughout the desert stretches. Locals rarely refuse you a patch of ground to spend the night. Sometimes they hope for a little money, sometimes not.

Official camp spots range from 50 pesos on a beach in Bahia Concepcion to 200 pesos per person per night in a dusty campground in Cabo San Lucas. On average expect to pay around 120 pesos or the equivalent in US dollars, which are accepted as widely as pesos

Baja – camping in a truck stop cactus garden.
© Sonja Spry & Aaldrik Mulder

everywhere on the peninsula. Most facilities will include a hot shower: a welcome luxury after a few nights of free-camping in the middle of nowhere.

Keep yourself well stocked with water at all times: in the desert regions you'll need even more. For less than a dollar, the one gallon plastic flagon is great value and can be purchased in even the smallest of villages. Some of the bigger towns have refill stations and for 20 cents you can fill your empty bottle with fresh drinking water. If desperate, waving an empty bottle from the side of the road will signal that you need either water or gasoline.

Baja is renowned for its fish tacos and you won't travel much more than 50km at a time before you stumble upon a run-down looking shack selling these or other local delicacies. The truck stops or ranchers' homes are not only a place to stock up on water, but also to get a taste of local cuisine and culture. You will see very few tourists in these places. Quite often there's no menu, no prices, so just ask what they have. Another Baja delicacy is ceviche, seemingly a risky choice in such a hot region, but with so much shellfish found on nearby beaches, it's usually very fresh. Meat is a staple here and seafood is devoured by the boat load. Vegetarians will fatten up on quesadillas, cheese omelettes and guacamole, there is very little else on the traditional restaurant menu to eat. Note that flour tortillas are made with lots of lard.

CENTRAL AMERICA
To the south of Mexico the Indian population increases as do the mountains; it's a great preparation for South America as you reach altitudes of over 3000m in Guatemala. Cyclists rave about the friendliness of Mayan villages in Central

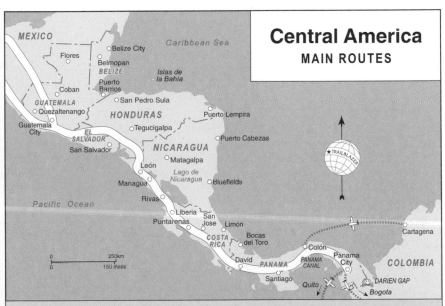

Riders generally travel on the Pacific side of this region, owing to its better climate and because most bikers are heading south and have taken a westerly route down Mexico. It's not necessarily an easier route – there are 4000m peaks in Western Guatemala.

America. You may be wary of crime, but the travellers' network is there to warn you of troubles ahead. With several borders in short succession there's petty bureaucracy to deal with; almost a quaint touch as the fees involved are not great. One of the worst offenders, Honduras, stretches from the Atlantic to the Pacific, so there's no avoiding it, but it's only a day ride through Honduras from El Salvador to Nicaragua if you're not in the mood to get stiffed for something else. Costa Rica will be a shock – a return to the developed world and light-skinned locals, American tourists and very few *indigenistas*. Beautiful beaches and national parks precede your big decision how to get across the Darien Gap to South America. Panama itself is well worth a visit to cross the canal, ride across to the Caribbean or Pacific, then see Panama City itself, from where most riders fly on to Colombia.

South America

Dominique Kerhuel

South America offers an extreme range of environments and topography: mountain passes rivalling the Himalaya, frozen deserts and extensive salt lakes in Bolivia, tropical rainforests, and the spectacular peaks of Chile leading on to the wilds of Patagonia and Tierra del Fuego. Compared with the trials and tribulations of getting visas in Asia or negotiating your way through checkpoints in Africa, South America has little in the way of bureaucracy and there are almost no restrictions on where you can go. Spanish is spoken across the continent except for Brazil, where Portuguese is the language, and you are definitely far off the beaten track when you reach Andean villages where only Quechua is spoken. Combine all these factors and you have a continent that is ideal for bike touring and camping with plenty of facilities for overland tourers.

Language
Learning some Spanish is highly recommended. It will enrich your trip as you will be able to communicate with people all over Latin America from California to Tierra del Fuego. Spanish will even be useful in Brazil as Portuguese is similar to Spanish in its written form (orally, it's a different story!). English is often spoken in South America, but having a grasp of the local language is definitely a big advantage. It enabled us to forge new friendships and encounter some great local characters who gave us directions, fed and put us up. South Americans are generally warm and welcoming people who will go a long way to help and assist you, should the need arise. Chatting with a Patagonian gaucho around a drink of maté must rate as one of the world's best travel experiences.

A phrasebook and school-Spanish will suffice for a short trip, but taking an *intensivo* course and living with a family is a good way to begin a long tour. Bolivia is the cheapest place to do this – expect to pay around €400 for 2 weeks of small classes and full-board with a family. Bolivia, Peru and Colombia share a clear and beautiful accent.

South America
MAIN ROUTES

WEATHER AND SEASONS

From the tropics to tundra, South America has an extremely varied climate – humidity, heat and rain in the north and formidable winds and cold from Bolivia southwards, owing either to the altitude or to the southern latitude in Patagonia.

Most of the continent is in the southern hemisphere, so anyone riding down from North America will most likely find themselves arriving as South America approaches winter. This means heavy rains for much of the tropical zone, though winter is the favoured season for the altiplano of Bolivia. To ride in one continuous journey, it's hard to avoid bad weather at some point. Some riders begin their journey in Buenos Aires to avoid the tropical region altogether, and many choose to visit only one part of the continent so they only need prepare for one region rather than carrying gear for every situation.

Seasonality is less important than altitude for the northern Andes; it's close to the equator. In Patagonia, the season is very short. Late spring through to early autumn is the time to visit Patagonia, though the winds are strongest at this time.

Public transport

A necessary but occasional evil for cyclists. You have come to ride a bike but sometimes you have to use local public transport for need of speed or convenience. The transport network is extensive in South America and is available in various forms:

Buses These are omnipresent and cheap all over the continent. For reasons of comfort and especially security in countries such as Peru, Ecuador or Colombia, it's best to use the most expensive bus companies (which are still very good value for money in comparison to Western prices). The more economical bus companies tend to stop to pick up passengers on the way and this is a risky business. Reports of mugging and assault by those 'picked-up' roadside travellers have been too frequent in Peru or Ecuador. It's especially true for night travel. It was always a bit daunting to be video-filmed and fingerprinted before boarding long distance buses in Peru. We were assured that this zealous procedure was for our protection. Somehow, the reasons are still obscure as to how this practice could have helped to ensure our safety.

It's usually not a problem to get your bike underneath or on the roof of a bus. With the amount of personal luggage South Americans take along on buses, it often looks as if they are moving house. Rules and regulations vary from country to country. In Chile, for example, when you purchase your ticket at the bus station counter, you have to pay a fixed luggage surcharge for your bike. The price varies according to the length of the journey. In Argentina, you pay the luggage handler, so there is some room for negotiation or occasional rip-off; a good reason to have a decent command of the Spanish language and a great opportunity to practise it! Nowhere will you be expected to have your bike boxed, bagged or dismantled. In some countries, your bus fare might also include a meal.

The only time bus companies might refuse to carry your bike could be in Patagonia in the busy summer holiday season (from Christmas to the end of February) when buses are often packed with local and foreign tourists. It's worth enquiring with the bus company before you purchase your bus ticket. To give a concrete example, only one out of five bus companies agreed to transport our bike from Santiago de Chile to Puerto Montt at that time of the year.

The main nuisance with bus travel in South America is the constant showing of low budget/low quality war or action movies. Unless you are a Jean Claude Van Damme fan, bring some earplugs or be prepared to be 'mentally' tortured for hours on end.

Boat Whether you are going down the Amazon River or crossing Patagonian lakes and fjords, it's always possible to take your bike along with you on a boat. Sometimes you won't even have to pay a surcharge.

Dangers and annoyances

South America is generally a fairly safe destination for cyclists. However, South American capital cities share some common characteristics: they are overpopulated and heavily polluted. They are choked with heavy traffic and surrounded by some fairly dangerous and deprived suburbs, both great sources of danger for cyclists. We were attacked by robbers at the entrance to La Paz, Bolivia's capital city. They threw stones at us in the hope of knocking us off our bikes. Luckily, we were riding downhill and were much faster than them. In South America, it's probably safer to travel the last stretch to the larger city centres by public transport.

Unless you are in the tropical jungle, there aren't any great predators or dangerous creatures. This obviously doesn't include hawkers of souvenirs who can be extremely persistent in some tourist spots. When camping wild, it's always wise to be discreet and look for a spot where you won't be discovered.

Acute mountain sickness may occur at altitudes above 2500m and is a potential health hazard for some cyclists. If you are planning to start your trip at high altitude, make sure that you follow the usual medical recommendations; mixing rest and light exercise at the beginning of your stay, drinking plenty of fluids and giving your body sufficient time to get acclimatised to the high altitude.

Food

South America is definitely a culinary destination. The range and quality of food available match the rich diversity of landscapes. Fruits (often turned into energising fresh juices) and vegetables abound in all shapes and colours. For carnivores, the continent offers among the best beef and lamb in the world and Argentina is the prime destination. The Argentinian *asado* is both a ritual and a celebration where half cows and entire sheep are barbecued. You can rest assured that you will be invited at least once on your trip. Wine will flow, food will be passed around, jokes will be exchanged and new friendships will be made.

Seafood is plentiful all over the continent with ceviche (marinated raw fish), fish (Chile is the largest salmon exporter in the world), lobsters, crabs and much more.

Wild food is also widely available from berries – notably the famed Calafate berry in Patagonia where, if you believe the legend, once you have tried one, you will be back for more – to seafood (invest in a bit of fishing line and some hooks).

When to go

The weather runs to extremes – sub-tropical in the north to sub-Antarctic in the far south, so climate considerations will determine when you'd want to travel in the region. The best time to cycle in Patagonia is from November to April when winter starts in the southern hemisphere.

For the rest of the continent, temperatures and precipitation vary incredibly as you climb from the Amazon basin to Andean peaks and back down to the Pacific coast. In general, there are two main seasons: the dry winter from April to October and the wet summer from November to March. Hence, the best time to visit the northern Andes (Bolivia to Colombia) will be winter when clear skies make for happier and drier cycling. During the rainy summer season, overland travel becomes extremely difficult in the lowlands, and at times even impossible in places like Bolivia.

As a general rule, the world's climate is becoming more unpredictable, so riders need to be prepared for just about everything.

PART 2 – ROUTE OUTLINES

Costs

Bolivia is the closest to countries like India in terms of poverty and low prices with the other northern Andean countries, Peru, Ecuador and Colombia being similar but a touch dearer. Chile is the closest to 'Developed World' standards and prices. Brazil is also expensive, especially in the cities. The whole of Patagonia is more expensive than average for South America, more so towards the south and in remote areas, though non-Patagonian Argentina is very cheap. Hostels cost from around €6, so a mix of wild camping and hostels will keep costs down.

PATAGONIA

Patagonia, the continent's southernmost region, is shared between Chile and Argentina, being divided by the Andes. Patagonia is South America's most popular cycling destination, often described as the icing on the cake by those who ride the full length of the American continent from Alaska to Tierra del Fuego.

Patagonia can be divided into three parts (northern, central and southern), each having distinctive and specific geographical features. In cycling terms, Patagonia's western side, along the Chilean-Argentinean border, is more attractive. The eastern region is flat, dry and featureless, the endless wind-battered Argentine pampa where you will find heavy motorised traffic and very little water. Unless you are fond of inhaling truck exhaust fumes, take pleasure in battling against frontal gales and enjoy riding a heavy bike loaded with gallons of water, I recommend Patagonia's western side. In addition to cycling, this latter region also offers a wide range of outdoor activities from trekking to sailing, horse riding to kayaking, and many more.

Northern Patagonia: the Lake District

This section lies on both sides of the Andes and is based around two big tourist draws: Pucón in Chile and San Carlos de Bariloche in Argentina. Good quality roads, most of them paved, criss-cross the Chilean-Argentinian border through spectacular mountain passes. This is one of South America's most scenic regions. The area is commonly called the 'Lake District' and the scenery is very much alpine with snowy peaks (often volcanoes), forests, green pastures and – you guessed it – lakes. This magnificent region attracts hordes of tourists in the Austral summer season (Christmas to end of February) and is best avoided by cyclists at that time. As the owner of a guesthouse where we stayed put it; 'Traffic-wise, it's like cycling in downtown Buenos Aires'. Springtime (November to mid December) and autumn (March to April) will be more enjoyable. Some of the mountain passes may still be closed for traffic in early spring, so make sure that you enquire with the local police before setting off. The road gradient is generally easy. Paso Mamuil Malal, the highest pass of this region, stands at 1207m. Accommodation and food are plentiful. With a reasonable budget and a carefully planned itinerary, you may be able to stay in solid accommodation and purchase a cooked meal every night. The weather is characteristically alpine with everything from warm sunshine to heavy snow falls; ensure you have a range of clothing to cover this diversity.

TRIP REPORT
SOUTH AMERICA

Name	Dominique Kerhuel
Year of birth	1968
Occupation	Teacher of French and English
Nationality	Breton
Other bike travels	UK, Tibet, South America, Swiss Alps
This trip	Patagonia, Bolivia, North Argentina
Trip duration	7 months
Number in group	Two (with sweet Swiss Olivia)
Total distance	6500km
Cost of trip	£2500 each excluding flights, gear & chocolate
Longest day	Villa Solano-Tupiza (South Bolivia). 14 hours, 92km, up 1187m, down 2100m. Highest point: 4265m
Best day	Difficult to choose – like 'What's your favourite song?'
Worst day	Bolivia's Central Highlands: 5km bumpy descent and 13km pushing bike uphill, crossing 30m-wide wild river. No water, hundreds of mosquitoes.
Favourite ride	See 'Best day'.
Biggest headache	Quite literally – in La Paz, Bolivia from the altitude
Biggest mistake	Descending from El Alto to La Paz city centre at night – attacked by stone-throwing robbers. Luckily we were riding downhill fast and they weren't Usain Bolt.
Pleasant surprise	The friendliness of the people everywhere
Bike model	Marin Muirwoods (male and female Cromoly frame)
New/used	9 months old
Modifications	None
Wish you'd fitted	Better luggage racks
Tyres used	Schwalbe Marathon Plus and XR
Punctures	13 for the 2 bikes, all in one day! Caused by 5cm long thorns in Bolivia
Baggage Setup	All Ortliebs: 4 panniers, 1 handlebar box, 1 canoeing dry bag (back rack)
Wish you'd brought	More spare parts for MSR stove, bike stand, a warmer sleeping bag for Olivia
Wish you hadn't brought	80Gb iPod which broke on first day on Carretera Austral
Bike problems	None
Accidents	None
Same bike again	Definitely!
Recommendations	Learn Spanish. Let go...

Central Patagonia – the Carretera Austral

The Carretera Austral is one of the world's legendary cycling routes. General Pinochet, Chile's former dictator, started the project in the 1970s and it was finally completed a few years ago. The Carretera Austral runs for 1240km from Puerto Montt south to Villa O'Higgins, where the Andes meet the sea.

In comparison to the north, this central part is less developed for tourism. This implies far less traffic and better opportunities for wild camping. The downside is the need to be more self-sufficient and carry enough food for two or three days at times. Water is plentiful in various forms; turquoise blue lakes, crystal clear streams, powerful waterfalls and heavy rainfalls! In high summer, expect plenty of rain coming from the sea. As a consequence, vegetation is luxuriant, ubiquitous and best appreciated in numerous national parks such as the Pumalin National Park which is privately owned by Douglas Tompkins, former proprietor of The North Face and Patagonia outdoor clothing empire. It's a textbook National Park with a virginal temperate rainforest, giving you an idea of how Patagonia used to look, before the systematic deforestation by settlers to create pasture.

Apart from the heavy rain, the other main nuisance has six legs, two wings and is known by the name *tábaños* – horsefly in English. Tiny but ferocious and tenacious, they will even bite you through two layers of clothing. The tábaños will eventually vanish as you go south.

You will have many opportunities to feel the force of nature along the Carretera Austral, but with luck, not on the scale of what happened to the inhabitants of Chaitén, a former regional capital and important ferry port. The town was destroyed by the eruption of Chaitén volcano in 2008. In February 2009, the Chilean government announced that it was going to rebuild Chaitén 10km north of its current location.

The entire route profile is hilly rather than mountainous; the highest point on the Carretera Austral is the Portezuelo Ibañez pass at 1120m. The difficulty is not so much the gradient as the state of the road surface. The tarmac is progressing further south each year, but there is still a substantial portion which remains unsealed. You will be glad if you have invested in a good quality bike and accessories (especially racks) which will be tested by bad road conditions. *Ripio* (gravel) is a word which will be part of your vocabulary from now on.

Carretera Austral © Dominique Kerhuel

Apart from Puerto Montt, Coyhaique is the only town where you can find spare bike parts and cycling accessories along the Carretera Austral. Most settlements provide accommodation and food supplies.

You will start to feel the pioneer spirit as you go south. Remoteness combined with dramatic landscapes make the Carretera Austral a challenging and rewarding cycling experience. There will definitely be a 'before' and an 'after' Carretera Austral in your cyclist life once you have ridden it. You might even have the chance – as we did – to meet a legend among touring cyclists; we came across Heinz Stücke (40+ years touring the world) on our last day, a few kilometres before Villa O'Higgins.

From Villa O'Higgins, cyclists and trekkers can continue onwards to Argentina. This involves taking a ferry at Villa O'Higgins (Lago O'Higgins, Chile) and a second one to El Chaltén (Lago del Desierto, Argentina). The good news is that they have now built a 20km rough track to join the two lakes (Lago O'Higgins and Lago del Desierto) where the respective customs offices are located. There is no need to dismantle your bike to sling it on the back of horses as before. The transfer from Villa O'Higgins to El Chaltén provides you with a

Glaciers and waterfalls on the Carretera Austral
© Dominique Kerhuel

wonderful vista (good weather permitting!) with breathtaking views of the Fitz Roy mountain range. There is a spectacular campsite at the end of Lago O'Higgins, just before the Chilean customs. We met a military road engineer who showed us some maps displaying a new road project to link Villa O'Higgins and Puerto Natales, in the 'Deep South'. This new track will go round the Campo de Hielo Sur, the third biggest extension of continental ice after Antarctica and Greenland. It's a gigantic project, even more colossal than the Carretera Austral.

The island of Chiloe, located south of Puerto Montt, could be a nice add-on or preparatory trip before tackling the Carretera Austral. Chiloe is compact and except for the central main road – the heavily motorised Pan American Highway – it offers some quiet coastal roads with magnificent views of the Andes. However, constant ups and downs make it hard work.

The Deep South: to Tierra del Fuego

As with its northern counterpart, this area is shared between Chile and Argentina, and cyclists will be criss-crossing the border as they head south toward Ushuaia, the last settlement attainable by road.

This southern part offers the most varied range of landscapes in Patagonia. The high mountain scenery around El Chaltén, with the Fitz Roy massif, gives way to a sierra of dry and dusty hills, leading on to a flat and windy treeless pampa and finally a Scandinavian-like panorama with glaciers and fjords as you enter Tierra del Fuego.

This wide variety of landscapes is blessed with a rich population of wildlife: birds (flamingos, ibises, eagles, condors, rhea ostriches); marine animals (dolphins, whales, penguins, sea lions) and mammals (foxes, coffee-coloured cousins of the llama called guanacos, pumas).

You are also back in tourist country with fairly developed towns (El Calafate, Puerto Natales, Punta Arenas, and Ushuaia) offering modern facilities and good transport (air, boat, bus) connections.

As if you needed to be told.
© Kyle Archer

It's here that you are the most likely to meet the famous and most feared Patagonian wind. Wind-battered half-bent trees and numerous comments in hostels' guestbooks will remind you that this is no myth. Provided you cycle from north to south, ie towards Ushuaia, you should have the wind to your side or even, with a bit of luck, at your back. The windiest time of the year in Patagonia is high summer (January and February), outside these two months, the winds aren't so strong. It's also the best time to avoid the hordes of motorised tourists with whom you will be competing for scarce accommodation, especially in Tierra del Fuego. As for the rest of Patagonia, the road gradient is fairly gentle.

BOLIVIA

Together with Patagonia, Bolivia is one of South America's favourite destinations among cyclists and this is fully justified. The country offers a wide range of landscapes and climates, many opportunities to escape from the beaten track in relative safety and is home to a fascinating indigenous population with a way of life almost unaltered for centuries.

Many travellers will start their Bolivian journey in La Paz, the capital. Downtown La Paz is located at 3600m and uptown (El Alto) is just above

---

FAR FROM THE BEATEN TRACK IN BOLIVIA

For the more adventurous cyclists, I recommend heading south through Bolivia's central highlands and crossing the entire length of the country to reach the Argentine border.

Starting at La Paz, make for Oruro, riding the altiplano on La Ruta 1, Bolivia's busiest road which links the capital city to the main towns in the country. Anticipate trucks, buses, cars, 24 hours a day. Oruro is a hideous mining town, and the first thing you

Roughing it in the Central Highlands of Bolivia. © Dominique Kerhuel

will want to do is to leave the place as soon as possible. However repulsive Oruro may appear at first glance, it offers some aspects of modernity – well stocked shops and markets, internet connection, postal service, banks, foreigners – and this is your last opportunity to enjoy these until you get to Sucre, three cycling weeks away. In between these two towns, as you go deep into the Bolivian mountains, be prepared to rough it. You will need to be self sufficient (tent, petrol stove, bike spare parts). The road profile is fairly consistent and easy to describe: up and down, down and up with a daily average vertical gain of over 800m. The unpaved tracks are so bad in places that there aren't any buses either – the terrain is too tough for them. Locals travel on the back of cattle trucks. Expect to meet people who don't speak Spanish (but Quechua or Aymara). On the other hand, you will be rewarded with sublime and remote high mountain scenery; you will be riding between 3000m and 4500m for most of the time.

Dominique Kerhuel

HIGH PLAINS DRIFTING

Some 500km from north to south, the Bolivian altiplano is an arid high plain trapped between two parallel Andean ridges: the Cordillera Oriental and Occidental. It slopes from around 4500m on the Chilean border down to the east. The wonderful bits include Lake Titicaca (3800m), beautiful multicoloured deserts criss-crossed by tracks and passes, the red Laguna Colorada and its famous flamingos, the arsenic-green Laguna Verde, volcanoes such as Licancabur, the Dali Desert and dry salt lakes such as Chalviri and the Salar de Uyuní.

Bolivia also claims the world's highest road, on the volcano Uturuncu, but this unsurfaced track is now so poor that the claim is debatable at best. Altogether the altiplano offers a tremendous cycling adventure full of experiences and sights unattainable elsewhere on Earth. Cycling across the blinding white Salar de Uyuní salt lake is the oddest, coolest experience. The illusion of cycling on a polar ice cap is hard to shake off.

In the south-west there are some passes approaching 5000m in altitude, but generally roads are no more than undulating. The altitude certainly takes it out of you, no matter how well acclimatised you are, but long-distance cycle tourists who stick to the 'path of least resistance' along the eastern edge miss most that is wonderful on the Bolivian altiplano. Tracks run across the plain but may not be marked on maps so this is the adventurous area to explore by bike. It's safer to stick with better-travelled tracks. If you stray west of Oruro or south of Uyuní you get into extremely remote areas where opportunities for getting supplies are limited or non-existent and water can be a serious problem.

There are no good maps of this area, making navigation difficult. Update your map from the Internet before you go and carry a compass.

Touring tips for drifters

• Take glacier glasses or strong sunglasses with sideshields.

• Use car petrol for stove fuel; allow about a litre per week.

• Refugios rarely offer food – carry several days' worth of dried food, depending on your route.

• Carry two days' water as lakes are mostly saline or volcanically poisoned. Treat refugio water with iodine. There are refugios at Lagunas Blanca and Colorada, and Quetena, Alota, Villa Mar, Isla Inkawesi and Uyuní.

• GPS receivers can be useful; look for waypoints to download from the web.

• Wide tyres are best for riding on the sandy desert tracks.

• Don't overestimate how far you can ride in a day – 60km is good in the mountainous desert areas.

• The corrugated altiplano roads will test the strength of all your gear, especially wheels and racks. It's no place for a breakdown.

• There are lots of sharp cacti around – bring a repair kit for your air mattress.

Steve Pells & Antony Bowesman
(photo © Antony Bowesman)

4000m, making it the highest capital city in the world, even higher than Lhasa in Tibet. Make sure that you take the time to allow your body to acclimatise to the high altitude. You may decide to use this acclimatisation period to explore the city and absorb its atmosphere. La Paz is, without doubt, one of the most interesting cities in South America. Where else would you find in the same street, witches selling dried llama foetuses, a coca museum ('coca' as in cocaine), merchants displaying Evo Morales' t-shirts (Bolivia's controversial president) along with fine alpaca woollen garments, women in traditional attire (including the ubiquitous bowler hat)? At first sight, La Paz might appear as a Hieronymus Bosch hell-scene, but beyond the general cacophony, it's possible to find quiet little corners with charming pedestrian alleys of wonderful colonial architecture.

La Paz is an ideal starting base for a wide of range of cycle trips. One of the 'classic' expeditions is the downhill ride to Coroico. Starting high in the ice fields above the Bolivian capital city, the steep and bumpy La Paz-to-Coroico road plunges down 3600m on its spectacular 65-km path to the lush, sub-tropical Yungas and the sleepy town of Coroico. The narrow – occasionally very narrow – track hugs the walls of the sheer valley as it snakes its way beneath waterfalls and rocky overhangs. Owing to the large number of casualties, this track has been labelled the 'most dangerous road in the world'. Local tour agencies have been keen to cash in on this reputation by offering this outing to an increasing number of 'adventure' travellers who bike it for the thrills. At the end of 2006, after 20 years of construction, a new alternative road from La Paz to Coroico was opened. This has considerably reduced motorised traffic and the risks of collision for cyclists. Nevertheless, the 'most dangerous road in the world' remains perilous. According to the Times newspaper, at least 13 cyclists have died on the road in the past 10 years.

A rather less commercialised trip would take you north from La Paz to Lake Titicaca, across the altiplano, a brownish treeless dry plateau framed by snowy peaks reminiscent of Tibet. At 3812m, Lake Titicaca is the highest commercially navigable lake in the world. In Inca mythology Titicaca is considered the place of their origin. These days, long after the Inca have disappeared, the lake is shared between Bolivia (to the East) and Peru (to the West). Witty Bolivians claim that they have the 'Titi' and the Peruvians the 'Caca'. The cycling will become more enjoyable as you leave the tarmac roads (and the ferocious traffic) and start exploring the surrounding countryside on secondary dirt roads.

Sucre will come as a real 'sugary' sweet treat. It is a fairly large town, blessed with a magnificent colonial architecture and all modern facilities. Bolivians say that it's their prettiest city, and we rate it as of one the finest (with Cartagena de Indias in Colombia) in the entire South American continent.

The Sucre-Potosí journey is without any real surprise except that you will be doing one of the highest daily climbs since the start of the trip (1500m in vertical ascent in a day). It is claimed that Potosí is the highest city in the World at 4090m. This mining town lies beneath the Cerro Rico ('rich mountain') – a mountain of silver ore, which was the main financial backbone of the former Spanish colonial empire for centuries.

It takes three to four cycling days from Potosí to Uyuní through a great landscape of colourful mountains, a rocky and dry pampa. Uyuni's claim to fame comes from the Salar de Uyuní, the world's largest salt desert at over 10,000km². Some cyclists cross this vast expanse of salt to get to North Chile. This requires careful planning as you will need to carry food and water in large quantities (see box p213 for more details). We chose an easier option and camped for one night on the Salar. This was enough to give us a taste of this salt desert and an opportunity for great photos. Bring your shades. You will need them on this dazzling salt flat, one of the planet's most hallucinogenic landscapes. For further surrealism, head towards San Pedro de Atacama in Chile where you will be able to appreciate en route flamingo-flecked lakes glowing in supernatural shades of red, blue and green, Dali-esque rock playgrounds, hot springs and volcanoes.

Uyuní features high on the list of dreadful Bolivian towns, so you wouldn't want to hang around there too long, except maybe that it has the best pizzas this side of Rome. From Uyuní, you can also reach Argentina via Tupiza. This unpaved washboard road surface is one of the worst in Bolivia: it is like cycling on a corrugated iron sheet. We feared our teeth might fall out. Fortunately, both the road surface and the landscape improve soon enough, and you will be riding in dramatic Wild West scenery.

It's a relatively smooth two-day ride from Tupiza to Villazon and the Argentine border. You will be welcomed to Argentina by a large sign stating 'Ushuaia, 5121km', an encouraging prospect if that's your goal.

Northern Argentina and Northern Chile share common characteristics – a dry and elevated area with scarce human settlements. You will need to lose height to reach larger towns (San Pedro de Atacama in Chile – Jujuy and Salta in Argentina). Due to the effects of altitude and the acclimatisation process, it will be more enjoyable to cycle in this region coming from Bolivia.

PERU
In the outdoor sphere, Peru is probably better known as a trekking and climbing destination. Nevertheless, the country has some very exciting cycling potential, especially if you avoid the Pan-American Highway, the monotonous and dry tarmac road that follows the hot Peruvian coast and is plagued by heavy traffic. Not for nothing is it the home of the first *Casa de Ciclistas* (see box p216). Better to leave the coast and gain altitude to expend your energy in the Peruvian Andes, the central mountainous region running parallel to the Pan-American Highway. The area is of astounding beauty with snowy peaks over 6000m and tiny swirling back roads which will take your breath away, in all senses of the word. Peru offers many fabulous archaeological sites and some world-class historical landmarks (like Machu Picchu and Cusco). Sadly, these places are also major tourist traps. Leave your bike in Cusco or Aguas Calientes and take transport to Machu Picchu or walk the final leg – buses crowd the road up and there's no safe place to leave your bike.

ECUADOR
Ecuador is far smaller than its neighbouring countries but it offers an amazing natural diversity. The elevated central highlands are sandwiched between the lush and balmy Pacific coast to the west and the tropical Amazon basin to the East. These central highlands are the most interesting area for cyclists both geographically and culturally. They are home to a colourful indigenous population who live among glaciated Andean volcanoes, separated by deep valleys.

COLOMBIA
Colombia suffers from a bad reputation abroad and many travellers tend to avoid the country for fear of their safety. We spent six weeks in Colombia and never felt frightened once. The safety situation has much improved in recent years, and provided you stick to the main roads, you should be fine. You just

TRUJILLO, PERU AND THE CASA DE CICLISTAS

We rode into Trujillo, Peru's second-largest city, looking for La Casa de Ciclistas and stopped at a bike shop to ask for directions. Inside, everyone knew where it was. The owner sent his nephews to lead us there, reminding them to be careful of thieves near the market.

The two boys delivered us to a plain-looking house, except for a painting over the door of two cyclists holding up the earth; one was a road racer and the other was a bike tourist. One of the boys knocked on the door. Someone opened it and we were rushed inside with our loaded bikes.

We entered a world of bike culture and felt accepted among our own kind. A man wearing a greasy shop apron and holding a dirty chain tool introduced himself as Lucho, the boss of the house.

He asked, 'Did you have a good ride today?' This was our first insight into Lucho's priorities: cycling first, everything else second.

La Casa de Ciclistas is a unique gathering place for long-distance travelling cyclists from around the world. It is not in a guide-book, but instead passed along by word of mouth from cyclists who meet on the road. Lucho has over a thousand cyclists in his guestbook. Inside there is a full set of bike tools and parts for a tired bicycle –

Lucho is a professional bike mechanic. Every inch of the house has decades of cycling memorabilia, including posters in several languages that covered the walls. Guests' touring bicycles are parked in every available space. Lucho, his wife Arecilli and daughter Angela were our hosts. Lucho said, 'All cyclists understand freedom, the wind in their hair, the wheels turning under them, the sound a bike makes when it is tuned to perfection, the agony of a head wind, and the frustration of a flat tyre. Anyone who understands these things is welcome in my house.'

We had originally planned to stay at La Casa de Ciclistas for only three nights, but found it so interesting and enjoyable we stayed for a week. I spent afternoons helping Lucho work on bikes and having long conversations about anything related to cycling.

We went on many rides, including a mountain bike outing around the ancient archeological ruins of Chan Chan that spanned over several square kilometres. They would have been difficult to see on foot, but it was easy on a bicycle. Other guests have been helped out with the bike races Lucho organises.

The success of the Casa de Ciclistas has spawned others – Cali in Colombia has one too.

Tim and Cindie Travis
⌨ downtheroad.org

Tim and Lucho
© Cindie Travis

need to avoid some identified danger zones controlled by the drug mafia and/or the Farc rebels (who are often the same people). There is no reason to cycle in these remote no-go areas located deep in the jungle or impenetrable mountains. Should you decide to cycle in Colombia, you should contact the tourist police located in each town. They are generally very helpful and will advise you of the latest information.

The Colombian landscape resembles that of its southern neighbour Ecuador. The central highlands aren't so elevated here, but you have the added bonus of the Caribbean coast with its pristine white sand beaches, clear blue sky and turquoise warm sea; a postcard from paradise. Colombians are kind and hospitable people with a great sense of fun and a contagious party spirit.

North Africa

Raf Verbeelen

From Morocco to Egypt, North Africa offers anything a biker could want. Just a short distance from Europe you'll find wild mountain ranges, sunny beaches and marvellous desert landscapes, often very close to each other. If you want culture besides historic mosques and medrassas, much of the northern coast is scattered with Roman antiquities, not to mention the pharaonic heritage of Egypt. Most riders return home raving about the rich culture and great hospitality of the people. And you'll never pay a fortune; many places are accessible on inexpensive charter flights and you can still travel on a modest budget.

For further information *Sahara Overland* (also from Trailblazer) has ten pages on cycling; you can visit the corresponding website and forum at 🖥 www.sahara-overland.com or my webpages: 🖥 www.verbeelen.net.

When to go
Even if you keep to the Mediterranean, summer is a season to avoid owing to the high temperatures. Winter temperatures are generally pleasant but it can be cold and rainy. In most cases the transitional seasons are the best choice in the north, especially if you want to cross the Moroccan High Atlas where the higher passes will be closed if it snows. Weather conditions may vary greatly from region to region, so taking the bus for a stage might help you get out of the rain. If you plan to cycle to sub-Saharan Africa (see p224) you're best off starting your trip in early autumn.

Food, health and accommodation
Health precautions are not too demanding and medicines are available in towns. It's sensible to get medical advice from your doctor or a travel health specialist and essential to check the country-specific requirements before you leave. In most cases your tetanus and hepatitis injections and a basic medical kit will do. During your stay you're most likely to encounter a degree of diarrhoea which can result in dehydration. Don't ignore the symptoms. To be on the safe side, stick to bottled water unless you have a good stomach. Rabies is present so avoid petting dogs and be careful not to get bitten. Some dogs can be persistent but in most cases you can get rid of them by speeding up. If not, an aggressive attitude or a stone might help (see p22).

Food is very good but in the poorer or desert regions you'll have to take what you're given which can become quite monotonous. Dates are found everywhere and are very nutritious snacks for cyclists. In the towns and villages you can also buy pasta, rice, canned food and fresh vegetables, but the more remote the village, the more expensive and the more limited the choice. Hygiene standards are not the same as in Western countries, so keep your eyes open and pray.

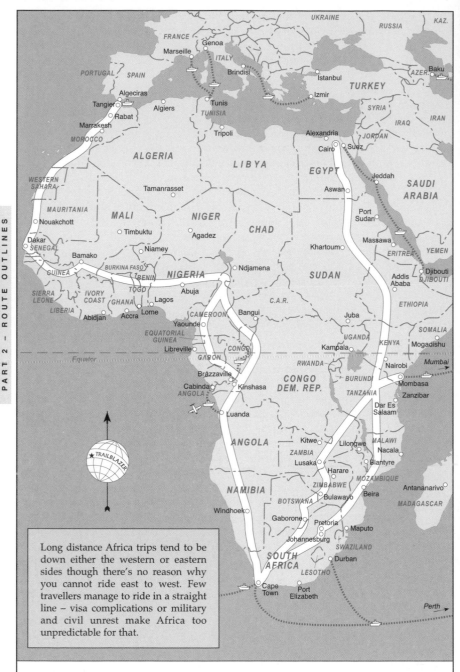

Long distance Africa trips tend to be down either the western or eastern sides though there's no reason why you cannot ride east to west. Few travellers manage to ride in a straight line – visa complications or military and civil unrest make Africa too unpredictable for that.

Africa   MAIN OVERLAND ROUTES

| 0 | 1000 | 2000 miles |
| 0 | 600 | 1200km |

Alcohol is forbidden to Muslims but this is not observed by everyone and it is certainly available in tourist centres. In Libya and Mauritania, however, it's illegal to bring in any alcoholic beverages.

As for sleeping, outside the tourist areas which are growing fast and where you can find any degree of Western luxury, your choice is limited to the local hotels which can range from very nice and clean to holes. They are, however, always cheap. Campgrounds are usually nothing to get excited about and wild camping is no problem in rural regions; just keep a low profile or ask a farmer

FIVE AFRICA MYTHS DEBUNKED

1 Africa is a dangerous place and its people are inherently violent.
Although there certainly are pockets of violence and no-go areas on the continent, cycling in rural Africa is as safe as cycling in rural areas in Europe or North America. In most places, you can leave your bike outside shops, have a stroll around the village and even hike up to see a waterfall and when you return your bike and belongings will still be there. Some African mega-cities such as Dakar, Johannesburg and Lagos live up to their reputations as dangerous places and you certainly wouldn't want to arrange a tour through conflict zones such as Darfur or Eastern Congo. Fortunately, with a little planning these places are easily circumnavigated. In most African capitals, keeping your wits about you will enable you to stay out of harm's way. During the two years I spent cycling around the continent, most Africans I encountered were gentle, humble and hospitable. They warmly welcomed me into their villages and shared generously of all they possessed.

2 African roads are so bad they're impossible to cycle on.
While it is true that Africa lacks a comprehensive paved highway network, that's part of the fun. Bouncing along on a narrow track waving at giggling toddlers, exchanging greetings with kids trudging off to school, stopping to chat with villagers on their way to the fields – the back roads are the best way to discover the real heart of Africa. Roads can be rough, especially after heavy rains, so you may not be able to cover as much distance in a day as you would in other parts of the world. With a little practice, though, you'll soon become a pro at cycling through seas of sand, navigating rock-strewn roads and steering a course through muddy, rutted tracks. And for those of you with overly-sensitive bums, don't despair. You can cycle almost 12,000km all the way from Cairo to Cape Town on smooth tarmac with less than 1000km on unpaved roads.

3 Africa is very corrupt and I will have to pay many bribes.
I never encountered any type of corruption in East or Southern Africa. Minor corruption in West and Central Africa is, however, quite common. I was regularly asked to pay miscellaneous 'processing fees' at border crossings and police checkpoints and sometimes asked to make a contribution towards a beer, soft drink or fuel for the generator. By standing firm, remaining friendly and being patient I never ended up paying any bribes or extra fees except on one unlucky occasion (see pp273-5).

4 I will have trouble finding food if I cycle through Africa.
Food shortages do occur in Africa, but as a cyclist with money to spend you are unlikely to be affected by them. Even in some of the very remote stretches where most of the local population was living off food relief provided by international aid agencies, I was always able to buy food locally. Markets may not be overflowing, but you'll find enough staples to get by.

5 Africa is too hot for cycling.
The African continent stretches 30 degrees north and south of the equator and thus varies greatly in terms of climate. The only region where it's really hot and sweltering all year round is the narrow band of lowland tropics that straddles the equator. Cycling through Namibia in July (the southern hemisphere winter) will mean frost on the tent; you'll encounter snow on the high passes in Lesotho in August and the highlands of Ethiopia are refreshingly cool all year round.
Amaya Williams

for permission. In remote areas put up your tent out of sight but even then don't be surprised if someone turns up out of nowhere full of curiosity or to invite you to their village.

What to bring
If you plan to go off the surfaced roads the best bike is a tough mountain bike on fat tyres. Bring spare parts and tools, too, because it will be hard or impossible to find anything decent there. On the other hand, there are little bike-repair shops in most towns and you'll be amazed what they can fix, albeit in a Heath Robinson way.

During the day, light shirts with long sleeves, sunglasses, a hat or local scarf, sun-cream and lip balm provide protection against the sun. But temperatures can drop considerably at night; you'll also need warm clothes and a good sleeping bag.

If you plan to camp, light free-standing tents are best. Speaking from personal experience, just make sure the tent can't be blown away by always leaving something heavy in it!

Muslim customs and etiquette
The version of Islam you'll experience in North Africa is far less strict than that of the indigenous Arab countries further east. Nevertheless, it's appropriate to wear baggy clothing – long sleeves and trousers – and not expose bare skin. If you can't live without them, cycling in Lycra shorts seems no problem, for a man at least, as long as you're actually cycling. People regard you as a sportsman anyway and you will normally only cause some giggling. However, attitudes may differ from region to region, so be cautious in your dress as you move into new territory.

Muslims regard other religions with much respect but atheism is not appreciated. During Ramadan, when Muslims don't eat, drink or smoke during the day, it's considerate not to do those things in public, though as a traveller (and a non-Muslim) you are permitted. Keep in mind that during this month it can be hard to obtain food before late afternoon in some places.

On the road
Roads are mostly in good condition due to recent 'tarmac fever' in the region. African drivers don't have a very good reputation and cycling in the big crowded cities like Cairo is an adventure on its own, though I've never felt more unsafe than in Western Europe. Where you have a choice, plan to ride on secondary roads; traffic beyond the main roads is mostly very light. Unsurfaced tracks or pistes offer a good alternative for exploring the countryside, providing they are not too sandy.

Stone-throwing is usually nothing more than a local kids' game, although someone badly hit would disagree. Once I sat by the roadside in a little Egyptian town with a local teacher who threw little stones at his own pupils cycling past. In Morocco's Draa Valley an attempt to chase after some stone-throwing kids ended up in a football game with them and an overnight stay in the house of one of their parents. Sometimes, you'll wish that the tourist who started to give pens to the local kids had been stoned before he had the chance to do it.

Some visitors are driven crazy by the hassling that goes on in Morocco, Egypt and Tunisia. This is mostly restricted to tourist hotspots and the general advice is to be firm without losing your good humour towards the hustlers. Especially when you get away from the tourist enclaves you'll be surprised by the hospitality of the people. The Berbers are famous for this, though some will take advantage of this reputation and try to sell you a carpet you don't need. During your trip you'll almost certainly be invited to have tea, a meal or even stay at someone's house. When this is the case, a little gift in the form of some tea, sugar, sweets or a present for the kids will always be appreciated.

Desert cycling

A successful bicycle trip in the Sahara starts with careful preparation and a realistic knowledge of your physical and mental limits. A look at a map such as the Michelin 741 can generate over-ambitious plans like crossing the central Sahara. Although it has been done, it's an expedition to be undertaken only by very experienced and committed riders and is next to impossible on your own. Other routes on the fringes of the desert can be far more rewarding but even then, it all comes down to knowing the difficulties that can be encountered and being prepared for them.

Major concerns for cyclists in the Sahara are the climate, remoteness and the terrain or track surface but the primary concern is that water resources are far apart and a cyclist's range is limited. Even in winter you will need 5-10 litres of water a day. However, if you envisage having to push a loaded bike through soft sand, you don't want to take much more than 20 litres in total, giving you a maximum of four days' range in winter with no washing. The distance covered on an average day in the desert can range from 100km or more on asphalt with a tail wind to a mere 10km or less pushing through soft sand with that same wind blowing in your face. The prevailing wind direction in the vast spaces of the Sahara is from the north-east but don't rely on this.

Once you're out in the desert, the success of your trip depends on economy of effort and good navigation. To save your strength and resources, rest in the shade during the hottest hours of the day and sip your water continually rather than drinking one full bottle every few hours.

Drinking water can get unpleasantly warm during the day but it cools off at night. A rope will prove very useful for getting water out of a well where nothing else is available, as you can tie it to a waterproof pannier. Note, however, that the technique is none too easy and it's a good idea to take a lesson or two with a local. Well water will need purifying. As you won't always be able to find wood, a fuel-stove is a must.

Navigation requires maps, a compass and even a GPS unit. For Morocco and Tunisia, maps to load in Garmin GPS units, based on tracks from travellers, are freely available on the internet. A donation to the authors or contribution to the projects of your own GPS logs is appreciated. Small binoculars may come in handy, too. Make sure you have experience in using all these things before you set off.

PART 2 – ROUTE OUTLINES

When the track becomes too sandy, you're lost. Have a laugh with your companion who will eventually fall down when stuck. Drink some water and start to push your 40kg loaded bicycle through the soft, deep sand. Convince yourself that it's the most normal thing to do on a hot day while everyone else is having a drink and swimming at the lake.

Where to go
Actually the choice is quite limited for the adventurous cycle-tourist. Restrictions on independent travel apply in Algeria and Libya (see box below and p255-8 for more on Libya). Egypt is described on p225. In addition, political problems can make some tours impossible. The Moroccan-Algerian border has been closed for many years now.

Northern Algeria aside, the North African countries are safe though you have to be alert as you would in any big city or tourist spot. In general theft or violence against tourists is far less common than in Europe. There have been terrorist attacks in most of the countries, but no more than in parts of North America, Europe and Asia.

TRANS-SAHARA
There are two main cycleable routes across the Sahara at the western and eastern borders of the desert. The Atlantic route, running along the coastline out of Morocco via Western Sahara to Nouadhibou in Mauritania and further on to Senegal/Mali, is fully sealed except for a few kilometres of no-man's land at the Moroccan-Mauritanian border. Make sure to follow the tracks here as landmines lie around just outside. Visas for Mauritania can be obtained in

---

FACT FILE – LIBYA

Distance: Across the country: 1100 miles.
Road conditions/traffic: Good asphalt, but bad drivers. Roads usually have a hard shoulder.
Maps/signage: 'Reise Know-How Verlag' and 'Gizi Map' have up-to-date maps. Neither is easily available in Libya. Road signs are almost non-existent and those that do exist are in Arabic. Fortunately there are few roads in the country.
Bike used: Cannondale Badboy with Blackburn racks and Ortlieb panniers.
Highlights: Leptis Magna/other Roman ruins and hospitality of people (very few people tour here so there is a friendly curiosity towards visitors).
Food and accommodation: Cheap youth hostels exist in all major towns and cities (£3 per night). Camping in the desert is safe. Food is cheap and shops are well stocked with supplies for the road.
When to go: Winter months are best (October-March). Winds can be a problem all

year round, but *ghibli* (a hot Saharan wind that blows from the south filling the sky with dust) season is mainly April/May. Summer months will be uncomfortably hot with little shade.
Logistics: Most visitors to Libya have their tourist visa arranged by a travel agent. This can be costly if travelling independently because a guide may be included as part of the deal. Only transit visas are issued for those without an invitation or arrangement with a travel agent. These are valid for anything between 3 and 15 days, depending on where you apply. Transit visas may be extended in most large cities. In both cases it is necessary to plan in advance. Libyan embassies don't issue visas very quickly.
Further information: ⌨ www.petergostelow .com. For general travel information about Libya use the Lonely Planet thorn tree forum. ⌨ www.lonelyplanet.com/thorntree.
Peter Gostelow

Rabat or at the border (slightly more expensively). All in all, this route should be quite straightforward. For the Eastern or Nile route, see p224.

MOROCCO AND WESTERN SAHARA

From the Rif over the Middle, High and Anti-Atlas mountains into the Sahara desert, Morocco's awesome range of landscapes makes it great cycling country. As there are infinite options, buy a good map and guidebook to plan your route. If things don't work out on the road, it's never a problem to put your bike on a bus. The four imperial cities of Rabat, Fez, Meknes and Marrakesh are all certainly worth a visit. If you want to visit the south of the country, Marrakesh is a great starting point, from where you can cross the High Atlas to end up at the borders of the Sahara, with green palm trees, beautiful kasbahs and strange ranges like the Jebel Sahro. Another good option is to start from Agadir and visit the wonderful Anti-Atlas unfolding dramatically into the desert. Never forget that parts of Morocco are very mountainous!

If you're cycling southwards, a strong tailwind will push you along and achieving distances of 150 to 200km a day is feasible. Service stations can be found at regular intervals in Western Sahara and once you get into Mauritania, every 50km you'll find rest stops consisting of canvas tents with comfortable cushions where you can relax and escape from the unrelenting sun.

If you're up to cycling in the desert and are well prepared (see p221), the region from Tan Tan near the Atlantic coast via Assa, Tata, Foum Zguid and Tagounite to the dunes of Merzouga at the Algerian border makes some great Saharan rides, with tarmac and piste stretches, or the choice between both. Contrary to remarks on the Michelin and IGN maps, the stretch on the piste between the Draa Valley and the Erg Chebbi is not forbidden and a beautiful ride, though not to be undertaken lightly. By the way, don't trust the main Morocco maps as to what is piste/tarmac, better inform yourself on the internet or recent guidebooks. Chris Scott's *Morocco Overland* (Trailblazer, see p311) will give you plenty of ideas.

The Western Sahara region inland from the coastal route is strictly for committed desert riders. Count on long monotonous stretches where in many cases you'll have to stick to the tarmac owing to the danger of landmines.

TUNISIA

Tunisia may have an unwelcome 'Ibiza factor' for the adventure cyclist but inland it offers many sights to see and is a relaxing place to travel in. It contains the tail end of the Atlas ranges in the north, the Sousse Plain with Kairouan in the east and the Sahara with the Grand Erg Oriental in the far south. This said, the Erg rules out off-road cycling, so for a desert adventure you're better off in Morocco. Nonetheless, the region of the Chotts (dried salt lakes), the Nefzaoua around Douz and the Dahar mountains between Matmata and Tataouine offer some very nice rides, not to forget the mountain oases around Tamerza. You will be entranced by beautiful desert landscapes and fabulous mountain villages, ksars and ghorfas (beautiful Berber architecture), all in a short distance from each other and the sea will never be too far away. South of Ksar Ghilane, there are restrictions on independent travel but you're better off there with a dromedary than a bicycle anyway.

Houmt Souk on the Isle of Jerba, a tourist trap but served by many cheap charter flights, is an ideal starting point for exploring the south of mainland Tunisia.

MAURITANIA

The area where Moorish Africa begins to give way to black Africa, this country is usually crossed on the way to sub-Saharan Africa rather than seen as a destination in itself. Although the cycling possibilities are limited, it certainly offers some great rides. From Nouadhibou close to the Moroccan border the new tarmac road to the capital, Nouakchott, is finished. But if you want a rewarding detour in the desert, you can take the iron-ore train east to Choum. The ride in an open wagon is free. From Choum you can try to cycle or get a lift south-east to Atar and from there a sealed road runs south to Nouakchott. The Adrar region around Atar also holds possibilities for off-tarmac riding, including a visit to the old Islamic town of Chinguetti.

From Nouakchott you can head into Senegal, which should be quite straightforward except for the intimidating border crossing at Rosso, or into Mali via Kiffa or Nema along the 'Route de l'Espoir', a harder route because of the state of the road and encroaching sand.

Cairo to Cape Town

Amaya Williams

Taking on Africa by bicycle may sound daunting to many. But for those who dare to take the plunge, Africa offers an unforgettable adventure that will be physically demanding, mentally challenging and immensely rewarding. Once you get beyond the clichés of a continent embroiled in ethnic conflicts and mired in poverty, you'll have the privilege of meeting some of the warmest people on earth and cycling through landscapes that range from dense tropical rainforest, to wide-open savannah, from windswept deserts to rolling hills covered in forests of eucalyptus. In Africa you can ride through great empty spaces and experience solitude and silence like nowhere else on the planet. You can pedal past herds of thundering elephants, loping giraffes and zebras and listen to hippos grazing outside your tent at night. You can experience a simpler way of life where smiles radiate, handshakes are warm and sincere and life is lived with a zest not often found in the West.

Africa is a vast continent, larger than the combined areas of China, the USA, Western Europe, Argentina and India. But rather than trying to take on the entire continent and its 53 countries in one go, most touring cyclists choose to focus on a particular region or route. By far the most popular Africa route is Cairo to Cape Town, taking in the diverse landscapes and cultures of East Africa and Southern Africa. West Africa and in particular Central Africa see far fewer cyclists and are good options for those seeking a bit more adventure and who are willing to deal with the vagaries of cowboy officials and changing regimes.

(Opposite) Top: Another glorious African sunset, Namibia (see pp227-8). (Photo © Amaya Williams). **Bottom**: Villagers' welcome in Ethiopia (see p226). (Photo © Eric Schambion).

The ride

One of the main advantages of this classic route is that, apart from a long stretch of rough road in Northern Kenya and a few hundred kilometres of unpaved highway in Sudan's Nubian Desert, it can all be done on tarmac. This route will be easier if done north to south due to strong prevailing northerly headwinds that blow down through the deserts in Egypt and Sudan. Set aside at least six months for the 12,000-km expedition.

White desert in Egypt © Eric Schambion

EGYPT

For many cyclists, Egypt's Western Desert is their first encounter with the beauty, silence and solitude of desert riding. Camping amongst the eerie wind-sculpted rock formations under an ocean of stars and watching the dramatic colour changes at sunrise and sunset is an amazing visual experience that will make you forget all those kilometres you've cycled with the wind whistling in your ear. The lush oases that punctuate this extension of the Sahara break up the monotony of the vast sandy expanses.

On the downside, Egyptians are slightly obsessed with internal security, especially along the Nile River. In the past, cyclists were regularly forced to take a ride in a convoy and were not allowed to cycle this route. Thankfully, the government has lightened up and cyclists are now being allowed to ride most of the way, albeit often with an annoying police escort trailing them at a short distance. If you don't enjoy uninvited company, and are keen to explore more of the desert, consider following the longer, but often spectacular Western Desert route where you will be allowed to cycle freely without escort or convoy.

SUDAN

If you've travelled much, you've probably discovered that the destinations the US State Department warns against most strongly are the same countries whose citizens are the most hospitable. It's certainly the case in Sudan, where you'll be showered with kindness. Everyone will want you to join them for tea; if you mention you're looking for a restaurant you'll be invited home

Roadside fish restaurant in Sudan.
© Tom Allen

for a meal; shopkeepers will refuse payment and strangers will offer you gifts of food and cold drinks. Encounters with these amazing people will lift your spirits after a tough day's ride through the Nubian Desert. Not long ago, when

(Opposite) Top: A stop for rest and shade on the plains of Tanzania (see p226), East Africa. (Photo © Daisuke Nakanishi). **Bottom**: The Nubian Desert, Sudan. (Photo © Eric Schambion).

Omo river, Ethiopia
© Eric Schambion

cyclists spoke of traversing the Nubian Desert in Northern Sudan they would invariably mention seas of sand, days without passing a single village and tell tales of heaving their bikes over steep, rocky and rutted tracks. Now that the Sudanese government has gone on a paving spree, with only a couple of hundred kilometres of rough road remaining between Dongola and Wadi Halfa, these experiences will be relegated to cycling lore.

ETHIOPIA

Ethiopia's highlands are the place to go if you like mountains. The climate is comfortably cool, the views are stunning and the 23-km climb out of the spectacular Blue Nile Gorge is unforgettable. Ethiopian kids, however, are infamous among cyclists. They're prone to pestering bikers for money and are easily worked up into a frenzy just at the sight of foreign tourists. You'll most likely have to dodge a few low flying stones, so this will be a good time to get some use out of the helmet you've got strapped to your back rack.

KENYA

If you're up for some real adventure that's truly off the beaten track, then a trip around Lake Turkana is perfect for you. The 'road' is just a sandy track and you won't encounter any package-tourists whizzing by in 4WDs. This area is in the heartland of tribal Africa and the colourful Turkana people still live much as they did centuries ago. It's a challenge to find water and you may end up digging in a dry river-bed (see box p227) just as we did. If you want to chalk up some tales that are worth telling, this is the place for you.

The Isiolo-Moyale road in Northern Kenya remains problematic owing to *shiftas* (as the local bandits are known) and rough road conditions. Many cyclists choose to hop on a bus for this stretch. We chose the alternative Lake Turkana route and were rewarded with some of the most memorable and challenging cycling of the entire expedition.

TANZANIA

Cycling through national parks is off-limits in many parts of the world owing to the perceived danger of encounters with wild animals. Mikumi National Park, not far from Dar es Salaam, has no such restrictions and you're free to come face to face with wild game including elephants, zebras, antelope, warthogs and lions. It's an exhilarating experience, but plan the 50-km ride for midday when you're less likely to run into a pride of lions lazing in the shade of an acacia.

MALAWI

This tiny country shouldn't be overlooked. If you like your cycling a little more relaxed, a ride around scenic Lake Malawi is ideal. Catch the sunset on the terrace of one of the numerous lodges lining the lake and put aside your

TRIALS AND TRIBULATIONS ALONG THE SHORES OF LAKE TURKANA

Bearing much similarity to the Sahel, Turkanaland is one of the most inhospitable parts of Africa. We had decided to cycle through this fascinating and unforgiving region, and there were many challenges to be faced. Our Michelin map showed no road skirting Lake Turkana. We knew that a rough track existed, having read the journal of two German cyclists who'd travelled that way in 2005. They'd spent a week covering a little more than 100km. Such a painfully slow pace seemed almost impossible to me. Why, I could walk faster than that!

No taps here... © Eric Schambion

Quite a few Turkana fishermen live along the shores of the alkaline lake, and we were armed with a map indicating water points along the way, so I wasn't too worried about the ride. Day one was tough – sand bogging us down being the biggest challenge – but we had still been able to knock back almost 50km. I optimistically thought that we'd be at the border within two days. We set up camp in a small Turkana village and my husband Eric went off with one of the local men to fetch water. After an hour he'd still not returned. It was getting dark and I asked the crowd of young men who had come to gawk if they had any idea what could be taking so long. My inquiry was met with shrugs. Just as the mosquitoes began

biting, he pulled up on his bike lugging our two 10-litre Ortlieb bladder bags and all our assorted bottles. Apparently, there was no water pump available for the village. Instead the locals had to go down to the dry riverbed and dig for water. Yes, dig for water. I'd heard about this desperate measure before, but had never thought I'd be drinking water that had been scooped out of the sand. In fact, the water was surprisingly clear and tasty. The trick was to watch out for the last few gulps in the bottle which tended to be a bit gritty, something like the end of a Turkish coffee when you get a mouthful of grounds. But we had water and I'd learned that, in Africa, that in itself was blessing enough.

fears of bilharzia (a parasitic infection caused by a worm sometimes present in tropical waters) and cool down with a quick dip in the lake whenever the pedalling gets too tiring.

ZAMBIA

Zambia bills itself as 'the real Africa'. Here's where you'll find yourself surrounded by the wild, untamed bush synonymous with Southern African scenery. South Luangwa National Park makes a great side trip, but be prepared. Riaan Manser, author of *Around Africa on my Bicycle*, says: 'A park ranger told me to mark my territory around the tent the way a cat would – to keep lions away.' Once you turn off from Chipata, the road goes from being perfectly paved to perfectly awful. Locals will warn you not to be on the road near sunset because that's when the elephants are out and they're a surly bunch in Zambia known to trample crops and invade unsuspecting villages.

NAMIBIA

While one best-selling guidebook claims that 'Namibia is desert country totally unsuitable for cycling', it stands out as one of my personal favourites. The harsh and unforgiving environment will test your resolve, but your efforts will

Unusual hazards to watch out for on the
roads in Namibia © Eric Schambion

be more than rewarded with a night camping in the desert under a canopy of stars and waking to a spectacular sunrise. The dunes at Sossusvlei are said to be the highest in the world and are surely one of the most awe-inspiring sights in Southern Africa.

If you decide to follow the main B1 highway heading south from Windhoek you shouldn't have any problems finding food or water, but you'll miss out on the real beauty of the Namib Desert. If you set off towards the desert and the dramatic dunes at Sossusvlei, as we did, your main concern will be finding water, although heat, high winds and sandy roads are other fun elements to deal with. Not far outside of Windhoek, the road turns to gravel. Conditions vary widely. If the grader has been through recently you're in luck, if not you may have to push at some points, as we did. Be sure to carry lots of water. At least six litres per rider for drinking, just to be on the safe side. We were there in October and it was over 40°C! When the real heat sets in around December you might want to think twice about tackling this route.

VILLAGE CAMPING

'Mzungu, Mzungu, Mzungu,' came the cry as soon as we were spotted on the outskirts of the village. The children were excited to see white tourists in such a remote corner of Western Tanzania. Night was fast falling and the sky was bursting with streaks of soft pinks and brilliant orange light. It was time to find a safe place to rest and recuperate from a strenuous day cycling over a sandy, rough and corrugated track. After a chat with the headman, to whom we explained our 'mission', we were shown to a small plot next to his simple mud-brick hut where we were told we should pitch our tent. As we started assembling the tent, word of our arrival had obviously spread and the crowd of curious on-lookers grew thicker. Everyone was chattering and pointing excitedly at our exotic gear and a few children called out timid 'hellos'. At one point an older man brandishing a big stick began to shoo the children away. The little ones seemed quite used to such treatment, and after momentarily fleeing the action they would sneak back to catch another glimpse of the odd foreigners. We soon got used to being treated like exotic ani-

mals in a zoo and went about cooking and setting up camp without any further thought of the curious crowd.

When it came time to do the washing up, I sprinkled a bit of Omo (a semi-toxic washing powder found throughout Africa) on the pots and pans and did a cursory job of getting rid of the rest of dinner. The chief spotted this and was obviously appalled at the Mzungu's lack of basic sanitary skills. He summoned one of his daughters who then disappeared with our MSR Teflon-coated cooking set. Later I found the industrious young girl scrubbing away at our now shiny pans, newly bereft of their non-stick coating!

At sunrise the crowd was back, not having tired of observing our antics. A few brave women reached out to touch my hair and marvel at its softness, straightness and odd blonde colour. The men were more interested in the bikes and each took a turn at prodding the tyres and testing the brakes and then nodding in approval. Finally we were ready to set off and rode triumphantly out of the village followed by a fan club of cheering children.

SOUTH AFRICA

The coastal Garden Route seems to be a favourite with cyclists, but I prefer the solitude of the semi-arid Karoo region. The sky goes on forever, locals are surprised and happy to see a foreign cyclist and hospitality is just a door knock away. You'll have to be as hardy as the Merino sheep that populate the area, because the distances between services are long and the heat can be oppressive in the summer months.

The Rainbow Nation suffers from a high rate of crime, but most of this is confined to large urban areas and targeted farm violence. Cyclists who keep their wits about them and take a few extra precautions, like finding a safe place to camp well before sunset and avoiding township areas, are unlikely to encounter any trouble.

BOTSWANA

The chief challenges in Botswana are steering clear of the abundant wild animals and obtaining water. You'll have your own mini-safari right from the saddle and will be sure to spot plenty of elephants, giraffes and zebras. Distances between settlements are long on the Kasane, Nata, Maun route and expect to put in 150km or more per day. Sleeping rough is probably unwise as lion sightings are not unknown.

West and Central Africa

I can count on one hand the number of cyclists I met during the 10 months I spent traversing West and Central Africa from Morocco all the way to Kinshasa in the DRC. Here the roads are rougher, the officials surlier and the adventures more thrilling. The further you travel from a capital city the more the roads will deteriorate. You'll be astounded and appalled at the utter state of disrepair of major thoroughfares which often resemble mountain bike trails rather than highways.

At checkpoints and border crossings you'll be asked to pay miscellaneous fees. Your vaccination card will be scrutinised. You may be told to pay a fine because your bike tyres are bald or you haven't got the registration for your bicycle. Patience and politeness are the keys to dealing with these minor hassles. Normally, officials will give up after a short while if you stand firm, accord them the proper respect and keep smiling. Remember, these are the moments when memories are made and you'll laugh about it later.

In this part of Africa a new adventure is always just around the corner. Maybe the ferry that was supposed to take you across the river has broken down and you'll have to load your bike and bags into a dugout canoe for the precarious journey to the other side. Perhaps the 'short-cut' road the villagers have indicated has suddenly run out and you find yourself surrounded by bush and an impassable track. Or perhaps the rains will hit early and you'll find yourself stranded in some far-flung village waiting for the water to recede. It's all part of the fun, and if you can keep a positive attitude most of the time, you'll never regret travelling this part of Africa on a bicycle. Just stopping at the local shop for a lukewarm coke and stale biscuits can be the starting point of an uplifting cultural exchange. Everybody will be interested in your trip and honoured that you've chosen to visit their remote corner of the planet.

For Morocco, Western Sahara and Mauritania, see pp223-4.

GUINEA

Guinea is paradise for cyclists. A pleasant climate in the highlands, spectacular scenery and mountains just steep enough to be a challenge, but gentle enough not to overwhelm less experienced cyclists. You'll probably want to spend most of your time in the Fouta Djalon region or in Guinée Forestière. We passed through grassy plateaux and lushly cultivated valleys, peered over sheer cliffs, wondered at fast-flowing waterfalls and conquered some mighty steep hills as we cursed the state of the road. The whole area had a wild, frontier feel to it that stoked my quest for adventure.

Roads are not always well-maintained, and if you're coming from Guinea Bissau you'll have 200km of rough roads before reaching the tarmac just outside of Labé. But don't let this put you off; the views are worth it and the hospitality is unbeatable. Be sure to check the security situation in Guinée Forestière as refugees from Liberia and Côte d'Ivoire sometimes cause tension in that area.

MALI

One of West Africa's most popular destinations, this landlocked country has been blessed with some outstanding geographical features to break up the monotony of the flat plains and scruffy bush. It has 1300km of the Niger River running through it and the sheer mesas and craggy rock formations found near Hombori have been compared to those in Monument Valley in California. The walled villages along the river are in the Sudanic style, moulded from the grey clay of the surrounding flood plain. We followed some minor gravel roads and tried to stay by the scenic river and its inland delta as much as possible. A highlight was our stopover in Djenné, with its Grand Mosque and animated Monday market. At dawn, farmers and merchants from far-off villages arrive via the river in wooden pirogues and begin spreading out their wares on the central square. The melange of different ethnic groups – Moors in their flowing robes, Peul with their pointy hats and the nomadic Tuareg on their camels – puts people-watching top of the list of activities.

Mali can be a challenging country for cyclists owing to the heat, dust, long distances between settlements and often monotonous landscapes. You may want to do as the locals do and wear a protective mask to keep out some of the dust particles. Depending on the season and the direction in which you're cycling, headwinds can be a real nuisance. The north-easterly *harmattan* blows down from the Sahara from December to February, and all the dust it kicks up can make cycling extremely unpleasant as well as unhealthy.

GHANA
The winding roads and dense vegetation around Kumasi probably make for the best riding. The ride to Lake Bosumtwi involves some steep hills, but there's light traffic and fantastic scenery. From Accra it's worth heading north towards Akosombo Dam and Hohoé for some fine scenery on your way to Togo.

TOGO
The cocoa triangle of Badou, Atakpamé and Kpalimé is highly recommended. Beautiful scenery, cool air and some nice side trips to waterfalls and lookout points. Roads are usually paved and in good condition.

NIGERIA
The best reason to cycle through Nigeria is to meet the people. They're amongst the friendliest on the continent and will be thrilled to chat with a foreign visitor. They'll be curious and full of questions and very impressed by your athletic prowess. You may receive small gifts such as fruit or biscuits and everyone will go out of their way to ensure your comfort. If you're looking for a hotel, someone will surely guide you, and there will be no expectation of a tip for the service rendered. In the remote countryside you'll see a fair number of frightened children who will flee at the sight of a white person on a bicycle.

Major roads are dangerous places, with drivers passing on steep uphill climbs, blind curves and basically driving all over the road at death-defying speeds. Secondary roads are altogether more pleasant and often paved. Road conditions can change dramatically – without warning the tarmac may end abruptly and you're left with a sandy track. Always try to get advance info from locals regarding the state of the road as the Michelin map is not always accurate.

CAMEROON
With its tropical coastal forests, cool volcanic plateaux and arid grasslands, the topography of Cameroon is as diverse as the entire continent. One of my favourite rides is the ring road that winds its way through the mountains in Northern Cameroon near Bamenda. We pedalled past terraced farmland and verdant rice paddies with volcanic mountains providing the backdrop. Conditions are rough and we found ourselves pushing more than pedalling on some rocky stretches, but the vistas were well worth the pain.

It is not advisable to enter Cameroon via Nigeria at the Ekang border post during the rainy seasons (Mar-Jun and Sep-Nov) owing to the extremely poor condition of the road. Sometimes giant potholes have to be negotiated, caused by heavy lorries

Gabon – flooded road © Amaya Williams

PART 2 – ROUTE OUTLINES

CHAOS IN THE CONGO

Cycling actually came to a halt as we pedalled into Loutete. This was the last town before the Ninja-zone, where drugged-up and well-armed rebels were known to hassle passing motorists. They were unpredictable, we were told, and although the peace process was underway it was best not to take chances. A freight train under military escort was leaving that evening and the officer in charge insisted we come along for the ride to the capital. We were given the place of honour right up front in the caboose next to the driver. Our bikes were securely tied down on the roof, just behind the machine gun which was mounted to deter would-be looters and sundry bandits. Our military escorts were a ragtag bunch, many in flip-flops, others with the soles of their boots worn through, some in ripped trousers and wearing an array of T-shirts and camouflage gear. They were keeping watch from the roof, with AK-47s casually slung over their shoulders and some armed with rocket launchers and grenades. The train was ancient, a cast-off from the South Africans and at the slightest incline we would slow to a crawl, going no faster than 20km an hour. The conductor relished pointing out the remains of various derailments and rickety bridges and a look of glee crossed his face as he watched me cringe. The exhausting 200-km trip took nearly 12 hours and the dark streets were almost deserted when we pulled into Brazzaville.

that get stuck and have to be dug out, creating walls of sand, mud and rock several metres high.

GABON

Much of this area is blessed with beautiful virgin equatorial rainforest. It's a treat to ride through, but you'll run into unpaved roads on your way to Congo, so watch out for the rains. From June to September is the best time to go.

CONGO-BRAZZAVILLE

The Congo is adventure cycling at its best and most brazen. Just getting into the country on the narrow overgrown and muddy track was a challenge for us. Then we nearly got lost in the labyrinth of customs, immigration, police and

Slow going on the Congo roads
© Eric Schambion

military posts all staffed by dodgy officials carefully scrutinising our documents and looking for ways to extract a bribe from us. One actually detained us for a couple of hours, insisting that we must somehow prove we were 'just tourists' in order to enter the country. It's a country of chaos, but if you've made it that far, you've surely got what it takes to handle this crazy corner of Africa.

Roads are tough going from the Gabon border to Brazzaville and during heavy rains progress will be slow. We heard mixed reports about the security situation around the Pool region where the Ninja rebels have their stronghold. This stretch of road is also notoriously rough, so taking the train, as we did from Loutete, might be the best option.

TALES FROM THE SADDLE

The Hungry Cyclist

Following a week-long sea voyage and a diet of dried noodles **Tom Kevill-Davies** *finds his culinary fortunes have picked up once on land and he is glad he overcame his doubts about Colombia. But then culture shock strikes as he meets another foreign bike tourer – and realises how much of a local he has become.*

After six nights at sea I longed to escape the claustrophobic conditions of our boat. As the orange glow of a city rose from the horizon, a feverish excitement overwhelmed the weary crew. We had arrived in South America and the port of Cartagena, an exquisitely preserved fortified colonial city, with a dark history of slavery and pirates. It was alive with energy, the perfect introduction to a new continent.

Allegedly I had just set foot in one of the most dangerous countries on earth, but as far as I could tell, Colombia was bursting with life and positive energy. And, for the first time since leaving Mexico, it looked like my culinary fortunes were about to pick up.

TOM KEVILL-DAVIES

As a 27-year-old devoted bike-rider and lover of food, in 2005 Tom quit his job in advertising and set off to explore the Americas through its diverse range of food. Having created his alter ego, The Hungry Cyclist, Tom travelled across the Land of the Free guided by culinary 'must taste' recommendations. The resulting *The Hungry Cyclist - Pedalling The Americas for the Perfect Meal* takes a heart-warming, humorous look at the hearts, minds and, most poignantly, stomachs of the people of the Americas.

Now living in south London with four bicycles Tom is busy on his next gastronomic quest, up the Mekong.

🖥 www.thehungrycyclist.com

Food seemed to be everywhere and Colombians clearly loved to eat. Gone was the monotony of rice and beans. In Cartagena I breakfasted on a calorie-packed arepa de huevo, the signature dish of Colombia's northern coast. A thick maize pancake filled with an egg and seasoned mince, deep-fried and eaten on the hoof, washed down with glasses of sweet orange juice squeezed by happy vendors on every corner.

I walked the city's ancient battlements, built by slaves to protect their colonial masters from invading English pirates, where vivid hand-painted stalls sold bowls of refreshing ceviche. Clams, octopus, conch and shrimp, drenched in lime juice, were the perfect antidote to the midday heat. Voluptuous black women wrapped in colourful robes stood behind towers of watermelon and cocada, a sugary treat made of grated coconut and molten *panela* (unrefined sugar) flavoured with tropical fruit. After a week of eating and enjoying Cartagena, the despondent thoughts that plagued me in the later stages of Central America vanished. Cartagena and Colombia restored my energy and reinstated my enthusiasm for the road. Pulling myself away from her plentiful charms, I packed up my bike and rode into the sultry heat of Colombia's coastal lowlands.

The coastal roads and palm-lined beaches of Cordoba soon morphed into the lush, damp meadows of Antioquia, where fine-looking cows, the happiest I had seen in some time, chewed the cud and rested from the heat of the day in the shade of ancient trees. The throbbing drone of cicadas replaced the rhythmic crash of the surf, and as I pedalled further inland, the quiet roads began to undulate over striking green hills. The calm qualities of my new surroundings filled me with enthusiasm, and as the hills rose and the valleys deepened, the dark shades of the Andean foothills began to fill the horizon.

I camped on a grubby piece of wasteland next to a petrol station, where the presence of a dormant, but heavily armed, security guard had provided me with some assurance of my safety during the night. I woke at sunrise when the soothing, nocturnal murmur of insects and amphibians was replaced by the disturbing and familiar din of the road. Old-fashioned jeeps skidded in the dirt; swarms of motorcycles revved their high-pitched engines. This was more than simply a place to fill up on four-star, the petrol station was bus stop, taxi rank, trading post and bustling social meeting-point. Children with heavy baskets of ripe mangoes and slices of sticky pineapple passed fruit through the windows of buses to the passengers trapped inside; men pushed self-decorated wagons, serving gloriously strong and horribly sweet shots of coffee from dusty Thermoses, and, against the odds, the familiar smell of frying food succeeded in overcoming the acrid odour of fuel and combustion.

Keen to sniff out the source of these delightful aromas, I packed up my tent and wearily made my way towards two multicoloured umbrellas, set up in the shade of a cluster of trees. A buxom black lady with a wide grin was hard at work. Her improvised kitchen was a temple to North Colombian street cuisine, and at her altar a noisy congregation of bus drivers, policemen, motorcyclists and truckers was grabbing at the food.

Buñuelos, perfectly fried spheres of cheesy dough, were piled into neat pyramids, while others bobbed up and down in a shallow vat of hissing oil. Carimañolas, deep-fried mashed yucca stuffed with minced beef, were stacked on dented metal trays like bullion in a bank vault, and towers of patacones sat next to mounds of golden arepas de huevo.

Plastic beakers of chilled fruit juice, guava, papaya, mango and maracuja (passion fruit), provided a fresh contrast to the otherwise oily flavours of the delicious deep-fried offerings. Reused bottles of home-made aji, a spicy salsa made with chillies and tangy tree tomatoes, were passed from customer to customer along with enthusiastic roadside banter, fuelled by a steady supply of strong Colombian coffee.

Colombian street food vendor
© Tom Kevill-Davies

It was as I was taking a bite from a buñuelo that the unmistakable outline of another cycle tourist became recognisable on the crest of the hill. Running from the shade of the trees, shouting and waving my arms like a crazed groupie, crumbs of breakfast spewing from my mouth, I gestured towards him and towards my bicycle as if to say, 'Look, look, I'm one of your lot.' But it became very clear, very quickly that, as cycle tourists go, Torsten, a middle-aged German, and myself had come from very different moulds.

'Desayuno?' I suggested, handing Torsten a delightfully warm arepa wrapped in a grease-stained paper napkin. 'No,' he replied unequivocally, pulling a plastic sack of what appeared to be birdseed and a bruised banana from the bag between his handlebars.

'Café?'

'No!' came another stern negative, and I watched his prominent Adam's apple bounce up and down as he emptied what remained of a bottle of fluorescent-pink energy drink into his mouth.

☆☆☆

Cycle tourists are like dogs, and with our brief introduction over we began sniffing each other's bottoms. How much weight are you carrying? What pedals are you using? Caliper or disk brakes? Drop handlebars or flat? Slick tyres or knobbly ones? A derailleur or internal gear system? *Sniff, sniff.*

Torsten's bicycle was brilliantly clean. Every dirt-free component glistened in the sun as though it had just come out of the box. His minimal equipment was meticulously packed in four clean Ortlieb panniers. His entire setup was as spotless and streamlined as he was, and together Torsten

His entire setup was as spotless and streamlined as he was, and together Torsten and his bicycle were a testament to German efficiency. I was not.

PART 3 – TALES FROM THE SADDLE

and his bicycle were a testament to German efficiency. I was not. As he ran his questioning eyes over my untidy rig, I could hear the white-coated technicians in his mind tutting in baffled disbelief at the dirty, overloaded, scruffy excuse for a cyclist and bicycle that stood before him.

'Vas is das?' I heard them say as he took in my colourful collection of souvenir stickers, which must have added a few grams of extra weight. 'Vas is dis?' they proclaimed at the chunky plastic hamburger bell, leather dream catcher, rosary beads and the various other lucky charms and trinkets that hung from my handlebars, weighing me down further.

'And vi are you not varing zee Lycra. Nein nein nein, Zis is very inefficient.'

This silent ritual over with, Torsten unclipped his multi-buttoned digital cycle computer and thrust it towards my face. 'Alaska!' he barked proudly, displaying his total distance. A figure close to 12,000 miles. 'Six meses,' he then broadcast in Spanglish. I hung my head in shame. In six months Torsten had cycled the same distance it had taken me over a year to cover. And it showed. We could not have looked any more different. Short, overweight, unshaven and clad in baggy shorts and a crusty, sweat-stained T-shirt, I was the antithesis of the man who towered over me. All elbows and knees, his tall, gangly frame of bones and sinew was tightly packed in a figure-hugging fluorescent Lycra outfit that accentuated every one of his lumps and bumps in disturbing detail. An oversized helmet dwarfed his long, thin face. He gave the impression of a man ready to be fired from a cannon in a circus.

We were an odd couple, but with Torsten's tortured Spanglish and my small anthology of German picked up from old war films, we established that we were heading the same way and would ride on together. 'Schnell! Schnell!' I cried, climbing back into the saddle. Leaving behind a bemused crowd of breakfasting locals, who had witnessed this bizarre roadside union, we rode together into the foothills of the Andes and towards Colombia's second city, Medellín.

☆☆☆

We gently climbed, our surroundings changing almost with each turn of the pedals. The near stagnant muddy water that meandered in the rivers and streams began to increase its pace as it ran downhill. Going in the opposite direction, we began to slow down.

No longer sharing the road with laidback, washboard-chested coastal locals in straw hats and plastic sandals, I was now cycling past barrel-chested farmers in heavy boots, jeans and ponchos.

Palm trees became thirsty plantain and papaya, their enormous translucent green leaves spread out around heavy bunches of fruit. The stony streams by the roadside came to life with running water that raced and gurgled its way downhill, this ever-increasing flow feeding the moist leaves of monumental ferns that fanned out from the moss-covered cliffs that rose above me. The road began to twist and turn through continual switchbacks that clung, precariously, to the sides of the steep valleys. For months I had been cycling in an oppressive, tropical climate, dripping with perspiration and operating in a permanent state of fatigue. But now, climbing higher into the foothills of the Andes, the altitude forced the temperature down. My sweat damp T-shirt was cool as it clung to my body on short-lived downhill runs, and as I advanced uphill, the invigorating air filled my lungs.

For all my apparent inefficiency, Torsten and I moved forward at more or less the same pace. Each day we came together for lunch, but Torsten was not a 'foodie'. He harboured a strong distrust of local cuisine and

'I could hear the white-coated technicians in his mind tutting in baffled disbelief at the dirty, overloaded, scruffy excuse for a cyclist and bicycle that stood before him'.
© Tom Kevill-Davies

insisted on surviving on a steady supply of biscuits, jam, birdseed and bananas. Sitting in the small family-run restaurants in the villages and towns along the way, stout vaqueros watched in silence across colourful tablecloths as Torsten carefully unfolded his spotless penknife, spread two biscuits with a flawlessly flat layer of jam, pressed each half together, wiped clean his blade, then slid this strange sandwich into his mouth. Opposite him I refuelled on generous plates of boiled cow's tongue smothered in tomato and onion sauce topped with a fried egg, and deep bowls of beef sancocho, a hearty Colombian stew loaded with meaty hunks of gristle and bone that I gnawed in my fingers. Of our opposing diets, mine was clearly the more indulgent, but if it was good enough for herding cattle on the steep slopes of the mountains, it was good enough for cycling up them.

Leapfrogging each other throughout the day, we reconvened in the evenings in pre-arranged towns and villages, and with the price of a room and a bed now halved, I took a break from my tent and wallowed in the relative luxury of the budget truck-driver dormitories and cheap guesthouses we settled on. Higher into the mountains the temperature dropped and at the end of each gruelling day cycling uphill I was always grateful for the heavy blankets and a soft mattress.

☆☆☆

The town of Valdivia perched precariously on a pass between two bottomless valleys. In the accelerating darkness the twinkling lights of its houses and the tolling of its church bells gave it an almost imaginary aura. Since crossing the gushing brown waters of Rio Cauca shortly after lunch, I had been cycling uphill for over thirty kilometres. I was ready to drop and the first sight of this small town could not have come too soon.

Torsten was waiting in front of the town's only guesthouse, a charmless, unfinished concrete premises that doubled as a canteen. A soap opera blared from an old television, a handful of unappetising empanadas, deep-fried pastry pockets filled with potatoes and mince, waited to be rescued from a grubby hotplate, and Torsten was meticulously scrubbing each link of his chain with an old toothbrush. A couple of rosy-cheeked children followed his every move, and they couldn't believe their luck when an additional Aryan athlete pulled up on another overloaded bicycle.

Our room was compact, with a glassless window that provided a view across the dark mountains. But for the stale smell of its previous occupants and damp-stained walls, it was almost romantic. The walls that separated us from our neighbours didn't reach the ceiling, giving the impression of being in a long dormitory, and two flimsy single beds, piled with heavy, woollen blankets, almost completely filled the space. Pushing my most important possesions under the bed, I kicked off my shoes. The pungent reek of long months of cycling filled the room, and doing what I could for Anglo-German relations I placed them on the windowsill, peeled off my clothes and collapsed into bed.

☆☆☆

'Up! Up! Thomas, *vamos*! *Vamos*!'

I opened my eyes and was greeted with the unsettling vision of a man in tight-fitting yellow and pink Lycra. It was a little after six in the morning. I pulled a heavy blanket over my head in protest. 'Das es verboten,' I quipped from inside my soft bunker, but Torsten was not amused. He wanted to get going and pulling my aching frame out of bed I waddled down the cold, concrete corridor to the communal shower where a vast, hairy man was rubbing his genitals with soap.

'Pardon! Pardon!' After waiting in turn, I did my best to wash under the ice-cold water that trickled out of a rusty pipe, pretending to be a shower. 'Aaah, oooh, aaah.' For the reaction it elicited, the water might as well have been boiling hot, but I cleaned the bits that needed cleaning and back in our room I dried off with an old T-shirt, put on most of my clothes and opened the wooden shutter to a morning of dense fog and the sound of rain. My heart sank.

In a country that was meant to run amok with merciless guerillas... somebody had run off with my shoes. Hardly an exciting story to recount to my grandchildren.

In over 10,000 miles of bicycle travel, I had had nothing stolen. But on a bitterly cold morning in the mountains of Colombia, someone had swiped the tatty, worn-out, fetid footwear that had been on my feet since New York. In a country that was meant to run amok with merciless guerillas and cold-blooded drug barons, where kidnappings were, apparently, commonplace, somebody had run off with my shoes. Hardly an exciting story to recount to my grandchildren when they pestered me for Werthers Originals and adventurous tales from the road. Slowly I came to terms with my loss and the depressing reality that I would have to continue cycling into the Andes in my socks and the only other footwear I possessed. A pair of sandals.

Outside, Torsten was ready to go, standing by his bicycle bulging in his finest Lycra. He looked down at my feet, and before he could take offence, that I was perhaps mocking his Germanic fashion sense, I explained my predicament and that I needed coffee. Bitterly cold, my toes were already curling up in protest at the icy rain that has soused my socks, and I skipped around the puddles and into a bar that had just opened its doors.

'Dos cafés, por favor.'

The owner poured two cups of black coffee from an ornate stainless steel urn festooned with complicated levers, valves and gauges, on top of which perched a large bronze eagle. I took my first sip, a few rays of morning sun broke through the cloud and drizzle, and what had been a miserable morning began to improve. Torsten went to use the loo, I gulped the last of my cup and was ready to take on the day.

Boisterous laughter shattered the peace of the morning, and a gang of men stormed into the bar. Wrapped in traditional Antioquian ponchos and wearing characteristic black and cream woven cowboy hats, they clumsily sat down at the table next to me and bellowed at the barman for beer. Judging by their smell and behaviour, they had been up all night.

I was handed a beer. I politely declined. The offer was made again. I declined once more. The offer was not to be resisted. Hoping for a little peace, and thinking it might warm my toes, I accepted. A small botter of Poker beer was placed in front of me.

'Colombia y paz!'

'Colombia y paz!'

I too raised my bottle and drank to Colombia and peace. The man beside me then pulled a thin test-tube from his trouser pocket. It was sealed with an orange bung and in its rounded bottom lay a drift of white powder.

'Colombian diamonds,' the man said proudly, holding the tube within inches of my face while gently tapping it with his fingernail like a mad scientist. Removing the rubber bung with his teeth, he ejected a small mound of pure, white powder on to the back of his hand. Holding down one nostril with a finger and implementing a short powerful sniff via the other, the white powder vanished up his nose. He offered me the tube. I politely declined.

'Take it,' he insisted. 'It's pure!'

I tried to explain that I was travelling by bike and that cycling through the Andes and cocaine were not a good combination.

'Take it!' The man's intoxicated demands became more pronounced. Taking hold of my shoulder he pushed me back into my seat. 'Take it! he shouted, showering my face with beer and spit.

... holding up my arm he tapped a substantial mound of white, crystalline power on to the back of my hand, and at gunpoint I sniffed.

When I declined again, he bent his other hand behind his back. When it returned it was gripping a gleaming, silver revolver. The heavy weapon hit the table and I stared in disbelief at the barrel pointing towards my chest. 'Tocarlo!' he said quietly, and holding up my arm he tapped a substantial mound of white, crystalline power on to the back of my hand, and at gunpoint I sniffed.

Rewarded for my efforts with a series of firm handshakes and forceful slaps on the back, I took a long pull on my beer, which helped to cleanse the unpleasant and bitter taste dripping in the back of my throat. My nose tingled in contact with the cool mountain air and the numbing sensation gently moved to my teeth and gums. My heart thumped in my chest. My cold toes began twitching in my sandals. I wanted to tell my new friends about where I was from, where I had been and where I was going. But soon bored by my broken Spanish ramblings they left me free to go, and I gestured to Torsten, who had witnessed this whole fiasco from the safety of the bar. 'Vamos! Vamos!' I reached an arm over Torsten's shoulder and we stepped out into the now bright sunshine. The valleys and mountains were breathtaking. Relishing the clean air that swelled in my chest, I pedalled out of town with unparalleled energy and enthusiasm on my way to Medellín.

☆☆☆

I never saw Torsten again ... I think the early morning drink and drug abuse was the straw that broke the camel's back...

I never saw Torsten again. We planned to meet for lunch but I think the early morning drink and drug abuse was the straw that broke the camel's back, and at the top of a long climb I lunched alone.

At the wooden shack of a home that doubled as a restaurant, a hand-painted sign leaning against its wall told me there was only one dish worth eating on the menu. Bandeja Paisa, and judging by the number of stocky vaqueros squeezed round its tables, they did it well. Considered by many, especially the proud people of the Paisa province, to be the national dish of Colombia, the bandeja Paisa isn't really a dish. Translated as 'tray of the Paisa', if rumours were to be believed this traditional feast was so riddled with fat and calories it made the full English breakfast look like a health plan. Considering the hedonistic path my day had taken, it seemed only right to put in an order.

The Paisa province of Colombia is also celebrated for its abundance of handsome women, and the Paisita that walked out of the busy kitchen, buckling under the weight of my lunch, was impossibly beautiful. Figure-hugging jeans, tight white blouse, rich ebony hair, hazel skin, exotic eyes and in her arms a tantalising array of Colombian home cooking. A perfectly braised skirt steak, a stack of crispy chicharrón, a ceramic bowl of slow-stewed beans, a heap of steaming rice, two still-sizzling chorizo, a pair of grilled arepas glistening in molten butter, golden shallow-fried plantain and a perfectly fried egg. The only visible greenery on this hazardously fatty platter was half an avocado.

Inside this small wooden building the rowdy banter of the vaqueros merged with the chink and clink of plates being scraped clean. Outside the dull clunk of cattle bells mingled with the sound of the wind, and with every gust, the view from the window changed, as dense billows of cloud and mist swirled and spiralled through the valley and over the top of the craggy ridges. The numbness of my toes reminded of the morning's events. I had no shoes. I had been forced to take drugs at gunpoint. I had cycled up a mountain in flip-flops. But here at the top I had enjoyed this remarkable Colombian tray of hearty local food, a testament to the hard-working people of the Paisas who filled the tables around me. In my wet socks, I raised my glass of milk and made a quiet toast.

Colombia y paz.

Extract reprinted by permission of HarperCollins Publishers Ltd. © Tom Kevill-Davies, 2009.

England to Australia:
unfit, unsupported and unprepared

Tim Brewer *is living proof that anyone can undertake a long-distance cycle tour without previous cycle-touring experience or even a great deal of planning and organisation. Sustained largely by buckets of enthusiasm, a yearning for adventure and that all-important sense of humour, in 2006 he set out to cycle from England to Australia.*

As I left university, and found myself staring down the barrel of 'graduate recruitment schemes', 'selection days' and reams of application forms, running away was an easy decision. I'd always intended to travel for a while, after three years in the damp of north-east England I was in dire need of a holiday. I'd saved enough cash, all I needed was a plan.

I'd worked in a call-centre, trying to flog people new electromagnetic spectrophotometers – always an easy sell. On the wall was a world map, one of my favourite sources of distraction. After long enough staring at a geographical, rather than political, world map, the familiar patterns – Africa there, Europe up to roughly that bit then it's basically Russia, India underneath, the Americas – start to disintegrate. Suddenly there's just a big chunk of land, undivided. If you start in Europe, and head south-east, you reach Singapore before you run out of land. If you're bored and susceptible to wanderlust, that's a thought that's going to fester.

I don't remember when I first thought of going by bicycle, but I do remember when I first said it out loud. I was drunk. It was not the culmination of a careful study of various possibilities, it was not well thought out, no charitable motivation or grand scheme beyond what, in the lucidity of midnight gin, was perfectly clear: 'Seriously, mate, how cool would it be to cycle to Australia?'

Over the next few weeks, I received various replies to this

TIM BREWER

Since completing his trip, Tim has been studying for an MSc in Globalisation and Development at SOAS, while working part time for the campaigning NGO 'Justice Africa'. Feeling the personal obligation to not abandon his girlfriend for two years again, Tim suppresses his wanderlust by trawling misty-eyed through old photos. His trusty touring bike was stolen in 2009, cementing London's position at the bottom of his personal league table of cities. His website is 🖥 www.random travels.co.uk

PART 3 – TALES FROM THE SADDLE

question, but it was the reply of my equally drunken companion that sealed my fate: 'Yeah! That'd be awesome! Seriously – you should do that! That would be *amazing!*'

Others were less supportive.

'You won't', 'You can't' and 'You'll die!' were the helpful contributions of three friends in a later conversation. That the feat was theoretically possible was nearly believable, but it was perfectly obvious that I was not the person to do it.

I was nominated for the award of 'sportsman of the year' at college, for services to darts, pool and poker. I was the 'king of pub sports'. A heavy drinker, I was 19 stone (266lb, 120kg), smoked an ounce of tobacco a week and was a stranger to exercise. One friend, in a voice that said 'I want to believe' asked incredulously, 'Are you at least doing some training?' My answer was simple. 'What would training involve? Cycling every day?'

Apart saving money, there didn't seem much I needed to do. At the beginning of August 2006 I made a single act of commission – I gave my notice at work. From that point on, as far as I was concerned, I was off. No-one seemed to understand how simple it was.

'Do you have a bike?' No. 'Do you have a route?' No. 'A tent?' No. 'Insurance?'

Details, details, details. Five minutes with the Yellow Pages gave me the numbers for all the local bike shops, five in all. The first four calls were brief:

'Do you sell touring bikes?' 'No'.

The fifth, however, was a winner:

'Yep, we've got everything from your one-day audax style to your full-on round the world tourer.'

'That's it – the second one – I'm pretty sure that's what I'm after, I'll be round in half an hour'.

Later that afternoon the internet provided me with insurance and a self-inflating roll-mat. I had to order sportswear and Lycras online from a specialist. In the world of cycling a 36-inch waist is 'extra large'. My Lycras were 6XL.

A fortnight before departure I popped into a camping shop and bought a tent and sleeping bag. Nothing flash – they looked small enough to carry on a bike and weren't too pricey. A couple of days before my departure I realised I'd probably need some inoculations for parts of India or Asia, so I dropped into the MediClinic in Waterloo station. The doctor took my form, which gave my intended destinations and departure date, scanned it, and looked gravely over his specs.

'I'm afraid I can't help you.'

'Why not?'

'It says here you leave on Friday, rabies inoculation is a month long course, and Hepatitis B is six months!'

'That's OK, I won't be anywhere risky for more than six months, all I want is the first jab, I'll pick the others up on the way.'

The doctor gave me a peculiar look – he seemed to be pleased with me, like I'd discovered the answer to a riddle. He'd never heard of anyone doing such a thing before, but the idea clearly appealed to him. He gave me the first course of my injections, and wished me well.

Cumulatively, my preparations took about three hours.

I packed my bags the night before I left. Looking back, my load was ridiculous – about seven changes of clothes and a pannier full of paperbacks. No cooking apparatus. No penknife. I didn't even have a bicycle lock.

> **Looking back, my load was ridiculous – about seven changes of clothes and a pannier full of paperbacks.**

Day 1 – Kent

My first day's ride was eight gruelling hours, covering the 50 uninspiring kilometres between my home in Dartford and Faversham, where an old friend had offered to put me up for the night. England being England, this involved nearly every source of discouragement I would face, including drizzle, headwinds, heavy traffic and aggressive drivers. It was also far further than was advisable for a man in my condition. Three nights later my legs and mind had recovered enough for me to move on. This taught me two vital lessons – 1. don't overreach, and 2. leave the country by the nearest port.

It took about a week for me to build up to 60 or 70km days, and that became my target throughout Europe. This, too, was a blessing in disguise; there are parts of Europe where 70km can take you through three countries. Unlike most of the rest of the world, interesting, historical or beautiful towns are crammed together in Europe – it would have been a shame to go faster.

Europe is the perfect training ground for cycle touring. Following rivers avoided long climbs, while cyclepaths kept me away from traffic; camping in campsites, which I look back on and cringe for the expense, meant I had safety and facilities at the end of every day, and often they were full of other cyclists. Carrying eleven paperbacks would be considered certifiable behaviour by almost all cycle tourers – all that extra weight could cut 10km from your potential day's ride! But since I set off too unfit to ride a full day on an unladen bike, this was irrelevant. The important thing was to have something to occupy the long afternoons of recovery.

On the road, those stones dropping off
© Peter Gostelow

My excessive wardrobe was discarded piecemeal as each item became simultaneously worn out and, thanks to weight-loss, unwearable. Although

I wasted a lot of money on restaurants, due to having no cooking equipment, the variety of local food is one of the highlights of western Europe, and was one of the things that kept me motivated. If I'd lived off Qwik-cook spagetti and tinned tuna all through Europe (as I later did in the Australian outback) I may well have turned back. It must be admitted that 'tuna surprise' would have given most eastern European food a run for its money.

The trick to being over-packed, I discovered, is to be overpacked with stuff you don't mind throwing away.

The trick to being overpacked, I discovered, is to be overpacked with stuff you don't mind throwing away. Almost none of what I took was new or of sentimental value, and nothing I bought along the way was expensive. So, as if by osmosis, my load fluctuated according to conditions and shrank without causing me pain.

Day 5 – France
My first night in France was also the first time I unpacked my tent, so I was pleased to find all its parts present and correct. Waking up with the sun in Calais, I *ranger*-ed my *choses*, opened the map of northern France my Grandfather had given me, and muttered to myself 'right... which way's Australia?' I identified a fairly straight road heading south-east, and set off.

'My first night in France was also the first time I unpacked my tent, so I was pleased to find all its parts present and correct'.
© Peter Gostelow

My first full day in 'abroad' I cycled 60km through green fields and very small villages to Clairmarais, near St. Omer, stopping at 2 o'clock to pitch my tent and find food. The former being accomplished with minimal hassle, since I had shrewdly stopped at a campsite, the latter proved nearly impossible. The outskirts of St. Omer, and particularly Clairmarais, are beautiful villages of canals, irrigation ditches, farmland. Not, however, of shops or restaurants. Eventually, I stopped at one of the roadside stalls selling homegrown produce which stand outside almost every house (presumably everyone buys from each other). I was looking for anything which could be eaten without preparation of any kind, since I still didn't even have a penknife. I asked for four figs and two plums, explaining when she began to weigh 2kg of plums that it was for my dinner and just two would suffice.

'For your dinner?'
'Yes.'
'How about some jam then.'
'I haven't any bread.'
Dark clouds passed overhead, thunder rolled somewhere. She gave me a

look of concern like I'd just told her I didn't have a face. She disappeared inside her house, and returned with a loaf of sliced white. The sun came out and birds sang again. I'm not ashamed to admit that I tore into these paltry rations like a pig at a trough. Cycling, it turns out, is hungry work. The fruit was sweet and juicy, even if the inside of figs does look like a botched operation, and bread dipped in jam is an underrated pleasure.

> ... I tore into these paltry rations like a pig at a trough. Cycling, it turns out, is hungry work.

Day 12 – Belgium
I reached St. Truidan, as planned, after a 66km ride, at 6pm. There was a festival going on in the main square; a festival of the clearly-unsafe-and-uninsured-thirty-year-old-travelling-fairground kind that we all know and love. The tourist office was closed, so I asked around for an internet café. After a couple of mistakes/miscommunications/downright lies, I was directed to the library. The internet, bless its little heart, tried hard, really hard, to find the nearest campsite. I know it did, I trust it. This campsite was, precisely, 41.5km further on.

I arrived at around 10pm, after only taking directions twice and backtracking once. To my delight, the campsite had a bar, and within 15 minutes my tent was pitched, and I was in it, boasting to the locals of how far I'd come. Unbelievably, I felt strong and loose, ready to ride another 100km if I needed to. This was a chimera, unfortunately, and the next morning I could barely move.

I should mention at this point, in case any of you should find it useful, that telling people you're cycling to Australia gets you free beer.

> I should mention at this point, in case any of you should find it useful, that telling people you're cycling to Australia gets you free beer.

This was my first 100km ride – I hoped the second would not be for a while. The next morning I was surprised to find I wasn't too sore; not stiff, nor aching, but weak. Very very weak. It took all my concentration to deconstruct the tent, let alone cycle anywhere. The 20km to Maastricht were painfully slow.

Day 14 – Germany
I arrived in Aachen after the tourist information office had closed. There were internet cafés all over the place, so I let Google be my guide. This, it transpired, was both foolish and serendipitous. The internet told me, in all good faith I'm sure, that the nearest campsite was 25km away, and that there were only three hotels in the town and that they were fully booked. I happened to have arrived in the middle of the world equestrian games, so the town was heaving with horsey people.

I set off following a cycle route which, in daylight, leads through open countryside, farmland, quaint little hamlets and traffic-free footpaths. At night it was a treacherous, pot-holed, unpredictable death-trap and at irregular intervals the devilish, iridescent gaze of satan's bovine sentinels would flash from the dark and a flap of bats rush past my face. When, after about an hour, I saw a small local pub with its front door open and heard chatter and laughter from within, there was no way I could just ride on.

As much for conversation as anything else, I asked for directions to the nearest campsite. Never has such a simple question produced such an energetic response. The bar was horseshoe-shaped, and barely fitted in the front part of the pub, so when people were sat around it was a squeeze to move. Everyone around the bar had an opinion – which way to go, where to go, it's too late, too cold, too far away. I drank my beer and chatted with the couple who owned the bar and a few locals. After about ten minutes, a man came into the bar and demanded, in rapid French, directions to the nearest main road. To my surprise, the man I'd been talking to in German replied in fluent French. I thought it strange that a French tourist would walk into a bar in Germany and assume that they would be understood. I said as much. 'Ah!' replied the landlord, 'but we are in Belgium. Germany is 200m that way!'

I found this fascinating. That the people in this pub lived in a different country from their neighbours, had a different government, different constitution, from those on the other side of the street. I tried asking them about it, whether straddling the border affects their lives, but the conversation was now being held simultaneously in French, German and English, depending on who was involved. It's hard enough for me to maintain coherence in one foreign tongue, so this was enough to make my ears bleed.

While I was talking to the people in my corner of the bar, in the background the problem of where I was to stay – my problem – had become the property of a conference of locals. Someone phoned a more local campsite, but they were full of horsey people. In the meantime, my glass was continually refilled. Never quite to the top, always just 'a little top up'. On the house. Some chocolate appeared, as if from nowhere, to keep me going.

Feeling thoroughly adopted into the fold of Chez Alito, I begin to entertain the hope that somebody would let me pitch my tent in their field. (This was a country pub – everyone has a field). Maybe they could see this in my eyes, maybe it was a current, an irresistible mental eddy around that horseshoe bar, but almost immediately the landlady turned to me and asked 'would staying in someone's garden be okay?'

She indicated the someones who made this kind offer, a middle-aged couple with whom I'd exchanged a few words but little conversation. I didn't waste any time protesting – they could change their minds. I was, instead, the very picture of surprise and gratitude; introduced myself, bought a round. The husband had a strange looking drink, a red liqueur with squirty cream on top in a shot glass with a long stem. I asked what it was, and while the rest of the bar tried to explain – 'its like strawberries, but smaller', 'do you know ´red berries'?' the landlady wandered off and returned with one for me to try. On the house. I think it was redcurrant based, but it tasted mostly of alcohol.

A short while later my hosts were ready to leave. 'Come, you do not make your tent tonight.'

So I collected what I needed for the night and parked the bike behind the bar. They lived two streets away, in Germany. A beautiful small house with an orchard in the garden. They made their sofa-bed for me, told me breakfast would be at nine in the morning and then they´d take me back to the pub. As I lay, mildly intoxicated, between crisp, clean sheets, already dreaming of the scrambled egg breakfast waiting for me in the morning, a treacherous thought stole into my mind: 'better preparation would have prevented this'.

> **As I lay between crisp clean sheets ... a trecherous thought stole into my mind: 'better preparation would have prevented this'.**

Day 35 – Prague
On my last day in Prague, I managed to get my penultimate Hepatitis B inoculation, rendering me completely invincible until February. My strategy for inoculations provided interesting experience, as it forced me to deal with the health services of different countries, without actually having to fall sick to do it. In socialist France I visited a doctor who ran his own practice from a terraced house, took the prescription he wrote to the pharmacy, who gave me the drugs to bring back to the doctor. It was a little inefficient, but empowering, all the people involved were autonomous agents, interacting. In post-communist Czech Republic, on the other hand, I had to find the special foreigner's section of the main hospital, where I was told exactly where to go and what to do. No autonomy, but organised, efficient equanimity. In the UK, with capitalist ideology running a nationalised service, there´s no autonomy and no organisation, but at least it's expensive.

Day 45 – Vienna
I arrived in Vienna after a 137km slog over hills. It was dark and I was exhausted. I wandered towards the first bar I saw, in search of directions to a hostel. A toothless, stooped, geriatric alcoholic was loitering at the door, so I asked him for advice.

'Where are you from?' was his reply. Clearly my German accent still needed work.

'London.'
'You come by bike?'
'Yep.'
'From London?'
'Yes.'
'Wow.'

'Well, it's not that fa...' I tried to be self deprecating but he interrupted me, 'Wow. Before you left you must have been *enormous!*'

I rode 137km in one day to be told I was still fat. Charming.

Day 85 – Istanbul

Reaching Turkey was a milestone. Cycling from the northwest corner of Europe to the southeast was, in my mind, a tremendous achievement, and I'd always told myself that no matter how much I hated it, I'd make it to Istanbul. No-one could say I'd 'given up' or 'failed' if I made it that far. In the event, there was no question of turning back. From the Bulgarian border to Istanbul was 250km of steep, gruelling hills. I covered the ground in two, 12-hour days. I was still overweight but fitter than I'd ever been and I'd made it across a continent under my own steam. I'd discarded most of my excess baggage, bought most of what I lacked, learned how to keep most of the bike working and could now trust my own legs to keep pushing. If nothing else, I'd shown that there are two ways to set out on a tour – you can begin with meticulous preparation, arduous training, and head straight for the nearest mountain; or, you can make a very, very slow start.

> **There are two ways to set out on a tour – you can begin with meticulous preparation and arduous training ... or you can make a very, very slow start.**

Through Asia to Australia

After six months, thanks to a spontaneous approach to route planning, I reached India via a circuitous tour of the Middle East, culminating in hitching a ride on a cargo ship from Suez to Mumbai. My workshy route had avoided all mountains thus far, and I was still around 100kg.

Ten months after my departure I tackled my first mountain. Since this was the Karakoram Highway, and followed immediately by crossing Tibet, I was glad of the extended run-up. By the time I reached the Kunjerab Pass, I was finally more fit than fat. Exactly one year after my lumbering departure I woke up, unzipped my tent and looked out at a turquoise lake. At 4500m elevation in the Himalayas, two days from the nearest village in the middle of a (technically) illegal ride through West Tibet, I had clearly changed my attitude somewhat. Along with the 50kg of bodyweight I'd shed, I'd lost half my preconceptions and most of my inhibitions.

By the time I met my long-suffering girlfriend at Hong Kong airport I was 70kg. This was the slightest I'd been since I was tall enough to ride a rollercoaster.

Crossing India © Peter Gostelow

High in Ladakh and the Spiti Valley

After an easy downhill ride on the Karakoram Highway in 2008, **Stephen Lord** *and* **Chris Scott** *set their sights higher in 2009, aiming to ride over some of the world's highest motorable passes. When illness strikes things don't work out quite as they'd planned...*

B ut I was going to do the Camino de Santiago!' I said when Chris reminded me we'd talked about a trip to Ladakh. 'You can do that when you're old!', he countered. We'd both enjoyed riding the Karakoram Highway the previous year and we had talked about Ladakh for this year. High altitudes are hard going at any age; it takes a lot of time and effort just to get there and acclimatise before the riding even begins and this was an opportunity to do one more high altitude ride in good company: we might not get a chance again.

We flew into Leh and checked into the Oriental, the best backpacker hangout in town, and spent a week getting to know Leh and visiting nearby monasteries. Although the passes would soon be snowed in, we thought that an extra day or two's acclimatisation would pay off and, after eight days in Leh, headed off towards Taglang La (5300m), one of the highest road passes in the world.

Tackling the Taglang La

We spent our first night near Upshi at the foot of the climb, no higher than Leh at around 3500m, under a parachute tent at the pashmina goat farm where we were made welcome. Next day a fairly effortless 700m climb led to the village of Rumtse, where we planned to spend a further day acclimatising. On our rest day we climbed a few kilometres up the pass and cached some water for the next day as Taglang La is a pretty dry pass on both sides.

Although the gradient is gentle, it's a long haul and the asphalt runs out at around 4900m but still 16km from the summit. We stopped for lunch when Chris, who'd always

STEPHEN LORD & CHRIS SCOTT

Chris Scott (right) also writes for Trailblazer and is the author of *Morocco Overland, Adventure Motorcycling Handbook, Sahara Overland* and the forthcoming *Overlanders' Handbook*. He has always had a sneaking admiration for people mad enough to go adventure-touring on a 'pushie' but his first bike trip was not until 2008, with Steve Lord and a fresh copy of Trailblazer's *Himalaya by Bike* by Laura Stone. Check out the videos on You Tube.

Stephen Lord – see p1.

doubted his ability to ride at such altitude, admitted he'd suddenly ran out of steam and didn't want to push on. We talked over our options: camping there and continuing the next day, or me riding on while Chris hitched a ride to the pass and waited. Camping without water would be a problem and it's never a great idea to ride solo at such heights, especially in the shorter days and colder nights of autumn. There was no certainty that I wouldn't run out of steam myself just round the corner.

I've twice run out of energy before at altitude ... It's entirely predictable, like running out of fuel in a car, but the exact moment it will happen is impossible to know.

I've twice run out of energy before at altitude while riding in Tibet. It's entirely predictable, like running out of fuel in a car, but the exact moment it will happen is impossible to know. If you're climbing a pass, you'll be struggling just to push the bike or more likely sitting down in a daze, wondering what to do next.

The very next Tata truck stopped for us and we hopped in the back with our bikes. We both knew we'd done the right thing when we saw how far it actually was to the pass. 'One of the great things about a bike is that you can always throw it in the back of a truck' said Chris, as we put on all our clothing for the ride down the far side.

'One of the great things about a bike is that you can always throw it in the back of a truck' said Chris

We detoured to Tso Kar lake, arriving at dusk with just enough energy to put up the tents. At around 4500m it was a freezing night and dawn brought with it a light sprinkling of snow. Back on the main road, a fierce headwind rose up over the dusty Morei Plains, taking the wind chill to well below zero. An Indian car rally was heading north which meant even more dust, but also lots of smiles and honks from balaclava-clad participants who were even less used to the cold than we were.

For 200km the central part of the Leh-Manali road lies above 4500m (14,800 feet) and there are no villages en route, just temporary encampments of parachute tents offering shelter and the Himalayan standards of pressure-cooked rice with dhal and chapatti omelettes. Any fixed toilet facility is a bonus, but once the water freezes, people prefer the al fresco option that comes with river views.

More 5000m passes

We'd been warned about the dawn reveille of revving trucks and so had brought ear plugs, but the belching smoke from the ageing Tatas was a real shocker. After yesterday's morale-sapping haul against the wind, at Pang we clutched our coffees in the warming sun, contemplating what this day would bring. Our goal was to get over the double pass of Lachulung La and Nakeela La, another 5000m+ col. We set off up a sandstone gorge which opened out into a broad upland valley. Chris was riding well and as we rounded a corner beyond the gorge he proclaimed we'd burst through the 5000-metre barrier and could see the summit prayer flags just ahead. I carried on to the pass, but a few hundred metres from the top I looked down to see Chris slumped against a rock. One-thirty, that's getting late I thought; we need some lunch in us or we could be in trouble again. I soon got some noodles on the boil; he'll be pleased to see lunch waiting for him, I thought as time slipped by. Twenty minutes later a car stopped and asked if I was 'Mr. Steve'. Chris had been laid low by stomach troubles and I was to go back.

From the top I looked down to see Chris slumped against a rock...

All I could think of was keeping his share of the cooked noodles, remote though the prospect was of him wanting them, and packed the pot carefully in my panniers before riding back down. Struck by sudden hunger, earlier he'd devoured a snack of his own but it had shot through rather than revived him and now, noodles were the last thing on his mind. Again, the first truck stopped for us, Chris got in the cab and I jumped in the back with the bikes. As I tried to lash them down the truck lurched off and before I knew it baggage and bikes were bouncing off the walls as I thought only of keeping the noodle pannier upright. I yelled at the driver to slow down, fearful that if I were knocked out I'd be found in a mess of blood, dust and spokes tangled with warm noodles. Chris told me afterwards they couldn't hear a thing and anyway the driver and his mate were busy sharing a spliff, immune to the carnage in the load bed worthy of a CIA torture manual. I managed to grab Chris's holdall and sat on that, rodeo style, with one hand on the pannier with the pot-noodles and the other free to balance. The truck hurtled from pothole to rut and as my noodle-preserving resolve waned, it pulled over at Nakeela La. This, I thought, was how the Fates punished me for the sin of hitching.

The driver and his mate were sharing a spliff, immune to the carnage in the load bed... This, I thought, was how the Fates punished me for the sin of hitching

The truck left me shaken by the road while Chris, indifferent to my Herculean noodle-saving efforts and himself wafting in and out of a high altitude and diarrhoea-induced hallucination, waited for me to get up for the count. Slowly I gathered my scattered baggage together and picked up the plot: a splendid afternoon sun cast rich colours over the valley below and ahead of us unrolled a hard-earned 800m descent on a good paved road: what's to be unhappy about? We cruised down, dawdling on the Gata Loops, a notorious/delirious (depending on your direction) stack of switchbacks, to take photos and suck in the views. Halfway down we passed a jeep taxi that had tumbled down the hillside a few hours earlier.

Sarchu and the Baralacha La
Sarchu is as charmless as any tent village but you have to look beyond the plastic- and post-digestive detritus at the incredible setting – and the fact that the 'English Wine & Beer' stall was open! We stayed in a very tidy Nepali-run tent and enjoyed an excellent *dhal baht*, while huddled round a fire, chatting with some truckers about life on the high roads of the Himalaya.

PART 3 – TALES FROM THE SADDLE

All that remained was one final pass before we turned off for Spiti. Baralacha La was only 25km away but, with a long run down the other side to Keylong, we decided to ride just 20km to the isolated tent camp at Bharatpur at 4750m, leaving only a 170-metre ascent for the morning. Surely we could ride twenty kilometres in a day? In Chris' case, only just; at one point he recorded a slurred and garbled video message as we struggled through the jumbled moraine onto the wide valley above.

Chris cooking cous-cous in a parachute tent

With the highway about to close for winter, at Bharatpur only two parachute tents were still standing and even they were busy packing up. We spent a happy evening with the Nepali family and surprised them by cooking some cous-cous with biltong for dinner and tsampa-porridge in the morning. By that time it was -10°C but to our relief an easy run led to the snowy crest of 4920-metre Baralacha La and a breathtaking view down the 1700m descent. We'd finally managed to pedal up a Himalayan pass and once wrapped up against the windchill, cruising down was euphoric, snapping photos of one another as we swung through the switchbacks and freewheeling for miles until the first shrubs, trees and even green grass appeared early in the afternoon.

From Darcha the valley became a deep, steep-sided ravine capped by snowy peaks and glaciers. After days of panting and effort, it was a heavenly ride towards the hoped-for fleshpots of Keylong where surely good food and fast internet awaited. We spent a couple of nights there, challenging the young boys left in charge of the kitchen to do their very best for us, but found only power cuts and no phone or internet, so we resorted to servicing the bikes and washing our clothes on the hotel roof.

☆☆☆

Into the Spiti Valley

Once let loose on the snows of Kunzum La, we were thrilled to be back in Tibetan Buddhist lands, dotted with chortens, prayer flags and mani walls. From Losar, the first village, the road improved dramatically but with winter setting in, we decided to stay in guesthouses: much easier and warmer than camping and a great way to see how local people live. Buddhists sometimes have a small chapel in their home, which means early morning prayers climaxing with drumming and a clash of cymbals fit to wake a hibernating yeti.

...with winter setting in, we decided to stay in guesthouses ... a great way to see how local people live.

Leaving iced-up Losar, we took a turn-off signposted to the village of Chicham, a track which, according to a tip in *Himalaya by Bike* (see p311), should lead on to Kibber when completed. At

4200m, Kibber claims to be 'the highest inhabited village in the world with motorable road and voting ballot' – this last qualification probably means there are several higher villages in neighbouring Tibet, where they have no ballot! We asked some motorbiking monks if we could get to Kibber this way. They said 'no', then 'yes' then 'no', typical of the way you sometimes have to ask three times to get an average answer. They then mentioned a 'span' and oddly, picked up my bike to assess its weight.

None the wiser but prepared to give it a go, by lunchtime we'd wheezed to a point high above the Spiti valley and rolled down to Chicham, a pretty Tibetan-style village facing nearby Kibber, just a few kilometres away as the crow flies.

'This will be fun' exclaimed Chris, but I was terrified by the prospect of dangling over the gorge like a Christmas light bulb on Regent Street...

Between the two hamlets lay a deep and as-yet unbridged ravine, perhaps 150m deep and around 100m across. We rode down to inspect the steel cradle and cable contraption used to cross the ravine; the so-called 'span'. 'This will be fun...' exclaimed Chris, but I was terrified by the prospect of dangling over the gorge like a Christmas light bulb on Regent Street and was rather hoping we'd have to backtrack. My hopes were based on the fact that one of the two ropes used to pull the cradle to and fro appeared to be broken and swung limply in the breeze. It was hard to know if it had snapped that day or months ago, but until it was repaired there was no way across. By now starving and cold, we cooked up the last of our food but even then it was my turn to feel feeble. I didn't have another 10km in me, let alone the 60km it would take to get to the nearest food at Kaza. We pushed the bikes back up to Chicham and after asking around, managed to arrange a homestay with the local schoolteacher.

Soon enough we were indoors shipping chai around a yak-dung fire while our new friend Tashi's wife made bread for dinner. As we chatted Tashi explained the Tibetan Buddhist logic of killing a single yak in wintertime: the merit that comes from feeding four or five families for several months greatly offsets having to take one life. The family had a young Bihari houseboy, and in a few days their own son, nine-year old Tenzing, was off to join a Tibetan Buddhist monastery in southern India – for life. Tashi explained he wouldn't see his son for a couple of years but that one of his brothers was a monk there and would look after him. I'd just finished another Dickens novel at the time and was amazed once more at how life for children in Victorian Britain had parallels in today's India. 'It's their industrial revolution, 150 years after ours,' suggested a traveller we met later, but it's a hard life, no matter how much the children smile.

Over the gorge

Next morning we rode down to the span to find it not only repaired but with a teenage girl patiently swinging in the cradle, waiting for someone to pull her in. Seeing her so relaxed in that helpless position set my mind at rest; I could manage the span. We pulled her in then Chris got in the cradle and slowly hauled himself across the chasm. The bikes and gear followed and finally Chris

Crossing the gorge.

pulled me over while I diverted myself by recording the experience on video.

From Kibber we dropped back to the Spiti valley and battled a freezing wind to the grungy town of Kaza where we needed to obtain a permit to transit the Tibetan borderlands. We spent our time in a cosy homestay by the creek, eating with the family around a warm stove. They, too, had a young Indian houseboy Pawan, hard at work cleaning and washing, though he joined the family for meals. It seemed as though he'd miss out on an education but compared with the near-destitute road workers we'd seen living in scrawny tents along the highway, Pawan was much better off.

One night snow fell in Kaza, a reminder that our cycling days this year were numbered. We left town and followed the now-turquoise Spiti river as it carved through a series of striking gorges towards the Tibetan frontier.

☆☆☆

At the former Raj-era hill station of Shimla we bought some sacks and string and disassembled the bikes for the flight home.

In Delhi, with our last rupees we hired an auto-rickshaw to get to the airport. I jammed my superbly compacted bike over the engine while Chris's filled the space between us and the driver, squashing his face up against the windscreen. With our legs poking out of the sides and our heads bent against the roof, the rickshaw puttered off into the mêlée to join Delhi's unending re-enactment of the Ben Hur chariot race, less the spikes, whips and body armour.

An hour or two later we were back in the fluorescent familiarity of Airport World, gnawing on a pair of fat pizzas, slurping lattes and watching Flight EK515 inch up the departure list.

Desert Blitz – across Libya on a transit visa

Nearing the end of a circuitous three-year journey home to the UK, **Peter Gostelow** *decided on one last twist in his route and rode down through Syria, Egypt and Libya before taking a ferry from Tunisia across to Italy. After kicking his heels in Cairo waiting for a visa, he found the Libyans had set him a record-breaking challenge.*

The statistics were against me. I had seven days to pedal 1100 miles across Libya on a fully loaded bicycle. A one-week transit visa was all the embassy in Cairo would give me, and I'd waited two weeks to get this. The truth is that unless you pay for a tour guide, getting a visa for Libya and travelling there independently is very difficult. Perhaps someone had taken pity on me when I said I was going to ride my bicycle across the country?

Libya is not an obvious cycle-touring destination. Africa's fourth largest country is almost all desert, there are very few roads and distances between places are vast. Coming to North Africa was just one of many detours I'd made during the last two-and-a-half years since starting my trip in Japan. Deserts weren't new, but this was the first time I was really being forced to rush across a country. Loading the bicycle on a bus might have been more sensible, but the challenge was half the reason I wanted to pedal across it. The fact that very few people have ever cycled across it was another reason.

There were two more challenges I'd been warned about – wind and traffic. I was entering Libya with a real threat of the *ghibli* blowing. This is a hot Saharan wind that blows from the south during spring and early summer, filling the sky with dust. As for the traffic... I'd received an e-mail from someone in Libya several weeks before who'd heard about my plan. Part of it read *'You probably get killed after some metres. Here exists no speed limit and no driving rules, the people drive in any direction'.*

It wasn't very reassuring, but stories of terrible traffic had existed in half the countries I'd already been to. Surely Libya could be no worse than the motorbikes in Vietnam or the trucks in India?

PETER GOSTELOW

Peter Gostelow worked as an English teacher in Japan before beginning a 3-year, 30,000 mile ride back home. In August 2009 he hit the road again to cycle to Cape Town. His journey can be followed at 🖳 www.thebigafricacycle.com.

PART 3 – TALES FROM THE SADDLE

Lunchtime rest-stop © Peter Gostelow

The Libyan immigration post stood lonely amidst the barren and flat landscape. Only the torn shards of plastic bags blowing against scrubs at the roadside offered some colour as the sun broke behind me. Mini-buses stacked precariously high with luggage were parked and waiting ahead of me. Their drivers and passengers were mainly Egyptians going to work in a country where oil, rather than tourism, is the backbone of the economy. A faded green flag frayed at the edges flew above the customs office. I was as unimpressed by the national flag as I was by the direction in which it was blowing – towards me. This wasn't the *ghibli*, just a headwind that would reduce my average speed to about 8mph. At the end of my first day I'd managed little over 70 miles and was exhausted. I needed to be doing nearer dou-

At the end of my first day I'd managed little over 70 miles and was exhausted. I needed to be doing nearer double this if I wanted to cross the country in a week.

ble this if I wanted to cross the country in a week. I knew then that my chances of making it were slim.

Riding at night was one option, until I realised the traffic warnings were true. Libyans drive quickly and there is only one major road across the country. I soon lost count of the number of overturned vehicles that lay burnt out or rusted at the roadside. Then there were the road kills. The stench and sight of bloated and rotting animals (nearly always dogs, but occasionally sheep, foxes, cats and the odd camel) was common throughout the country. The only time traffic slowed down was when passing through police checkpoints, of which there were many. I was often asked where the rest of my tour group was whilst the visa in my passport was examined. Confused looks came when I pointed to myself, explaining that there was only one person in my group.

On my third day in Libya the bleak scenery dramatically improved. The Jabal Akhdar (Green mountains) rise up from the Mediterranean in the northeast of the country. I was finally changing gears as I climbed from sea level to about 700 metres. Low clouds had formed over the tree-covered slopes, out of which the ancient Greek city of Cyrene appeared as I reached the top. Two plain-clothed men whom I'd never seen before were waiting for me here beside a black BMW. It was an ominous sign. 'You are Pizza Anduru Gasutero?' I corrected their pronunciation. 'It's Peter, not Pizza.' The police at the last check-post must have informed them about me. It made me feel important when I heard they'd been waiting all day, but the reality was that the Tunisian border was still over 700 miles away and I only had four days left on my visa. They asked my opinion about Libya and I explained people drove very quickly. They took this as a compliment before I too sped on towards the city of Benghazi in the hope of getting a visa extension.

The next morning was spent in a Libyan immigration office where I managed to gain an extra week on my visa. This was great news, but the onset of the *ghibli* wasn't. The sky was now a yellow haze of dust, the temperature way above 40°C and the wind would have reduced cycling to walking speed. I was invited to a family event in the neighbouring town of Ajdabiya by a local man from Benghazi who'd helped with the bureaucracy of getting a visa extension. He didn't tell me it was the funeral of his brother in-law until we'd nearly arrived. It explained why his wife had been crying throughout the journey. Many mourning family members gathered to watch me take my panniers and bicycle out of the car. They were probably as confused as I was about why I was here. Ahmed, my host, treated me like royalty, and when the *ghibli* continued the next day he insisted I stay. I had encountered similar hospitality in a number of other Muslim countries – Pakistan, Iran and Syria. Libyans might drive without much sense, but I was warmly welcomed during my short time here.

> They asked my opinion about Libya and I explained people drove very quickly. They took this as a compliment...

★★★

Tailwinds in monotonous landscapes are a cyclist's dream. When I finally set off the following day the wind was pushing me along at 15-20mph. I'd covered 130 miles by the time I wheeled my bike off the road to pitch my tent – the longest day on the entire trip. The road followed the Gulf of Sirte coastline, a part of Libya where the desert often meets the sea. Any romantic notions of cycling past sand dunes and camels silhouetted against sunsets were soon dissipated. Even the blue waters of the Mediterranean, which lay close by, were mostly out of view. Instead it is oil fields that are the most notable feature of the arid landscape. Construction of the 'Great Man-made River' also continues close to the road. This colossal engineering project, described by Muammar al-Gaddafi as the 'Eighth Wonder of the World', consists of a network of pipes to pump underground water from the Sahara to the coastal cities of the north. Trucks transporting huge cylinders thundered past me at the roadside as I raced on westwards towards the capital Tripoli.

The wind was in my favour for a second day, before it switched to the

> Tailwinds in monotonous landscapes are a cyclist's dream.

Desert camping © Peter Gostelow

south and the *ghibli* began again. The sand in my mouth and eyes was less of a concern than the fear of dehydration. Police at a check post offered me sliced melon and chilled water. It felt like a luxury and I filled all 10 litres of various bottles I was carrying before heading off again. Several hours later there was a lull in the wind, then a moment of calm before the temperature dropped by about 15°C. The wind then suddenly started blowing from the north. It was a refreshing change, but not helping me get to the capital any quicker.

Near Tripoli lies Leptis Magna, one of the most extensive and impressive Roman cities still remaining. With so few tourists in Libya I almost had the site to myself. I wanted to stay longer, but my visa was expiring the next day and there were still 200 miles to the border. I tried for a second extension in Tripoli, but got pointed from desk to desk before the immigration office closed at lunchtime. During my time in Libya I'd been wondering what

I wanted to stay longer, but my visa was expiring the next day and there were still 200 miles to the border.

would happen if I over-stayed the visa's exit date? There were rumours of big fines and I already knew Libya wasn't the most tourist-friendly of countries when it came to issuing visas. The visa's exit date was written in pen – 15th April. What if I just touched it up a little and made that 18th April? It was a simple, but potentially very dangerous thing to do. Under the light from my head torch the night before reaching the border I went ahead and did it. I thought it looked pretty convincing, although wouldn't get a second opinion until arriving at the Tunisian border the next morning.

It was a chaotic scene with vehicles stretching back half a mile. Fuel in Libya is almost free so Tunisian drivers come across the border to fill their tanks up. Beads of sweat formed on my brow as I handed my passport over for inspection. The immigration officer was more interested in the flag stickers on my bicycle than the forged visa though. The stamp went down with a smile and I was soon breathing a huge sigh of relief. I pedalled into

The immigration officer was more interested in the flag stickers on my bicycle than the forged visa.

Tunisia and found shade under an olive tree to rest and reflect. It was the first moment of real relaxation in weeks. Crossing Libya had been one of the biggest challenges of the trip. Now I could continue at a more leisurely pace. Tunisia had small roads and I wasted no time in finding them.

On the run in Tibet

Being told it was impossible only added to **Corsair***'s determination to get to Lhasa from the east, but it wasn't just the police who were after him. His ride, as he puts it, was at times like Frodo's mission to get to the heart of Mordor in 'The Lord of the Rings'.*

The Dutch veteran cyclist wished us good luck with a smile of doubt on his face. He had warned us of the impossibility of getting into Tibet from the east, giving us zero per cent chance of making it all the way to Lhasa. I looked at the single page 'guide book' a German female biker had given us some weeks back. She had also failed but at least she'd given us some up to date news about the area. 'Bayi – most dangerous place, crawling with PSB. Bomi – big military town. Watch out! Yanjing – difficult checkpoint at the beginning of town. Mi La. Second highest pass. Good camp spots on the left. Chuka – safe. Good restaurant and small shop', and so on. This wasn't much but for someone with no clue about the area it was a great help. If nothing else, it showed that someone had made it through and that it wasn't completely impossible as people had led us to believe.

Into Tibet in the dark

We left the last open outpost of civilisation before the sun was up. Dead set on taking no risks we hadn't told anyone in Zhongdian where we were headed. The city was now only a few dim lights far behind us and I felt triumphant. First obstacle gone. We were on our way. The feared topography started to prove the rumours were true. 'No flat metre', someone had told us but fortunately, I love uphills! The scenery got more dramatic by the day and we started to feel we were in for a great adventure in all ways. We passed Deqen without any trouble, even if we got searching looks from people in uniform there. The Meili/Kawa Korpo range was astonishingly beautiful and we soon forgot the paranoia about being caught.

CORSAIR

As shy as a snow leopard, 'Corsair' is well known to China's Public Security Bureau and has been deported several times for exploring areas closed to foreigners. He has been cycling throughout the high mountains of Asia since the early 1990s and still rides the same bike, a 1991 Scott. He is equally devoted to mountaineering and is particularly tempted by off-limits peaks.

PART 3 – TALES FROM THE SADDLE

Raid on East Tibet © Corsair

According to our information we were soon in for the first real test of the journey: Yanjing. Some road workers had given us an incorrect distance and when we cycled around a corner the red and white barrier over the road came as a nasty surprise. The guards had seen us. No choice but to ride up to them acting innocent and stupid. They were polite but strict. We had to go back the way we had come. No room for discussion. With heavy hearts we started to roll down the hill we had just cycled up. An old woman who'd seen the incident gave us some food and pointed at the hills to the right. There was a track up there and she advised us to go at night. Later that day, hiding under a small bridge waiting for dark, we suddenly noticed a familiar figure struggling up the long climb – Chris, the Swiss cyclist we had met in Dali some weeks earlier. When he'd heard our story he was all for joining us in a clandestine venture when dark had fallen over the Yunnan-Tibetan border town.

The first scree hills were steep and very hard to get up in the dark. Chris's packing was a disaster and he kept dropping things which he had to go back for. The narrow trails along the mountain sides were precarious and probably quite dangerous in places but we couldn't tell as we didn't dare use any light. By dawn, after a full night of pushing, pulling and worrying about being caught we reached the road on the other side of town. We snatched a few hours of sleep in a small sheltered riverbed. The hill continued up for what felt like eternity and the gorge in the west got deeper and deeper. On the other side of the pass the plains of Markham awaited us. We had been warned about the place by some who had been caught there but the travellers' grapevine had blown up the tales into crazy proportions – the valley was populated with deadly mastiffs, informers and extremely zealous PSB officers.

> **The narrow trails along the mountain sides were probably quite dangerous in places but we couldn't tell as we didn't dare use any light.**

The mad dogs of Markham

We camped about 10km outside town and Chris climbed a small peak to get an overview of Markham. He could see it was a large town and that it would be very difficult to get past. Night fell and the silvery light of a full moon looked like spoiling things for us. There were dogs everywhere. It wasn't just that we wanted them to stop barking and not wake the whole of Markham, they were also very dangerous. Some would attack without being provoked and it was hard enough just defending ourselves, let alone making any progress. I don't know how many I clubbed or hit with rocks that night, but fortunately none of us was bitten. Help arrived unexpectedly. A horse and rider with cloth wrapped around his head came slowly along the road. He gestured to us to follow. The dogs seemed to hate the horse even more and frantically attacked the new target. The mysterious rider calmly rode on while the horse skilfully kicked at the dogs. From time to time howls and whines indicated the hooves had hit home. The whole scene was like something out of Tolkien: riding under the full moon, being attacked by evil, semi-invisible creatures and being helped by a cloaked stranger who communicated only with short unintelligible grunts.

The whole scene was like something out of Tolkien: riding under the full moon, being attacked by evil, semi-invisible creatures and being helped by a cloaked stranger ...

When we reached the outskirts of the city, the dog attacks got fewer and without warning the rider took off. We dodged some dangerous sources of light and late into the night realised we had passed the last houses of the settlement. Now we were climbing steeply it was hard to find a camping spot. When the first morning light hit we took refuge behind some small pine bushes we hoped would give us enough protection from being seen from the road.

The group gets smaller
Over a double pass and flying down a long switchback section, being pelted with rocks by obnoxious kids, Katja decided she'd had enough. She gave up in the a settlement, Chuka, and hitched back the same way she'd come. Chris and I continued the journey and after a full day's climb we found a good camping spot. Next morning, however, required a new take on things. Chris had been vomiting all night and was too weak to continue. He almost forced me to go on on my own and reluctantly I finally did. We made some vague plans to keep in contact with notes sent by truck drivers and meet later, further down the road. I passed the turnoff to Lhasa and continued north. For some reason I had no interest in going to central Tibet. I wanted to head for the more interesting unknown back roads and my final destination in China was the oasis town of Kashgar, still thousands of kilometres away. The rock throwing and the dog attacks continued. The weather was miserable and I was starting to feel worn out. Without really caring I went straight through Qamdo in the middle of the day and was stopped by a

The rock throwing and the dog attacks continued. The weather was miserable and I was starting to feel worn out.

police officer. He wondered where I was going. I thought my ride was over, but the young officer was genuinely helpful and didn't seem to care at all about the presence of a foreign cyclist. I was surprised when he showed me a shortcut through the city towards Riwoqe.

Rumbled in Riwoqe
Chinese and Tibetans alike warned me about the next stretch of road. They talked about 'crazy people', highway robbers and murderers. I must admit I

felt uncomfortable on some occasions, getting strange and hostile looks. The fact that there was no traffic whatsoever later in the evening made me think it was a dangerous area. Someone was outside my tent that night, quietly sneaking around but fortunately not making any moves against me. Many coinciding factors had exhausted me and I didn't realise I probably should have taken a break for a day or two. I guess it was the tiredness which made me cease caring as I cycled into Riwoqe in broad daylight. I had a great meal of hot noodles and when I was about to pay a man who had been staring at me blocked my way and demanded to see my ID. He said he was a PSB officer. I told him my passport was on the bike and as soon as I reached it I made a run for it. The man came after me, shouting. I thought I'd got away but my heart sank when I turned the next corner: a major checkpoint blocked my way. Search lights, a sturdy chain over the road, a box with a soldier armed with a machine gun and some sort of spike mat. Taking a chance even though I knew the race was over, I smiled and tried to cycle straight through it, only to be firmly grabbed by a soldier. He didn't return my faked smile.

The only policeman in town who spoke any English was very friendly, but after he had left me under arrest in a small cold hotel room I felt really miserable. So, this was how my grand plan had ended. Half asleep, with brooding thoughts about an escape without my bicycle and passport, a knock on the door woke me up. A very dirty and worn out Chris was escorted into the room. My hopes for him making it were dashed but I was happy to have some company again.

Under arrest

The following day we were transported back to Qamdo. This gave us some hope again. Perhaps they didn't care about us and would let us go? The help I had got finding the way there some days earlier indicated that. That faint hope evaporated when we were informed that we were under arrest for breaking the laws of China. Days of interrogations followed. Our entire luggage was thoroughly searched but I was lucky and managed to hide my rolls of film thanks to an unexpected power cut. After four days we got our verdict: fines and transport to Chengdu, where we would be further questioned. The officer in charge didn't answer my question about our expulsion from China, but I took his non-answer as a yes. We couldn't allow this to happen!

We got our passports back after we had paid the fines but the police still had our bikes. We told the police we had to clean them before we entered the bus early the following morning and they agreed. We washed them for hours in the police compound and when all the big wigs had left we told the low rank officials we had the right to take the bikes back to the hotel where we were being held as we were going on the bus early the following morning. Reluctantly they let us take the bikes. At last we had some reason to feel hopeful.

The Great Escape

We were locked up in the old wing of a central hotel. Amazingly, Chris had a large and sturdy cable cutter. There was a padlock, connected to some thick wire on the outside of the double door which separated us from the corridor leading to the main lobby. At 2am we nodded in agreement, held our breath and pushed the cable cutter through the tight gap in the doors. We knew there was no way back and no explanation would be good enough if we went on from there. The wire gave way and slowly we pushed our bikes through the dark corridor. There was no one in

> **We held our breath and pushed the cable cutter through the tight gap in the doors.**

the lobby. The courtyard was dark but the gatekeeper was at his post. Sleepily he opened the gate without challenging our story that we had been ordered to go to the bus station on our own. Then a motorcycle arrived. The man was in uniform. A police uniform. Our hearts sank. Now we were really in deep shit. I decided not to even try to make up a story as to why we were where we were. The race was over. The policeman was behaving strangely and almost fell off his bike. Stinking of alcohol, he cracked a joke with the gate keeper and paid no real attention to us.

We quickly cycled off into the maze of streets of central Qamdo. We didn't have much time before the sun came up and we were supposed to be at the bus station. We needed somewhere to hide and I remembered a bridge some 20km before Qamdo. After a lot of fast cycling on back streets we found the route south and pedalled as quickly as we could. We finally reached the bridge just as the sun spread its light over the barren landscape of east Tibet.

Cat and mouse amongst the fish

Chris was ill for two days. Lots of police jeeps passed over our bridge and it was a long and nervous wait. We didn't dare cycle anywhere and Chris really wasn't in a condition to do so, anyway. We felt reasonably safe where we were and it was better to play it cool and wait. On day three we saw a truck slowly coming up the hill towards our bridge. I jumped up on the road and flagged it down. The driver smiled at us as we got in. Smugly he told us the Qamdo police were looking for us, but that we needn't worry. He would take us to Bamda airport. But that was a military airport and once again I was alarmed. The driver realised and explained that he'd drop us at a safe distance from the place. At our lunch stop with our new friends another scary incident occurred. A PSB jeep stopped right in front of the restau-

Dwarfed by the peaks © Corsair

rant and we almost panicked. Chris went into the kitchen and suddenly became very interested in the food the cooks were preparing. I jumped into the hole in the ground where they kept fresh fish for the restaurant. An old Chinese man looked curiously at me when I appeared from out of nowhere. I pretended I was interested in learning the Chinese names of the fish he had down there and he was happy to teach me. Finally, after a lot of fish name-learning the PSB departed. Our driver and his friends laughed hard when we came out of our respective hiding places and we continued our journey.

Caught again

Only a week after our escape from Qamdo our time was up again. A police jeep overtook me and two men jumped out. I smiled and tried to cycle on, like a stupid tourist not understanding what they were on about. The young soldier pointed his machine gun at me, giving me an expressionless look. I stopped.

> **The young soldier pointed his machine gun at me, giving me an expressionless look. I stopped.**

Chris was the lucky one. His interrogator was only interested in football and the world's geography and I could hear them laughing and talking about famous goalkeepers in the next room. The woman who questioned me never smiled. After hours of hard questioning the toughest question came.

'Have you been to Qamdo?'

'No, no. As I said we're on our way from Lhasa towards Yunnan'.

I stuck to my story, hoping that it might at least mean we'd be sent in the right direction. Unverified travellers' tales had told us that the PSB always sent you back to where you started.

The final word was that next morning we would be sent by bus to Chengdu. My trick hadn't worked. I was depressed. Chris had had enough of it all and had decided not to risk his bike and his mission to cycle back to Switzerland. I was still defiant and wanted to make a go of it at night. The last blizzard had given me a high fever and bad cold so I slept right through the 3am alarm clock. It was light when I heard the knock on the door. OK, that was finally it. Life would go on, but hell I was disappointed with myself. I had failed.

Forced to cycle – to Lhasa!

The police officer informed us that it was illegal for foreigners to ride on public buses in Tibet and so we must cycle to Lhasa. We were not allowed to leave the main road. I was completely flabbergasted. What? I couldn't believe what I had just heard! Cycle to Lhasa? I asked him to repeat it. Yeah, it was like that. The way things work out sometimes can't be explained and this time it was a real enigma.

> **The police officer informed us that it was illegal for foreigners to ride on public buses in Tibet and we must cycle to Lhasa.**

We were nervous riding through Bomi where there were hordes of drunken army guys who didn't seem to care about our existence, or they might've been too drunk to really notice. The ride in the dark past Rawu nearly killed us. At one point I almost cycled off the road where a landslide had removed half the road's surface; I noticed the gaping hole only seconds before I would've disappeared into it.

Somehow Chris and I once again got separated and after three solid days of cold rain I reached the outskirts of Bayi, the most feared place of all along the route. It was a very dark night. The rain was torrential and in a way I was thankful for the conditions.

> The ride in the dark past Rawu nearly killed us. At one point I almost cycled off the road where a landslide had removed half the road's surface...

Visibility was down to a couple of metres and even the strong lights of the checkpoints didn't cut well through the downpour. Tired, chilled to the bone but happy, I collapsed in a perfect camping spot 8km out of town. I had my first rest day since the days under the bridge close to Qamdo. I was happy. I ate a lot of food and tried to regain some strength for the last 300km to Lhasa. It felt unreal that I had made it. It wasn't the original plan, but what the hell; I really was almost there.

Lhasa by bike – but not for everyone

About 60km out of Bayi my trip through east Tibet ended abruptly. A police car stopped just in front of me and there was no chance of escape. Once again, questioning. More fines, but after some negotiations at least I managed to get a visa extension and was to be sent to Lhasa instead of the very scary alternative, Qamdo.

The bus ride to Lhasa was absolutely miserable. I had already pictured myself arriving there on my bike, slowly cruising around looking for nice places to eat and a cool place to stay. Now I arrived in utter defeat and I felt like shit.

Five days later Chris arrived. By bike! To be honest, I was a bit annoyed that Chris made it through OK. Not so much because he'd *made* it but for the way he did it. Before Bayi he had been invited for a drink by some road workers. After numerous shots of hard liquor Chris's confidence was on a high and he had cycled straight into Bayi in broad daylight. Still half drunk he had marched into a noodle shop for another drink and something to eat. The PSB had arrived and even talked to Chris. I guess they couldn't believe anyone was courageous or stupid enough to arrive in a closed town drunk and in the middle of the day, so they hadn't even asked for his passport. I had done my utmost to be careful and I'd still got caught. Chris had done the opposite and made it.

Life can be so unfair!

> ...they couldn't believe anyone was courageous or stupid enough to arrive in a closed town drunk and in the middle of the day, so they hadn't even asked for his passport.

A long day to Sihanoukville

Near the end of a tour of the backroads of South-East Asia, **Jonathan Waite** *and his wife, Alexandra, leave Kampot for Sihanoukville. When you're cycle-touring, a lot can happen on a ride of just one day.*

The road was in good condition; a bit dusty, perhaps, but flat and sealed for the most part. With a bit of luck we should make it to Sihanoukville, Cambodia's premier and only beach resort, before dusk. We were now well into our fourth month of cycling and the prospect of covering distances in excess of the magic 100km mark no longer seemed so daunting. With a restful few days behind us we were very nearly looking forward to a challenge.

Leaving Kampot

We woke up early the following morning. Bleary-eyed, I made my way on to the balcony and looked out. Elephant Mountain was nowhere to be seen, shrouded in thick, rolling mist. In amongst the maze of tiny back yards below our balcony, immaculately dressed schoolchildren in crisp white shirts were being loaded onto the backs of motorbikes, wet clothes hung up on washing lines, shutters shut, and wailing babies being plumped unceremoniously into buckets of water. The inhabitants of Kampot were going about their daily business and it was time we were off.

It was mid-winter in Cambodia. Since crossing over the border from Vietnam, the weather had been dry and tolerably hot – as opposed to monsoon rains and unbearable heat in the summer. The vagaries of tropical weather were still, however, a considerable source of mystery to me. The promise of a violent storm would often come to nothing at all, lightning was only sometimes accompanied by thunder, or vice versa, and on occasions it seemed as if it was raining when actually it wasn't. That morning the sky wasn't

JONATHAN WAITE

Jonathan Waite's first taste of long-distance cycling was a ride home from the Côte d'Azur to Cardiff whilst in his late teens. With no map, he took a disastrous wrong turn through the Massif Central range of mountains and had to rely on local hospitality to keep himself going – mainly in the form of illicit, pre-dawn visits to local vegetable plots. Twenty years later, and determined to do better, he and his wife embarked on a six-month meander around the former Indochina. Jonathan is an actor and now lives in the Loire Valley, France.

giving anything away: an unbroken layer of thick white cloud interspersed with sudden bursts of intense blue sky.

The going was good for the first twenty or so kilometres and we were soon bumping along the dusty track at an impressive rate of knots. The road was busy with early morning traffic, and as always at that time of the day, those clinging on to the backs of the various overloaded forms of transport were in upbeat mood.

Rain, rain, rain ...
Before long, however, the road took a sharp turn inland, towards the evergreen foothills of Elephant Mountain, and the weather began to change. The sky suddenly went a dirty, lead-grey, as heavily-laden rain clouds rolled in above our heads. Soon the first blobs of warm rain came splashing down.

Before the rain © Jonathan Waite

There were no houses around, just the occasional lean-to bamboo shelter situated at the edges of one of the fields. Unfortunately, it was a case of no room at the inn. Every available square inch of space under the rooves of these shelters had been taken up with families escaping the rain. Another mile or so down the road, however, our luck changed when we spotted a small roadside canteen.

The place was empty and, as was often the case whenever we went in search of food, we weren't quite sure whether we had actually stumbled into someone's back yard. There was a small cooking area, of sorts, consisting of a mis-shapen wok perched on top of a bucket of charcoal and a glass display box, with a few coils of rice noodles and some half cut vegetables on one of the shelves. Behind us stood a single windowless hut with a mud floor. We sat down at the wobbly table and waited.

A girl eventually appeared, carrying a baby. She hesitated and began slowly making her way over towards the table. She then stood there in front of us, for what seemed like a very long time, silently taking us in; during this time the baby reached up from her arms towards the sagging undersides of the blue tarpaulin roof, and began gently prodding a tiny finger into the deep puddles. The girl very nearly smiled, turned and went back inside.

The road was almost deserted now. In between the heaviest bouts of rain the odd motorbike slid past, with riders dragging their feet through the mud in a desperate attempt to keep upright. The family's piglet did his best to entertain, hurtling back and forth between the puddles before scuttling blindly across the road, down the ditch and off into the fields.

It rained and rained and rained. That day we were to spend the best part of four hours sitting on the plastic stools, watching successive waves

That day we were to spend the best part of four hours... watching successive waves of torrential rain slowly wash away the road...

Before the mud © Jonathan Waite

of torrential rain slowly wash away the road...and with it our hopes of reaching Sihanoukville before nightfall.

It did eventually stop raining, though by now it was so late we had no real idea where we were heading. Sihanoukville was still over 100km away and, judging by the lack of place names on our map, our prospects of finding accommodation along the way were very slim indeed. Added to this, was the fact that the road had disappeared – or at least was lying somewhere between the adjacent ditches.

An unsettling encounter

Just as we were preparing to leave another woman came out from the doorway. She was older, in her fifties, tall and thin, and wearing simple, faded clothing. She took a few uncertain steps towards us, held out the palms of her hands, and began stroking Alexandra's forearms. She then began saying something, murmuring a few words at a time, her soft voice barely audible over the pitter-patter of the last drops of rain on the tarpaulin. With a sharp intake of air her focus then suddenly shifted upwards – to Alexandra's face – her long, bony fingers gently tracing the curve of the nose, cheekbones and temples. Tears were streaming down her face now and she began hugging Alexandra, over and over again, smothering her forehead in kisses. The younger girl eventually came out, placed a free hand on the woman's bare shoulders, smiled – half apologetically – and lead her back inside.

Neither of us, of course, knew why the woman had reacted in such a way. She certainly wasn't mad. Seeing Alexandra that day had perhaps awakened in her a distant memory. By my calculations the woman would have been in her early twenties when the Khmer Rouge came to power. Perhaps Alexandra reminded her of someone who was once dear to her – a sister, for example. Whatever the truth, this latest encounter was as unsettling as it was moving.

Mud-wrestling

During the next couple of hours my mind went into a strange, dream-like state. I can only guess that foot soldiers caught in the midst of a fierce battle must experience a similar feeling. A kind of numbness. Or a mountaineer perhaps, trying to battle his way through deep snow, great gusts of wind threatening to knock him off balance with every step. Flailing around in calf-deep mud that day was our very own slice of oblivion.

Flailing around in calf-deep mud that day was our very own slice of oblivion.

Each lumbering cement lorry or truck that passed by carved up the road into steep-sided ruts, making it extremely difficult just to keep upright. Pedalling had also become an exhausting business, the wheels spinning wildly in the mud. Each time we went up an incline, no matter how slight, the space between the tyres and the mudguards then quickly filled up with mud and before long the wheels soon stopped turning altogether. The only solution was to try to keep the wheels as clear of mud as possible. After every dozen or so energy-intensive pedal strokes I would dismount and go off in search of twigs or folded-up banana leaves with which to break up the sticky clods caught between the tyres and the mudguards. Needless to say, the main supply of twigs and leaves lay underneath the trees…which meant crossing the by-now, very deep roadside ditches.

Then the sun came out, with a vengeance. Within the space of a few minutes our bikes, bike bags and bodies were baked in a thick, indestructible layer of terracotta mud. Every moving part on our bicycles began to squeak, and with it came the disquieting thought that each stroke of the pedal that day was doing more damage to the chains and gear sets than on the entire trip.

Then the midges came out. Every time we stopped to look for new twigs we fell victim to thick clouds of the little rascals, eager to suck on our salt-encrusted upper bodies.

> **Then the midges came out...we fell victim to thick clouds of the little rascals, eager to suck on our salt-encrusted upper bodies.**

Indeed, our list of woes at that moment was a particularly long and exhaustive one, and had there been any bystanders present, a tangible drop in morale amongst the troops might well have been in evidence. I would go on to describe the difficulties of applying suntan cream to mud and grit-covered limbs but some readers may think I am milking it.

…And then there it was, standing before us, beckoning us to come closer. Just when we had been least expecting it, when the chips were down, when our backs were well and truly up against the wall and all hope lost, what we least expected had appeared on the horizon, and we knew we'd be saved …

At the car wash

The car wash itself bore little resemblance to the standard Western model. There were none of the the familiar oversized, rotating brushes or hydraulic swinging arms, and there was certainly no set of miniature stop-go traffic lights. In its place was an oily generator, a water pump with a pipe leading from it to a nearby puddle, and a small army of cloth and sponge-wielding young children. Amidst a great flurry of activity, our bikes were handed over, de-bagged and appropriate-sized plastic bags placed over the dynamo, gear shifters and seat. The generator then spluttered into action and the woefully under-aged team set about their task with gusto, each of

> **The car wash was a water pump with a pipe leading to a nearby puddle, and a small army of sponge-wielding young children.**

them taking responsibility for cleaning a particular area of the bikes. We watched, with a mixture of glee and incredulity, as the thick coating of mud and silt disappeared before our very eyes. With the aid of a few final blasts of water to remove any stubborn clods our bikes, bike bags and bodies were soon as good as new. The whole transformation process was not over yet, however. The water hose was swiftly replaced by an air hose – of the kind used to inflate tyres – and the bikes were then treated to a quick blow dry.

... the owner then came under siege from the car wash staff, each of them jumping up and down in an attempt to pluck the bank notes from his hands.

When it came to settling up for services rendered the owner suddenly appeared – from under the engine block of a lorry. I handed over the necessary riel to the owner, who then came under siege from the various members of the car wash staff, each of them jumping up and down in the air in an attempt to pluck their share of the bank notes from his hands. He was unflustered, though, and with the appropriate thin wad of bank notes held just high enough to be out of reach, methodically set about placing a few thousand riel within the grasp of each pair of tiny, snapping fingers.

Lunch with the car wash staff

Just as we were about to continue on our way the owner disappeared off somewhere, and then reappeared. He began making vague, flapping-of-the-hand gestures aimed roughly in our direction. As far as I could tell, he was beckoning me, or us, to follow him somewhere. I got off the bike and went over. He then led me round the back of the garage, to a back yard area currently in the shade. There was the car wash team – sitting at two plastic tables, staring expectantly in the direction of three large saucepans. Two places had been laid for us. We didn't need a second invitation. The rigours of the morning's mud-wrestling had been such that we had given up all hope of ever sitting down to lunch, and by this time we were ravenous. Lunch consisted of fish soup, stir-fried vegetables and lots of rice, and was delicious.

Our young hosts also made for exceptionally good company. I don't think they stopped giggling for the duration of the meal. With the aid of our maps, and my miming skills, I was able to find out a little about their lives. The children were all related to each other, in ways which I was unable to fathom, and originated from the Preah Vihear province in the remote, mountainous north. Like many other rural families, they had got wind of a job prospect somewhere very far from home and had arrived en masse. Looking around at the makeshift car wash, out here in the scrub, miles away from the last electricity pylon, it seemed like a huge sacrifice to make just to earn a few riel.

Cham country

The remainder of the journey, on tarmac now, took us through a bewildering array of different landscapes, both physical and human. First and foremost though, we needed to make up for lost time. The rounded hump of Elephant Mountain, our roadside companion for the last few hours, eventually subsided and we soon found ourselves whizzing through a beautiful, fertile area of land, covered in a patchwork of emerald green paddy fields. We were now currently in the rain shadow of Elephant Mountain – if my memories of O-level geography serve me right.

The villages, or more accurately the villagers, we encountered also had something different about them. The women waving to us from their porches or from the backs of carts were now wearing tasselled headscarves (as opposed to the checked *krama*), and the customary groups of young boys sprinting alongside us often had small, white caps perched on the backs of their heads. At the entrance to one village we passed by the local mosque, the call to late-afternoon prayers blaring out from crackling speakers.

We had entered an area of southern Cambodia with a particularly high concentration of 'Cham' villages – the Chams being the ethnic group to which around 80% of Cambodia's million or so Muslims belong. Almost everyone suffered in some way under the Khmer Rouge but the repression of the Chams was particularly savage. Looking across at the scenes of happy village life it was hard to imagine the horrors of the recent past.

Made in Cambodia

The landscape then changed again, from rice fields to immense flood plains. Suddenly, we could see for miles around us. The plains themselves lay under a uniform covering of perfectly still, crystal-clear floodwater and were breathtakingly beautiful. Sounds travelled across the water with uncanny clarity. A large, heron-like bird clicking its wings, way off in the distance, or a solitary water buffalo, splashing water over itself, grunting with pleasure.

Up ahead now large numbers of people were crossing over the road in front of us. After kilometre upon kilometre of open countryside and scattered villages, seeing so many people in the same place was something of a

> **After kilometre upon kilometre of open countryside and scattered villages, seeing so many people in the same place was something of a shock.**

shock. The crowd numbered upwards of seven or eight hundred people, nearly all young women. As we weaved our way through the crowd, the source of this sudden influx of people became clear. A very large, modern-looking shoe factory had opened its gates, and the entire workforce was on its way home. Dozens of stalls lined the road, selling everything from CDs to cigarette lighters, saucepans to siphons, and bras to bike tyres. The mood was an upbeat one – it felt as if we had inadvertently wandered into the village carnival.

Home, for most of the girls, lay not very far away. On the opposite side of the road lay rows and rows of identical wooden huts laid out in grid-like fashion. The huts themselves consisted almost entirely of bunk beds, rising to a height of five or six beds, each with its own mosquito net tied into a neat bundle overhead.

A few kilometres further down the road we came across two more of these giant, warehouse-like factories. At least now whenever I see the words 'Made in Cambodia' on the inside of a pair of shoes, I have a better idea of what this means.

> **...now whenever I see the words 'Made in Cambodia' on the inside of a pair of shoes, I have a better idea of what this means.**

Stumbling into Sihanoukville

Sihanoukville, in the meantime, was still nowhere to be seen. As was often the case in Cambodia, the scarcity of signposts, and even more so those written in the Latin alphabet, meant that we never quite knew where we were. In the absence of any plausible alternatives, we battled on. With a good eight or nine hours' worth of not uneventful pedal-pushing behind us, however, we were growing increasingly anxious to bring the day's proceedings to a close.

The road then started to creep uphill, which was not good news at all. Particularly as we were supposed to be heading towards the coast. The hills we encountered were of the long and sustained, lingering variety and our last reserves of energy began to dwindle – in addition to our thirst for life in general.

By the time we reached our fourth consecutive hill, we gave up. Our chances of reaching our destination before nightfall were nil and there was no point in pushing ourselves any further. Ahead of us now lay an uncertain, and potentially dangerous ride in the dark.

A roadside drinks stall presented itself just at the right moment, so we decided to drown our sorrows in a couple of bottles of fizzy coin-cleaner. As we sat there, crunching the last of our supply of peanuts, a hired jeep pulled up. In it were four Westerners – British by the sound of their voices – the boys in the front and the girls in the back. Once the wheels had ground to a halt one of the girls, dressed in bikini top and a denim hot pants – and who probably worked in PR in Chelsea – clasped her hands round the roll-bar and deftly lifted herself up and out the jeep. She strode up confidently towards the stall holder and asked 'Got any cold beers, mate?'

Sihanoukville
© Jonathan Waite

The girl then came back out to the jeep, handed round the chilled booty, and once again levered herself – Dukes of Hazzard-style – into the back. The jeep then sped off into the distance, leaving the sound of generic, non-descript techno blasting out across the night air.

Sihanoukville was evidently not as far away as we thought.

No pay, no pass:
on the edge in Central Africa

In 2006, **Amaya Williams** *and her husband, Eric Schambion, set off on a three-year cycle-tour of Africa. Despite Eric's concerns about the dangers of Africa, they found that politeness, patience and a friendly smile would see them through all manner of social encounters – until they reached one particular police road block in Equatorial Guinea.*

Most people have never heard of Equatorial Guinea. This tiny land straddles the equator, squashed in between Cameroon and Gabon. With a population of under a half a million, it's one of the least populous countries in Africa and the only African nation where Spanish is the official language, a legacy of its colonial past.

Despite a per capita GDP of more than US$30,000, Equatorial Guinea ranks 121st out of 177 countries on the United Nations Human Development Index. The 'curse of petroleum' has made a few wildly rich and left most in poverty.

Few Westerners, apart from oil industry experts, travel to Equatorial Guinea. The country is truly 'off the beaten track', seeing only a trickle of intrepid backpackers each year. Corruption is rife in this tiny nation. The consensus among posters on Lonely Planet's Thorntree travel forum was that in Equatorial Guinea, bribes were unavoidable: 'No Pay, No Pass', was how one jaded Africa traveller put it.

Equatorial Guinea lies deep in the heart of tropical Africa: our cycling route followed fast-flowing rivers spanned by rickety wooden bridges, the winding roads lined by impenetrable rain forest. As we pedalled, exotic bird calls and

AMAYA WILLIAMS

Amaya Williams grew up in Big Sky Country and is a graduate of the University of Montana. She set off to explore the world in 1995 when an old high school friend (thanks Tracy!) asked her the probing question,'Is this really what you want out of life?' Caught up in the corporate rat race at the time, the answer was an emphatic 'No!' Within weeks she was off to Asia to teach English and explore the continent.

She met her future husband, Eric Schambion, in Laos. Their first cycle trip was to Africa: 40,000km and 40 countries. As Amaya says, 'Traveling by bicycle means I can experience Africa with all my senses, and at a pace that's slow enough to take in humanity. Cycling takes me to far-flung villages that almost no foreign tourists ever get to see'.

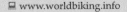 www.worldbiking.info

monkey cries provided the background music and insects buzzed, bit and sucked our blood until our limbs became big red blotches. Cycling across the country as quickly as possible seemed to be the best strategy. That way there would be less chance of hassle from police, military and any other officials who might be keen on emptying our pockets.

Ten. That's the number of police road blocks we'd successfully cycled through in 24 hours. We were feeling quite smug. Others caved into requests for bribes, but we stood our ground and got away with it. Already on the road for almost a year, we'd had plenty of experience dealing with dodgy officials and their crafty methods of extortion.

We weren't expecting trouble as we neared our 11th roadblock. The sound of our pedalling roused the soldier on duty, who was dozing in the shade of a tree by the side of the road. The soldier looked like he was barely out of his teens and was dressed in scruffy fatigues and flip-flops. He quickly slipped on a tattered t-shirt before motioning for us to approach.

We put on our friendliest smiles and donned a slightly subservient manner that seemed to go down well with low-level officials.

We put on our friendliest smiles and donned a slightly subservient manner that seemed to go down well with low-level officials.

'*Buenos tardes, senor*'.

'*Pasaportes*', he grunted in reply.

From a battered desk in his outdoor office, he drew out a faded ledger. The same tiresome rigmarole…name, nationality, passport number, date of birth, profession, coming from, going to. Developing countries feed on bureaucracy. Ledgers to be dutifully filled in and then filed away to be forever forgotten.

As the soldier laboured to fill in the ledger, we glanced anxiously at our watches. A storm was approaching and we wanted to make it to the border before nightfall. Some twenty minutes later, when the young man had checked and double-checked his work, and then asked us to check his work, we checked our watches and concluded that if we rode hard and fast, we might just make it to the town we were aiming for before sunset.

But the soldier refused to return our passports.

'*El Jefe*. You wait.' he said, thumping the ledger for added emphasis.

Wait for the boss? Not possible. You've got all the information you need, we assured him. And we really must be on our way, a storm is rolling in, we pleaded. *Adios, amigo. Nos Vamos*. But he was adamant that we wait.

We contemplated making a break for it. Our passports were lying on the desk, within easy reach. Our soldier had returned to his tree. Should we just grab our precious documents and speed off? What could the young man do? Sprint after us? He had no vehicle at his disposal, so surely he'd never catch us on foot if we fled on our bikes.

He had no vehicle... but what he did have was a menacing-looking AK-47. We waited.

But what he did have was a menacing-looking AK-47. We waited.

A small crowd of curious onlookers had gathered. Western tourists are rare in the remote villages of Equatorial Guinea. In fact, more than once we'd been welcomed by exuberant children calling out 'Chinos, Chinos' as we pedalled past. Apparently the only foreigners those kids were used to seeing were the ubiquitous Chinese road crews paving routes through the thick equatorial jungle. I'm blonde-haired and green-eyed and with my hard-to-place accent have often been taken for German or Dutch, but never Chinese.

In his own good time, the boss stumbled in, obviously back from a drawn-out drinking spree in the local watering hole. El Jefe was a stout man, prone to shameless belching, who had a wild look in his eyes. He was slurring his Spanish so badly we could hardly make out his words. But *dinero* we clearly understood. Two thousand francs (about $4) was the going price for the privilege of passing his checkpoint. It was a measly sum, but we'd not paid a single bribe since we began cycling 20,000km back, and stood by the principle of not contributing to corruption.

> **It was a measly sum, but we'd not paid a single bribe since we began cycling 20,000km back...**

We pointed out to El Jefe – as politely as we could, given that we were seething under a façade of friendliness – that none of his counterparts at the previous ten roadblocks had requested a special checkpoint processing fee.

Giving us the evil eye, El Jefe broke into a rant about the disrespect of foreigners.

'You foreigners think you own the world. My country must be free of imperialists. We Africans are not the white man's servant.'

That was the gist of it, for as much as we could make out his Spanish.

Eric and I skulked in our corner, trying our best not to provoke further wrath. It was a game, one we had played many times. If we were patient, we were sure to prevail.

> **It was a game, one we had played many times. If we were patient, we were sure to prevail.**

Suddenly El Jefe disappeared – passports in hand – only to reappear a moment later toting his Kalashnikov. Flinging the weapon casually over the back of his chair, he crossed his arms and smirked.

Quickly we took stock of the situation. We were at the outskirts of a remote village in a tiny African country that most people have never even heard of. Apart from the officials at the previous ten checkpoints, nobody knew of our whereabouts. And, we were at the mercy of an inebriated and well-armed lunatic.

Perhaps it was time to rethink our hardline stance on the paying of 'miscellaneous fees'. Hands trembling, I fumbled in the bottom of my handlebar bag to dig out the requested 2000 francs. With a wave of his hand, El Jefe refused my offering.

'You give double.' Quickly I handed over the cash, El Jefe rewarded us with the return of our passports and we sped off down the bumpy road.

Guess that guy on the Thorntree forum knew what he was talking about after all. No Pay. No Pass.

Now check your brakes

Edward Genochio *had planned to finish his ride in Hong Kong but instead stayed to find work and rebuild his bank balance as well as his strength for the return ride home on a more mountainous route. That's when he found out that it's not just other people who are out to get you – sometimes your own efforts, or lack of them, can get you into just as much trouble.*

When you get a puncture, you fix it right away. Because you have to. When your brake pads wear down, you leave it till tomorrow. Because you can.

Three roads lead out of Moc Chau, a small town on the edge of Vietnam's north-western highlands. I arrived from the north-west, on the road which climbs from Son La and Dien Bien Phu.

The second road, running south from Moc Chau to the Vietnam-Laos border is 32km long, uphill all the way, and very hard work. At the top, a scrupulously polite Vietnamese border official will inform you that this border crossing is not open to foreigners, and you will have to go back down again.

The final road leads east. Beyond the motor repair shops that fringe the town, the road runs level along the plateau for a few miles, climbs gently to a small pass and then plunges helter-skelter down the mountainside to lowland Mai Chau and the coastal plain beyond.

On the plateau my brakes were OK. True, I had to squeeze the levers right to the handlebars to get the blocks to bite on the rims, but they did their job, just about: they slowed the bike down on a flat, dry road.

That was good enough for me. Brake-adjusting is a fiddly, mucky job and was a bike chore I avoided whenever I could. And on that particular day I had another excuse to postpone the exercise: I was in a hurry. My visa was ticking. I had a day and a half left to get out of the country, and I'd just been turned away from one border crossing; my back-up exit point was 250km away. I didn't have the time, I told myself, to be digging out my toolbag from the depths of my pannier and messing around with the brakes.

Brake-adjusting is a fiddly, mucky job and was a bike chore I avoided whenever I could.

So I kept riding, along the plateau out of Moc Chau, and up in the sunshine to the pass. And then the downhill began. Immediately, the weather was transformed. The clouds had banked up against the seaward side of the mountains, and now suddenly I was descending through rain and near-whiteout fog. My wheel rims were instantly wet and I had no brakes: my brake blocks were just skimming water off the rims; I was captive to the pull of gravity down the slope.

To begin with this is OK. The road is straight and there is no traffic. I'm going fast and fast is good. But the wind is behind me too and I'm going faster and faster, a little bit too fast because the visibility is really bad now and it would be nice to slow down just a little because I can't see what happens to the road up ahead. I have both brake levers pulled right down to the handlebars, but there's just an arc of spray coming off the wheels and I can't slow down, in fact I'm still accelerating and this really is getting much too fast. The road in front of me

I have both brake levers pulled right down to the handlebars, but there's just an arc of spray coming off the wheels and I can't slow down...

looks like it ploughs straight ahead into the forest, but then only just in time I see that it swings to the left, and I have to lean hard to get the bike round the corner. We make it, my bike and I, but we're still rushing downhill and this is becoming a proper mountain road now. There is a low roar up ahead and moments I later I flash past a heavy truck struggling up the hill through the rain.

With the truck behind it's just the roar of the wind now as I plummet down-wards, and a greeny-grey blur as the forest rushes past in the mist, and the sting of the raindrops as they impact on my face. The road runs straight for a while but then I see it is bending again, this time to the right. I throw myself across to the right but it is a tight bend and surely I'm going much too fast to make it round, with all the weight in my panniers this is more a careering juggernaut than a bicycle. I am slipping out to the left side of the road, and through the mist I can see that beyond the edge of the road there is perhaps six foot of dirt shoulder, and then – nothing. From the edge of the road, the mountain just drops away, sheer, into the fog. Whether the drop is 100 foot or 1000, I can't see, but it probably doesn't make much difference – either way, it's too far to fall. Somehow I'm two-thirds round the bend now and if my tyres can keep their grip I might just keep on the road. But I'm flying along right up on the edge – the left-hand edge, the wrong side of the road, and if that truck had come half a minute later I would have had the choice of hitting it or going over the cliff. I lean a little harder to the right, and pray that my tyres will hold on the wet road and that there won't be another truck. Every muscle in my

EDWARD GENOCHIO

Edward Genochio was born in Belgium and has been trying to come to terms with it ever since. He spent three years at Cambridge University gazing at maps, for which he was awarded a degree in Geography. He spent five years working as a self-employed website programmer. He spent a while herding reindeer with the Chukchi people of Kamchatka, and another while researching the conflicts between human communities and monkey conservation on the Tibetan plateau. Concluding that neither Chukchi nor Tibetans nor monkeys were much better off for his meddling, he bought a bicycle and a lot of bananas, and poddled off to China by bike.

The road is strewn with obstructions...
© Ed Genochio

body feels taut as I fight to keep the bike leaning hard into the bend, while at the same time straining to achieve the opposite, holding the bike up to stop the tyres slipping out from under me. And then gradually the bend eases and I think I've made it round. But the road is even steeper here and then a little further on up ahead a heap of rubble is blocking the right side of the road. I see it in time, but only just, and I have to swerve suddenly and hard to the left to get past and again I imagine or try not to imagine what would happen if there was something coming up the mountain on the other side.

The rubble turns out to be the start of a long stretch of roadworks, and the road ahead is strewn with obstructions – more rubble, deep craters, steamrollers, diggers, bitumen boilers – and effectively it is down to a single vehicle-width, though that width switches from one side of the road to the other unpredictably. At the speed I'm going through the fog, fifty, sixty kilometres an hour now, and on a mountain road on a laden bike with no brakes, that feels very, very fast and I'm only just managing to swing my bike across in time. Then up ahead there is the sound of another engine coming up the hill. If it's a truck there's no way I'll get past it, and I start to size up my options. My brakes are still on full and still they're having no effect, there's virtually no rubber left in them. Going off the cliff to my left is one way out. Leaping off the bike and rolling down the road is another. At this speed I'd surely break some bones but I might survive it; hitting a truck head-on would give me worse odds. And there's another bend to the right now, if it's a slight one I

Going off the cliff to my left is one way out. Leaping off the bike and rolling down the road is another.

might be able to get round OK but that engine is sounding close now, just around the corner and it's going to be very tight. The curve flings me out left near the drop and into the path of the truck, but right on the apex of the bend I see it and it's not a truck, it's a Minsk motorbike struggling up the mountain and the rider edges to his right and just squeezes past between me and the edge of the mountain. I imagine he turns to see what lunatic has just come flying down the mountainside right into his path, but my eyes are fixed on the road ahead and I can't look back to see.

My hands are trembling as they squeeze on the brakes, but it's heavy rain now and gravity is pulling me down the slope with far greater force than any remaining friction that my brakes can apply to the wheels. Rushing towards me is a big yellow JCB parked in the middle of the road. As I get close I reckon I can get past that on the inside, away from the precipice, but then beyond that there are figures in the mist on the road. A fraction later and I can see they are people, road-workers, some of them walking along the road and others resting on the heap of gravel I'm heading right for. I open my mouth to let out a warning scream but the sound seems to slip backwards behind me and I don't know if they can hear me coming. I'm screaming and screaming as one of them gets up and makes to cross the road in front of me. As I'm almost upon him he sees me and leaps back and in that same instant I flash past and he is behind me. I'm still screaming like a banshee, and other people on the road ahead are waving and calling at me to slow down.

This goes on for seconds, minutes, hours, I can't tell. I have no sense of time passing, it's all just a present-tense out-of-control terror. And then, gradually, the gradient seems to ease

> **I have no sense of time passing, it's all just a present-tense, out-of-control terror.**

and though I'm still going fast, too fast, and though my brakes still aren't biting, the bike seems to have slowed a little: I have a little more time to think, a little more time to anticipate swerves and to avoid the cow which has wandered onto the road ahead. I try using my feet as friction brakes, scuffing the soles of my sandals on the road, but they keep catching on the uneven road surface and being pulled violently backwards and I feel this could easily break my legs.

And then at last the blur of passing tarmac, vegetation, people, rock slows a little more and the sting of rain in my eyes lessens and though my brake blocks are no longer even touching the rims I'm able to get onto the crossbar and run along astride my bike, gradually taking more strain on the legs and pulling the bike up with my arms.

Gradually the bike came under control. Slower, and slower, and, then, at last, I was at the bottom of the mountain and I brought my bike to a stop. Trembling and dizzy, I sat down by the roadside, shaking more and more as I began to realise how much I had ridden my luck on that descent: it was only by sheer good fortune that I had come through alive and unhurt, that I'd not hit the oncoming truck, or the steamrollers or the road-workers or the cow, that I'd not gone over the edge on the big right-hand bend.

A little later, dazed and still sitting there, I found I was sobbing. I saw one of the road workers coming down the hill towards me. He sat down beside me at the side of the road, and put his hand on my shoulder. He spoke not a word of English, and I not a word of Vietnamese, and so there we sat, he with his hand on my shoulder and I still trembling and trying to stop.

And then after a few minutes he remembered that he knew a word of English: just one word, gleaned from the international language of road-signs. He pointed to my bicycle, which lay on the road by our feet, and said, 'Stop'. We chuckled, and then we laughed, and then we laughed and laughed helplessly and the other road-workers came and joined us and we were all pointing at the bike and saying 'Stop' and laughing and laughing.

☆☆☆

Memo to any other cyclists as foolish as me: do not let your brakes get to the point where they are at full stretch to stop you in the dry. When you're going down a mountain in the rain, they will not stop you.

A truck probably will.

Check your brakes now. Because you can.

Tour Fatale?
Extracts from the diary

A dog bite and the theft of his bike marked the end of **Igor Kovše***'s 2004 ride between Xinjiang in Western China and Kyrgyzstan. A return to Kashgar the following year for an attempt on one of the world's hardest rides, the 3000km trans-Tibet road to Lhasa, ended in a broken collar bone after a crash early on. Undeterred, Igor planned a gruelling ride for 2008 taking in some of the dream routes for cyclists, the Pamir Highway and the Karakoram Highway.*

Day 1: First day in Tajikistan – 130km
The plane landed in Dushanbe early in the morning. It was a quick flight from Istanbul, just about 4 hours, and there was no time to take a nap. The box my bicycle was in arrived pretty beaten up but there was no apparent damage to the bike. I put it together, changed some money (got 3.42 Tajik somons for US$1), bought a bottle of water and pedalled off. For the first 50km the road was rough, the traffic busy. At midday my thermometer showed 37°C.

Day 3: Kaburabot Pass – 89km   [total to date: 319km]
A catastrophic day. By the end of the day I felt totally weak and knackered. I can't explain why, I drank a lot of water, there must be something wrong with my system. Maybe lack of salt. Also, the little and ring finger on my left hand went numb and I knew it was going to stay that way till the end of tour. This happened to me three years ago in Argentina; it took six months to recover.

The altimeter stopped working. The front shifter didn't work well either, sometimes after shifting up to the middle ring the lever wouldn't return to its position. Since it's a combined shift/brake lever I was reluctant to shift too much, being afraid that I would lose the braking function as well. As a result I was either spinning like a rat in cage in the small ring on flat parts or grinding in the middle ring uphill.

I got over Kaburabot pass (30km long and 1600m of climbing, top at 3253m) by 14:00. That was the best

IGOR KOVŠE

A civil engineer from Ljubljana, Igor Kovše took up cycle touring at the age of 35 but jumped in at the deep end, with long and hard rides. He is known on internet forums as an ultralight tourer, choosing to ride narrow-tyred racing bikes. See p287 for his packing list and weights for this trip.

part of the day. Going up from the west it's constant gradual climb through alpine-like pastures with wild flowers and singing buntings. On the other side you drop through a wild ravine on a gravel road and you need to stop every ten minutes to wiggle fingers numb from constant braking. As it turned out this first pass was the only real pass of the whole tour.

...you need to stop every ten minutes to wiggle fingers numb from constant braking

After Kalaikum the road follows the Pyanj river – the border river between Tajikistan and Afghanistan. The scenery along the river is fantastic, yet I was impatient to find a proper camping space. Putting up a tent required much of my energy. I crawled in for an early night and took a couple of aspirins, hoping for a health improvement by the beginning of the next day.

Day 6: Khorog – 53km   [total: 591km]
In the morning I went to the OVIR office to get registered with the police. What I expected to be a swift process took half the day.

I spent an hour cleaning and oiling the chain, and then I lay down in my room thinking how the trip was going so far. Not particularly well. I was behind schedule, my left hand was numb, my back was aching, my arse was in blisters, Tajiks appeared to be not so much hospitable as curious and their dogs quite annoying. I decided to go the fastest way through Tajikistan.

At 15:00 I got the little piece of paper from OVIR and jumped on my bike eager to leave this unfriendly town. Then 5km further on there was a police check point. The policeman examined the OVIR certificate and decided that it was no good – some stamp was missing. I should go back, he said. I gave him 20 somons which transformed him into a friendly, smiling person, wishing me good luck on my way. So, the OVIR pulled a little scam on me. The seed of anxiety sneaked into me. I don't suppose they played this little game just for 20 somons. There will be more checkpoints ahead, and some of them might insist that I turn back, all the way to Khorog.

Day 10: Other cycle-tourists on the Akbaytal Pass – 76km [total: 1007km]
Another cold night, below zero, but again, I was happily warm in my sleeping bag. Just after starting out I met the first cyclist on the road. He was a German whose plans were drastically altered by the new Chinese visa policy – he couldn't get one. I got mine at home. As usual, he was surprised how little I was carrying. 'Unbelievable', he said. It was unbelievable to me what stuff he had in his four big panniers, one big waterproof sack atop of panniers and a big handlebar bag. At least he

As usual, he was surprised to see how little I was carrying.

arranged everything very neatly. He and his bags looked so clean and fresh as if he had started the trip just around the corner. Cleanliness, that's one thing I'm starting to miss.

Half an hour later, starting a gentle climb I see an unmistakable silhouette of a cyclist, coming down the opposite side. As he approaches I recognise him: yes, it is my friend Zlato. We both don't seem too excited about the encounter;

14 days ago we were sitting at one of Ljubljana's cafés discussing our upcoming trips. He tells me the terrible news: from 1st July Kyrgyzstan introduced obligatory visas for Slovenian citizens. I started my trip on 26th June when Slovenians still didn't need the visa. Just what I needed! So what was I to do? There is a 17km stretch of 'no-man's-land' between Tajik and Kyrgyz immigration points. Should I go through the Tajik immigration, get an exit stamp and try to enter Kyrgyzstan without visa? If they don't let me in Kyrgyzstan, I'm stuck in between, as I have only single entry visa to Tajikistan. Should I try it anyway and in the worst case forge my Tajik visa so it reads 'double-entry'? Should I bribe the Tajiks not to put an exit stamp in my passport? Should I turn back and make a shortcut to China by somehow crossing the Kulma pass? Or should I just drop it all, go back to Dushanbe and end this trip, which has already given me more than enough headaches?

Or should I just end this trip, which has already given me more than enough headaches?

Day 11: Border: Tajikistan to Kyrgyzstan – 71 km   [total: 1078km]

I started early in the morning in a cold and strong headwind. A couple of hours later I reached the Tajik immigration post. There is a three-stage procedure. First you face the drug-squad. They turn up your luggage inside out, pretending to search for drugs but are in fact just amused at what sort of idiotic stuff the foreigners are carrying with them. They were most impressed with my card reader – as with all of my other stuff it is stripped of unnecessary plastic and appears as a mysterious microscopic electronic gadget. The card reader was confiscated but as compensation they warmed up a tin of beef meat for me to devour right there and gave me another tin to take away. After the drug-squad there is customs. They meticulously copy data from your passport into their big ledger book. Then there is immigration where they do the same thing as customs, only they are much more important, so it takes longer.

...as with all of my other stuff it is stripped of unnecessary plastic and appears as a mysterious microscopic gadget

I went through all this, still worried about what would happen on the other side of the 17-km no-man's land. These 17km are quite scenic, it's this part of the road which made Janne Corax proclaim: 'This shits on KKH!'. But as I said, I was too worried to appreciate the view, I had even lost interest in taking photos. From Tajik immigration there is a short climb to Kyzyl-Art pass with the famous monument of big-horn sheep. Then it's a big downhill on a terrible surface and quite a lot of water. Some 8km further the asphalt starts and lasts until the Kyrgyz immigration point. While waiting for the gate to open I was very polite and friendly to the young border soldier and it seemed to have worked, as he recommended me to higher ranked officer for mild treatment. I started babbling right away about no-visa regime for Slovenia and managed to persuade the officer. He nodded and gave my passport to a subordinate to put in an entry stamp. So there it was, I was let into Kyrgyzstan without the visa!

Day 12: Into China – 86km [total: 1164km]

Down 'memory lane' day. I rode in my own tracks traced back in August 2004. The last few kilometres to the Chinese border have been recently paved. I ride this impeccable piece of asphalt with utmost respect. I feel like I am in one of those car commercials where a car is driving through magical desert landscape on traffic-free road. At the

I ride this impeccable piece of asphalt with utmost respect.

Kyrgyz immigration post they remind me of the new visa regime but it's too late to be worried. They wave me out of Kyrgyzstan.

Day 13: Long ride to Kashi – 224km [total: 1388km]

Last night I decided to try cycling to Kashi in one day. The road stone close to where I camped indicated 208km. That was just the number of kilometres till the end of road No 309; there were another 40km to Kashi. If I started at 6:00 and cycled until 20:00, I could manage it by doing 18km every hour. The ride was 20km shorter than I expected, so I was in Kashi around 19:00.

Tomorrow's my first rest day. I feel filthy as a pig; there's going to be a big wash up.

Day 14: Rest day in Kashgar

In the morning I went over to a Qinibagh hotel to ask for a room. The cheapest was 360 Yuan, but I said I was looking for something around 100. I got a room with two beds, clean sheets, air-conditioning, TV, tea, separate bathroom, toilet paper, towels, soap, toothbrush, toothpaste, comb, bathroom slippers and cloth for cleaning shoes. Unheard-of luxury for 80 Yuan!

I then proceeded with a long list of chores lined up for today. I washed myself, washed my cycling jersey, shorts, socks, gloves and cap, charged up the battery, patched up the holes in my clothes, plastered the blisters, changed money, called home, sent a couple of emails, went for a lunch, bought cigarettes, cleaned the chain, borrowed a book and read much of it. A busy rest day!

Day 19: Leaving Gilgit – 101km [total: 1971km]

That great day came, after all! It didn't look like it from the beginning. I had a late start from Gilgit, I was waiting until 11:00 for the money changer to open his shop. Money business is really curious in Pakistan: the banks don't change money at all, and there are just a few money changers in bigger towns.

I cycled the first 30km down the KKH in a strong headwind that was constantly blowing each day from noon to 5pm. I tried to be as resigned as possible. After 37km there is turn-off to the left for Skardu. Until yesterday I was quite certain I wouldn't take this detour but now I was not so sure. I took a half-hour break, smoked four cigarettes, and then turned left.

Approaching Muztagh Ata © Igor Kovše

PART 3 – TALES FROM THE SADDLE

As soon as I left the Gilgit river valley the wind turned and was now behind me. The road was leading along the Indus river upstream, and it seemed that my predictions about the wind always blowing upstream were correct. I had a fantastic rest of the day. I wasn't complaining about the road going predominantly uphill. The surface was excellent, even better than on most of the KKH, and the presence of the wild roaring river was energising. I entered into a cycling frenzy. With the bursts of adrenalin I spent half the time out of the saddle, frequently playing games with the trucks, overtaking them uphill and downhill, letting them overtake me only when I took photographs or just stood there amazed at the sight.

Day 22: Sadpara to Deosai Plains – 44km   [total: 2153km]

The climb to Deosai plains awaited me today. This was the only part of my itinerary on which I had no information and which was a bit 'original'. A gardener from the neighbouring hotel advised me to start early, at 5:00, to avoid the heat. I was happier to start at 8:00. The first 6km to the village of Sadpara are still paved and flattish, and then a long 25km climb starts. It is a great climb with fine views down the valley towards Skardu, although the road is in places so bad that you have to push. I think it was the only true climb after Kaburabot pass, 1800km before. My 25mm slick back tyre skidded on a couple of steep sections with loose gravel. It is the tyre with cuts in the thread in two places now. I've been patching it with pieces of duct tape every 50km for over 1000km now and it's holding well, even on a surface like this. It is just proof that anything can work, no matter how unorthodox it seems.

The top of the pass is around 4000m. There is an office to collect $4 for the Deosai NP. 'Where are the bears?', I asked, and got the answer that they are on the other side of the mountain, individually controlled and kept away from the tourist path. A group of Pakistani tourists invited me for lunch, fried rice and onion salad, and after that they took photographs of me with each of them in a row. I felt like a movie star.

I moved on through wavy Deosai plains on the road with fewer stones but still unridable in a couple of places. After a while I descended to the river with a suspension bridge, the ranger station and tourist camp. I got a round of applause as I was coming down to the camp – I was already accustomed to my reputation as a champion. I stopped for a lunch here, even considered camping, but when I heard the price (1000Rs), I moved on and few kilometres further on I put up my small tent for free.

Day 26: Chilas to Dasu – 122km   [total: 2491km]

It was a hard day today. The weather was ideal though – a bit of drizzle in the morning, then overcast day with no wind. But somehow I was slow as a snail. It seems that my motivation tube for this tour had a slow leak right from the beginning and was now almost completely flat.

It seems that my motivation tube for this tour had a slow leak right from the beginning...

I searched for a cheap hotel in Dasu and got a hole of a room for 150Rs. I rode through Kohistan today. The kids were more aggressive than usual and they even threw a few stones after me, but obviously not aiming to hit me.

Day 27: Rest day in Dassu

My god, what a night! The fan didn't work. The mosquitoes ate me alive. That's the price of a cheap room. In the morning I spent an hour in the toilet, vomiting yesterday's dinner and having attacks of diarrhoea. I felt too weak to walk or cycle. Leaning against the bike I walked over to another hotel, checked in, fell on the bed and spent the most of the day in it.

Day 28: Dasu to Besham – 74km   [total: 2565km]

I've lost weight terribly. I look like a skeleton. The problem is that you can't get proper food here. Even the sight of the hole-in-the-wall restaurants makes my stomach turn.

I've lost weight terribly. I look like a skeleton. The problem is that you can't get proper food here.

In the morning the hotel owner takes me for breakfast. Tea and miserable paratha made yesterday in a restaurant into which you enter through the corridor stinking of human faeces. I've lost too much weight and must eat, so I force myself to do it.

The ride starts promisingly. The road climbs high above Indus and stays there almost all the way to Besham. Halfway I stop in a hotel in Pattani and have a big plate of rice and three drinks. It weighs me down considerably. The rest of the day I spend grinding, panting and resting in the shade.

Day 31: Islamabad to Jhelum – 151km   [total: 2966km]

I waited until 9:00 when bursts of diarrhoea finished. While waiting, I replaced the back tyre with a 20mm spare one. The old one could probably make it through the tour despite the now increasing number of cuts in the thread but if it tore, the tube would explode and that would be bad, bad as I had no spare tubes left. On the other hand, the miraculous circle of weight reduction appeared again: having thrown away two tubes, I am about to leave behind another 400g of the tyre.

Heat, diarrhoea & traffic: Highway No 5 in Pakistan © Igor Kovše

Right from the start I took off in wrong direction and ended on a motorway No 2, which is closed to cyclists. Police stopped me and turned me back. At noon I came back to the starting point in Islamabad – called 'Zero point', ironically – making it a pointless 41km. I don't remember much of the rest of the day. If I must describe it, I'd say: heat, dirt and exhaust fumes.

Day 33: Lahore – 77km   [total: 3151km]

I was at the very edge yesterday. I wanted to call a doctor. Today was better, although cycling was far from enjoyable. Today I discovered a heavenly refuge: CNG filling stations. They are extremely clean (because they're not for trucks), they have air-conditioned stores where the prices are the same as in street stalls, and extremely friendly staff, who will turn on the fan for you, invite you into cooled office, offer you juice and even give you medical advice. I reached Lahore today. I was too tired to take my bike upstairs to my room – a hotel boy had to help me with it.

> **I was at the very edge yesterday. I wanted to call a doctor.**

Day 35: Rest day in Amritsar   [total: 3187km]

I spent the morning in the Golden Temple and the afternoon lying in my room. My appetite returned and I managed to eat some food – I opted for bananas and French fries and not for Indian food, to be on a safe side.

When I was undressing that evening the bicycle computer fell from my jersey pocket, bounced a few times on the ceramic floor and went blank. It stopped working. Someone was trying to tell me that this tour was over. I didn't object.

> **Someone was trying to tell me that this tour was over. I didn't object.**

Epilogue

Bicycle tours always look better viewed from the distance of a few months. Well rested, well fed, the travellers' diarrhoea receding, the (slightly touched-up) photos looking much better than when you took them, re-thinking the good and the bad moments seen from the adventure-less present, you seem to enjoy your tour much more now than at the time it was happening.

When I look at the picture of an asphalt strip running through the middle of the stunningly coloured hills of high Pamir, or the dramatic road cut into the Indus canyon, I feel the urge to jump up and get back there again. I forget that at the time when I took the photograph I hated every metre of the gravel road, I was fed up with cycling, with dirt and sweat, with kids stalking me at every village, with answering the same basic questions over and over again.

This was 'le tour fatale', after all: fatal for future trips. At Day 34, the last cycling day, I was sure I'd never come back to the 'developing' world, to dirt roads and to places where you can't cycle through a village without being an attraction to every man, woman, child and dog.

But now, over a month later, I start to dream of a big tour again ...

> **But now, over a month later, I start to dream of a big tour again ...**

ULTRA-LIGHT PACKING LIST

Igor Kovše shows how it is possible to ride for over a month and camp with less than 7kg of gear. In fact, he had less than that as he includes the clothes he wore in the total. His total check-in weight for the flight was under 20kg, so he would have had no excess baggage charges. This was the gear list and where he packed it on his Dushanbe to Delhi trip:

Item	Weight (g)	Position	Item	Weight (g)	Position
Bicycle			**Clothes**		
Bicycle alone	9600	bike	Cycling cap	34	myself
2 bottle cages with bolts	116	bike	Glasses	40	myself
Rear rack with bolts	576	bike	Cycling jersey	160	myself
Bike computer with holder/receiver	35	bike	Arm warmers	30	myself
Altimeter	32	pocket	Cycling shorts	188	myself
Lock	48	bike	Cycling gloves	28	myself
	10,407g		Socks	20	myself
Carriers			Shoes	662	myself
Underseat bag used as handlebar bag	90	bike	Rain/wind jacket	370	rear rack
Main stuff sack (30ltr)	156	rear rack	Polar fleece jacket	248	stuff sack
Stuff sack for tools	10	tent	Long trousers	314	stuff sack
Stuff sack (medical kit), spare glasses, etc	10	stuff sack	Rain pants	112	rain jacket
Bungee cord for main stuff sack	70	rear rack	Underwear	32	stuff sack
Spare nylon belt	6	tent	Rain shell gloves	10	rain jacket
Spare velcro straps	6	stuff sack	2 pars of light fleece gloves	66	rain jacket
Plastic bags	50	stuff sack	Overshoes	78	handlebar bag
1 ltr and 1.5 ltr plastic bottles	90	bottle cage	2 pair spare socks (light & woollen)	78	stuff sack
	488g		Nylon stockings as leg/arm warmers	16	jersey pocket
Tools and spares			Fleece cap	34	stuff sack
Flat screwdriver	30	tool sack	Spare T-shirt	122	stuff sack
Spoke key, allen keys	42	tool sack		**2612g**	
Razor blades (instead of a knife)	2	tool sack	**Photography**		
Pump	72	tool sack	Digital camera with battery	336	handlebar bag
Patch kit	20	tool sack	Spare camera battery & charger	126	stuff sack
15 mm pedal wrench (cut in half)	50	tool sack	Card reader	10	stuff sack
8 mm & 10 mm wrench	20	tool sack	Bubble-wrap protection	4	handlebar bag
2 tyre levers	10	tool sack		**476g**	
Hypercracker	24	tool sack	**Paperwork**		
Chain tool	40	tool sack	Passport, air tickets	70	myself
Bolts and nuts	6	tool sack	Notebook, calendar and a pencil	38	jersey pocket
Oil	10	bike	Photocopies of town plan maps	6	jersey pocket
Duct tape	10	seatpost		**114g**	
3 spare spokes	10	rear rack	**Miscellaneous**		
2 spare tubes	196	bike	Toothbrush	6	handlebar bag
Spare tyre	296	rear rack	Skin cream	20	handlebar bag
	838g		Sun screen	10	bike
Camping			Razor	6	handlebar bag
Tent	888	rear rack	Dish washing cloth used as a towel	10	handlebar bag
Sleeping bag with compression bag	972	stuff sack	Lighter	10	jersey pocket
Strip of bubble wrap (sleeping pad)	72	stuff sack	Pen water filter	20	stuff sack
Mini flash light (= bike taillight)	8	stuff sack	Spare glasses in soft case	40	stuff sack
	1950g		Medical kit* & sewing kit	88	stuff sack
Food and water				**210g**	
Water in two plastic bottles	2500	bike			
Emergency food	200	stuff sack	**Total**	**19,795g**	
	2700g		(without bicycle, water and food) 6,688g		

* After the bad experience with gut infection, I would add water purifying tablets too.

For Igor's philosophy of lightweight cycle-touring see: 🖥 http://www2.arnes.si/~ikovse/weight.htm.

'I may seem fanatical about this lightweight business but, in fact, I don't take it too seriously and to those of you who wish to follow, I suggest that you don't either. I do take great pleasure in cutting things, though'.

Igor Kovše

PART 3 – TALES FROM THE SADDLE

The Great Fig Hunt

A great believer in living off the land, **Alastair Bland** *has written about the delights of home-made wine and is also a keen mushroom hunter. Here he finds he can not just survive but flourish on one of nature's gifts to cyclists – figs.*

The smells of the Central Valley, the length of the road, the sweetness of unfettered youth and the endless abundance of figs: I still relive those days like it was last month, but, alas, how the years have flown! I was a boy when I set out upon my bicycle with little more than a sleeping bag and a map of the state, with my eyes peeled for the autumn fruits that would sustain me for many weeks, and today those echoes of my past and the long shadows of my age meld into a remembered two-month time of golden sunlight and a sheer exuberance for life. I manage to overlook the dark times: the pit bulls in pursuit, the vile slums of Los Angeles, the vagrant near Chico who threatened to brain me with a crowbar, and the crushing misery of the Central Valley heat. To the contrary, I have mostly remembered the figs.

It's this inverted flower of a fruit, in fact, that drew me out on the road again this August. I left home with a sleeping bag and tarp on the rear rack of my bicycle, with my travel panniers filled with the basic tools of the simple life, and I aimed for the delta's Brannan Island, precisely where I began my 2004 journey. Brannan Island, home to a state park campground and an uncanny number of fig trees around its levee-lined perimeter, is the premiere destination for those pursuing the noble sport of fig hunting.

I was encouraged to find that, although I was out of practice, I had not lost my touch; the old magic was still there. As I pedalled I scanned the roadsides, and the slightest sprig of fig foliage visible over the roof of a barn would reveal the presence of a tree that the common man couldn't have detected. And I could still identify a fig tree a quarter of a mile away by its thickly textured appearance and the jungly pattern of outward growth common to many feral figs. Nor had I lost my olfactory powers, and more than once I caught a whiff of that thick hay-like odour before catching sight

ALASTAIR BLAND

Alastair Bland is a freelance journalist in San Francisco. He cycles almost everywhere and travels often but can always be reached at 🖥 allybland@yahoo.com.

of the fig tree itself, furtively growing amongst the roadside shrubbery. Yep, thought I, this old dog's got some kick in him yet!

The hunt was good that day. I struck up about a tree per two miles, and I only selected the best figs – those so ripe their skins were taut under their own sagging weight, the sort so soft and jammy that they never reach grocery stores – and after 15 miles of riding my basket was brimming with fruit. A common misconception about figs holds that there are two varieties: black and green. Actually, there are hundreds – purple, brown, yellow, red, striped like the Kremlin steeples, thin-skinned, thick-skinned, pink inside, magenta inside, figs the size of Bartlett pears, and countless combinations in between.

There are hundreds – purple, brown, yellow, red, striped like the Kremlin steeples

I also rediscovered that day how the avid fig hunter disapproves of all trees but the fig. I snorted at apples, oranges, plums and other such fruits of the year-round grocery aisle. I even cast judgment upon the people who lived in each house I passed by the looks of their yards. Those with no trees at all were managed by hopelessly lost souls. Those with non-fruit trees were fools. Those with apple trees, social conformists. Walnuts, boring. Lemons, spare me. Mulberries, I condoned, but likely the fruit all went to waste, and thus, idiots. I feel it's an able system of character analysis.

I also rediscovered some of the ugly points of fig hunting. The heat was oppressive, and I passed the afternoon in a shady park in the dismally slow town of Isleton. I only returned to camp at dusk, when the delta air was balmy – and swarming with insects. I settled in at my picnic table and, before dinner, picked the bugs from my eyes. I ate figs stuffed with cheese, then went to sleep among dust, grime and ants. The mosquitoes came out around midnight. I had no repellent, and they feasted.

The sun rose from a brilliant scarlet flood over the eastward horizon, but it boded only of the blistering heat to come. I loaded up on Kadota figs west of Lodi and passed through several smaller villages. I say 'villages' experimentally, to see if the connotations of the word – like bakeries, mules, town plazas and old women carrying the day's milk – ring true in any way. They don't. In rural Europe, espresso machines, cobblestones beyond number, ancient church steeples and other charms of Old World village culture make for an almost universally pleasing bicycling experience. It's in Europe, too, that fig tree roots take readily to the perimeters of historical castles and fissures in stone bridges. The trailer shack shanties of rural America, with their gas station coffee and the pit bulls and broken appliances in the front yards, only offend the senses. It's an unfortunate juxtaposition of beauty and beast that this land is prime fig country.

It's an unfortunate juxtaposition of beauty and beast that this land is prime fig country.

Northeast of Lodi, the earth began to roll. A subtle change at first, my legs felt it, then my eyes caught it. Bluffs grew at the roadsides and quickly the flat manure lands of the valley transformed into lolling hills of chaparral and oak trees, and scattered pines told of the jagged high country ahead. I stayed that night with a friend and winemaker in El Dorado County. On my trip of four years ago I enthusiastically fermented my own wine in a plastic Nalgene bottle and got satisfactorily drunk several times. I have since matured into a gentleman with expensive tastes, and we drank fine beer and Pinot Noir that evening. We ate wild rice, pasta and figs wrapped in prosciutto, and we discussed real estate.

With a gift the next morning of two bottles from Toogood Winery, I departed for the high country and would see no more figs for days of weary journeying. The foothills country changed just as fast as I pedalled. The agricultural elements were buried by pine forests, and through the trees I saw the bald peaks and sheer cliffs of the Desolation Wilderness to the north, and Mark Twain's favourite lake and my evening's goal – Tahoe – lay somewhere beyond those summits.

A cyclist burns an average of 45 calories per mile, I have read. Carrying 35 pounds of gear and going uphill must nearly double that rate, and by mile 60 my granola breakfast had burned through and I was desperately hungry, thousands of calories in the hole. Each store I saw on highway 88 was closed. I climbed over one high pass after another, finally dropping into the town of Meyers where I stumbled into a supermarket. I bought dinner – wholewheat bread and sandwich makings – before I attacked Luther Pass. Still, as I circled Lake Tahoe's west shore, I faced another 600-foot climb. At last, gravity drew me down the final miles and I barely made it to Sugar Pine Point State Park before dark. I drank a bottle of Primitivo and ate a salmon sandwich at sunset. I enjoyed eight more, then expired for the night.

I rolled into campgrounds looking theatrically overdrawn and beaten by circumstances – any cyclist knows the technique – and I won several bottles of beer...

I explored the high Sierras for several days. I climbed from the dry east side up through Markleeville, home base of the annual Death Ride – a century-and-a-half bike ride comprising over 14,000 feet of elevation gain. I drifted over high stony plateaus and along the green shores of still mountain lakes. I rolled into campgrounds looking theatrically overdrawn and beaten by circumstances – any cyclist knows the technique – and I won several bottles of beer with my efforts. I watched for black bears at night, and triumphed over high passes by day, and stared awestruck toward the peaks of giant sequoia trees. I wound in circles through the scrub-less high country and built up tremendous appetites and went to sleep on huge and nourishing dinners.

But I missed the figs of the lowlands, and the call to duty soon brought me back. Fig season, after all, wouldn't last forever. I smacked my lips in anticipation of breakfast as I sailed at almost 40 miles per hour down Highway 4 one morning, yet my heart sank as the mountains vanished. First the craggy cirques disappeared. Then the pines of bear country transitioned into the chaparral of tick country, and my disappointment was tangible. As I arrived in the Gold Rush town of Murphys, the sweltering heat gripped me and assured me that the change was complete; I was back in the Central Valley, for better or for worse.

I camped near Plymouth at Bray Vineyards, where the winemaker – also a friend of mine – met me at the gate and left me with a door open to the office, with email access, and with 10 opened bottles from the day's tastings. If only such moments could last forever. But night time in the Central Valley is a great swindle; the air is so cool and silent, and the stars above speak of tranquility the world round. Drinking wine on a comfortable patio furthers the deception and makes one forget that the sun will rise again, and I was momentarily deceived into thinking that here was heaven. In fact, the sun was prowling behind the Earth, in flames and fury, mobilising for another day of hell. She looked sublime and harmless enough at dawn, but I knew what she had in store for me, and I decided I would ride 90 miles to the coastal Napa Valley for relief. I arrived that evening – alas, in the midst of a terrible heat wave; there would be no relief here.

I paid homage to my former years by dabbling in the infamous craft of making road wine.

For several days I bore the weather and rampaged about the country, devouring the figs, laying waste to the crop and taking note of feral trees for future pillages. I stuffed myself to the gills, camping each night at Napa Valley State Park. I paid homage to my former years, too, by dabbling in the infamous craft of making road wine – sort of. I started with a ready bottle of Simi Winery 2007 Sauvignon Blanc. This lightly acidic wine, with delicate notes of citrus, tropical fruit, spice and all that drivel, can be improved by adding fresh Calimyrna figs. I transferred the wine into my wide-mouthed water bottle and added eight smashed fruits and a day later I enjoyed the result – a robust and tawny beverage with an earthy sweetness and flavors of oak, pine, mead, and, well, figs. I drank the last of it on the ferry ride home, from Vallejo across the largest estuary on the continent, to San Francisco.

Figs: something about them holds mysterious powers over my imagination. My carnal instincts say it's the taste and texture, but my wiser side tells me it's something more essential – a combination of lore, biology, history and geography. It's the durability of the trees, certainly, which will sprout in the driest, stoniest places, with an affinity for European castles, and it's their productivity, as they'll generate perfect fruit for three months of the year and live, though neglected, for centuries.

By now I've eaten 10,000, but my fascination persists. My attempt last September to relive a fig-hunting adventure of years prior taught me that journeys are sweetest in memory, but I will surely be compelled someday again to brave the baking Central Valley – or perhaps the

My attempt to relive a fig-hunting adventure of years prior taught me that journeys are sweetest in memory...

scorched plains of Spain or the rocky ruins of Greece – for another taste. The fig, after all, is a sweet blessing, but, so it seems, it's also my bitterest curse.

APPENDICES

Appendix A – Bicycle maintenance

MAINTENANCE ON THE ROAD

At home, maintenance can be put off forever. On tour, you're covering much greater distances and need to keep your bike running efficiently. Rest days are a good time to keep up with maintenance on your bike, at the campsite or in a cheap hotel courtyard. At the very least you want to be checking the '3Bs': bolts, brakes and bearings. Maintenance can be a chore but on the road it's much more satisfying when you have no distractions or time constraints and know that your work will ensure the smooth continuation of your trip.

Cleaning your derailleur drive train

Cleaning the chain and exposed gears is an important and rewarding task. Your bike will ride a little faster and more quietly and the drive train will certainly last longer and be less messy if you keep it clean. You may have one of those chain bath gadgets to wash the chain but on the road it's easier to give the chain and gears a dry clean using an old toothbrush (or the specialist brushes from manufacturers like Park), a tiny flat screwdriver and a rag. Working with everything dry makes far less mess.

With your bike standing upright, pick away at the grime on the chain and gears; if you have some WD40 or similar solvent spray, this will help

---

CHAIN OIL

Convenient free supplies!

Instead of carrying your own chain oil, you might look around petrol/gas stations for discarded motor oil containers. You need only a few drops and there's usually enough in one plastic container for one or two bikes. In the developing world motor oil is sold in bulk so you won't find discarded bottles but you will find fellows who will part with a few drops from their oil cans, either at no charge or for the equivalent of pennies, in roadside repair shops.

Motor oil is not the most ideal lubricant but many long-distance tourers have managed for years with this low-cost method, which also spares you the risk of an oil spill inside a pannier, if you miss tightening a bottle top!

How much chain oil to use

Sprays like WD-40 are not really good enough to properly lubricate a chain alone; they are not thick enough to protect the metal of the chain, cogs, and chainwheels. Chain oil (especially the thicker formulations, such as 'Phil Tenacious Oil') should be applied sparingly: a maximum of six drops, over the entire length of the chain (while backpedalling, by hand, 2-3 turns of the crank when the chain is in the large chainring). If a chain looks wet after you've oiled it, you've used waaaaay too much! Wipe off the excess or your chain will become a sticky magnet that attracts abrasive dirt and grit, and that defeats the whole purpose of lubrication: reducing wear.

Paul Woloshansky

loosen any crud. Hold the flat end of a small screwdriver against the side of the jockey and pulley wheels of the rear derailleur and rotate the pedal backwards to scrape off dirt, as if you were working a lathe. If you can, do the same to the rear sprockets, cleaning each one in turn. It's harder to get in behind the largest chainring but be persistent and your efforts will pay off. Do the same with the chain itself; you need to poke and scrape every link, especially in between the plates.

Next, lay the bike down. Fold your rag in two and pull it tight to create a straight line along the folded edge. Use the rag like dental floss to 'floss' between the sprockets of the rear cassette. You don't have to remove the wheel and can use the rag to move the sprocket around when you have cleaned one side. Wipe off any excess muck and let everything dry, then add a few drops of whatever lubricant you're carrying (see box on p292).

Checking bolts
Some riders check nuts and bolts daily, especially for their racks, but unless you're riding off-road it's excessive except if you've noticed persistent loosening (either visible loosening or a wobbling rack). Checking all bolts every rest day is certainly a good idea.

Brake maintenance
Brake pads have a much shorter life on tour – you're riding greater distances, and though there's hopefully less stop-and-start riding, your bike is heavier and you might be making some long descents. Wet weather is also very hard on brake pads and so they need frequent attention.

Fine tuning, which normally means tightening the brakes as the pad wears, is done by turning the small barrel adjuster on the brake cable anticlockwise to tighten the brakes. You might find the adjuster next to the brake lever if you have mountain bike bars, or they'll be by the brakes themselves. Over time, this fine tuning is not enough as the pad becomes so worn that it does not fully engage with the rim. Check after a big descent or a rainy day that the pads have not become dislodged. Brake pads can move out of position and in the worst case rub on the fragile tyre sidewall. If the pad is wearing unevenly you won't get good braking performance and should replace it.

Replacing brake pads
Good quality rim brakes have metal brake shoes that take thin rubber pads while the shoe remains fixed in place and needs no adjusting. If you have the older type of brake block that has a metal bolt fixed into the pad, look for after market brake blocks such as Kool Stop Tectonics that will take standard V-brake pads, which are less bulky and easier to fit.

Fitting new brake shoes is not easy as the pad can move around while you are tightening it, and you need near-perfect positioning. Don't feel you have to push the perpendicular bolt on the brake pad all the way into the cantilever so that the brake pad rests against the cantilever arm; the brakes will have greater mechanical advantage if you extend the brake pad out from the arm a little – try it that way and adjust later.

Half-tighten the brake shoe, push the brake against the wheel and adjust the pad to where you want it to hit the rim, allowing a little toe-in (ie: the

Adjust bolt to set brake pad

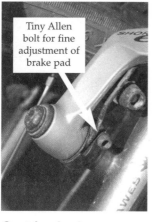

Tiny Allen bolt for fine adjustment of brake pad

front, leading edge of the pad is a little closer to the rim than the rear). Tighten it fully, then pull the cable through the anchor bolt, holding both brake arms with your other hand almost against the wheel. With luck the cable will not slip back through the anchor bolt while you reach for your Allen key to tighten it. If it does, you either need a friend to help or a pair of locking pliers – but be careful not to damage the cable by clamping it too hard.

Cleaning brake pads

Brake pads build up with grit and tiny scraps of metal to act like sandpaper on the wheel rim, which reduces braking power. Using any sharp tool, carefully scrape or dig out as much grit as you can from the brake pads which you may have to remove beforehand. Occasionally cleaning the wheels is a good idea as it allows you to see any damage to the rim and also makes wheel truing easier (see p298).

Brake squeal

Brake squeal is an annoyance but not usually a safety issue. It could be a toe-ing in problem – see bottom of p293 for how to set cantilever brake pads. Other causes of brake squeal are dirty or damaged rims, damaged or badly worn brake pads, loose brake arms (tighten the bolt attaching the brake arm to the boss on the fork or frame), or even the type of brake blocks.

Centring brakes

Brakes touching the rim unevenly is a common problem; usually one pad is dragging lightly on the rim. It may be that one pad is out of position and catching on the rim, or the wheel was not properly centred in the dropouts when you last put it in but, most of the time, a simple adjustment solves the problem. Look for a tiny Allen bolt (usually 2mm) on the side of one or both brakes – see illustration. Tightening that bolt on the brake that is rubbing will push it away from the rim. Alternatively you may have to loosen the small bolt on the opposing brake. Experiment but be careful not to over-loosen these bolts – it can release a spring inside the brake, and you'll need to remove the brake from the brake boss, dismantle it and reset the spring.

Replacing brake cables

Not a difficult job but make sure you have the right cables you need – brake cables are longer for rear brakes and different for mountain bike and dropped bar setups. Note how your brake cable fits into the brake lever when you push it out. You may have to squeeze the brake a little to see where the cable nipple fits into the brake lever.

Weak brakes

There are many possible causes. The longer cable on rear brakes reduces power – there's more stretch in the cable and also more chance for dirt in the cable housing, causing friction. The brakes themselves could be set in a position giving little mechanical advantage, or the straddle cable (older brakes have a thick cable linking the two brake arms) may be too long. It's usually possible to set the spring inside each brake arm in two different positions on the brake boss, so remove the brake from the boss, see where the coil spring fits into a hole in the boss, and make sure it is in the hole that gives it greatest resistance. An over-tight bolt or grime in the brake could also reduce efficiency.

Derailleur adjustment

As derailleurs have become indexed (click-shifting) and built to higher standards and narrower tolerances, they've become more fussy and in need of more regular adjustment. It's minor work but you might need to make small adjustments every couple of days. For a derailleur to work well, the chain, sprockets and derailleur mechanism (or 'mech') all need to be clean. A dirty cable will also stick and cause problems, and a kink in a cable can only be rectified by replacement. Manufacturers advise not to lubricate gear cables but if they are rusty or slightly damaged a squirt of spray or oil would be a quick road fix. Common problems include:

Noisy or poor shifting Assuming everything is clean, you need to look at the alignment of the mech and check it's tracking exactly in line with the sprocket carrying the chain. A mech feeding the chain a little to the left or right will be noisy and cause friction.

Turn the bike upside down and turn the pedal with one hand. By rotating the barrel cable adjuster one way or the other, the derailleur will move up or down the cassette – a few turns of the adjuster and it will jump into the next gear. Keep adjusting it till the derailleur is centred for each gear. It's easier if someone else shifts gears using the handlebar gear control while you pedal and experiment with the barrel cable adjuster – you'll soon get the hang of it as the gears run most quietly when all are correctly aligned with the mech.

Many gear shifters have a second barrel adjuster next to the gear shifter on the handlebar. On a long straight stretch of road where there's nothing but the sound of your gears chattering, try adjusting it on the fly – you'll soon be in the habit of listening out for gear noise and doing some fine tuning to eliminate it.

Chain comes off the cassette This is caused by loose limit screws (see illustration) allowing the rear mech to move too far. These limit screws can work loose over time; tighten them so they only just allow the chain into the highest and lowest gear. The limit screws are at the back of the rear

Limit screws

Barrel cable adjuster

Rear derailleur adjustment

BIKE MAINTENANCE

mech and are usually marked 'L' and 'H'. Screw in 'L' a touch to stop the chain jamming into the spokes and screw in 'H' to stop the chain going off the smallest sprocket (highest gear).

Chain skipping This might be caused by a tight link not articulating fully as it goes round the sprockets; it could have got damaged by the chain getting stuck in the spokes. Lubricate the tight link and prise it apart. If the plate on the side of the link looks damaged, you may have to replace that link. Sometimes your chain and/or sprockets are so worn that the chain comes off, especially during hard pedalling. There'll be no apparent damage, but examine your chain for stretch and check your sprockets too – see 'chain stretch' below.

Front derailleur

Front derailleurs don't have the fine-tuning adjustment of a rear mech, only the limit screws, but it's usually possible to move the cage (the curved plates which sit around the chain) while you're riding if they're rubbing on the chain. If you hear a clattering sound, it may well be the front derailleur and you can look down while riding and check if the cage is rubbing. Half-shifting the gear control on the left handlebar will usually shift the cage out of the way.

To move the chain over such large jumps between chainrings, the cage has to over-shift, that is, it needs to move a little further than the ideal position in order to push the chain onto the next chainring. That's when you need to give it a click or half-click to push it to a centred position for the ring you want to use. Very occasionally an extra push is needed when going up into larger rings or a click in the other direction to pull it back. Again, let noise be your guide and adjust it any time you can hear it.

Limit screws

Front derailleur limit adjustment

Limit stop adjustment

As with rear derailleurs, tightening either screw moves the limit inwards, so if the chain is falling off the chainrings tighten the screw on that side. Note that the limit for the large chainring tends to be right on the ring, whereas for the smallest chainring you have to set the limit a millimetre or two left of the ring itself.

Don't alter the height of the derailleur on the seat tube on the road, this needs doing only if you change the chainring or fit a different size. The cage should be about 1mm above the large chainring when set for the highest gear.

Chain stretch

Chains don't actually stretch like knicker elastic, but the rivets and collars around them wear out over time, allowing each link to lengthen and so effectively stretch the chain. Measure your chain using a 12" rule held at the centre of one rivet in the chain link. The 12" line on a new chain will be exactly in the centre of the twelfth link. More than 1/16" (nearly 2mm) over and it's time for a new chain and more than 1/8" (3mm) over, you'll more than likely need new sprockets as well. If you can see daylight between the chain and sprockets or chainring, your chain and the sprockets/rings are on the way out.

Headset maintenance

Paul Woloshansky

Headset maintenance is mostly ignored by touring cyclists, who are usually more concerned with how their wheels and drive-trains are holding up. Generally speaking, on shorter tours the bearings that allow a bicycle to be steered shouldn't require servicing or adjustment. On long journeys, however, ignoring an out-of-adjustment headset can ruin this component, damage a frame and fork, and negatively affect your bike's handling. A bicycle burdened with very heavy front panniers exacerbates the potential for harm so you need to recognise the problem early on in order to prevent or minimise damage.

The following advice is really 'an ounce of prevention' so you won't have to look for 'a pound of cure' out in the middle of nowhere:

Threaded headsets

If your bike is equipped with a threaded headset you'll need a tool that fits the flats of your bike's headset adjusting cone to adjust or service the bearings. Wrenches much smaller than the ones bikeshops use are available and are a good choice for a touring toolkit (e.g: Park Tool's RW3, which has a 36mm headset wrench on one end and a 15mm pedal wrench on the other; make sure you get one that fits your bike!).

Ideally two wrenches are used to adjust a headset, but you can usually find an adjustable spanner (crescent wrench) in most roadside repair shops to fit a headset's locknut, which is tightened down clockwise against an adjusting cone held securely by either a 32, 36, or 40mm headset wrench.

Don't fret if your first adjustment results in an overtight headset: adjustment is by trial-and-error, try again, backing off the adjusting cone a little before re-tightening the locknut against it. To check if your adjustment is too loose, grasp the front brake lever and rock the bike forward and backward to detect any play, and adjust it out with the adjusting cone. Keep on checking and adjusting until you've got it right, but be aware that a headset that's been loose for a while will probably have pitted bearing surfaces, so the final adjustment will often be a compromise between too tight and too loose.

Aheadsets or threadless headsets

Threadless systems are adjusted from the very top; tightening down the Allen-head bolt (visible in the centre under the top cap) drives the stem downwards on the smooth, threadless steerer tube. This action compresses the Aheadset and eliminates bearing play. It's possible to over-tighten, so watch that there is no play but that the handlebar moves freely.

The golden rule is this: you must loosen the Allen-head bolts on the side of the stem (they attach the stem to the steerer) before you snug down the top bolt. This step allows the stem to move freely down the steerer. If you forget to do this, you risk damaging or dislodging the star-nut (the barbed nut that has been driven down inside a steerer tube, that the adjusting bolt screws into).

Also, before snugging down an Aheadset, check to see if any plastic or rubber seals are protruding. If they are, centre them so they aren't damaged or sheared-off during adjustment. If the seals are damaged the system will be less weather-proof.

Wheel truing

Because of the extra payload and rough roads it's normal for wheels to go out of true on tours. Squeezing pairs of spokes gives a very rough idea of spoke tension but should help identify any loose spokes. They'll also need some minor truing should a spoke require replacement. To do so without a truing stand or any tools other than a spoke key follow these instructions. Of all bicycle maintenance procedures, this essential skill is worth learning before leaving home as it does require a certain knack.

1. With the panniers off, stand the bike upside down.

2. Spin the wheel and push one brake pad towards the wheel. As you push it closer, it will probably make contact in one or several places on the rim.

3. Select the biggest point of contact to work on first. As the wheel rubs against the brake pad, it slows down and comes to rest on the biggest bump.

4. Slowly turn the wheel back and forth to find the centre of this bump. If it looks as if the bump is on the other side of the wheel, go round to that side and start there.

Wheel truing takes a little practice. It's easiest with a proper spoke key (shown here). Turn anticlockwise to tighten; clockwise to loosen.

5. Bear in mind that though you're tightening the spokes, you're actually turning the nipples that the spokes screw into, so you tighten the opposite way. Turn the key **anti-clockwise to tighten spokes**, and clockwise to loosen them.

REPAIRING A BROKEN FRAME WITH GLUE

British bike designer Mike Burrows writes that two-part epoxy glue (such as Araldite in the UK) can make a good repair on broken frames or racks. First, clean the frame using petrol or something similar to remove all grease. File or scratch the surface thoroughly to give good adhesion. Wrap with strips of woven glass fibre, binding it as tight as possible on the frame. Use a knife to spread the mixed epoxy on, warming it up beforehand if necessary. PVC insulating tape can be used to bind the epoxy resin onto the frame, pricking the tape to allow excess resin to escape. A clean break in a rack can be strengthened by using a tent peg as a splint before binding with glass fibre and glue. (From CTC's *Cycle Magazine* January 2005).

6. Tighten or loosen in quarter-turn increments. Turn just past 90°, then back off in order to loosen the spoke in the nipple, as sometimes the spoke twists but does not turn in the thread. Lightly lubricate the nipple if necessary. Check the rim frequently by spinning the wheel to check on your progress, so you don't overtighten and risk a broken spoke or round off the nipple so the spoke key can't grip.

7. For small bumps, turning only the one spoke at the centre of the deviation may work, but you may have to slightly loosen the spokes either side of it. Be careful loosening spokes as this is as dangerous as over-tight spokes in causing metal fatigue (and hence breakages) and allowing the wheel to go out of true.

8. Work around the wheel until all large deviations are eliminated. Once you can rotate the wheel and feel numerous tiny bumps, there is probably not much more you can do yourself. If you can get the deviations from true down to 1mm, that is excellent for a roadside repair.

Fixing a puncture

You'll need a pump to match your valves (these days nearly all pumps fit both Presta or Schrader valves), glue, chalk or talc, patches or old inner tube to cut a patch from, sandpaper and two tyre levers.

Most people on day rides simply fit a spare tube rather than repair a puncture on the spot and hold up their friends. It saves a few minutes. Even then remember to check the tyre for thorns or broken glass which might still be embedded.

To repair an inner tube

1. Loosen the brakes by pulling the brake cable out of its guide. Open the quick-release on the wheel and remove the wheel.

2. Remove the cap on the tube valve or locknut around the base of the valve, if there is one.

3. Loosen the tyre from the wheel by hand, squeezing the tyre as you go round it with your hands.

4. If the tyre is loose in relation to your wheel, you might be able to remove it by hands – the safest way to do so and rather satisfying too!

5. If not, use plastic tyre levers. These are soft and less likely to damage rims or tubes. The kind with a hook on the other end allows you to clip it to a spoke and free your hands to insert the second tyre lever – see illustration.

6. Work your way slowly round the tyre with the tyre lever, bringing the tyre off the rim on one side only.

7. Remove the inner tube and pump it up. You can probably spot anything

Using plastic tyre levers to remove tyre.

larger than a slow leak. Mark it or hold your thumb over it and keep searching in case there are more punctures. If you can't dip the tyre in water to look for escaping bubbles, you'll have to use your ears or try to feel the air rushing out if you hold the tyre up to your eyes or wet lips.

8. Rub round the hole with sandpaper, making sure you eliminate any raised edges running down the centre of the tube.

9. Apply a thin layer of glue to an area around the hole larger than the patch. Let it cure till it becomes tacky, then apply the patch, removing any backing plastic or foil first on the side which goes on to the tyre. Hold it tight for a minute or two. If you have chalk or talc, spread a little on the excess glue. Or if there is some very fine soil around, crumble it to dust in your fingers and use that.

10. While you let the glue dry a little longer, check the tyre for foreign objects. Rips in the tyre can be reinforced with patches of old inner tube glued on the inside, though this may only work as a temporary repair.

Before resorting to tyre levers refit the tyre as much as you can by hand.

11. The glue will be dry within five minutes. Partially inflate the tube and stuff it back in the tyre and seat the valve in its hole.

12. Begin fitting the tyre bead back behind the rim. Go as far as you can around the wheel with both hands. Before resorting to the tyre levers to push the last bit of tyre bead over the rim, push the lever in between tyre and rim to make sure the inner tube is not trapped.

13. Partially inflate the tube then deflate it quickly to free the inner tube, should it be trapped. Inflate the tyre to full pressure, hope it stays that way and refit the wheel and the brakes.

TOOLKIT

Your toolkit should be chosen with your own bike in mind so that it comprises only the tools you need. It will be based around the following essential items:

Multi-tool with sufficient Allen keys, screwdrivers, chain tool, blade
Leatherman or similar
Spoke key
2 tyre levers

It's easiest to build your toolkit around a multitool such as the **Topeak Alien II**, one of the most popular bike tools available, with 26 functions on it. Having them all in one place makes it harder to lose the small tools, such as the 2mm Allen key you may need to fine-tune your brakes. Check all over your bike to see if you have the necessary screwdriver or Allen key to fit everything. Something as big as the Alien II will have all those keys, and in long enough sizes to reach all the places you need to reach.

A few **extra Allen keys** or a small **wrench** for the most commonly-used sizes would not hurt – you may lose or damage keys and wear out their edge. You may need a particularly long Allen key to reach into certain places, such as the stem, and the short keys that multi-tools have are sometimes not long enough. Pedro's of the USA makes an excellent set of long individual Allen keys with ball ends for working at odd angles. Having a few individual 'L'- shaped Allen keys enables you to use either end depending on

A lightweight tool and repair kit: – CoolTool, hose clamps, valve adaptor and cable ties.
© Robin Wielder

whether you want extra length or leverage. You could also buy an extension collar to gain more leverage on your Allen keys. I use these in combination with an adjustable wrench to remove pedals. Pedals need a 15mm wrench to remove them, but pedal wrenches are normally about 30cm long as force is usually required. Most people balk at carrying such a long tool and my alternative is to be able to extend the length of the wrench that I carry. Grease your pedals' threaded spindles before fitting them to the crankset, every time you re-assemble your bike for a long trip. If you are going to box your bike for a flight or train trip, (it may be required for trips on Amtrak in the USA, for instance) you must be able to remove the pedals. The right tool must be slim to fit in the gap beside the pedal but strong enough to apply sufficient force. Another great bike tool that has been around a long time is the **CoolTool** made by Gerber but it can be hard to find outside the USA. The CoolTool has an adjustable wrench opening up to 19mm that can handle pedals, and you can combine the tools to make a long lever, more so if you buy a short section of tube to extend your 6mm Allen key. Since this is a rare need, you could instead use the 10cm piece of 10mm diameter aluminium tubing you should have brought for repairing broken tent poles.

The second multi-tool you need is a **Leatherman** or something similar. This gives you good quality screwdrivers that bike-specific multi-tools usually lack, and in different sizes. It serves as a backup for several tools and has

ESSENTIAL SPARES

- Puncture kit
- Hose clamps
- Electrical ties/zip ties
- Duct tape (may fit around your water bottles or loose around the seatpost)
- Brake pads
- Brake cables
- Gear cables
- Cable ends
- Old toothbrush for cleaning gears
- WD40 or similar solvent

- Small tub of grease
- Spare spokes: several of each length used on your bike
- Various extra nuts, bolts and washers
- Glue – Loctite, SeamGrip, Epoxy and blue Loctite for locking threads on racks etc.
- Small patches of fabric – canvas, old inner tube or tyre wall, nylon for tent or mattress
- Sleeve piece of aluminium to repair tent poles

BIKE MAINTENANCE

A fabric tool roll is a convenient way to pack your tools and keep them from rattling.

wire cutters and pliers that are essential for removing and installing gear and brake cables. It also has one or more sharp knives for emergency roadside repairs. Having good knives for working on your bike means you can keep your penknife clean for using on food. Some riders swear by a multi-tool with built-in locking pliers, such as the **Leatherman Crunch**, which is probably the best choice for a biker. I was once saved in a remote part of Wyoming by using locking pliers as a clamp to hold a broken rack on my bike. Locking pliers damage nuts, bolts and cables very easily though and should not be used when a proper wrench is available.

A **dedicated spoke key** is another luxury, as you will have one on your bike multi-tool, but it is for emergencies only. When you are truing the wheel on a rest day, you will appreciate having a high quality spoke key. Even the best ones are not expensive; just make sure it fits your spokes before you buy it. A **cassette removal tool**, still sometimes referred to as the Hypercracker long after the firm stopped making them, is a necessity. When spokes break, the ones next to the gears go first and these cannot be replaced without removing the cassette. In a workshop, you would use one tool to immobilise the cassette and another to remove the lockring. On the road, you have no space for these tools. Instead, buy either the NBT2 or the Unior pocket lockring.

FURTHER LEARNING

Books
● *The Bike Book*, Fred Milson. Good simple introductory text. Colour photos.
● *Zinn and the Art of Mountain Bike Maintenance*, Lennard Zinn. Very comprehensive, good for older bikes and components.
● *Pocket Mountain Bike Maintenance*, Mel Allwood. Focussed on contemporary mountain bike topics such as discs and suspension. Lots of colour photos.

Bike maintenance courses
It's easier for most of us to learn practical things by doing. In Britain, CTC runs bike maintenance classes (💻 www.ctc.org.uk), as does the London Cycling Campaign (💻 www.lcc.org.uk). A week-long course will greatly increase your proficiency in many tasks and many classes encourage you to bring your own bike, so you will learn how to dismantle and service it before taking it on tour. 💻 www.cyclewales.net can provide customised classes for tourers at their Snowdonia workshop.

Online
💻 www.sheldonbrown.com
 Excellent primary source of all reference information.
💻 www.parktool.com
 Good 'how to repair' articles.
💻 www.bikemagic.com
 Click on 'how-to.'

Forums
💻 www.lonelyplanet.com/thorntree The hub for adventure cycling. Dedicated branch for touring and excellent country-specific branches.
💻 www.bikeforums.net Separate branches for technical, touring and all aspects of cycling.
💻 forum.ctc.org.uk Lots of branches and good 'For Sale' section.
💻 www.bikeradar.com All aspects – road, mountain biking and touring.
💻 www.thorncycles.co.uk/forums The best place for advice on Rohloff hubs.

Appendix B – Staying in touch on the road

BLOGS, WEBSITES AND GALLERIES

You'll have to set all this up before you leave, so think through what you really need. It's easy to go overboard with an ambitious website only to find later on that you'd rather be riding or relaxing than sitting in an internet café.

Email Everyone has email, your parents and friends *demand* you use it and you might need to keep them sweet in case you need funding later on. Only quirky or cantankerous travellers like travel writer Paul Theroux refuse to use it.

Web gallery The next level of commitment to entertaining friends and family back home. A gallery is also a good way to ensure your best photos are saved in case you lose your digital media cards. Galleries like Flickr and Picasa are easy to use but expect to spend a few hours while your images upload to the server – internet cafés run slow in much of the adventure-touring world. Pay for extra storage space at your chosen gallery, the free amount will be insufficient. You'll save a lot of time if you can batch-resize your photos before uploading, and burn DVDs to send home full-res images. Internet cafés or camera shops will do this very cheaply for you.

Blog You could learn how to write a blog on the hoof at some of the easier sites but it's better set up at home. Again it means more hours that could profitably be spent in cafés, museums or sleeping in are taken up in slow, smoky internet cafés with occasional power outages, but a blog can be fun for everyone back home – possibly more fun to read than it is to write. The best blog for cyclists has to be 🖳 www.crazyguyonabike.com, it's a massive site that allows you to do what cyclists want – tell the story chronologically with text in a long column and photos as big as you like. It's all indexed so people can find your blog and is generally regarded as one of the easiest blogs to learn.

Website A full-featured website may look easy but many of the cyclists who do really professional jobs are, in fact, out-of-work programmers and website builders, so their ride becomes what Brits would call 'a busman's holiday'. Unless you have those skills, you could find you're in deep water. Starting your trip with a big website can create expectations, so make sure you can deliver the goods. It's much easier if you bring along a small computer so you can do the bulk of the work offline in your tent or guesthouse and spend minimum time in the internet café uploading. A computer will allow you to run your own software such as Dreamweaver for web-building – the good sites tend to use expensive software like this, though you can use WordPress blogging software and come up with a much more customised look than a typical traveller's blog.

Blogs and websites give friends and family back home a lot of pleasure, but this book's about riding and we say: keep it simple, go for a gallery at most and don't spend too much valuable off-bike time as an internet-slave!

CONTRIBUTORS

Tom Allen left home in 2007 to see where he'd end up. He has since contented himself with inching his way little by little round the globe, even finding a wife en route to come with him. 💻 www.ride-earth.org.uk

Tim Barnes started out as a cycling sceptic, but was quickly converted and he and his wife Rowena have since toured extensively in Europe, South America and Central Asia. Tim runs a charity distributing computers to African schools. 💻 www.timbarnes.ndo.co.uk 💻 www.adventure-cycling-guide.co.uk

Jean Bell Born in 1907, Jean graduated from the University of California in 1929 before becoming a cycle-touring pioneer in Europe. During WWII he was an intelligence officer, then later went into cattle ranching and real estate. He continued to travel to Europe regularly. Jean died in California in 2009.

Alastair Bland (see p288)

Antony Bowesman British-born Antony has lived in Finland, Japan and is currently working in western Australia. 💻 www.thorntothehorn.org/

Tim Brewer (see p241)

Adam Chalupski, an architect from Krakow, Poland, is currently on the road. 💻 www.roborelanium.cyclingnomads.org/

Adrian Cooke Currently saving up for his next big trip, Adrian has a blog at 💻 http://triptracker.net/trip/2285

Janne Corax has spent most of his time since 1994 travelling the world by bicycle, having cycled through over 60 countries. He has ridden all the major routes in western China and made the first bicycle crossing of the Chang Tang high plateau in northern Tibet 2003-4 with his partner, Nadine Saulnier. 💻 www.stormkorp.se/

Philip Davis got his first taste of adventure touring on a trip across Jordan, Syria and Lebanon. He has since bike toured in northern India, looped around southeast Asia, ridden in Japan, Taiwan and the Friendship Highway from Lhasa to Kathmandu.

Bastien Demange was last heard from in Finland and favours any kind of travel as long as it's difficult and non-motorised. 💻 www.bastiendemange.com

Mark Elliott wrote Trailblazer's *Azerbaijan with excursions to Georgia*. He also co-wrote the ground-breaking *Asia Overland* and has published or contributed to many other travel guides for Lonely Planet. He lives in Belgium with Danielle, whom he met in Turkmenistan.

Edward Genochio (see p277)

Peter Gostelow (see p255)

Simon Hill, a corporate escapee, hails from Leigh-on-Sea in Essex and enjoys several long trips a year to warm places.

Roy Hoogenraad lives in beautiful Timaru on New Zealand's South Island. He enjoys bicycle and motorbike touring and occasional visits from Warm Showers List bike tourers.

Björn Josk & Even Verrelst specialise in the art of 'disposable cycling' – buying a cheap bicycle on the road when the urge takes them and selling it as their mood changes. Their Asian trip in 2007 lasted 17 months and they conquered the Himalayas for 6 months.

Dominique Kerhuel In a bid to escape 'Middle England' on his bike, Dominique has so far battled ferocious Patagonian winds; braved the cold in Tibet; and learned to escape the drenching rain in the Outer Hebrides by burrowing like the locals in a pub.

Tom Kevill-Davies (see p233)

Igor Kovše (see p280)

Scott Morris has been a pretty obsessive mountain biker since the age of 14, and he plans to keep riding in the mountains as long as he is able. Between rides he's studying for a PhD in Computer Science at the University of Arizona. 💻 www.topofusion.com/diary/

Tim Mulliner wrote about his return by bike to New Zealand in 'Long ride for a pie'. An inveterate traveller, he is now working on a masters in Environmental Science at Dunedin University.

Álvaro Neil left a law office in Madrid for life as a cycling clown on a 10-year world trip. 💻 biciclown.com

Steve Pells has cycled extensively in Europe, the Americas, Asia and Oceania, and prefers riding in mountainous regions. 💻 www.sentient-entity.org.

CONTRIBUTORS (cont'd)

Salva Rodriguez is a gym teacher from Spain, and is three years into a nine-year trip round the world by bike.

Luka Romih & Manca Ravnikar, from Ljubljana, have done several long rides together, starting with trips in Slovenia, Croatia and Romania and later travelling as far as Kyrgyzstan, the Pamir Highway and west Tibet.

Friedel Rother & Andrew Grant Friedel has pedalled some 50,000km by bicycle through 30 countries, including much of the Middle East, Central Asia and Southeast Asia. She owes a debt of gratitude to her husband Andrew, who keeps her going through rainstorms, and the people of Iran and Kyrgyzstan for some of her most enjoyable riding to date. ▣ http://travellingtwo.com

Chris Scott (see p249)

Luke Skinner Between August 2004 and April 2006 Luke cycled 29,169km from London to Cape Town with Anna Heywood, raising money for Link Community Development, a UK-based charity working on education projects all over Africa. ▣ www.africabybike.org

Cameron Smith recently backpacked for two months in western Australia and is currently lining up his third year-long bike tour.

Peter Snow Cao travelled for three years on his Grand Asian Tour and met his wife in China. They live in Chengdu, where Peter runs Bike China Adventures. ▣ www.bikechina.com

Sonya Spry & Aaldrik Mulder Australian-born Sonya and Dutchman Aaldrik met in San Francisco and married in London. With inescapable wanderlust, in July 2006 they packed up their bikes and left their home in Holland for a grand world tour which they hope will take at least five years. ▣ www.tour.tk/index.htm

Laura Stone is the author of Trailblazer's *Himalaya by Bike – a route and planning guide*, which was the perfect excuse to cycle very slowly between Pakistan and Bhutan for two years. Laura is now based in London and runs Greenrock, a cycle challenge events company. ▣ www.himalayabybike.com and www.greenrock.co.uk.

Tim & Cindie Travis left their home in Arizona, USA in March 2002 to live their dream of cycling the world. Since then they have travelled through 23 countries on four continents and have no plans to stop. While on the road they have written two books, *The Road That Has No End* and *Down the Road in South America*. ▣ www.DownTheRoad.org

Peter van Glabbeek has cycled more than 80,000km in Europe, Asia, Australia, South and North America and expects to continue travelling for many years more.

Raf Verbeelen started his cycling holidays with some friends in Belgium and neighbouring countries. Now trying to combine this with his passion for the Sahara he puts his bicycle on planes to North Africa. He has visited the deserts of Morocco, Egypt, and Tunisia. ▣ www.verbeelen.net

Jonathan Waite (see p266)

Bill Weir Lifelong touring cyclist Bill Weir has roamed extensively across North America, the Pacific, Asia, and Europe, yet dreams of still more rides. Travel writing helped finance his long journeys. He has links to recent epic bike tours in Asia and beyond at ▣ www.arizonahandbook.com/Bill's_travels.htm.

Amaya Williams (see p273) **& Eric Schambion** Eric has had a passion for travel ever since he was a small boy accompanying his lorry-driver father throughout Europe. After meeting Amaya in Laos they eventually gave up their regular lives to become self-confessed 'bike nomads' and are still cycling round the world.

Dave Wodchis has toured by bicycle in Tibet, South-East Asia, Northern Europe and Australia as well as his native Canada. ▣ www.oneworldphotography.com

Paul Woloshansky began bicycle touring in 1970, at age 16. A poorly-equipped and badly-planned trip up the Alaska Highway before it was paved turned out well, in spite of everything, and was the beginning of a life-long passion. When at home in Calgary, Canada, Paul writes cycling- and travel-related articles, with an Asian focus: *Sharing the Road: A Cyclist's Guide to India* is a current work-in-progress.

GLOSSARY

Note: some of the terms used below are illustrated in the photograph on p24

• **Anodised** Anodising is a method of coating and hardening aluminium at room temperature. This also makes it corrosion resistant.

• **Audax ride** Long, fast ride with minimal gear. Bikes designed for audax rides have the comfort of a touring bike but are designed for speed.

• **Bar-ends** Bolt-on extensions to handlebars to provide extra hand positions to straight / mountain-bike handlebars. Available in many shapes and almost a necessity for touring on a bike with a straight (ie non-dropped) handlebar.

• **BOB** (as in 'Beast of Burden') is a maker of single-wheeled trailers; their Yak model is the most popular among tourers, particularly for off-road use.

• **Bottle cage** Metal or plastic drink-bottle holder that screws onto bike's frame.

• **Cartridge bearings** A sealed ring-shaped unit containing ball bearings. Easy to replace, no need to service but no standard sizes and you will only find them in good bike shops while touring.

• **Cassette sprockets** The small gears at the back, also known as cogs. Used to be fitted individually into a cluster so that you could change the sizes of individual sprockets if you wanted, but these days the cluster of gears is produced in one unit which is known as a cassette.

• **Chainrings** The large rings between the pedals at the front of the drivetrain. Controlled by the gear shifter on the left of the handlebar.

• **Chain stays** Tubing connecting the bottom bracket to the rear dropout.

• **Cones** screw onto the axles and tighten against the bearings to hold them in place and give the wheel the minimum amount of play while allowing it to rotate freely. They rarely need adjustment but require thin (15 and 16mm) wrenches.

• **Derailleur hanger** The place on the frame immediately behind the rear dropout where the derailleur is bolted onto the frame. This is a vulnerable point because it projects and if bent in an accident or in transit will badly affect gear shifting. Aluminium frames usually have a replaceable hanger owing to the difficulty of repair.

• **Drivetrain** Sounds as if a motoring journalist made up this term but it simply refers to the gear system considered as a whole.

• **Dropouts** Dropouts are the wrench-like ends to the forks and at the corner of the rear triangle on the frame, into which the wheels fit.

• **Groupset** An anglicised version of the Italian Gruppo, referring to the entire set of gears, usually in connection to the name brand and quality, eg Shimano Deore LX.

• **Headset/Aheadset** The headset is the bearings supporting the front wheel, one set being at the bottom of the head tube and one at the top. The Aheadset is the most modern type of headset and is found on almost all quality bikes, and differs from the headset in that the steering tube is not threaded but uses a bolt instead to pull the steerer up into the head tube, making it easier to adjust. Note, however, that the handlebar cannot be raised at all on an aheadset. You have to buy a new stem to do that.

• **Quills/stems** A quill-style stem is the old style in which a narrow handlebar stem fits into the head tube rather than around the top of the steerer.

• **Recumbent** Bicycle design where the rider lies back rather than sits in the traditional fashion.

• **Sag wagon** Support vehicle; what you get when you sign up for a typical guided bike tour. It carries your bags, spare parts and emergency supplies and gives exhausted riders a lift.

• **Seat stays** Run from the top of the seat tube to the rear dropout.

• **SPD pedals** Shimano's style of pedals that lock onto cleats in the bottom of cycling shoes designed especially for Shimano SPDs. They are the most common kind of pedal designed for cleated shoes. Undoubtedly efficient but some bike tourers like them, some don't.

• **Swaged spokes** Where the metal is worked to make it thinner in some areas to save weight.

• **Threaded steerers/brake shoe posts** Where the steerer tube is threaded, as in old headsets. Bikes with large (32-36mm) nuts around the head which lock the steerer into the head of the bike have threaded steerers. Similarly, some old brakes had metal posts (the short metal piece perpendicular to the rubber pad) which were threaded.

• **TIG-welded frames** TIG welding uses electricity rather than oxy-acetylene: the metal is welded at a higher temperature.

• **Truing** The art of making a bicycle wheel true: perfectly round with no kinks or wobbles.

• **29er** A 700c/28" wheel or frame built for fat tyres.

• **Wheel 'dishing'** Wheels are 'dished' in that the side of the wheel has a saucer shape, giving it greater strength. The left side of the rear wheel is more dished than the right side on a bike with derailleur gears, and the more derailleur gears a bike has, the less 'dish' to its shape and the weaker it will be.

INDEX

Acute Mountain Sickness
(AMS) 20-1, 207
Adventure Cycling Association
(ACA) 185, 191, 195
adventure touring 88
Afghanistan 124-5
air mattresses 80
air travel 65-6
Albania 95
Algeria 222
Allen, Tom 107, 304
altitude sickness 20-1, 207
Argentina 208-11
Armenia 111, 114
ATMs 15
Australia 178-84
Ayers Rock (Australia) 184
Azerbaijan 111-14

Baja California 199-203
Baku (Azerbaijan) 113
Balkans 95-6
Bangkok (Thailand) 167, 169
Barnes, Tim 124, 304
batteries 84, 85
Bekaa Valley 110
Bell, Jean 7, 92-3, 304
bicycle maintenance 292-302
bike helmets 71
bike touring tents 75-7
bike transportation
    by air 65-8
    India 137
bikes 23-39
    accessories 55-62
    bags for 68
    boxes and boxing 65-8
    brakes 42-4
    components 30-1, 39-48
    frames 25, 29-30, 36-7, 298
    gears 39-42
    handlebars 27, 52, 54
    pumps 60
    racks 55-9
    spares 301
    tools 60-2
    wheels 44-8
Black Sea route (Turkey) 105
Bland, Alastair 288-91
blogs 303
Bolivia 212-15
Botswana 229
bottle cages 81, 82

Bowesman, Antony 213
brakes 42-4, 276-9, 293-5
Brewer, Tim 241-8
Bruce Gordon bikes 32
Bruce Gordon racks 57
budgeting 15, 16
Bulgaria 95
bush camping 182

Cambodia 166-7, 266-72
Cameroon 231-2
Camino de Santiago (Spain)
    90
camping 73, 101, 178, 182, 228
    see also bush camping/wild
    camping
camping gear 73-85
Canada 187-8
Carretera Austral (Chile)
    210-11
cash 15, 17
Central Africa 229, 232
Central America 203-4
Central Asia 116-31
chain oil 292
Chalupski, Adam 125, 304
Chile 208-11
China 117, 141-59
Chonqing (China) 158
clothing 69-73
coffee-making 82
Colombia 215-16
comfortable cycling 51-3
component groups 30-1
Congo-Brazzaville 232
Continental Travel Contact
    tyres 47-8
Cooke, Adrian 16
Corax, Janne 141, 145, 146,
    304
Corsair 259-65
Coroico (Bolivia) 214
credit cards 14-16
Croatia 95
'crotch rot' 21
Cuba 198
cycle components 30-1,
    39-48
cycle helmets 71
cycle racks 55-9
cycle...see also bike...
cycling companions 9-11
cycling position 51-3

cycling shorts 69
Cyclists' Touring Club 7

Dalton Highway (Alaska) 185
Damascus (Syria) 109, 110, 111
Danube route 89, 91
Darjeeling (India) 133
Darwin (Australia) 181, 182,
    183
Davis, Philip 107-11, 304
Dead Sea Highway 110
debit cards 14-16
Demange, Bastien 104, 304
Dempster Highway (Canada)
    185, 188
derailleur drive chain,
    cleaning 292-3
derailleur gears 40, 295-7
desert cycling 221-2
Diamox 21
diet 21-2
diphtheria 18
disc brakes 43-4, 45; and racks
    58
dishing 45
dogs 22, 107, 156, 217
drinking water 82

Eastern Europe 95-6
Eastern Tibet 153-5
Ecuador 215
Egypt 225
Elbe River route 91
Elliott, Mark 111-14, 304
emails 302
Ethiopia 226
Europe 89-96
Everest Base Camp 147, 150
expedition touring bikes 27-8

footwear 72-3
frames 25, 29-30, 36-7, 298
France 89-90
Friendship Highway (Tibet)
    146-50
fuel (for stoves) 81

Gabon 232
gear, transport of 55-8
    weight of 62-5, 287
gears 39-42
Genochio, Ed 97, 100-5, 159-
    61, 276-80

Georgia 111-13
Germany 91
gers 160
Ghana 231
Gilgit (Pakistan) 129
gloves 72
Gobi Desert 160-1
Gostelow, Peter 163-73, 174-8, 222, 255-8
GPS 85-7, 221
Grant, Andrew 94, 305
Great Divide Mountain Bike Route (USA) 185, 188, 195-8
Great Northern Highway (Australia) 182
Great Ocean Road (Australia) 178, 181
Guangxi (China) 159
guidebooks 13
Guinea 230
Guizhou (China) 158-9

HACE & HAPE 20
handlebar bags 60
handlebars 27, 52, 54
headgear 72
headsets 48, 297-8
health 17-22
heavy gear 64-5
helmets 71
hepatitis A and B 18
Hill, Simon 168, 304
Himalaya by Bike (Stone) 136, 137, 138
Himalayan foothills 133
Hokkaido (Japan) 176
Honshu (Japan) 177
Hoogenraad, Roy 184-5, 304
HP Velotechnik Street Machine GTe 35-6
hub gears 41-2
hubs 44
Hungry Cyclist, The (Kevill-Davies) 233-40

India 131-41
Indonesia 171-3
inoculations 17-18
internet banking 14-15
internet forums 11-12
Iran 115-16
Israel 110

Jandd racks 57
Japan 175-8
Japanese B encephalitis 18
Jordan 107-11
Josk, Bjorn 118, 305

Kailash, Mt (Tibet) 152
Karakoram Highway 126-31
Karakum Desert 114
Kashgar (Kashi) 131, 150-2
Kathmandu (Nepal) 146, 147, 150
Kazakhstan 116, 117, 119, 121-2
Kenya 226
Kerhuel, Dominique 204-16, 304
Kevill-Davies, Tom 233-40
kickstands 61
Kings Highway (Jordan) 109
Kinnaur (India) 139, 140
kitchen equipment 83-4
Koga-Miyata bikes 33
Kovše, Igor 280-7
Kyrgyzstan 116, 119, 122-3, 124
Kyushu (Japan) 177

La Paz (Baja California) 199, 201
La Paz (Bolivia) 212, 214
Ladakh (India) 138, 139, 140
Laos 169-70
Las Vegas (USA) 193
layering (clothes) 69-71
Lebanon 107-11
Lhasa (Tibet) 146, 147, 150-4
Libya 219, 222, 255-8
liquid fuel, transport of 81

malaria 18-19
Malawi 226-7
Malaysia 170-1
Mali 230
Manali-Leh route 138, 140
maps
  Africa 218
  Asia 98-9
  Australia 179
  Central America 203
  South America 205
  South-East Asia 163
  USA 189
Marin County (USA) 193
Marin Muirwoods bikes 36
Markham (Tibet) 153, 155, 156
Mauritania 219, 222, 224
Mawson Trail (Australia) 178, 181
medium weight gear 63-4
Mekong Delta (Vietnam) 166
Melbourne (Australia) 181
meningitis 18
Mexico 199-203

money 14-17
Mongolia 159-61
Montenegro 95
Morocco 217, 220-1, 222-3
Morris, Scott 195-8, 304
mountain bikes 23, 25-7
  mid-range 35
  used, adapting 37-9
Mulder, Aaldrik 188, 305
Mulliner, Tim 179, 304
multitools 60-1
Munda Biddi Trail (Australia) 178
Muslim customs 219, 220
Muslim hospitality 108
Myanmar (Burma) 173

Nakhchivan (Azerbaijan) 114
Namibia 227-9
Neil, Álvaro 64-5, 304
New Zealand 184-5
Nigeria 231
Nomad S & S bikes 32-3
North Africa 217-24
North America 185-98
North Sea cycle route 91
Northern Pakistan 126-30
Nullarbor Plain (Australia) 179-81

Old Man Mountain racks 56
online research 11-12
outback tour (Australia) 181-4

Pacific Coast Highway (USA) 185, 188, 190-2
Pakistan 126-30
Pamir Highway (Tajikistan) 117,123-6
panniers 59-60
passports 13
Patagonia 208-12
PayPal account 15
Pells, Steve 213, 304
Peru 215
planning schedule 12
polio 18
Prague-Vienna Greenway 91
pump-horns 61
pumps 60
punctures 299-300

rabies 18
racks 55-9
Rajasthan (India) 134
Ramadan 128
Rando-Cycles Globe-Trotter 36
Ravnikar, Manca 96, 305

ready-made routes (Europe) 89
recumbent bikes 28
Repack Road (USA) 193
riding position 51-3
rim brakes 42-3
rims, wheel 45
River Danube route 89, 91
Roberts Roughstuff bikes 34
Rodriguez, Salva 125, 172, 305
Rohloff Speedhubs 41-2
Rohloff-based bikes 36
Romania 95
Romih, Luke 96, 305
Rother, Friedel 94, 116-23, 305
Rover Safety Bicycle 7
Russia 97, 100-5

saddles 51-4
Sahara 221-4
saunas, Russian 102
'Sayan Loop' route 104-5
Schambion, Eric 305
Schwalbe Marathon tyres 46-7
Scott, Chris 148, 178, 180, 249-54
Serbia 95, 96
Shandur Pass (Pakistan) 129
Shangri-la (China) 156-7
Shikoku (Japan) 177
Siberia 97, 101, 103-5
Sichuan (China) 158
Sikkim 133-4
Singapore 171
Skardu (Kashmir) 128
Skinner, Luke 85-7, 305
sleeping bags 79-80
sleeping pads 80
Slovenia 95
Smith, Cameron 62, 150
Snow Cao, Peter 141, 142, 305
solar power 85
solo travelling 9
South Africa 229
South America 204-16
South Australia 181
South-East Asia 163-73
South-Western Australia 180
Southern India 135
Spain 90
SPDs 72
Spiti Valley (India) 139, 140
spokes and spoke holes 46
Spry, Sonja 188, 305
St Helen's, Mount 192
Stone, Laura 50, 136, 138, 305
stoves 80-2
Stuart Highway (Australia) 183, 184

Sudan 225-6
Sumatra 172
sunburn & sunstroke 19
sunglasses 84
Surly Long Haul Trucker 31-2
Surly racks 57
suspension 49-51
synthetic materials 70
Syria 107-11

Tajikistan 116, 119, 123-6
tandems 28-9
Tanzania 226
Tbilisi (Georgia) 112
tents 73-7
tetanus 18
Thailand 167-9
Thorn racks 57
Thorn Raven 32-3
Thorn Sherpa 34
Tibet 141-2, 144-56, 259-65
Tierra del Fuego 211-12
Titicaca, Lake (Bolivia) 214
toe clips 72
Togo 231
tools and toolkits 60-2, 300-2
torches 84
touring bikes 23-5, 27-8
trailers 55
trans-European routes 89
trans-Sahara routes 222
travellers' cheques 15
travelling companions 9-11
Travis, Tim & Cindie 200, 216, 305
Trujillo (Peru) 216
Tsetang (Tibet) 154
Tunisia 221, 223-4
Tubus racks 56
Turkanaland 227
Turkey 105-7, 112
Turkish baths 105
Turkmenistan 116, 117, 119, 120
typhoid 18
tyres 46-8

ultralight gear 62, 287
unboxed bikes 68
USA 188-98
Uzbekistan 116, 119, 120-1

van Glabbeek, Peter 186, 305
Vantage Highway (USA) 192
Verbeelen, Raf 217-24, 305
Verrelst, Even 118, 305
Via de la Plata (Spain) 90
Victoria (Australia) 181

Vietnam 165-6
visas and permits 13-14
  see also name of country

Waite, Jonathan 266-72
water bottles & cages 82
water purification 82
waterproof clothing 71
websites & galleries 302-3
weight limits (air travel) 65
Weir, Bill 131, 141, 157, 162, 305
West Africa 229
Western Europe 89-91
wheels 44-8
wild camping 78
Wilder Ranch State Park (USA) 193
Williams, Amaya 219, 224-32, 273-5
Wodchis, Dave 198, 305
Woloshansky, Paul 39, 187-8, 292, 297, 305

yellow fever 18
Yukon Territory (Canada) 188
Yunnan (China) 157-8
Yunnan Highway 156-7

Zambia 227
Zhongdian (China) 156-7

TRAILBLAZER

OTHER GUIDES FROM TRAILBLAZER – see p312 for full list

Azerbaijan – with excursions to Georgia
Mark Elliott, 368pp, 200 maps, 30 colour photos
ISBN 978-1-905864-23-2, *4th edition*, £14.99
Fourth edition of this acclaimed practical guide with over 200 detailed maps.
What to see, where to go, how to get there, where to stay, where to eat. History,
language and cultural tips. This is still the only dedicated guide to Azerbaijan.
Includes excursions to Georgia.

The Silk Roads – a route & planning guide
Paul Wilson, 448pp, 50 maps, 40 colour photos
ISBN 978-1-905864-32-4, *3rd edition*, £14.99
The Silk Road was never a single thread but an intricate web of trade routes
linking Asia and Europe. This guide follows all the routes with sections on
Turkey, Syria, Iran, Turkmenistan, Uzbekistan, Kyrgyzstan, Kazakhstan,
Pakistan and China.

Nepal Trekking & The Great Himalaya Trail *Robin Boustead*
1st edition, 320pp, 8pp colour maps, 40 colour photos
ISBN 978-1-905864-31-7, £14.99
This guide includes the most popular routes in Nepal – the Everest, Annapurna
and Langtang regions – as well as the newest trekking areas for true trailblaz-
ers. This is the first guide to chart **The Great Himalaya Trail**, the route which
crosses Nepal from east to west. Extensive planning sections.

Trekking in the Everest Region *Jamie McGuinness*
5th edition, 320pp, 30 maps, 30 colour photos
ISBN 978-1-873756-99-7, £12.99
Fifth edition of this popular guide to the Everest region, the world's most famous
trekking region. Includes planning, preparation and getting to Nepal; detailed
route guides – with 30 route maps and 50 village plans; Kathmandu city guide
– where to stay, where to eat, what to see.

Kilimanjaro: the trekking guide to Africa's highest mountain
Henry Stedman, 3rd edition, 368pp, 40 maps, 30 photos
ISBN 978-1-905864-24-9, £12.99
At 19,340ft the world's tallest freestanding mountain, Kilimanjaro is one of the
most popular destinations for hikers visiting Africa. It's possible to walk up to the
summit: no technical skills are necessary. Includes town guides to Nairobi and
Dar-Es-Salaam, excursions in the region and a colour guide to flora and fauna.
Includes Mount Meru.

Inca Trail, Cusco & Machu Picchu
Alexander Stewart, 4th edition, 352pp, 74 maps, 40 photos
ISBN 978-1-905864-15-7, £12.99
The **Inca Trail** from Cusco to Machu Picchu, is South America's most popular
trek. Practical guide including detailed trail maps, plans of Inca sites, plus
guides to Cusco and Machu Picchu. Route guides to other trails in the area: the
Santa Teresa Trek and the **Choquequirao Trek** as well as the **Vilcabamba
Trail** plus the routes linking them. This entirely rewalked and rewritten fourth
edition includes a new history of the Incas by Hugh Thomson.

Tour du Mont Blanc
Jim Manthorpe, 224pp, 60 maps, 30 colour photos
ISBN 978-1-905864-12-6, *1st edition*, £11.99
At 4807m (15,771ft), Mont Blanc is the highest mountain in western Europe,
and one of the most famous mountains in the world. The trail (105 miles,
168km) that circumnavigates the massif, passing through France, Italy and
Switzerland, is the most popular long distance walk in Europe. Includes
Chamonix and Courmayeur guides.

TRAILBLAZER

OTHER GUIDES FROM TRAILBLAZER – see p312 for full list

Himalaya by Bike – a route & planning guide
Laura Stone 368pp, 28 colour & 50 B&W photos, 73 maps
ISBN 978 1 905864 04 1, *1st edn*, £16.99
An all-in-one guide for Himalayan cycle-touring. Covers the Himalayan regions of Pakistan, Tibet, India, Nepal and Sikkim with detailed km-by-km guides to main routes including the Karakoram Highway and the Friendship Highway.
❑ **Route descriptions with detailed mapping** – Unique hand-drawn GPS maps show distances between villages, altitudes, places to eat and accommodation, water sources, fuel stations and points of interest along the way. Elevation profiles for each 100km section and route overview profiles to get you training!
❑ **Town guides** – Islamabad, Kashgar, Manali, Leh, Srinagar, Shimla, Gangtok, Darjeeling, Lhasa, Shigatse, Kathmandu and Guwahati.
'Inspirational guide' **Cycle Magazine** *'Rammed full of in-depth information'* **Adventure Travel Magazine** *'Indispensable'* **LCC Magazine**

Morocco Overland – from the Atlas to the Sahara *Chris Scott*
1st edition, 288pp, 24 colour & 170 B&W photos
ISBN 978 1 905864 20 1 £15.99
Morocco Overland is a guide to 49 routes through southern Morocco's spectacular landscape – from the snow-clad High Atlas to the dunes of the Sahara and right down to the Mauritanian border. With easy-to-follow routes ranging from sub-alpine trails to arid canyons winding past hidden Berber villages and from the Atlantic surf to former Dakar Rally pistes, this comprehensive route and planning guide will appeal to both the seasoned adventurer and to the first timer.
❑ **Route guides with GPS waypoints** – Covers 49 routes for 4WDs, motorcycles and mountain bikes with 100s of GPS waypoints. Each route is reversible and is graded for suitability for mountain bikes. Includes fuel stations, restaurants and places to stay. With over 40pp of mapping. *'The bible for off-roading to and across this corner of North Africa'* **Wanderlust Magazine**

Sahara Overland – a route & planning guide *Chris Scott*
2nd edition, 640pp, 24 colour & 170 B&W photos
ISBN 978 1 873756 76 8 Hardback £19.99
Covers all aspects Saharan, from acquiring documentation to vehicle choice and preparation; from descriptions of the prehistoric art sites of the Libyan Fezzan to the ancient caravan cities of southern Mauritania. How to 'read' sand surfaces, using GPS – it's all here along with detailed off-road itineraries covering 26,000kms in nine countries. *'THE essential desert companion for anyone planning a Saharan trip on either two wheels or four.'* **Trailbike Magazine**

Australia's Great Ocean Road *Richard Everist*
1st edition, 416pp, over 500 colour photos
ISBN 978 1 905864 26 3 £19.99
Co-published with Australian-based BestShot! this is a lavishly-illustrated full-colour guide to one of Australia's top tourist regions. The Great Ocean Road follows the southwest coastline of Victoria from just outside Melbourne. Sights, activities and background context with strong emphasis on sustainable tourism. Route guide from Geelong to Portland: towns, villages and places of interest.

Norway's Arctic Highway – Mo i Rana to Kirkenes
John Douglas 320pp, 30 colour photos, 53 maps
ISBN 978 1 873756 73 7, *1st edition*, £13.99
Norway's Arctic Highway stretches 900 miles from Mo i Rana to Kirkenes, almost all the route within the Arctic Circle. At its most northern point the road comes to within 19.5 degrees of the North Pole. This is a region of intense physical beauty – tundra plateaux, vast glaciers and magnificent fjords. Includes km-by-km route guide with maps plus detailed guides to Tromsø, Bodø, Hammerfest and other towns along the route.

TRAILBLAZER

Adventure Cycle-Touring Handbook	2nd edn out now
Adventure Motorcycling Handbook	5th edn out now
Australia by Rail	5th edn out now
Australia's Great Ocean Road	1st edn out now
Azerbaijan	4th edn out now
Coast to Coast (British Walking Guide)	4th edn out now
Cornwall Coast Path (British Walking Guide)	3rd edn out now
Corsica Trekking – GR20	1st edn out now
Cotswold Way (British Walking Guide)	1st edn out now
Dolomites Trekking – AV1 & AV2	2nd edn out now
Inca Trail, Cusco & Machu Picchu	4th edn out now
Indian Rail Handbook	1st edn late 2010
Hadrian's Wall Path (British Walking Guide)	2nd edn out now
Himalaya by Bike – a route and planning guide	1st edn out now
Japan by Rail	2nd edn out now
Kilimanjaro – the trekking guide (includes Mt Meru)	3rd edn out now
Mediterranean Handbook	1st edn out now
Morocco Overland (4WD/motorcycling/cycling)	1st edn out now
Moroccan Atlas – The Trekking Guide	1st edn mid 2010
Nepal Mountaineering Guide	1st edn late 2010
Nepal Trekking & the Great Himalayan Trail	1st edn late 2010
New Zealand – The Great Walks	2nd edn out now
North Downs Way (British Walking Guide)	1st edn out now
Norway's Arctic Highway	1st edn out now
Offa's Dyke Path (British Walking Guide)	2nd edn out now
Overlanders' Handbook – worldwide driving guide	1st edn early 2011
Peddars Way & Norfolk Coast Path (British Walking Guide)	1st edn late 2010
Pembrokeshire Coast Path (British Walking Guide)	3rd edn out now
Pennine Way (British Walking Guide)	2nd edn out now
The Ridgeway (British Walking Guide)	2nd edn out now
Siberian BAM Guide – rail, rivers & road	2nd edn out now
The Silk Roads – a route and planning guide	3rd edn mid 2010
Sahara Overland – a route and planning guide	2nd edn out now
Scottish Highlands – The Hillwalking Guide	2nd edn out now
South Downs Way (British Walking Guide)	3rd edn out now
Tour du Mont Blanc	1st edn out now
Trans-Canada Rail Guide	5th edn mid 2010
Trans-Siberian Handbook	7th edn out now
Trekking in the Annapurna Region	5th edn late 2010
Trekking in the Everest Region	5th edn out now
Trekking in Ladakh	3rd edn out now
Trekking in the Pyrenees	3rd edn out now
The Walker's Haute Route – Mont Blanc to Matterhorn	1st edn out now
West Highland Way (British Walking Guide)	4th edn out now

For more information about Trailblazer and our expanding range of guides, for guidebook updates or for credit card mail order sales visit our website:

www.trailblazer-guides.com

ROUTE GUIDES FOR THE ADVENTUROUS TRAVELLER